Eastern Europe's Uncertain Future

edited by
Robert R. King
James F. Brown

Published in cooperation
with Radio Free Europe

The Praeger Special Studies program,
through a selective worldwide distribution
network, makes available to the academic,
government, and business communities significant and timely research in U.S. and
international economic, social, and political issues.

Eastern Europe's Uncertain Future

A Selection of Radio Free Europe Research Reports

PRAEGER SPECIAL STUDIES IN INTERNATIONAL POLITICS AND GOVERNMENT

Praeger Publishers   New York   London

Library of Congress Cataloging in Publication Data

Main entry under title:

Eastern Europe's uncertain future.

(Praeger special studies in international politics
and government)
   Includes bibliographical references and index.
   1. Europe, Eastern—Foreign relations.   2. Europe,
Eastern—Foreign economic relations.   3. Europe,
Eastern—Economic conditions.   I. King, Robert R.
II. Brown, James F., 1928-   III. Radio Free Europe.
DJK50.E17   309.1'171'7   77-10666

PRAEGER SPECIAL STUDIES
200 Park Avenue, New York, N.Y., 10017, U.S.A.

Published in the United States of America in 1977
by Praeger Publishers,
A Division of Holt, Rinehart and Winston, CBS, Inc.

789   038   987654321

How will historians a quarter of a century hence view developments in Eastern Europe in the 1970s? Most probably they will
divide the decade into two fairly equal parts. The first, beginning
in early 1971 and ending in mid-1976, will be seen as a period of
extraordinary stability—Soviet-dominated and Soviet-controlled stability. This was principally a result of the Soviet decision to invade
Czechoslovakia in August 1968. Thereafter the USSR's policy toward
Eastern Europe was aimed at preventing a repetition anywhere in the
region of the events that took place in the CSSR between 1965 and 1968
and made the invasion of that country inevitable from the Soviet point
of view. Thus in the first half of the 1970s there was an extensive
Soviet-led campaign for cohesion involving not only economic integration under the Council for Mutual Economic Assistance (Comecon) but
also political, military, ideological, and foreign policies. The USSR
therefore sought to cast detente as a bloc-to-bloc affair and attempted
to coordinate East European relations with the West.

A key aspect of the attempt was the policy of "consumerism"—
the ensuring of a standard of living relatively higher than had previously
prevailed throughout Eastern Europe. For the most part this policy
was extremely successful—by regional standards—owing largely to
what one might call objective economic circumstances. In the first
part of the 1970s the world as a whole was going through an economic
upswing, and the recession that was to hit the West affected Eastern
Europe only later. In some regards, however, consumerism was
very clearly motivated by political considerations. This was the case
in Czechoslovakia, where it was an important element in the whole
postinvasion normalization process, which has achieved a certain
degree of success. The same considerations lay behind the consumerism in Poland after the riots at the end of 1970. As a result of these
circumstances, in 1971 Eastern Europe entered the most prosperous
period of its history. By the beginning of 1977, the standard of living
had risen higher than at any time in the communist or even the precommunist past.

In the mid-1970s, however, Eastern Europe appeared to be
entering a period of important change, and our future historian will
probably record that the second half of the decade was a period of
considerable instability. There are several reasons for this. First,
there was a marked and sudden economic deterioration in the area.
At the beginning of 1975 the Soviet Union, upon which Eastern Europe

v

depends heavily as a source of supply, raised the prices of its raw materials sharply. The blow the economies of Western Europe suffered as a result of the Organization of Petroleum Exporting Countries (OPEC) states' decision to increase oil prices in 1973 is in many respects comparable to the effect on Eastern Europe of the Soviet decision to increase the prices of its raw materials (and particularly oil).

There were other reasons for the economic decline, of course, including inflation imported from Western Europe—a reflection of the degree to which East-West economic relations have developed. These were things for which the East European leaders could not be blamed. There were other things, however, for which they were responsible, such as insisting upon maintaining a command-style economic management (Hungary was the exception in this regard). For these and other reasons, then, Eastern Europe entered a period of economic deterioration at the beginning of 1975. The effects of this decline became evident in 1976, and are likely to continue.

In view of this, the rise in living standards will surely level off, even if it does not actually drop. The rising expectations of the East European populations, fed by the success achieved with regard to consumer goods during the first half of the 1970s, may thus also contribute to the problems facing their governments in the second half. The unrest in Poland in June 1976, when food price increases were announced, was certainly one aspect of this general problem. Although the government and the party hastily rescinded the proposed increases, the fundamental economic and political problems remained unresolved. While a repetition of such events in response to divergencies between rising consumer expectations and declining economic capability cannot be anticipated elsewhere in Europe, it cannot altogether be ruled out.

There are also noneconomic reasons for the growing instability. First in importance in this connection are the consequences of the Conference on Security and Cooperation in Europe, which culminated in Helsinki in the summer of 1975. If that conference had taken place in 1971, it is probable that we would have heard little about it thereafter. But it took place just as the economic decline in Eastern Europe was setting in—at a time of questioning, when, owing partly to the economic situation and partly to other circumstances, there was growing dissatisfaction. It is ironic that the Soviets, who were the most consistent advocates of the Helsinki conference, came to see that it took place at just the wrong time. Thus the societies of Eastern Europe, which must not be confused with the states or regimes, have reacted to Helsinki in a manner far different from that anticipated by the Soviet and East European governments.

The second interesting—and related—development was Eurocommunism. This is not the place to analyze the emergence of this complicated phenomenon, however. Suffice it to say that whatever dangers Eurocommunism may represent for Western Europe, it also represents a very considerable danger to the established order in Eastern Europe. It has the kind of attraction for elites both inside and outside the communist parties that Yugoslav revisionism had for the elites in Eastern Europe during the 1950s. The pull of Eurocommunism is perhaps stronger because the East European elites are certainly more attracted to Rome, Paris, and Madrid than to Belgrade and Zagreb.

The East European state most subject to Western influence is the German Democratic Republic (GDR). The proximity of the Federal Republic, their common language, and the penetrability of the border between the two German states give Western ideas almost unhindered access to the GDR. In the past, these factors inhibited the development of an East German national consciousness; by the early 1970s, however, there was some indication that such an identity was developing. But, although impressive successes in sports contributed to that sense of identity, there have been other signs that it is not as strong as might have been thought. The fact that dissident popular singer Wolf Biermann was denied the right to return after a trip to the West and the reports of large numbers of GDR citizens seeking permission to emigrate to the West suggest nervousness on the part of the East Berlin leadership. The diplomatic and domestic confidence that marked the GDR in the early 1970s seems to be giving way to a growing uncertainty.

Other less well-defined fears and expectations may well have a serious effect as the decade of the 1970s wears on. Most significant is the uncertain result a Soviet succession crisis, or even succession issue, might have. Since World War II changes of leadership in the USSR have been marked by uncertainty and instability; this was true after the death of Stalin in 1953, and after the removal of Khrushchev in 1964. Although in the latter case the succession was very well conducted from the Soviet point of view, between 1964 and 1968 the new Soviet leadership was understandably so concerned with internal affairs that East European developments were not given the attention they would have received had the Soviet leaders been less preoccupied with strengthening their own position. This period saw the advent of the Prague Spring in Czechoslovakia and Romania's successful enlargement of its foreign policy autonomy.

History, of course, does not always repeat itself, but in the case of the USSR it may well do so. It is a question of not merely the retirement of one man, but the impending departure of the whole senior ruling oligarchy. The first man in that oligarchy to go was

Marshal A. A. Grechko, who died in 1976. Prime Minister Aleksei Kosygin has had a heart attack, and although he was back in his office by mid-1976 it is unlikely that he will continue for long. Mikhail Suslov is 75, Nikolai Podgorny is 74, and Leonid Brezhnev is 71. And indeed, the man who is often mentioned as an interim successor to Brezhnev, Andrei Kirilenko, is older than the present party head. The Soviet leadership need not face a crisis like the one that followed Stalin's death, but any important leadership changes must lead to a preoccupation with internal problems that will, at least to some degree, create a power and authority vacuum in Eastern Europe. In combination with economic deterioration, the impact of Helsinki, and Euro-communism, this could result in considerable instability.

There will be succession problems whose solution cannot be long delayed in Eastern Europe as well. Yugoslavia will have to face one fairly soon, despite the fact that Marshal Tito has defied expectations and fears thus far. It is difficult to see how an internal crisis can be avoided when Tito goes, and it is also difficult to see how that crisis can avoid having repercussions on at least some parts of Eastern Europe, and particularly the Balkans. Even Bulgaria, ignored though it often is, has one of the most important geopolitical and strategic locations in Eastern Europe, bordering as it does on Yugoslavia and on two not particularly stable members of NATO (Greece and Turkey). It too will face a succession crisis before long, since the Bulgarian leadership is almost as old as that of the USSR. Albania, another Balkan country important because of its strategic location, faces the same problem, and even Hungary, which with good reason is considered the most stable state in Eastern Europe owing to the greater degree of rapport between rulers and ruled, depends largely on one man—66-year-old party leader Janos Kadar, who is not in particularly good health. The question here will be: Can Kadarism survive Kadar?

For all these reasons Eastern Europe appears headed for a period of considerable instability, whose beginnings have already become apparent. A certain degree of tension already exists between the societies of Eastern Europe and the regimes that govern them; it is evident in the relationship between the Soviet Union and some of its satellite regimes, and perhaps also in the relations between some of the East European states.

To achieve stability in Eastern Europe would require three things, the first of which is a harmonious relationship between the individual states and the Soviet Union. This is perhaps the easiest to achieve, and in fact several of the East European states have done so at various times. Second in importance is a harmonious relationship between the individual East European state and the society it rules. This has been difficult to achieve in the past, and for most East European states it remains elusive. Third is acceptance of Soviet hegemony by the East European societies. If these three elements were present, there would be stability in Eastern Europe, but they have not been over the past 30 years—at least not all together—and the consequences have been evident.

Unless there is a great change in the Soviet Union's attitude toward Eastern Europe and in its estimate of what its long-term interests are in relation to the region, it is unlikely that real stability will be achieved. The consequences of this state of affairs are difficult to predict, but it could well result in a repetition of events similar to those that transpired in 1956 or 1968; it is also conceivable, though less likely, that the events of 1914 or 1939 could repeat themselves.

The studies that make up this volume give a good picture of Eastern Europe in this period of transition. They are revised versions of Background Reports that originally appeared in the Radio Free Europe (RFE) Research series in 1976 and early 1977, and their authors are all members of the RFE Research and Analysis Department. They are not intended to give a complete picture of the individual countries, but taken together they do provide a mosaic of the problems facing both Eastern Europe as a whole and the individual states in the region. Although there are a number of indications that instability may be increasing, in many respects life continues very much as usual. Any effort to give an accurate sense of present developments must also consider the less dramatic events that demonstrate that despite potentially significant impending changes, much remains the same. A number of the chapters highlight areas in which one finds the seeds of instability—the response to Helsinki, Eurocommunism, the economic slowdown, the Polish price-increase crisis, and the civil rights movement. At the same time, however, other aspects of life in the region that point to the continuation of past trends are dealt with—relations with the Soviet Union, expanding economic relations with the West, new emphasis on ideology, and Church-state relations.

The entire Research and Analysis Department of Radio Free Europe contributed to this book. While its members cannot be listed individually, the following deserve particular mention: Miss Rada Nikolaev and the Bulgarian Research Unit; Mr. Hanus Hajek and the Czechoslovak Research Unit; Mr. Charles E. Kovats and the Hungarian Research Unit; Mr. Kazimierz Zamorski and the Polish Research Unit; and Mr. Ion Gheorghe and the Romanian Research Unit. Unity Evans edited and proofread the manuscript, and the final draft was typed by Urszula Stefanowski. These acknowledgments would not be complete without special thanks to Mr. Richard Rowson, the former president of Praeger Publishers, who has consistently supported and encouraged the publication of this volume.

CONTENTS

PART V: CHURCH-STATE RELATIONS

LIST OF TABLES AND FIGURES

LIST OF ABBREVIATIONS

ADN   Algemeiner Deutscher Nachrichtendienst (East German Press Agency, the official East German news service)

AFP   Agence France Presse (a French news service)

Agerpres   Agentia Romana de Presa (Romanian Press Agency, the official Romanian news service)

AIC   agro-industrial complex

ANSA   Agencia Nationale Stampa Associata (National Press Association Agency, Italian news service)

ATA   Albanian Telegraphic Agency (Agjensija Telegrafike Shqiptare, the official Albanian news service)

BCP   Bulgarian Communist Party

BIS   Bank for International Settlements

BR   Background Report

BTA   Bulgarska Telegrafna Agentsia (Bulgarian Telegraph Agency, the official Bulgarian news service)

CC   Central Committee

CCP   Chinese Communist Party

Comecon   Council for Mutual Economic Assistance

Cominform   Communist Information Bureau

COPMIM   Coordinated Five-Year Plan of Multilateral Integration Measures

CP   communist party

CPCS   Communist Party of Czechoslovakia

CPSU   Communist Party of the Soviet Union

CSSR   Czechoslovak Socialist Republic

dpa   Deutsche Presse-Agentur (German Press Agency, a West German news service)

EEC   European Economic Community

FRG   Federal Republic of Germany

GATT   General Agreement on Tariffs and Trade

GDR   German Democratic Republic

GMT   Greenwich mean time

GNP   gross national product

ha.   hectare

HPR   Hungarian People's Republic

HSWP   Hungarian Socialist Workers' Party (the Hungarian communist party)

IAC   industrial-agricultural complex

IBEC   International Bank for Economic Cooperation

IIB   International Investment Bank

Kcs   Czechoslovak koruna (the monetary unit of Czechoslovakia)

kg.	kilogram
KIK	Klub Inteligencji Katolickiej (Club of the Catholic Intelligentsia in Poland)
LCY	League of Communists of Yugoslavia (the Yugoslav communist party)
MBFR	Mutual and Balanced Force Reductions
MFN	most-favored-nation
MTI	Magyar Tavirati Iroda (Hungarian Telegraphic Agency, the official Hungarian news service)
MW	megawatt
NAIC	national agro-industrial complex
NATO	North Atlantic Treaty Organization
NEM	New Economic Mechanism (in Hungary)
ODiSS	Osrodek Dokumentacji i Studiow Spolecznych (Center for Documentation and Social Studies)
OECD	Organization for Economic Cooperation and Development
OKPIK	Ogolnopolski Klub Postepowej Inteligencji (All-Polish Club of the Progressive Catholic Intelligentsia)
PAP	Polska Agencja Prasowa (Polish Press Agency, the official Polish news service)
PCE	Partido Communista de Espana (the Communist Party of Spain)
PCF	Parti Communiste Français (the French Communist Party)
PCI	Partito Communista Italiano (the Italian Communist Party)
PGR	panstwowe gospodarstwo rolne (state farm, in Poland)
PKIK	Polski Klub Inteligencji Katolickiej (Polish Club of the Catholic Intelligentsia)
PPSh	Partija e Punes te Shqiperise (the Albanian Party of Labor—the Albanian Communist party)
PRC	People's Republic of China
PUWP	Polish United Workers' Party (the Polish Communist party)
RAD	Research and Analysis Department (of Radio Free Europe)
RCP	Romanian Communist Party
RFE	Radio Free Europe
RL	Radio Liberty
RSR	Romanian Socialist Republic
SALT	Strategic Arms Limitation Talks
SED	Sozialistische Einheitspartei Deutschlands (the Socialist Unity Party of Germany—the East German communist party)

SFRJ	Socijalisticka Federativna Republika Jugoslavija (Socialist Federative Republic of Yugoslavia)
SKJ	Savez Komunista Jugoslavije (League of Communists of Yugoslavia)
SPC	scientific-productional complex
TASS	Telegrafnoe Agentstvo Sovetskogo Soiuza (Telegraph Agency of the Soviet Union, the official Soviet news service)
TR	transferable ruble
UCY	Union of Communist Youth (in Romania)
UN	United Nations
UNESCO	United Nations Educational, Scientific, and Cultural Organization
UPI	United Press International (a U.S. news service)
U.S.	United States
USSR	Union of Soviet Socialist Republics

EXTERNAL INFLUENCES AFFECTING EASTERN EUROPE

Although no area of the world is today immune from external influences, Eastern Europe is particularly subject to them. Throughout their history, the peoples of the region have had to bow to more powerful neighbors; in centuries past they were incorporated into other states, and even in the present century, in which they have for the most part existed as independent entities, foreign influences have played a dominant role not only in their external relations but in their domestic affairs as well. Since 1945, the Soviet Union has been the preponderant power in Eastern Europe. Recently, however, other external influences have begun to make themselves felt in the region. The effects of contact with Western Europe and the communist parties of Western Europe now interact with the Soviet factor.

For the Soviet Union, Eastern Europe remains a critical protective glacis, and thus it is the USSR's most important preoccupation so far as foreign policy goes. Soviet influence over this region is maintained through a number of related means. Military power, which is augmented by the stationing of some 30 divisions in East Germany, Hungary, Czechoslovakia, and Poland, remains the ultimate guarantor of its influence. At the same time, however, the Soviet Union has sought to consolidate and legitimize its domination and render the exercise of brute force unnecessary by fostering political, economic, and ideological unity.

Attempts to achieve an "organic relationship" with these client regimes in Eastern Europe—never completely successful—have encountered a growing number of problems as the impact of other external factors upon the area has increased. The influence of Western Europe and North America has increased as economic relations have expanded and as detente has weakened many of the barriers that in the past kept these states relatively isolated from Western contacts. The Helsinki Conference on Security and Cooperation in Europe in the summer of 1975 was important in intensifying these tendencies. Also not to be underestimated is the influence the communist parties of Western Europe have begun to have upon the parties in the eastern half of the continent. Particularly significant is the impact of those Western parties that have established their independence from Moscow and begun to pursue policies consistent with their own domestic interests—the so-called Eurocommunists. The Italian, Spanish, and other parties institutionalized their autonomy from the Soviet Union gradually over the last two decades, but the

2

French party did so quite abruptly in 1976. The Eurocommunists are particularly significant because of the traditional close "fraternal" ties between East and West European parties.

The first chapter in this section deals with the current impact of three external influences upon Eastern Europe—the problems the Soviet Union faces in attempting to maintain its traditional sway and the measures it has taken to do so; the effects of the expansion of East-West relations in the wake of the Helsinki conference and preparations for the follow-up gathering in Belgrade; and the Eurocommunist phenomenon with its influence upon Eastern Europe.

The part of Eastern Europe in which these external forces have been particularly evident is the Balkans. This area, which in the past was a focal point of conflicting great-power interests, continues to be in many ways more subject to these diverse external influences than is the remainder of Eastern Europe. Bulgaria is the Soviet Union's most consistent and staunchest ally. Romania, though a member of the Warsaw Pact and Comecon, has over the last decade successfully achieved a degree of autonomy in foreign policy. Yugoslavia, which considers itself both socialist and nonaligned, shares certain broad foreign policy interests with the Soviet Union, but at the same time senses a Soviet threat to its independence. The Yugoslav party is close to the Italian Communist Party so far as its attitude to interparty relations and its view of Moscow go. Isolated Albania remains perhaps the closest ally of China, although increasing signs of strain in this relationship have been apparent lately. In addition to this disparate agglomeration of communist states, the region includes (geographically and economically, as well as historically) Greece and Turkey, both members of the North Atlantic Alliance, both with links to Western Europe and the United States. Thus the Balkans reflect more dramatically than the rest of Eastern Europe the conflicting influences at work in the region.

Chapters 2, 3, 4, and 5 highlight some of the major foreign policy problems facing this part of Eastern Europe. The Balkan conference in Athens in January 1976 (Chapter 2) was an attempt to implement on a regional scale some of the principles accepted in Helsinki. The limited results of this gathering are largely attributable to external influences coupled with and exacerbated by bilateral problems. In the face of the Soviet drive to achieve cohesion among the Warsaw Pact/Comecon states, Romania has shown itself willing to improve, at least atmospherically, its relations with the USSR (Chapter 3). While no fundamental shift in foreign policy has been apparent thus far, there are indications that Romania is interested in expanding its economic relations with the Soviet Union and the other Comecon states. Yugoslavia, too, has made attempts to improve its ties with the USSR (Chapter 4). The regular hot-to-cold fluctuations that have marked their relationship in the past, however, continued even after Soviet party leader Brezhnev visited Belgrade in late 1976; the basic areas of difference between the two countries remain. Albania, long China's closest ally, also appears to be undergoing a rethinking of its foreign policy (Chapter 5). Since the party's seventh congress in November 1976, there has been evidence of increasing strain in relations with China, and at the same time a better attitude toward Albania's Balkan neighbors (except Bulgaria) has become noticeable. The Albanian leadership, however, adamantly persists in its determination not to mend its diplomatic fences with the Soviet Union.

1

THE MAJOR EXTERNAL INFLUENCES: THE SOVIET UNION, EAST-WEST COOPERATION, AND EUROCOMMUNISM

J. F. Brown
Charles Andras
Kevin Devlin

SOVIET-EAST EUROPEAN RELATIONS IN 1976

Pat periodization invites charges of schematism. Rightly so, since the affairs of men, public or private, are too mercurial and volatile to lend themselves to rigid compartmentalization. But, without losing sight of this relevant truism, we may, in the context of Soviet-East European relations, divide the year 1976 into two fairly neat halves: the first half, in which Moscow was on the defensive in the preparations for the conference of European communist parties, ultimately held in East Berlin in June; and the second half, when, on the state level, Moscow sought to strengthen its control over Eastern Europe and to bring Yugoslavia closer to its orbit.

Objections, of course, will immediately be raised. The Soviet Union did not suddenly after July 1976 crank up the wheels of cohesion. The European communist party conference was a matter of parties, anyway, rather than states, and an essential role in opposition to the pretensions of the Communist Party of the Soviet Union (CPSU) was played by West European parties. Such arguments are well taken, but, while cautioning against, they do not undermine the generalization made. More to the point would be a warning against

---

This chapter is composed of three sections of "Survey of East European Developments in 1976," RAD Background Report/260, Radio Free Europe Research, 23 December 1976. The sections in question are J. F. Brown, "Soviet-East European Relations in 1976"; "Between Helsinki and Belgrade: The East European Course in East-West Cooperation"; and Kevin Devlin, "Change and Challenge in European Communism."

taking 1976 as a year in isolation. In terms of Soviet aims, the year should be seen as part of the whole period since 1969, during which the Soviet Union conducted an energetic yet sophistocated policy of comprehensive integration in Eastern Europe.[1] This policy may not have achieved the results desired. But it is still being pursued and is, in any case, seen by its initiators as a long-term process.

East Berlin Positions

It was undoubtedly the preparations for East Berlin that dominated observers' attention in the first months of 1976. Indeed, well before the beginning of the year it was evident that the Soviet view of the conference—one that would solidify the CPSU's mastery over the European movement—was totally unrealistic. On the contrary, a situation was developing that embarrassingly revealed Soviet inability to dominate or even decisively influence some of Europe's most important parties. The Soviets' arithmetical majority remained, of course, impressive. But, if ever there was a genuine case for distinguishing arithmetical from political majorities, it was during the preparations for the European communist party conference. The Yugoslavs, Italians, Spaniards, Romanians, French, British, and Swedes opposed Soviet hegemony and stood for the independence of each party: 7 out of 28. But it was this decisive minority that handed the CPSU its biggest humiliation since the great schism with China.

The two East European parties in this decisive minority represented states already well known for their resistance to Soviet domination. The Yugoslav and Romanian attitudes, therefore, came as no surprise. Nor did those of the "ultra-loyalists"—the Czechoslovaks, the East Germans, and the Bulgarians: In fact, at different times each of these parties appeared to be pressing the case for CPSU domination harder than were the Soviets themselves. Also loyal to the Soviets, but with a more nuanced and restrained approach, were the Poles and Hungarians. These two parties at least kept contact with the Italians and Yugoslavs when the negotiations were at their most acrimonious.

The varying stands of the East European parties on the European conference, therefore, accurately reflected the positions they generally take toward Soviet hegemony in the numerous contexts in which it seeks to assert itself. In this sense, East European politics have been fairly predictable for several years now: Yugoslavia behaves as an independent state; Romania as if it wants to be; Poland and Hungary have supported Soviet initiatives undeviatingly in substance, but have effectively shown a poise and flexibility of manner that has distinguished them from the Bulgarians and Czechoslovaks.

The case of East Germany is not so simple. For the German Democratic Republic (GDR), loyalty to Moscow is a matter of survival—
literally an Existenzfrage. But the Moscow its leaders prefer is the
cold-war Moscow, unequivocally hostile to the West and particularly
to West Germany. A period of detente, therefore, creates a
dilemma for the GDR's leaders. Analogies are dangerous, but there
is some similarity between Pankow and Tirana. No one was more
loyal to the Soviets when they were bristlingly hostile to the Yugoslavs
than the Albanian leaders. When Khrushchev began his courtship of
Tito, the Albanian attitude changed. What Yugoslavia is to Albania, the
Federal Republic of Germany (FRG) is to the GDR. But geopolitics,
of course, routs the analogy. Albania could get away with it; East
Germany dares not try.

The Tightening

The Soviets must have drawn several conclusions from the
reverse at East Berlin, some of which may not yet be apparent.
But, drawing on a formidable diplomatic tradition, they publicly
ignored the reverse, preferring to posture as if it had never happened.
In this they were aided by the vagueness of the final document agreed
upon at East Berlin. Some have claimed that, for present and potential dissident parties, this document is indeed a Magna Carta of their
liberties. But the 1215 Magna Carta was—or was supposed to be—
binding. Its 1976 counterpart was not—and it was considered a great
victory for the dissident parties when the Soviets were forced to
agree that it should not be. But this, of course, means that it is
not binding for the Soviets either; and since East Berlin they have
either ignored the document, stressed those parts agreeable to themselves, or put their own interpretation on those parts deliberately
left ambiguous. Deliberate omissions, such as the pregnant term
"proletarian internationalism," they have continued to use in all their
hegemonistic connotations.

But still, the Soviet leaders, sometimes good at deceiving others,
do not often deceive themselves. Their nonchalant attitude toward
the East Berlin document probably does not denote an equally nonchalant attitude to the political realities and dangers the document
represents. The reverse at East Berlin, therefore, among other
things, must have reinforced the USSR's determination to strengthen
its grip on Eastern Europe, the region closest to it and perceived as
most vital to its national security. The specter of "Eurocommunism"
might not be stopped from haunting Western Europe, but it must be
repulsed closer to home. What the dissidents gained in East Berlin
would result in greater Soviet pressure for conformity in Eastern
Europe.

Thus a new dimension was added to a Soviet policy already in evidence for several years: that of seeking to enforce cohesion in Eastern Europe. The determination to avoid another Czechoslovak Spring and its consequences was perhaps the main determinant of this policy. Another was the need to "shore up" Eastern Europe against the assumed dangers of detente, the "contaminating influence" of contacts with the West.

Now another danger, "Eurocommunism," was added, although the Soviets may perceive this as nothing basically new but just another poisonous refinement of this whole Western "contaminating influence." They may now indeed, in rueful perspective, consider two of their most spectacular foreign initiatives in recent years—Helsinki in 1975 and East Berlin in 1976—as mixed blessings indeed. East Berlin was a definite reverse. Helsinki brought its advantages, but it has also become a rallying cry for self-assertion or even disaffection in Eastern Europe to an extent the Soviets probably underestimated. Both Helsinki and East Berlin were seen by Moscow as securing, even legitimizing, its dominance in vitally important aspects of international politics. But already in the negotiating stages of both conferences it became obvious the Soviets were not going to get matters entirely their own way. The consequences of both conferences might well make them wish they had never originated them.

The Narrower Field

But the defeats, frustrations, and fears on the larger fields of European politics logically lead, in this case, to a closer Soviet concentration on the narrower field of Eastern Europe. And, because Eastern Europe is perceived as so vital to Moscow, this concentration is comprehensive or multidimensional. It embraces party and state in Eastern Europe and every walk of public life encompassed by party and state.

Eastern Europe now, therefore, is the only geopolitical area in which the Soviets make no distinction between state and party interests, between the USSR's interests as a traditional power-oriented state and as the leader of the world communist movement. Outside Eastern Europe, for various reasons, it is reasons of state that now largely motivate Soviet policy. Even in Western Europe, this seems to be more and more the case. And in this context, "Eurocommunism" is by no means an unmitigated disaster from the Soviet point of view. What is lost on the roundabouts may be made up on the swings. Enrico Berlinguer, Georges Marchais, and Santiago Carrillo—heads, respectively, of the Italian, French, and Spanish communist parties—may be terribly rude to Soviet Party Secretary Boris Ponomarev. This

is unfortunate and humiliating. But measure that against the disarray
in the Western alliance if communist parties come to power in Italy
and France. Weighing up considerations of this sort must be common
practice in Moscow these days. But for Eastern Europe, Caesaro-
papism still prevails, with Moscow the seat of both pope and emperor.

The whole logic, therefore, of a complex political situation pointed
in 1976 toward a closer Soviet concentration on Eastern Europe that
aimed at solidifying Moscow's predominance. And there is no doubt
that Soviet policy has been facilitated by the economic difficulties of
the East European states themselves.

These difficulties began to occur after a period of notable economic prosperity in the first half of the 1970s. This prosperity had
several causes, economic and political. But one of the basic ones
was a plentiful flow of relatively cheap raw materials from the Soviet
Union. This ended in early 1975, when the Soviets drastically increased the prices of these materials. Allowing for the obvious
differences, an analogy might be drawn with the West European situation. The unprecedented West European prosperity from the beginning
of the 1960s was, to a considerable extent, based on supplies of cheap
oil. Although cheap oil for Western Europe ended in 1973, it ended
for Eastern Europe in 1975. True, there are other reasons, of both
external and domestic provenance, for the recent economic recessions
in the two parts of Europe, but the enormous and sudden increase in
the prices of raw materials was undoubtedly the catalyst of both.

The political consequences of both these disasters have been far-
reaching. In Eastern Europe, the most important was a strengthening
of the Soviet grip. The economic deterioration that began in 1975
accelerated in 1976. The real cost of the Soviets' pricing policy
became more evident, as did the effect of worldwide inflation and
recession. Poland, which since early 1971 had enjoyed enormous
economic expansion under Edward Gierek, also had its third poor
harvest in a row. The economy was badly overheated; serious,
domestically generated inflationary pressures became irresistible;
the foreign (Western) debt was assuming almost terrifying dimensions.
The GDR, too, had a very poor harvest and showed more basic signs
of faltering in other economic branches. In Czechoslovakia, where
economic prosperity had been Gustav Husak's one positive success
in the whole normalization program, the situation was similar. In
Hungary, where the New Economic Mechanism (NEM) had brought
unprecedented prosperity, the government openly warned the population that more austere times lay ahead. The Bulgarian leadership,
never as frank with its population as the Hungarian, was nevertheless
clearly signaling that the good years were over. Romania was seriously affected by various economic weaknesses, some domestically
induced, others over which it had no control. Only Yugoslavia, which

during the years of general boom had been experiencing serious difficulties but now appeared to be pulling out of some of them, showed
a more cheerful economic countenance.

The Soviet leaders were not slow in seeking to exploit the opportunities presented them. Just at the moment Eastern Europe was
beginning to seem more vital to them than at any time since the end
of World War II, it had also become economically more vulnerable
than at any time since the early 1960s. The steps taken by Brezhnev
to strengthen the Soviet hold in Eastern Europe are too well known
to warrant recounting in detail here. Most took place in November.
They included the bailing out of the Gierek leadership that month,
after its disastrous blunder in June; the visit to Yugoslavia; the visit
to Bucharest, where <u>Vozhd</u> met <u>Conducator</u> after the latter had made
some much publicized concessions in the summer; the Warsaw Pact
meeting, also in Bucharest, which saw the first institutional innovations in that organization since March 1969 and a further Brezhnev
essay in "directed consensus." Finally, the symbolic opportunities
presented by Brezhnev's 70th birthday in December were not missed
by the political stage managers in Moscow.

Success Only Temporary?

How successful will these Soviet efforts turn out to be? Will the
last part of 1976 be remembered as the period when that success in
controlling Eastern Europe that had eluded the Soviet Union for three
decades was finally achieved?

It would be imprudent to underestimate the advantages Moscow
presently holds over an economically weakened Eastern Europe.
Just two years ago, in 1974, for example, a self-confident Gierek
leadership in Poland, although loyal to Moscow, was conducting its
external policy, economic and perhaps political, in a manner that
must have caused Soviet misgivings. Now, that self-confidence has
been shattered and Soviet supremacy—particularly psychological
supremacy—has been reasserted. Romania continues to insist that
its relative independence in foreign policy will be maintained, but
some have argued that economic weakness could begin to affect its
political will. Tito apparently resisted Soviet attempts to encroach
on Yugoslav sovereignty with success. But will Yugoslavia, with its
potential for instability, even disruption, always remain so immune?
Albania, a country whose strategic value far outweighs its intrinsic
importance, is weakened by domestic dissension, economic distress,
and uncertainty over the future of its alliance with China. The view
of Tirana from Moscow may be now more promising than it has been
for many years. As for the other East European countries, they have
presented few problems of assertiveness to the Soviet Union.

The appearance, therefore, at the end of 1976 is one of safety and stability from the Soviet point of view. But this could be grossly deceptive. Paradoxically, Eastern Europe could be moving into a period of pronounced instability, with the traditional Soviet aim in the region—to achieve cohesion and viability—seeming even further than ever from attainment.

In the first place, the Soviet Union itself cannot long delay a change of leadership that might degenerate into a succession crisis. Enough has already been written about this possibility elsewhere. What might be mentioned here, however, is that in 1976 the breakup of the ruling Soviet oligarchy actually began with the death of Marshal A. A. Grechko and the serious illness of Aleksei Kosygin, to add to the known physical corrosion of Brezhnev himself. The two- to three-year periods after the departures of Stalin and Khrushchev were marked by a lack of Soviet decisiveness in Eastern Europe and the inevitable loss of control. The same need not happen again, of course. But the possibility of its doing so should not be overlooked, especially if a change in Soviet leadership interacted with other destabilizing factors at work in the region.

The most dangerous of these factors would probably be a serious decline in living standards. The "consumer spree" of the early 1970s is over, and the East European leaders (not just the Polish) and above all the Soviet leaders, who possess so much economic advantage, must be careful to ensure that living standards do not fall below the tolerable minimum. And their dilemma, of course, is that no one knows what the tolerable minimum is, especially with populations strongly infected by the disease of rising expectations. Other potentially destabilizing factors tend to be less general and confined to one or more countries. But instability after Tito's death, for example, would certainly have repercussions beyond the borders of Yugoslavia. Because of the Macedonian issue, it could most seriously affect Bulgaria, whose ruling gerontocracy must soon begin to fall apart. (And before Todor Zhivkov asserted his supremacy in the early 1960s, leadership instability in Bulgaria was the rule rather than the exception.) In both Romania and Hungary, it would only need the death of the party leader to transform radically the unique, but totally different, situations that prevail in those two countries.

A long list of possible sources of instability could be compiled without necessarily straying into fantasy. Two intriguing latecomers to this list could be mentioned here.

One is the potential effect on intellectual elites in Eastern Europe of precisely that "Eurocommunism" that challenged the Soviets in East Berlin. This should not be exaggerated, but neither should it be ignored. In fact, there is evidence already suggesting a rapport between the PCI and some of the dissident Czechoslovak reformers

of 1968. At the moment, the political effect of this may be slight
because these Czechoslovak reformers are powerless. But in two
or three years' time, there may have been sufficient movement on
the scene in Prague and Bratislava for this interaction to have some
impact. More important at present is the interaction between "Eurocommunism" and the dissident intellectuals in Poland. This has
already begun, and the influence of Italian and Spanish intellectual
communists on their Polish counterparts is likely to grow. This
influence could spread to East Germany and Hungary; indeed, it may
already have done so. "Eurocommunism" could become for East
European intellectuals in the late 1970s and early 1980s what Yugoslav
"revisionism" was in the 1950s, and its impact might, in fact, become
even greater.

The other latecomer is "Helsinki." If the agreement on European
security and cooperation had been signed in the summer of 1971 instead of 1975, the chances are that it would now be remembered as
a Soviet diplomatic victory—because then, it would have coincided
with the beginning of the four-year period of prosperity in Eastern
Europe, a prosperity that was the lubrication of the Soviet Union's
cohesion drive. But the Helsinki agreement was actually signed just
when Eastern Europe's prosperity was seen to be coming to an end,
when the new era of dissatisfaction, uncertainty, and restlessness
was beginning. It was East European society in this mood that was
ready to take advantage of those articles in "Basket Three" (cultural
and humanitarian contacts) for which the Western side negotiated so
strongly during those last few months before the ceremonies in
Helsinki. If the West continues to remain firm on Basket Three, the
popular response in Eastern Europe could be extraordinary.

Triangular Relationship Needed

What all this only serves to show is that, in East European
politics and in Eastern Europe's relations with the Soviet Union, the
East European societies are a factor not just of great importance
but of clear and separate distinctiveness from the East European
states or ruling authorities.

If Soviet-East European relations were a matter to be settled
between the Kremlin and the official capitals of the region, then one
might look forward at the end of 1976 to a period of growing Soviet
hegemony in Eastern Europe, more and more stable because less
and less disputed. But a truly "organic" relationship between the
Soviet Union and Eastern Europe depends on three factors: (1) a
harmonious relationship between Moscow and the individual East
European regimes; (2) a harmonious relationship between the individ-

ual East European regimes and their societies; and (3) an acceptance
by the East European societies of Soviet hegemony over their countries.
An essay, even a book, on Soviet-East European relations within the
framework of those three factors might one day be worth writing.
In the meantime, it can safely be maintained that, if we take the
region as a whole, an organic relationship with the Soviet Union
seemed, as far away at the end of 1976 as it ever was. That year,
like so many others in the past, saw the mounting of an ideological
offensive, at Soviet inspiration, in most of the East European countries.
At the end of the year, an important conference on ideological purity
was held in Sofia. One of the main aims of this offensive has been
to produce or catch the elusive "socialist man." Presumably such
a "socialist man" would enable factors two and three outlined above
to be attained. The more sensible East European leaders know the
task is impossible. But they go through the motions, partly at least
to please Moscow.

As for the Soviet leaders, present and future, they will go ahead
building their infrastructure of integration, stability, and control in
the alliance they dominate. But at the end of 1976, despite all the
appearances of Soviet strength, there seemed even less assurance
that this infrastructure would not in the end turn out to be nothing
but a superstructure weakly set down in a soil that rejects it.

BETWEEN HELSINKI AND BELGRADE: THE EAST EUROPEAN COURSE IN EAST-WEST COOPERATION

At the end of 1976, with only six months remaining before the
Belgrade conference—the Helsinki follow-up scheduled for mid-1977
in the Yugoslav capital—any discussion of East-West relations can
hardly avoid the subject. The idea of the gathering resulted from a
compromise in the long series of East-West diplomatic talks that
paved the way for the Helsinki summit. Most of the Warsaw Pact
regimes pressed for a sort of standing committee to help in the
implementation of the Final Act, but the majority of Western participants refused to accept this proposal because they thought it might
lead to the institutionalization of Warsaw Pact interference in European affairs. In the end, the diplomats from East and West agreed
that the signatory governments would organize multilateral meetings
among their representatives "to exchange views on the implementation
of the provisions of the Final Act" and on "the deepening of their
mutual relations, the improvement of security, and the development
of cooperation in Europe." It was also resolved to hold the first
such meeting "at the level of representatives appointed by the ministers
of foreign affairs" and to convene it in Belgrade in June 1977.[2]

Differences of View

It now appears, however, that the two sides do not agree about
the role such a follow-up meeting should play, about how a review
of the implementation of Helsinki should be accomplished. But this
difference of views should not surprise anyone. It stems directly
from the difference between the Eastern and Western concepts of
European security and detente, and their ideas on what practical
steps should follow from the Helsinki agreement in the field of East-
West interaction.

In the West there is a strong conviction that, although Helsinki
has improved the general atmosphere in East-West relations, its
practical results are lagging behind original expectations and that
this is mainly true with regard to Basket Three, because the socialist
regimes are reluctant to comply with the recommendations of the
Final Act. The Belgrade conference, therefore, should look deeper
into this matter and do something to speed up East-West cooperation.
Various steps have been taken in the West to monitor the implementation of Helsinki and provide material for Belgrade. The most prominent among them is the U.S. Congressional Commission, which was
set up in the summer of 1976. In November members of the commission spent two weeks on a fact-finding tour of Europe and returned
with the conclusion that Helsinki "offered an unprecedented opportunity
for broadening a dialogue with the nations of Eastern Europe" but
that "real progress lags far behind the potentialities," especially in
areas covered by Basket Three. "What is needed at this stage," the
commission's report stated, "is further progress at the Belgrade
back-up meeting without vituperation or rocking the boat."

Members of the Soviet alliance do not concur. Except for the
Romanians, they claim that progress has been considerable but that
in order to assess it correctly the Final Act must be taken as a whole:
One must not concentrate on only certain aspects of it, like Basket
Three, and gloss over the others; such an attitude cannot but lead to
a deliberate distortion of reality, to indulging in hostile propaganda.
The regimes' views of Western efforts to monitor Helsinki and line
up their findings in Belgrade crystallized in their handling of the
U.S. Congressional Commission. The Warsaw Pact states refused
to issue visas to the members of the commission and charged that in
establishing it the United States was "trying to secure the right for
itself to interpret the Final Act in an arbitrary and unilateral manner"
and that the commission's work was out of line with the principle of
noninterference in the affairs of other nations. Regime media have
also claimed that members of the commission were acting "in the
spirit of the cold war," attempting to find "violations on the part of
others while forgetting about their own commitments."[3] Preparatory

work for Belgrade was in order, but it should be a common effort
leading to a "constructive exchange of experience and opinions about
the positive results achieved to date in the realization of the Final
Act." Only such an approach could ensure continuation of the course
of detente set off by Helsinki and protect it from cold war forces
wanting to wreck the follow-up conference.[4]

Despite their calls for a common approach, the Eastern regimes
seem to be busily preparing for Belgrade. Apparently they are
anxious not to appear there as potential defendants, but rather to
assign this role to the West. Hence the new efforts in Eastern media
to restate the Warsaw Pact concept of European security, to shift
the responsibility for any failure to the West, to stress the regimes'
unwavering willingness to cooperate, and to impress public opinion
with a set of fresh measures.

Five Points

On the whole, there are few new elements in these maneuvers;
generally speaking, they reiterate what has been said many times
before. Below are some of the points most frequently made:

First, Helsinki has been a great contribution to European security,
detente, and peaceful cooperation. A problem is posed, however, by
the fact that forces in the West distort the meaning of the Final Act,
and stress the importance of Basket Three at the expense of the other
sections of the document and use it as a pretext for interfering in the
internal affairs of the socialist states. But the Helsinki agreement
must be seen as a single act, no part of which can be separated from
the others. In fact, the introductory chapter of the Final Act deals
with the basic principles of interstate relations—such as noninterference in domestic affairs of other states—which constitute the precon-
dition for all cooperation and thus must be given priority, not ignored,
as forces in the West have tried to do.

Second, under the present circumstances, when political detente
has progressed so far that it would be difficult to stop or reverse it,
detente in the military field takes on primary importance. In the
terms used by Brezhnev, "political detente must be complemented
by military detente." The idea is to move gradually toward total
disarmament, by reviving the deadlocked Mutual and Balanced Force
Reductions (MFBR) talks in Vienna, bringing the SALT talks to a
conclusion, taking other nuclear control measures, and so on.
Another urgent task is to pay more attention to Basket Two, which
covers cooperation in the economic, technical, scientific, and environmental fields. Brezhnev's related proposal, made at the Polish party
congress in December 1975, has been advocated as the ideal solution.

Third, cultural-humanitarian cooperation and freer flow of information have been overemphasized by the West, which—it is claimed—has accused members of the socialist community of violating the Helsinki agreement and lagging far behind the West in the fulfillment of the provisions of Basket Three. But, so the regimes claim, the facts prove just the opposite. The socialist countries have translated more Western books, shown more Western films, and so on than vice versa; the Eastern visa policy is more liberal than that of the West; and people in the East are better informed about life in the West than are their opposite numbers in the West. Hence, only the socialist countries can complain about "gross disproportions."[5]

Fourth, East-West cooperation, particularly in the humanitarian-cultural field, must not be confused with ideological capitulation on the part of the socialist regimes, or with convergence between the two social systems. The Marxist-Leninist concept of peaceful coexistence, of East-West detente, relates only to state-to-state contacts and does not include the opposing ideologies and social systems. It is the capitalists who want to extend the idea of coexistence into the field of ideologies, and in doing so their aim is to subvert socialism and undermine socialist unity. In reality, under conditions of peaceful coexistence, antagonism between East and West shifts into the ideological fields; it intensifies rather than diminishes, but the struggle—and this is a new facet—is carried on with nonmilitary means. Similarly, peaceful coexistence does not guarantee the continuation of the existing system of social exploitation. The intensification of social conflict is a natural law, a historical process; thus class warfare will not cease and social progress will expand even in a world governed by the principles of peaceful coexistence. The socialist regimes, permeated by the spirit of proletarian internationalism and solidarity, cannot play the role of bystanders in this conflict. Again, these formulations are not new, but the impression is that in the fall of 1976 they were reiterated with new emphasis. The many repeats should not be attributed solely to the imminence of the Belgrade conference; they are also a reaction to the decision of certain European communist parties to drop the term "proletarian internationalism."

Fifth, in order to fulfill their obligation to promote East-West cooperation and detente and to avert threats to the forces of detente, the members of the socialist community must consolidate their unity and increase their might and worldwide influence. This is all the more important since it is precisely their unity that is the prime target of the imperialist opponents. In the consolidation process, the two most topical tasks are coordinated action in foreign policy and ideological cooperation. The latter must lead to an ideological counterattack against imperialist efforts to distort socialist reality

and show the world the real face of established socialism. The
questions of how to do this and what the characteristics of "real
socialism" are dominate this aspect of the intrabloc discussion.6

A New Bucharest Declaration

Most of the points listed above reappeared in the form of concrete
proposals addressed to the West in the document issued by the last
session of the Warsaw Pact Political Advisory Committee, which
was held in Bucharest on November 25-26. The purpose of this conference, convened half a year before Belgrade, was to impress the
world with the degree of unity achieved by the socialist community
and its interest in peace. The document issued at the meeting, officially called the "Declaration of Warsaw Treaty Member Countries,"7
is being treated by the regimes as crowning the Bucharest Declaration
of ten years ago that set off the subsequent East-West negotiations
on European security and cooperation. In the new document, the
regimes try to regain the offensive, to put an end to the present
period of wavering in the domain of European security and cooperation, and to enlarge the content of the general concept.

To begin with, the participants in the conference expressed their
determination to "strictly abide by and carry out all the provisions
of the Final Act [of Helsinki]." Speaking of economic cooperation,
they criticized "some" capitalist countries for maintaining "discriminatory restrictions on trade with the socialist countries" and
urged further development of trade based on reciprocity. Moving
into the next area—science, technology, the environment—they
embraced Brezhnev's idea of holding large-scale European conferences on cooperation in those three sectors. They also endorsed
the continuation of cultural-humanitarian cooperation but added two
notes of warning: (1) using these contacts for purposes that undermine
"understanding and friendship among peoples" or in order to "inter-
fere in the domestic affairs of states" is a "road without a future";
and (2) the mass media should "truthfully inform the public" and
help to "bring people closer together."

But it is disarmament with all its ramifications that really
dominates the conference document. First of all, there is the well-
known argument that political detente should be complemented by
military detente. This is followed by calls to speed up the MBFR
negotiations in Vienna and the nuclear weapons talks, and by the
vague offer ultimately to dissolve the two opposing military alliances
in Europe. The list ends with two specific and relatively new suggestions: first, the two alliances should refrain from admitting new
members—a move obviously directed against possible NATO member-

ship for Spain; and second, the signatories of the Helsinki agreement should conclude a treaty "on not being the first to use nuclear weapons against each other." Post-Bucharest comments in the regime media have played up the conclusion of such a treaty as the most urgent of the many tasks involved in consolidating peace in Europe.

The declaration ended with a statement expressing "great satisfaction" at the all-round cooperation among the socialist countries, among the members of the Warsaw Pact, urging that it be intensified. It also reported that the Political Advisory Committee has resolved to set up a "joint secretariat" and a "committee of foreign ministers." These new organs will, as the document put it, "deepen the political contacts among the fraternal peoples." In the opinion of the Political Advisory Committee, all-round cooperation is "in full accord with the interests of peace on the European continent. It is a factor that stimulates all-European cooperation in strengthening peace and security, in promoting economic progress, culture, and the spiritual enrichment of peoples."

Two questions come immediately to mind in connection with this latest Warsaw Pact declaration.

In the first place, what sort of united front lies behind the facade of the pact? No one can ignore the fact that the session of the Political Advisory Committee was preceded by an almost three-day-long bilateral conference between Brezhnev and Romania's Nicolae Ceausescu. While all their differences cannot have been reconciled, their meetings represent a long step toward "normalization of relations." Romania has always warmly supported the basic Eastern concept of European security and cooperation, but on specific issues, at least until recently, it followed a course of its own, jealously guarding its national identity. For example, the Bucharest regime hesitated to join in collective Warsaw Pact campaigns against the "capitalist-imperialist forces," or to identify itself with all the aspects of socialism promoted in other states belonging to the community. Also, the Romanian leadership has been less satisfied with the general state of East-West relations than have the other regimes. For instance, in a speech delivered in Tulcea, Ceausescu complained that "very little has been done to implement" the Helsinki Final Act.[8] It is not to be expected that these events in Bucharest will lessen Ceausescu's interest in specifically Romanian solutions, but perhaps his means and methods will change. In any case the fact that in the context of socialist cooperation the Warsaw Pact document refers to "respect for the equality and sovereignty of each state, nonintervention in internal affairs, and comradely understanding," is considered a concession to the Romanian leader.

National self-interest and tradition have also induced Hungary and Poland to become more active in regard to East-West cooperation, especially in the economic field, than certain other members of the community. There is no reason to believe that such discrepancies will disappear in the future. Party First Secretary Janos Kadar's trip to Austria (his first official visit to a Western country), which took place only two weeks after the Warsaw Pact summit, has also been interpreted in the West as a signal that, despite the pressure for socialist consolidation, the Hungarian regime wants to adhere to its present tested course in East-West cooperation.

Another question is: To what extent can the Warsaw Pact proposals speed up East-West negotiations and ease the climate of the Belgrade conference? In Western eyes the real problem with East-West interaction is that it often stumbles into concrete difficulties, and usually Eastern "rescue actions" do not provide concrete solutions, or, if they do, their solutions work out to the disadvantage of the West. The first reactions to the latest Bucharest declaration have made a similar point: They have noted the general character of the proposals and the fact that the most important of them (agreement not to be the first to use nuclear weapons) would weaken Western Europe and expose it to the numerically overwhelming conventional forces of the Warsaw Pact. The Frankfurter Allgemeine Zeitung[9] called the Eastern offer a "strategy of intimidation." Later NATO Secretary-General Joseph Luns and representatives of the member states rejected the Warsaw Pact proposals as "unacceptable." On the other hand, despite such obvious snags, the declaration may provide Western nations with useful clues to Warsaw Pact thinking about the future course of detente.

Progress and Retrogression

Since the Belgrade conference is intended to promote security and cooperation, it will have to prepare a dispassionate and objective assessment of all aspects of East-West relations. These can be characterized as an uneven mixture of small steps in the right direction and recurrent staggering setbacks ideologically motivated or simply bureaucratic interference by the East, and limited awareness in the West of all the potentialities of the Final Act. In the view of several Western observers, the socialist regimes have made "carefully portioned and controllable concessions" in various sectors of East-West cooperation without, however, changing anything in their basic political position.[10] It has also been noted that in a few marginal sectors the positions of the individual regimes may differ slightly from each other, a phenomenon that cannot please the centralist forces in the community.

Progress and retrogression are most easily discernible in the wide area covered by Basket Three. The number of East-West cultural cooperation agreements has markedly increased since Helsinki. On the other hand, writers, poets, and other cultural workers in the East are still subject to severe limitations imposed by the regimes.

Also in the area of Basket Three, the Soviet Union eased the working conditions of foreign journalists and began granting them multiple-entry visas. Their direct access to government sources has been facilitated. Under a reciprocal agreement, United Press International (UPI) opened a new bureau in Leningrad, and TASS did the same in San Francisco. More recently, a newspaper exchange agreement was concluded between a daily newspaper in Bremen, West Germany, and one published in Riga, Latvia (Soviet Union)—an interesting new venture. It is based on exchanges (and publication) of material produced by each side. Western newspaper sales in the Warsaw Pact countries have slightly increased; the largest importer of Western journals is Poland, but in terms of per capita sales Hungary and Czechoslovakia lead the way.

Even in the sensitive field of human contacts—such as family reunion, ethnic emigration, and travel in general—the recommendations of Helsinki combined with Western insistence, public protest, and economic pressure have brought about some success. U.S. State Department figures issued in August indicated that Soviet exit visas for Israel, West Germany, and the United States have been issued at a higher rate this year than in 1975. The Polish-West German package deal allowing the resettlement of 125,000 ethnic Germans in the Federal Republic of Germany (FRG) was also facilitated by the spirit of the Final Act of Helsinki, and there is some hope that even the rigid Czechoslovak regime will allow some of its 80,000 ethnic Germans to emigrate.

The case of Romania deserves special attention. It ranks second (after Poland) in Eastern Europe as a harborer of ethnic minorities. Hungarians, Germans, and Jews predominate, and the two latter groups are the most actively interested in emigration. The issue attracted the attention of the U.S. Congress and was connected with the granting of most-favored-nation status to Romania. The flow of resettlers has remained relatively slow, however, giving rise to repeated criticism of the regime in Congress and in the Western press. In a speech in the summer of 1976, party and state leader Ceausescu pledged to resolve the question, but he also took exception to "propaganda from abroad" whose intention, he said, is to obtain "cheap skilled labor" for the "great capitalist monopolies." In recent months public protests staged by private individuals and organizations in the West have speeded up the issuance of Romanian exit visas to a considerable number of persons who for one reason or another wanted to emigrate.

But if some progress has been registered in regard to the freer flow of people, there have also been retrogressions, violations of both the letter and spirit of the Helsinki agreement. The list of bureaucratic interventions is long and varied and includes such actions as refusal by the Warsaw Pact states to grant visas to members of the U.S. Congressional Commission, the USSR's refusal to admit an interreligious delegation of 14 American Christian and Jewish leaders, and Hungary's withholding of permission for an Italian literary group to organize a meeting in Budapest. All in all, the East's performance in the field of human contacts and human rights in general has been rather disappointing. In a report to the U.S. Congress, former President Gerald Ford severely criticized the regimes for their basically unaltered stand on human rights matters. "They continue to act on the philosophy," Ford said, "that individual rights must be subordinated to the collective good as defined by the communist party."11

In the area of Basket Two, a sharp increase in East-West economic cooperation has marked the period under consideration. Among its most distinctive features are purchases of foreign technology and a growing interest in industrial cooperation agreements. If a Czechoslovak figure is correct, in all about 1,000 such agreements have been concluded since the mid-1960s, a good proportion of them in the last year. On the socialist side, the most frequent partners are the Soviet Union, Poland, and Hungary, and it now appears that Czechoslovakia wants to join the line. Hungary and Romania both permit joint ventures with Western companies, with the latter owning 49 percent of the enterprise and having a share in management. The first mixed West German-Romanian company began operating in October 1976 and is said to be a model.

Some observers suspect, however, that the upsurge in economic contacts would have taken place even without the security conference, since it is a logical consequence of the present trend in international relations and the pressure exerted by modern industrialization and scientific-technological progress. The expansion has also brought problems, one of which is that the East's debts to the West have risen to the point where they might well undermine the confidence of Western financial circles. This danger has been widely discussed in the Western press but is rarely mentioned in the East.

While Helsinki has not given any obvious impulse to the MBFR talks in Vienna, it has generated cautious confidence-building measures in the military field. Members of the Eastern alliance have issued three invitations to Western countries (some of them NATO members) to send observers to their maneuvers, but access to the actual scene

of operations has been limited. Similar invitations from the West
have so far been rejected or ignored by members of the Soviet bloc.

In speaking of the "concrete," "positive" results of Helsinki,
one should not overlook the spread of a new awareness among the
peoples of Eastern Europe that Helsinki has made certain things
possible that were not possible before. This phenomenon is connected
with the seventh principle, governing interstate relations, in which
the signatories reaffirmed the validity of human rights and fundamental
freedoms and pledged themselves to "promote and encourage the
effective exercise of civil, political, economic, social, cultural,
and other rights and freedoms, all of which derive from the inherent
dignity of the human person and are essential for his free and full
development." The Warsaw Pact regimes like to insist on the fundamental importance of the ten principles, but they do not stress this
one; if it is a question of refuting Western concern about the handling
of human rights in the Eastern part of Europe, their usual answer is
that they are building the most humane political system mankind has
ever known.

Nevertheless, the seventh principle has caught the attention of
Soviet and East European citizens, who tend to regard it as something of a yardstick. In reflecting on developments at home and
abroad, they frequently allude to the promises written into the Final
Act. Helsinki crops up in the protest actions of Soviet dissidents
and plays a role in the "dialogue" between Polish intellectuals or
Church representatives and the regime. But, as the Western press
recently reported, even in the rigid political system of the GDR,
individuals seeking exit permits do not shrink from reminding the
regime of the commitments it made in Helsinki concerning the freer
movement of people. Just before the latest clash between the GDR
regime and the intellectuals, the number of such exit permit demands
reportedly went over the 100,000-mark by a considerable number.

CHANGE AND CHALLENGE IN EUROPEAN
COMMUNISM

In the chronicles of the international communist movement,
1976 may become known as the Year of the European Conference—
although that title would have gone to 1975 if the Kremlin's original
plans had not been thwarted by an alliance of independent parties.
This alliance cut significantly across the familiar East-West division,
since it consisted of the Yugoslav and Romanian regimes in the East,
plus the Italian,* Spanish, British, and Swedish parties in the West,

———

*In such interparty matters, the small but locally important
San Marino CP can be regarded as an extension of the Italian party.

joined in the closing stages, at least on some important issues, by
the French. The stubborn resistance by these parties to repeated
attempts by the pro-Soviet majority to introduce something like a
"general line," expressed in ideological terms, prolonged the preparatory process—at least 16 sessions over 20 months—so that the conference that was originally supposed to have been held "not later than
mid-1975" did not take place until the end of June 1976. More important was the fact that, when it did take place, it was obviously not
the kind of conference that the Kremlin had sought to achieve, but
instead one that marked the "institutionalization of diversity" in the
European communist movement.

By the end of 1975, it had become clear that the crucial issue
was the new procedural principle of "decision-making by consensus,"
which the Soviets and their supporters accepted at the initial consultative meeting held in Warsaw in October 1974—largely as the price of
Yugoslav participation. If the independent parties could successfully
insist upon observance of the consensus rule, they would get the kind
of conference, and more specifically the kind of conference document,
that they wanted; and other demands that they put forward during the
preparatory meetings would also be met. It would be a lowest-common-
denominator text; it would emphasize the principles of autonomy,
equality, and noninterference in interparty relations (with the important corollary that no special status should be accorded to the CPSU);
it would contain no criticism of any party, present or absent (for
example, the Chinese); it would deal with political action and not
with ideology; and in any case it would not be binding upon any party.

During 1975, the Soviets had made repeated attempts (acting
through the East Germans, who, as hosts at the East Berlin preparatory sessions, were charged with producing the successive draft
texts) to wear down the resistance of the independent grouping. The
latter rejected the first two "general line" drafts (April and July 1975),
and in the closing months of the year successive shifts in Soviet
positions betrayed uncertainty in the Kremlin over how to deal with
this challenge. Thus, a basically acceptable "soft-line" draft produced in October was unexpectedly followed in November by a return
to a harder line, which in turn gave way to more conciliatory positions
in December.

The New Year opened with a marathon preparatory session
(January 13-22), which evidently brought considerable progress
toward a consensual text but left major issues still unsettled. After

----

One may note also that on various issues the independent alliance
appears to have been supported by several other Western parties,
such as the Swiss and Belgian CPS.

that session, the Yugoslav delegate Aleksandar Grlickov told Austrian journalists that no agreement had been reached on the principles of interparty relations, the role of nonaligned countries, relations between communist and social democratic parties, disarmament, and the evaluation of "the crisis of modern capitalism"—and the list could obviously have been extended (for example, to the assessment of NATO and the EEC, or to such concepts as "anti-Sovietism" and "proletarian internationalism").

Shortly afterward, however, the Italian delegate, Antonio Rubbi, claimed[12] that agreement had been reached on "the fundamental lines" of the document, although there still remained "questions to be clarified." And, in a mid-February report to the Italian Communist Party (PCI) Central Committee, Sergio Segre said that "the agreement that now seems to be taking shape [is] consistent with the stand defended from the first by the PCI"—which held that the document must be based upon consensus, "without claiming to delineate general lines and strategies, to take on a binding character, or to tackle themes—such as ideological ones—on which there exist diverse and divergent positions."

The contrast between these assessments seems to have been more apparent than real—a question of different viewpoints. A genuine debate over the document was evidently going on; and, while Grlickov pointed to the important questions still under discussion, the Italians were stressing that it was now a matter of hammering out a consensual, nonbinding text.

Fitful progress toward an agreed text in the early months of 1976 was not facilitated by the fact that the confrontation was not a clear-cut one between loyalist and independent parties; other sectional interests were coming into play. The French Communist Party (PCF) offers a good example. Although by this period it had adopted positions of demonstrative independence vis-a-vis Moscow (an important development to be discussed later), it still disagreed with the Spanish, Italian, and Yugoslav parties on some basic issues—such as NATO, the United States, the European Economic Community (EEC), and the class struggle in the West. At the preparatory meeting in mid-March the French reportedly submitted a memorandum criticizing the current draft for its lack of a "class analysis": It demanded a more militant text, with particular reference to "the crisis of capitalism," and (as the PCF later confirmed) it warned that the French had not yet decided whether to attend the conference.

Nevertheless, the central question was still whether the new rule of consensus would prevail; if it did, there could be only minor, verbal concessions to French recalcitrance.

At the Editorial Commission session on May 4-6 the ironing-out of remaining differences continued. The communique said that the

"final" meeting of the commission would be in early June, and that
the conference itself could take place "in the near future." But there
were still clouds around the summit. On May 12, Grlickov reported
to the Executive Committee of the League of Communists of Yugoslavia
(LCY) that "an important step forward" had been made in coordinating
views on certain parts of the draft through "satisfactory formulations,"
but that the questions on which agreement had not been reached were
mainly "issues of principled and fundamental significance." A few
days earlier, he had expressed the hope that the remaining problems
would be "solved" at the early June session and in this connection
expected "other parties to take the LCY's position into account, and
to accept it."13

 That implicit demand set the scene for the final turning point in
the prolonged drama. This was Konstantin Katushev's visit to Belgrade in early June for talks during which, according to a Yugoslav
source, he "ended by unexpectedly accepting all the demands which
until that moment the Soviets had opposed"14—demands expressed
in what Grlickov later termed "seven decisive amendments"15 presented at the May session.

 When the pan-European conference finally convened in East
Berlin on June 29-30, it turned out that, with regard to the conference
document, the independent parties had had their way on almost every
major issue. It was a lowest-common-denominator text based on
the new principle of consensus, itself a formal recognition of the
equality and autonomy of all communist parties; it contained no criticism of the Chinese and no praise of the Soviets; it dealt with political
action and not with ideology; and it was not binding upon the participants (in fact, it was not even signed by any of them). The victory
of the independent parties on these central issues was emphasized
by the unexpected arrival of a 29th delegation, that of the independent
Dutch party, which had boycotted all the preparatory meetings, so
that in the end the only absentees were the isolationist Icelanders
and the intransigent Albanians.

 The document was more important for what it did not say than
for what it did say. Most striking was the fact that the sacrosanct
formula, "proletarian internationalism," was omitted and replaced
by a distinctly "Italian" one.* Again, no special status was accorded

---

 *"[Communist parties] will develop their internationalist, com-
radely, and voluntary cooperation and solidarity on the basis of the
great ideas of Marx, Engels, and Lenin, strictly adhering to the
principles of equality and the sovereign independence of each party,
noninterference in internal affairs, and respect for their free choice
of different roads in the struggle for social change of a progressive
nature and for socialism."

to the CPSU or the USSR. But what it did say was also significant—
for example, the "Eurocommunist" emphasis on communist parties'
dialogue and collaboration with "all other democratic forces, each
of these forces fully retaining its identity and independence." Finally,
for the first time in a collective communist document, there was
recognition of "the nonaligned countries' movement [as] one of the
most important factors in world politics"—an important point for the
Yugoslavs. On the other hand, the long list of political objectives
was broadly in harmony with Soviet foreign policy goals (but then the
differences between independent and loyalist communist parties are
generally concerned not with foreign policy but with ideology, domestic
policies, and interparty relations).

The main interest of the conference, however, lay not in the
largely anodyne text but in the "institutionalized diversity" of positions
manifested in the speeches. At one end of the spectrum, loyalist
speakers, having reluctantly agreed to the dropping of proletarian
internationalism and the abandonment of special status for the CPSU/
USSR, proceeded to insist on the continued validity of both. At the
other end, the most provocative was Santiago Carrillo of the Spanish
Communist Party: He explicitly rejected Soviet authority, made an
obvious reference to former Soviet support for Enrique Lister's
splinter party, and suggested that socialist states should set an
example by withdrawing their troops from foreign countries. Marchais
of the PCF declared flatly: "Conferences like this one do not appear
to us to correspond any longer to the needs of our time"; instead—
"since any elaboration of a strategy common to all our parties is
henceforth absolutely ruled out"—they should consider holding ad hoc
consultative meetings that "would not always end with the adoption
of a document."

The most complete presentation of independent Western communist positions at the Berlin conference came from Berlinguer of Italy;
and he made it significantly clear that he was not speaking only of or
for his own party. He noted that other West European communist
parties now shared the PCI's perspective of a socialist society based
upon "the principles of the secular, nonideological nature of the state
and its democratic organization, the plurality of political parties and
the possibility of alternation of government majorities, the autonomy
of trade unions, religious freedom, and freedom of expression, of
culture, and of the arts and sciences."

Berlinguer's speech in that forum can be said to have summed
up another important development in communist affairs during 1976—
the emergent ideological challenge posed to Soviet authority, and
more generally to the East European regimes, by what came to be
known as the "Eurocommunist" parties of Western Europe: a challenge
that grew in coherence and vigor during the preparatory process for
the Berlin conference.

Eurocommunism might be described as the tendency for communist parties in advanced societies of constitutional democracy to adapt to their sociopolitical environment by committing themselves to a gradualist, nonviolent struggle, in collaboration with other political forces, for the creation of a "socialist" democracy in which existing bourgeois liberties (opposition, protest, alternation of governments, and so on) would be guaranteed and extended. This commitment involved an effort to establish electoral credibility by emphasizing each communist party's independence, by rejection of the East European "model," by criticism of repressive regime policies, and by the development of an ideological rationale increasingly divergent from that of the ruling parties.

The most striking manifestation of this tendency during the year was the dramatic change in the PCF's interparty positions. For years, the French party's proclaimed commitment to pluralistic democratic liberties had been undermined by its traditional loyalty to Moscow. The change came quite suddenly in late 1975, within the framework of preparations for the 22d PCF congress (at which the party provoked Eastern ideologists by formally abandoning the doctrine of the dictatorship of the proletariat). In December 1975, successive statements criticizing specific instances of regime repression were climaxed by a Politburo declaration expressing "most formal reprobation" of Soviet labor camps. At the 22d congress, Secretary-General Marchais referred to "certain developments in the Soviet Union" and said: "We cannot admit that the communist ideal . . . should be stained by unjust and unjustifiable acts. . . . That is why we express our disagreement when violations of human rights occur in a country that made its socialist revolution 58 years ago."

A few weeks later, the 25th congress of the CPSU gave Marchais another chance to emphasize the growing gap between the two parties— by declining to attend. He explained that he took this decision "because there is a divergence between our two parties on the problems of socialist democracy [and also] on the evaluation of French foreign policy." Santiago Carrillo of the Spanish Communist Party also declined to attend the 25th congress, finding it "more important" to go to Rome with other Spanish opposition leaders for political talks.*

---

*While in Rome, Carrillo gave an interview (Corriere della Sera, 16 February 1976) in which he spoke of the "primitive stage" of Soviet socialism. Asked if he did not fear that his views would be condemned by Moscow, he replied: "By what right could they condemn us? They can criticize us, as we criticize them. Condemnation is excommunication from a Church, and the communist movement was a Church but now no longer is one."

The third major Eurocommunist leader, Berlinguer, did attend the congress—to make a challenging statement of the PCI's "revisionist" positions, including its commitment to work for pluralistic socialism "within the framework of the international alliances of our country" (that is, NATO and the EEC).

Some Soviet speakers at the congress made guarded criticisms of "right-wing opportunism," but in the course of the year the developing debate between loyalists and Eurocommunists found more explicit expression in statements by regime spokesmen—notably Soviet, East German, Bulgarian, and Czechoslovak—and in Western communist reactions. The debate, which at times reached the level of open polemics, generally concerned such doctrinal questions as proletarian internationalism, the dictatorship of the proletariat, and "general laws" for the building of socialism. Another controversial question was the extent to which Western communist parties should seek political progress through "compromising" alliances with other forces. But behind these lay a more basic issue: the challenge to Soviet authority posed by major Western CPs increasingly determined to give their own political interests priority over those of the Kremlin, and to reinforce their claim to independence by selective criticism of regime policies. This challenge was the more significant in that it came at a time when the Soviets were making obvious efforts to strengthen integration among the East European regimes in many areas—a fact that had much to do with the vigorous Yugoslav interventions in the ongoing debate, on the side of the Eurocommunists.

The influence of Eurocommunist ideas was strengthened during the year by political developments in various countries. In the Italian national elections of June 1976, the PCI maintained the advances made in local elections a year earlier by getting almost 34 percent of the vote, only narrowly failing to overtake a demoralized Christian Democratic Party now dependent upon communist collaboration in tackling the country's grave crises. In France the PCF's commitment to Eurocommunism (a term it rejected) was strengthened by the prospect of leftist successes in 1977 local elections and the 1978 national elections—and by the fact that François Mitterrand's Socialist Party was now the strongest force in the tripartite alliance, outpolling the PCF by roughly three to two. The most striking transformation came in post-Franco Spain, moving toward constitutional democracy with unexpected impetus: The opposition front, "Democratic Coordination," stood with the now semiclandestine Spanish CP in the demand that it, too, should be legalized. Finally, events in Portugal strengthened the Eurocommunist tendency through a negative example, so to speak, as the political setbacks suffered by the hard-line, pro-Soviet Portuguese CP apparently demonstrated the impracticability of a revolutionary strategy in Western Europe.

The reaction of the major West European CPs to the death of Mao Tse-tung in September demonstrated their concern to extend their freedom of maneuver vis-a-vis Moscow. While Pravda gave the news in one paragraph, l'Unità and l'Humanité devoted four pages to the passing of what Georges Marchais called "one of the greatest figures of history," and in sending warm messages of condolence to Peking both the PCF and the PCI indicated readiness to reestablish normal relations with the Chinese CP.* The mild response of the French, in particular, to the Chinese rejection of messages from "revisionist" parties made it clear that this was a move away from Moscow rather than toward Peking.

One obvious reason for regime concern over the growth of Eurocommunism is the "subversive" influence that Western communist ideas may have in Eastern Europe. During the year, support for the positions of the Italian, Spanish, and French CPs was expressed by leading East European dissidents in a position to do so (for example, Andrei Sakharov and Roy Medvedev of the USSR, Wolf Biermann and Robert Havemann of East Germany, and Edward Lipinski and Adam Michnik of Poland). As the year's end approached, Lucio Lombardo Radice of the PCI Central Committee, in an interview on Eurocommunism, spoke of this sensitive factor with rare bluntness:

> It is inevitable that the socialist opposition to socialist governments in the East . . . should link itself at least ideologically with Eurocommunism. It is equally inevitable that the Italian, French, or Spanish "model" should become a political problem for the ruling communist parties of Eastern Europe.16

NOTES

1. On the period since 1969, see J. F. Brown, Relations Between the Soviet Union and Its Eastern European Allies: A Survey, Report R-1742-PR (Santa Monica, Cal.: Rand Corporation, November 1975).

2. See the Final Act's concluding chapter: "Follow-up to the Conference."

3. Izvestia (Moscow), 21 November 1976.

---

*The Spanish CP had already made an unsuccessful attempt to reestablish normal relations with the Chinese party, by sending a delegation to Peking in September 1971.

4. Dietrich Guhl, "Helsinki und die friedliche Koexistenz in Europa," Einheit (East Berlin), November 1976.

5. See, for example, Mlada Fronta (Prague), 23 November 1976; Trybuna Ludu (Warsaw), 6 December 1976.

6. See, for example, Tamas Palos, "On Ideological Cooperation Among the Fraternal Parties," Tarsadalomtudomanyi Kozlemenyek (Budapest), no. 4, 1975, and Yu. Kandalov, "Socialist Ideological Cooperation Needed to Fight Capitalism," Sovetskaya Kultura (Moscow), 26 November 1976.

7. TASS, 26 November 1976.

8. Radio Bucharest, 27 August 1976.

9. 4 December 1976.

10. For example, Neue Zuercher Zeitung, 10 December 1976.

11. The report was released in Washington on 8 December 1976.

12. In a Rinascita (Rome) article of 6 February 1976.

13. Politika (Belgrade), 8 May 1976; emphasis added.

14. Frane Barbieri's dispatch from Belgrade in Il Giornale (Milan), 20 June 1976.

15. Radio Belgrade television interview, 26 June 1976. Grlickov said that one of these amendments, dealing with proletarian internationalism, "was concerned with whether it was possible to describe any one country as a major factor, or the main force."

16. La Stampa (Turin), 8 December 1976.

2

THE ATHENS CONFERENCE
AND REGIONAL COOPERATION
IN THE BALKANS

Robert R. King
Rada Nikolaev
Slobodan Stankovic
Louis Zanga

For the first time since World War II, a conference of Balkan government experts was held in Athens at the end of January 1976. It was attended by representatives of Bulgaria, Greece, Romania, Turkey, and Yugoslavia—only Albania declined the invitation to participate. The conference produced some 150 suggestions for cooperation in such nonpolitical areas as joint exploitation of solar energy, improvement of transportation and communication links, and joint efforts in the area of tourism to be considered by the individual governments; and at some (unspecified) time in the future, representatives (the level of which was also unspecified) may meet to consider further cooperative efforts. Although such results would normally be considered rather meager, in light of the significant differences between the countries involved and their previous unwillingness to meet together, the conference must be considered a success.

PREVIOUS POSTWAR EFFORTS AT
REGIONAL COOPERATION

It took more than 30 years for such a gathering to materialize, although efforts in this direction had been made periodically since

---

This chapter is a shortened and updated version of the following Radio Free Europe Research Background Reports: Robert R. King, "The Athens Conference and the Balkans: Old Variations on an Old Theme," RAD BR/55, 1 March 1976; R. N. (Bulgarian Unit), "Bulgaria and the Balkan Conference in Athens," RAD BR/41, 12 February 1976; Slobodan Stankovic, "Yugoslav Paper's Critical Appraisal of Balkan Conference," RAD BR/40, 12 February 1976; and Louis Zanga, "Albania Reacts to the Balkan Conference," RAD BR/78, 5 April 1976.

the late 1940s. After 1945, the establishment of Soviet client regimes
in Romania and Bulgaria and of pro-Moscow governments in Yugoslavia and Albania led Yugoslavia and Bulgaria to plan and carry out
initial steps toward the creation of a Balkan Federation, which was
to include Yugoslavia, Bulgaria, Albania, and perhaps also Romania.
Stalin, however, vetoed the scheme, fearing that a unified bloc of
Balkan states would be more difficult for Moscow to control. Good
relations came to an abrupt end in June 1948, when the Yugoslavs
were expelled from the Communist Information Bureau (Cominform),
and the division in the region became explicit when Greece and Turkey
decided to become members of NATO in the early 1950s.

The possibility of regional cooperation was raised again in September 1957, when a series of Khrushchev-inspired proposals for the
reduction of East-West tension were made. The Poles proposed ban-
ning nuclear weapons from all nations bordering on the Baltic except
the Soviet Union and closing the sea to ships of all non-Baltic states,
and a related proposal called for a nuclear-free zone in Central Europe. At the same time, Romanian Premier Chivu Stoica addressed
messages to Albania, Bulgaria, Greece, Turkey, and Yugoslavia
proposing that they join in a conference aimed at improving relations
through Balkan detente. Albania, Bulgaria, and Yugoslavia accepted
the proposal, but Turkey and Greece declined to participate. When
NATO missiles were installed in the latter two states in 1959, Romania,
under Soviet auspices, revived the Stoica proposal, calling for a top-
level conference to discuss the creation of a nuclear-free, missile-
free zone in the Balkans.[1]

In the 1960s, Romania and Bulgaria periodically revived the issue
of furthering multilateral cooperation and creating a nuclear-free
zone, and as the Romanians began to pursue a more active and
autonomous foreign policy this became a frequent theme. A formal
proposal to this effect was made in June 1970, when the Romanian
government sent notes to all Balkan states and to the UN secretary-
general.[2] The response was hardly encouraging, however, and the
Romanians did not attempt a similar initiative thereafter.

CHANGING CONDITIONS AND THE
SUCCESSFUL GREEK INITIATIVE

By mid-1975, changed conditions in the Balkan Peninsula favored
renewal of the proposal for a multilateral conference. This time the
initiative came from the new Greek government of Constantine Karamanlis. A number of important changes were responsible for both
the suggestion and its culmination in the Athens conference.

First, the proposal was formally made only a few weeks after the final stage of the Conference on Security and Cooperation in Europe had ended in Helsinki. This gathering created a climate conducive to further collaboration between the various states of Eastern and Western Europe. In such an atmosphere, both the Soviet Union and the United States could hardly object to their allies' participating in an exercise of regional detente.

Second, the internal changes in Greece after the collapse of the military junta in the summer of 1974 made the possibility of regional cooperation more palatable to the communist states, although all had managed, despite initial aversion, to improve state and economic relations with the military regime in Athens. The Karamanlis government was also more interested in furthering regional cooperation and lacked the ideological attitudes that had inhibited the military leaders.

A third factor that helped to bring about the conference was the strained state of Greek and Turkish relations with the United States in the aftermath of Turkey's invasion of Cyprus that summer. Both states sought to demonstrate their disapproval of U.S. foreign policy by engaging in more independent action. As a result, both have recently undertaken moves toward rapprochement with the Soviet Union and the East European states. Also, this attitude on the part of Athens and Ankara undoubtedly made Moscow more willing to see the conference take place.

The fact that changed conditions favored the holding of the conference, however, should not be taken to mean that there was an identity of views among the participants. Many of the factors that influenced their divergent attitudes in the past continue to affect their hopes and expectations for the future of collaboration in the area.

ROMANIA: THE LEADING PARTISAN OF MULTILATERAL COOPERATION

Romania has perhaps been the most consistent advocate of multilateral collaboration in the region, and its stance at the Athens conference reflected this. The response of Romanian President Ceausescu to Karamanlis's invitation was particularly enthusiastic, and the Romanian press build-up also reflected the government's endorsement.[3]

During the conference itself, the Romanians were also apparently among those willing to go farthest toward regional collaboration. In addition to the usual detailed list of potential areas of cooperation, they apparently called for the creation of new organizations to encourage it. Ceausescu made the same proposal in his foreign policy speech to the Grand National Assembly shortly before the Athens conference,[4] and a Yugoslav paper reported that the Romanian delegation had proposed the creation of a Balkan highway organization and other agencies.[5]

Although its hopes were certainly not realized at the Athens gathering, the Romanian government believes that the situation is now propitious for further progress. It was agreed in advance that the Athens meeting would deal with cooperation in nonpolitical areas, and while the Romanians accepted this as a necessary first step, their desires go considerably beyond this limited sphere, into areas that are clearly political. Ceausescu, in his foreign policy speech just a month before the Athens conference opened, reiterated interest in "turning this area into a zone of peace and cooperation without nuclear weapons."[6] The same theme was emphasized in an article in the foreign policy weekly Lumea[7] at the time the Karamanlis proposal was initiated.

Romania's concern for good relations in the Balkans goes well beyond the desire to have friendly links with its neighboring states and obviously involves its perception of relations with the Soviet Union and Romania's place in the world. Concern to maintain and expand its autonomy vis-a-vis Moscow is a consideration that enters into most of Bucharest's calculations with regard to foreign policy. Improving relations with other Balkan states is seen as a means of overcoming the physical isolation the RSR's (Romanian Socialist Republic) position imposes. The repeated suggestion that a zone free of nuclear weapons and foreign military bases be created in the Balkans is seen in Bucharest as a way of reducing Romania's strategic significance in Moscow's eyes by lessening its insecurity along the southern flank. Also, a group of closely cooperating Balkan states would form more of a barrier to great-power politics in the region. This was hinted at in the Lumea article mentioned above. The author noted that in the past, efforts to achieve regional interdependence have been prevented by the "intervention of foreign interests, by a certain viewpoint on the part of third parties and larger powers which reduced the zone of the Balkans to a field for political maneuvers and haggling" by means of Diktat, force, and pressure. The evolution of political conditions in the peninsula and the generally improved climate resulting from the Helsinki conference, however, have altered the situation: "For the first time the Balkan countries are in the position of being able to reject, firmly and successfully, any attempt at brutal interference, intimidation, or threat to use force."

Given this attitude on the part of Romania, the prospect of greater Balkan cooperation is unlikely to be considered reassuring in Moscow. The very fact that the Romanians and Yugoslavs are among its most enthusiastic supporters would tend to raise Soviet doubts, and it was certainly in an attempt to forestall this that Romanian Foreign Minister George Macovescu, in response to a query during an official visit to Austria, stated: "We are against blocs and we stand for the dissolution of blocs. We are not working to build a bloc in the Balkans."[8] Despite this gesture toward the Soviet Union, Romania's aims with regard to regional cooperation are clearly intended to further its own foreign policy goals.

YUGOSLAVIA: THE OPTIMISTIC SKEPTIC

The Yugoslavs have likewise been staunch advocates of Balkan cooperation, but, while their view has been hopeful, they have shown considerably more skepticism with regard to the possibilities than have the Romanians. They have shown a greater awareness of the complexities and difficulties inherent in any attempt to introduce cooperation in the area but at the same time have encouraged such efforts. They particularly praised the Romanians and the Greeks for their stands on regional cooperation during the Athens conference, and they were harsh in their criticism of Bulgaria's reticence.[9]

The Yugoslav attitude toward Balkan collaboration is influenced by two problems—first, the fear of great-power involvement in the region and the need to stress Yugoslavia's nonalignment; and second, the need to resolve outstanding bilateral issues in relations between states in the peninsula, and in particular the quarrel with Bulgaria over the Macedonian question. This fear of the great powers and their past manipulation of the Balkan states is constantly expressed in articles on regional issues. As one Yugoslav foreign affairs specialist noted: "The amount of success achieved . . . will depend on the degree of independent action of each of the countries concerned. Or conversely, the more liable those countries are to foreign influence, the less their success in overcoming mutual misunderstandings will be."[10] In commenting on the Athens conference a Yugoslav daily noted that "every act of foreign interference, regardless of the motives and arguments that might be offered as justification, would fundamentally impede inter-Balkan cooperation."[11] In their criticism of foreign influence in the peninsula, the Yugoslavs have implicitly but clearly attacked Bulgaria for putting "its foreign policy in the Balkans at the service of the strategic needs of non-Balkan factors."[12] This, the Yugoslavs maintain, hampers the evolution of real cooperation in the area.

Yugoslav commentators frequently refer to the second problem mentioned above—the need to resolve outstanding bilateral issues between Balkan states before regional cooperation can become a reality. The dispute between Greece and Turkey over Cyprus is of course a matter of concern, but their main preoccupation is the Macedonian question. The argument is advanced that regional cooperation is hampered by "the Bulgarian attitude toward Yugoslavia, which contains many elements of territorial pretension and negation of the provisions of the Helsinki declaration on national minorities."[13] Unless the Macedonian and other unresolved issues are settled, the Yugoslavs see little hope that regional cooperation can come about.

Under existing circumstances, they claim, "bilateral cooperation is obviously the most effective way of advancing relations between the Balkan countries."[14] They argue that since two countries in the region are members of the Warsaw Pact and two are members of the Atlantic Alliance, multilateral cooperation would necessarily reflect the interests and influences of these military blocs. Thus the only way to "multilateralize" regional collaboration is by severing bloc ties: "The way to multilateral cooperation clearly leads through emancipation from bloc affiliations and promotion of bilateral collaboration." The Yugoslavs go still further, suggesting that the divisive bilateral questions that also hamper general regional cooperation are exacerbated by external influences and that if left to themselves the Balkan states could resolve their own conflicts more easily: "The present insufficient stability in the Balkans is probably due to the activities of extra-Balkan factors rather than to the divergencies between the Balkan states themselves." Although the Yugoslavs at present see bilateral cooperation as the only possible area of progress, this has not limited their willingness to discuss possibilities of multilateral efforts. This is particularly apparent in the Yugoslav reports on the Athens conference, which were highly critical of the Bulgarian delegation's refusal even to raise the possibility of multilateral cooperation.

BULGARIA: THE LOWEST COMMON DENOMINATOR

Commentaries on the Athens conference described it as a success, although in actual fact the conference was a success mainly for the Bulgarian delegation, which seems to have consistently defended the Bulgarian government's policy of not going beyond noncommitted consultations and apparently managed to have this policy accepted by the other participants. Bulgarian policy, however, was not always so oriented. Sofia responded favorably to the Khrushchev-inspired Stoica proposals in the 1950s, and the first half of the 1960s was marked by repeated and persistent expressions of Bulgarian support for a nuclear-free zone in the Balkans. This support was essentially a matter of principle, however, and was not accompanied by concrete suggestions on how to reach agreement on the subject.

Nonetheless, there are certain indications that despite the lack of concrete action during this period Bulgaria had not abandoned the idea that many of the Balkan countries' problems could be solved on a multilateral basis. A statement advocating "steps of a regional Balkan character—e.g., multilateral Balkan parliamentary and government meetings," was made by Foreign Minister Ivan Bashev in 1970, in an interview with a representative of the Hungarian radio network.[15]

A year later, an incident in connection with the tenth Bulgarian Communist Party (BCP) congress provided an indication that Todor Zhivkov was still (or again) in favor of a high-level Balkan conference but was prevented from making a suggestion to this effect, presumably because of Soviet disapproval. A passage in his report to the congress was obviously deleted at the last moment, but through an error became known to Western newsmen.[16] The passage in question called for a common declaration by the Balkan countries on respect for territorial integrity, noninterference in internal affairs, and renunciation of the use of threat of force. It went on to say that the preparation of such a declaration "could provide a favorable occasion to discuss these questions on a bilateral basis and to hold a multilateral meeting of government representatives or heads of government of the Balkan states."

Although Zhivkov renounced his original advocacy of a multilateral meeting of Balkan leaders, his report as read and printed still contained outspoken support for multilateral undertakings:[17]

> In addition to developing bilateral relations with its neighbor countries, Bulgaria will continue to support and actively participate in all multilateral Balkan undertakings that might lead to the expansion of economic, political, and cultural relations among the Balkan countries and to the transformation of the Balkan Peninsula into a zone of lasting peace and stability, understanding and cooperation.

The positive attitude to multilateral undertakings expressed at the tenth BCP congress was soon reversed, however. In an interview with Finnish journalists, Premier Stanko Todorov said that despite the favorable atmosphere prevailing in the Balkans "one must be satisfied with strengthening bilateral neighborly relations."[18] In an interview with Le Monde,[19] Todorov repeated this view, stating still more explicitly that "the situation is not yet ripe for establishing multilateral relations in the Balkans." Thereafter, Bulgaria consistently advocated bilateral relations as the only possibility for the Balkan countries.

The first sign of a more faceted Bulgarian attitude to the question
of bilateral versus multilateral undertakings in the Balkans was shown
during Greek Premier Karamanlis's visit to Bulgaria at the beginning
of July 1975. Later, when his proposal for the Athens conference
was officially announced, it became apparent that during his talks in
Sofia he had made preliminary soundings and had obtained a
preliminary favorable answer from Zhivkov. Bulgaria's acceptance
of multilateral undertakings in certain spheres did not seem to be
definitive, however. When Foreign Minister Petar Mladenov visited
Turkey at the beginning of September 1975, he told a press conference
that "Bulgaria has supported and will continue to support both bilateral
and multilateral initiatives," but in a speech during that visit he said
that "developing good-neighborly relations among the Balkan countries
on a bilateral basis is the real way to establish confidence and mutual
understanding in the Balkans."[20] The joint communique on Mladenov's
Turkish visit did not mention the issue at all.

After a brief initial report on the Karamanlis invitation,[21] however, Bulgarian media more or less ignored the issue until 26 January
1976, the day the conference began. They failed to mention Zhivkov's
acceptance of the invitation,[22] which had been reported in Athens on
September 29, Bulgaria being the second country (after Yugoslavia)
to answer favorably. According to reports from Athens, Zhivkov
called on Karamanlis to conduct bilateral negotiations to decide when
the conference should be held and to work out the details of the issues
to be discussed. It is not known whether such bilateral consultations
were actually held, although various official visits by government
heads and foreign ministers did take place.

The level of the delegation to the Athens conference reflected
the importance each country attributed to the gathering. Greece's
delegation was headed by an undersecretary for coordination and
planning; Romania's by a first deputy minister of foreign trade, Yugoslavia's by an undersecretary of the Ministry of Finance, Turkey's
by a diplomat with ambassadorial rank, while the head of the Bulgarian
delegation, a department head in the Ministry of Foreign Trade,
appears to have been the lowest-ranking of the five delegation leaders.
This can be taken as illustrating Bulgaria's desire to play down the
importance of the conference.

On January 27, the Sofia daily press reported the opening of the
conference, and two days later published a dispatch from the Bulgarian
Telegraph Agency (BTA) correspondent in Athens. Thereafter, there
was no mention of the conference until it ended on February 5. The
next day, what was apparently the full text of the official communique
was published. Such coverage was quite in line with Bulgarian press
practice, and as a matter of fact, in the case of the Athens conference,
publishing the communique represented a deviation from protocol in

deference to the political importance of the gathering. Unlike Yugoslav and Romanian news media, neither Bulgaria's daily press nor
its radio news services commented on the conference. The only
commentary appeared in the weekly Pogled on February 9, linking
the Athens conference with the post-Helsinki spirit and assessing it,
from this point of view alone, in positive but rather vague terms.

Little became known of the conference proceedings in general or
of the role played by the Bulgarian delegation in particular, since
the sessions were held behind closed doors. The scanty information
provided by Greek and Yugoslav sources and Western press reports
indicated, however, that Bulgaria sought to keep conference discussions and decisions to a minimum. The Bulgarian and Turkish wish
to leave aside all issues of a predominantly political character[23]
seems to have been readily accepted as realistic by the other delegations. The Bulgarian delegation was said to have insisted on excluding
cultural cooperation from the conference agenda,[24] and it was also
the Bulgarians who wanted it to be purely consultative in nature.[25]
All the other delegations seem to have found it difficult to accept this
point, but, as the communique revealed, the Bulgarian position finally
prevailed. The Bulgarians even refused to agree to a proposal for a
second meeting to be held in Sofia.[26]

The attitude of Bulgaria in this case appears to be more a reflection of Soviet concerns and policies than of its own interests or desires.
There have been indications, including Zhivkov's censored proposal
at the 1971 party congress, suggesting that Bulgaria would in fact
favor closer cooperation with its neighbors. In foreign policy matters,
however, Sofia has shown itself a devoted follower of the Soviet line,
and it is presumably this consideration that led it to play a role at
the Athens conference.

ALBANIA: THE NONPARTICIPANT

Albanian reaction to the Balkan conference was expressed in a
commentary that appeared in the party daily, Zeri i Popullit.[27] It
was at once intransigent and promising: multilateral action of the
kind exemplified by the conference was totally rejected, but there
was some receptivity to the idea of bilateral contacts. In view of
Albania's habitual distrust of any meaningful form of contact or
cooperation with the outside world, the editorial should be assessed
in light of its more hopeful features.

Albania's distaste for multilateral conferences is the product of
its theory of the evils of superpower supremacy, which is today the
central core of its foreign policy. The main thrust of the Zeri i
Popullit editorial was aimed against the alleged direct or indirect

influence exerted by the two superpowers on the convening of the conference. Seen from this angle, Tirana's decision to shun the Athens
gathering was no great surprise and was a logical outcome of a European policy that had led to the earlier boycott of the Helsinki conference. The editorial said that the Balkan conference was an outgrowth
of the body of its northern predecessor, and as one of Tirana's main
objections to the Helsinki conference was the presence there of the
two superpowers, it was doubtless considered that some of that taint
was inherited by the Athens gathering.

As long as the Albanian regime's foreign policy is based on distrust and rejection of the superpowers, its attitude toward multilateral
conferences is unlikely to change; and as long as Enver Hoxha remains
party leader, the chances of any slackening of this rigid line are very
remote, although evidence that there are differences on this critical
issue can be found in the many recent changes made in the top ranks
of the Albanian leadership.

The editorial left little doubt that the superpower most feared
by Hoxha is the Soviet Union and that it is Moscow's dark intentions
in the Balkans that give Tirana its greatest cause for concern. One
reason for this is that the Soviet Union is the only major power with
a reliable ally in the Balkans, namely Bulgaria. While the editorial
claimed that both superpowers were interfering in Balkan affairs, it
is clear that it considered the Soviets the real meddlers. The presence of Bulgaria, Moscow's most faithful ally in Eastern Europe, at
the Athens conference was by itself sufficient cause for Tirana to
allege Soviet interference in Balkan affairs; in the eyes of the Albanians, Moscow had forged a direct link with the conference through its
Sofia connection.

In dealing with traditional Balkan problems, the article spoke of
"chauvinistic policies and policies of suppressing national minorities."
This may have been primarily directed against the Yugoslavs, who
have launched a major crackdown on Albanian irredentist elements
in Kosovo, where the antinationalist campaign has put some strain
on Yugoslav-Albanian relations following a revival in the early 1970s
of good-neighborly relations between the two countries.[28] An earlier
Zeri i Popullit editorial,[29] without mentioning the Yugoslavs by name,
condemned anti-irredentist policies in a neighboring country, and
warned against the pursuit of a policy of "persecuting national minorities." Tirana has yet to react to the trial and subsequent sentencing
of 19 Albanian irredentists in Pristina in February and of two others
in March.[30] The relatively low-keyed response to the events in
Kosovo may indicate that, for the time being at least, Tirana wants
to avoid an overt political confrontation with Belgrade.

Turning to the other participants in the Balkan Conference, the
March 23 editorial charged that "territorial claims and sharp differ-

ences of opinion exist between several countries," which would seem to be a reference to the dispute between Greece and Turkey and possibly Bulgaria and Yugoslavia. The editorial also denigrated in rather vague terms the policies of other Balkan states: "Some countries fuss about independence but rely on social imperialism and play its game"; others "asked for the participation of Hungary and Italy, even of the Soviet Union and the United States, in these intra-Balkan talks." The unnamed countries in this case appear to be Romania and Yugoslavia, but once again these slightly outlandish allegations may have been intended for internal consumption as justifications of the rigid line on the question of multilateral meetings.

The one positive feature of the editorial—and it is an important one—was its endorsement of the policy of bilateral contacts between Balkan countries. Tirana's record on this matter is not very distinguished, and Zeri i Popullit's imprimatur is therefore all the more significant. The editorial observed:

> The problems of the Balkans must be solved by the Balkan
> countries themselves, without interference by the super-
> powers and in spite of them. It cannot be said too often
> that bilateral collaboration is the only form of coopera-
> tion that is advantageous. It alone can help to strengthen
> the freedom and independence of all nations and the cause
> of peace and security in the Balkans. By dealing with the
> most acute bilateral questions, the road can be cleared
> for a joint meeting later on.

Will Tirana put into practice what it preaches? Although Albania's relations with Greece, Romania, Turkey, and Yugoslavia may be considered reasonably cordial (in the case of Bulgaria only a total break could make them worse than they are), there is much room for improvement, and Belgrade in particular has shown untiring willingness for rapprochement and greater cooperation with Tirana. In the early 1970s, new ground was broken by the two countries, but subsequent Yugoslav efforts to cultivate the seeds then planted were met with sudden mistrust in Tirana, especially in 1974 and 1975. In part, this may be explained by a renewed lack of Albanian self-confidence in the face of the "revisionist magic" of its northern neighbor. The unprecedented rigor of the campaign mounted by Albania against the "fierce bourgeois-revisionist" ideological pressure alleged to have been exerted upon it suggests that Tirana feared ideological infiltration and decided to apply the brakes for that reason; another factor was probably Albania's internal turmoil in recent years and the leadership changes that have accompanied it.

The comments made by Albanian party leader Enver Hoxha at the party's seventh congress in November also reflect a renewed Albanian concern about improving the country's standing in the Balkans. The signs of further interest in expanding relations with Greece and Yugoslavia—albeit coupled with concern for ideological contamination—have increased. Although the political situation in Tirana remains far from certain, even after the party congress, the regime's reaction to the Balkan conference and the statements about the region during the congress give some cause for optimism about Albania's future policies on Balkan affairs and about the prospects of cooperation with some of its neighbors.

THE SOVIET UNION: EMINENCE GRISE

There is some evidence that the Soviets consider the efforts to achieve Balkan cooperation undesirable in terms of their own interests. In the past, the Soviets certainly viewed similar efforts negatively. In 1948, the Soviet party daily Pravda[31] denounced Georgi Dimitrov's proposal for a customs union for the communist states of the Balkans and the Bulgarian-Yugoslav suggestions for a South Slav federation and urged instead that the independence and sovereignty of the individual states be strengthened. Somewhat later, however, as Soviet-Yugoslav differences became more pronounced, Stalin called for a Bulgarian-Yugoslav federation in an effort to infiltrate and ultimately dominate the recalcitrant Yugoslav party organization. Thus the Soviets were opposed to any Balkan moves that might be outside their control or might create a bloc of states more easily able to resist them, but were quite willing to encourage mergers or joint ventures that would serve their interests and that they could manipulate. The Soviet policy toward Balkan cooperation appears to follow essentially the same logic today—if the Soviets can utilize and control joint efforts they are in favor; otherwise they oppose.

The changes in the Balkan Peninsula over the last few years have left the Soviets in a somewhat awkward position. The aftermath of the 1974 Cyprus crisis engendered considerable disenchantment with the United States in both Turkey and Greece, and both have moved in the direction of a foreign policy course less exclusively oriented toward Washington. One facet of this is that both countries have improved their relations with the Soviet Union and Eastern Europe. The possibility of weakening the southern flank of the Atlantic Alliance is especially attractive because of its proximity to the strategically important and unstable Middle East. The postjunta government in Greece has been particularly keen on regional cooperation, and thus the Soviet Union has been put in the awkward position of seeking to establish closer ties with the two NATO states in the Balkans but not favoring multilateral cooperation. Unless considerably stronger ties are established between the Balkan capitals of Athens and Ankara and Moscow, the Soviets are unlikely to give much support to serious collaboration in the area.

While the political evolution in Turkey and Greece is positive from the Soviet viewpoint, Romania and Yugoslavia present more complicated problems. In balancing its assertions of autonomy in foreign affairs with judicious acceptance of crucial Soviet positions, Romania has evidently managed to avoid moving beyond the limits of the acceptable (from Moscow's point of view), but there is a continual attempt to create conditions favorable to greater foreign policy autonomy. The various efforts at regional cooperation in the Balkans— as well as Romania's drive to be accepted in the nonaligned movement, to identify itself as a developing country, to strengthen the United Nations, and to foster more rapid disarmament—must be seen in this context. And the Soviets probably view Romania's intentions in connection with regional collaboration in this light.

A measure of Moscow's feelings about Bucharest's intentions may be found in a Soviet article[32] on nuclear-free zones that appeared in August 1975—the month in which the Helsinki conference ended and the Karamanlis invitation was issued. The author spent some time discussing proposals to create nuclear-free zones submitted to the United Nations. Significantly, the Balkans were mentioned only once, and in passing—as one of several regions regarding which such proposals had been made in the past—and Romania's overtures were not mentioned at all, though in 1970 one of its proposals was made to the UN secretary-general. Proposals relating to Africa, the Middle East, southern Asia, northern Europe, and Latin America were discussed, however. A Polish writer[33] reflected a similar aversion to mentioning the Romanian proposals in an article on the 1957 Rapacki plan for a nuclear-free zone in central Europe; he made no mention of the simultaneous proposals put forward by Romanian Premier Chivu Stoica and renewed periodically since that time, although he did make a passing reference to the less well-known 1958 "Tito Plan for the Balkans." Such pointed omissions can hardly be interpreted as indicating anything but Soviet disapproval.

The other Balkan state of concern to the USSR is, of course, Yugoslavia. The approach of the post-Tito era will no doubt produce domestic instability, and the Soviet Union is undoubtedly watching the situation closely and at the same time seeking to influence through all available means the evolution of this key Balkan nation. Moscow seems content to await the departure of Tito before committing itself to a Balkan policy, however, but Bucharest is anxious to establish some kind of regional framework before he goes.

In Soviet eyes, the best approach to Balkan cooperation is one of
waiting. The likelihood of Turkey and Greece reversing the decline
in their relations with the United States does not at present appear
great. There is a real possibility that Greece and Turkey will forge
closer relations with the Warsaw Pact states; if they should do so
before any firm decisions on Balkan cooperation are made, this would
be all the better from the Soviet viewpoint. The question of post-Tito
Yugoslavia will probably be answered before long, and a change in
the Albanian leadership (also something that is not likely to be too
long delayed) might conceivably also bring about a situation more
favorable to the Soviets. Romanian foreign policy remains an irritant
to the Soviet leaders, but thus far its international deviation has been
contained. Romania's decision to participate more actively in Comecon
and recent indications of better relations with Moscow give the Soviets
reasons to hope for reversal or at least moderation of past Romanian
policies. Under such circumstances, the best thing from the Soviet
point of view is to defer action until the political evolution of the region
becomes clearer, and Bulgaria's behavior at the Athens conference
seems consistent with this approach. While Sofia did not preclude
multilateral cooperation, it prevented the taking of decisive steps in
that direction and focused on bilateral cooperation. Further steps
toward regional collaboration may come, but the Bulgarians have
effectively slowed movement in this direction, and for the present
that seems to be the primary Soviet desire.

NOTES

1. The Stoica proposals appeared in Scinteia (Bucharest), 17
September 1957 and 7 June 1959.
2. United Press International (UPI)/Athens, 8 June 1970.
3. Scinteia, 3 October 1975 and 20, 24, 28 January 1976.
4. Agerpres, 28 January 1976.
5. Vjesnik (Zagreb), 8 February 1976.
6. Scinteia, 19 December 1975.
7. (Bucharest), 28 August 1975.
8. Reuter, 28 January 1976.
9. See Vjesnik, 8 February 1976; Radio Belgrade (28 January
1976) voiced the same criticism.
10. Ranko Petkovic, "Factors of Balkan Security and Cooperation,"
Review of International Affairs (Belgrade), 5 March 1975.
11. Vus (Zagreb) and Tanjug, 12 January 1976.
12. Miro Draskic, "The Balkan Topics," Review of International
Affairs, 20 July 1975.

13. Vus and Tanjug, 12 January 1976.

14. Petkovic, op. cit. The remainder of the unreferenced quotations in this paragraph are from the same article.

15. Rabotnichesko Delo (Sofia), 18 February 1970.

16. Sueddeutsche Zeitung (Munich), 23 April 1971.

17. Rabotnichesko Delo, 21 April 1971; this statement was included in the resolution of the congress—see ibid., 27 April 1971.

18. Helsingin Sanomat (Helsinki), 1 April 1973; see also Robert R. King, "Multilateral Cooperation in the Balkans: Differences of Views Between Bucharest and Sofia," Eastern Europe Background Report/6, Radio Free Europe Research, 5 April 1973.

19. (Paris), 21 July 1973.

20. Zemedelsko Zname (Sofia), 3 September 1975; see Bulgarian Situation Report/25, Radio Free Europe Research, 10 September 1975, Item 2.

21. Rabotnichesko Delo, 22 August 1975.

22. A brief BTA dispatch, however, did report Zhivkov's reply on 27 September 1975.

23. See the Frankfurter Rundschau, 3 February 1976.

24. Frankfurter Allgemeine Zeitung, 31 January 1976.

25. Radio Belgrade, 28 January 1976.

26. The Times (London) and Handelsblatt (Duesseldorf), 2 February 1976.

27. (Tirana), 23 March 1976.

28. See Louis Zanga, "Irredentism in Kosovo as Tirana's Policy Toward Belgrade Hardens," RAD Background Report/166, Radio Free Europe Research, 2 December 1975.

29. 22 January 1976.

30. Tanjug, 7 February 1976; Rilindja (Pristina), 19 March 1976.

31. (Moscow), 29 January 1948.

32. Y. Tomilin, "Nuclear-free Zones: How to Make Them Effective," International Affairs (Moscow) no. 8, 1975, pp. 67-72.

33. Lech Niekrasz, "Reflections Under an Atomic Parasol—The Career of a Polish Proposal," Zycie Warszawy (Warsaw), 8 September 1975.

CHAPTER

3

ROMANIA AND THE SOVIET UNION: TOWARD A RAPPROCHEMENT?

Robert R. King
The Romanian Research Unit

For the past decade and a half, the pattern of Romanian-Soviet relations has by no means been either consistent or unambiguous. At the same time, however, the general policy line that underlies the zigging and zagging that has marked the relations of the Romanian Socialist Republic (RSR) with its powerful neighbor since the early 1960s has been the desire to increase its autonomy from the Soviet Union and pursue policies more consistent with Romanian national interests. With great skill the Romanians have managed to institutionalize a certain degree of independence from the USSR despite attempts on the part of the Kremlin leadership to limit and contain their deviation. At the same time, however, the two countries have converging interests in certain areas, and the Romanian leaders have been most sensitive in balancing their relationship with the Soviet Union.

Romania's foreign policy in recent years has been geared to establishing good relations with as many states and groups of states as possible. This has been done in an effort to provide broad support for Romania's policy vis-a-vis the Soviet Union and to bolster its international status. The attempt to generate as many favorable international points of reference as possible has involved extensive efforts to establish and maintain good relations with individual coun-

This chapter is a shortened and updated version of the following Radio Free Europe Research Background Reports: Robert R. King, "Romania and the Soviet Union: Assessing the Balance," RAD BR/226, 3 November 1976, and Robert R. King and Romanian Unit, "Soviet Party Leader Brezhnev Pays First 'Friendship' Visit to Romania," RAD BR/247, 2 December 1976.

tries in Western Europe, the European Economic Community, the
United States, West European communist parties, the United Nations,
non-Warsaw Pact communist states (notably Yugoslavia, China, and
North Korea), and—most recently—individual third-world countries
and the nonaligned as a group.

In the 1960s the focus of Romanian policy was upon bettering
relations with Western Europe and the United States, and in this
regard Bucharest was a step ahead of Moscow and its East European
allies. While detente and the European security conference in Helsinki
have narrowed differences in this area, Romania is still beyond the
limits the Soviets have set—for example, on the question of cooperation with the EEC. Recently the RSR's attention has centered on its
relations with the individual countries of the third world and the nonaligned nations as a group. While an improvement in Romania's
bilateral relations with developing countries would not be a source
of serious concern to the Kremlin, its relationship with the nonaligned
bloc certainly is. In January 1976 it was admitted to the "Group of
77" developing countries, which frequently act together in the United
Nations. In fact, in its UN activity Romania has pursued many policies that are consistent with the interests of this group. In August
1976 the RSR was granted permanent guest status at the nonaligned
summit in Colombo, which further strengthened its ties with these
countries. Its professions of political and military nonalignment—
and the third world's acknowledgment of these professions—are hardly
seen in Moscow as contributing to Soviet attempts to strengthen the
Warsaw Pact and the cohesion among East European states. Overt
Soviet disapproval has not been manifest, but private disapprobation
has undoubtedly been voiced.

While its policy of establishing and maintaining points of contact
with as many states and groups of states as possible has in large
part been predicated on the desire to bolster Romania's international
position in order to enhance its autonomy vis-a-vis the Soviet Union,
relations with Moscow have been handled with great care. Areas of
conflict exist, but the disagreements have not been permitted to
escalate beyond manageable bounds. Relations have been satisfactory
or normal, but they have not shown the warmth and cordiality that
mark the Soviet Union's relations with the other East European states.

During the last half of 1976, however, subtle changes were
apparent in the Bucharest-Moscow relationship. While such tactical
shifts have been frequent in the past, [1] there are certain features of
the present one that mark it from the previous efforts. Hitherto,
periods of accommodation with the Soviet Union have frequently been
preceded by Soviet pressure. The Romanians' intransigent stand
against Soviet intervention in Czechoslovakia in 1968 was moderated
within days of the military action after threats against the RSR had

been uttered by the USSR and other Warsaw Pact states. Bucharest's relations with Peking cooled noticeably, and those with Moscow were "normalized" in the wake of a Soviet-led campaign to pressure Romania after Nicolae Ceausescu's visit to China in 1971. The present apparent improvement in Soviet-Romanian relations, however, does not appear to have been preceded by strong pressure of this kind.

At the same time, however, there are certain general political conditions that may have contributed to Romania's interest in reducing friction with the Soviet Union. The uncertainty regarding some of the RSR's traditional friends may have been one such factor. Although the death of Mao Tse-tung and the subsequent political upheavals in the Chinese leadership took place before the Soviet-Romanian improvement had become apparent, problems within the Chinese leadership had already come to the fore with the death of Chou En-lai in early 1976. Another traditional Romanian ally facing similar succession problems is Yugoslavia, where Tito continues in office, but uncertainty about the future increases with the approach of his demise. The quadrennial ritual of the American elections may also have added a further aspect of uncertainty—an uncertainty perhaps heightened by doubts over official U.S. interest in Eastern Europe.

A number of political factors also appear to have prepared the way for the improvement in relations. The conference of European communist party leaders in East Berlin at the end of June was clearly significant in this regard. The ostensible Soviet compromise on certain questions, which was essential to secure the participation of a number of West European parties and those of Yugoslavia and Romania, helped to prepare the way for better Romanian-Soviet relations. At the same time, Ceausescu's moderate and rather low-keyed address in East Berlin avoided extreme statements that might have offended the Soviet Union. During that conference Ceausescu met individually with Brezhnev, a meeting to which some significance has subsequently been attributed by the Romanian mass media. A more friendly tone toward Moscow, however, was evident even four weeks before the East Berlin gathering, in Ceausescu's speech to the Congress on Political Education and Socialist Culture. That speech followed meetings in Bucharest between Ceausescu and Konstantin Katushev, CPSU Central Committee (CC) secretary for interparty relations, and Aleksei Yepishev, former Soviet ambassador to Romania and now political director of the Soviet military forces. One should not exclude the possibility that Soviet pressure or even threats were conveyed during these meetings. In any case, they undoubtedly helped to clear the way for Ceausescu's visit to the USSR.

CEAUSESCU'S VISIT TO THE SOVIET UNION
AND MODERATION OF THE POLEMICS
OVER BESSARABIA

The key indication of improving relations was the visit paid by Romanian Communist Party (RCP) leader Ceausescu to the Soviet Union in August 1976 for talks with party chief Leonid Brezhnev. The official announcement of their meeting[2] noted that "special attention was paid to deepening the relations between the two parties" and went on to say the "closer unity of views on the problems discussed was noted with satisfaction." As if to emphasize the closer relations between the two parties, Romanian CC Secretary (in charge of foreign relations) Stefan Andrei met in Moscow with his Soviet counterpart Katushev. In the past, Romania and the USSR have maintained normal and correct state-to-state relations even when interparty relations were rather cold. (A reflection of this was the fact that in 1970 the new Soviet-Romanian friendship treaty was signed only by the premiers of the two states, and at the last minute Brezhnev canceled his planned visit to Bucharest for the signing ceremony.) Despite these indications of high-level determination to improve relations, however, the major improvements seemed to be atmospheric—such as the attention given to a Soviet Komsomol delegation's visit to Bucharest and a new upsurge of activity in the Romanian association for friendship with the Soviet Union.

One of the more significant results of better relations with the Soviet Union was a visit by Polish party leader Edward Gierek to Bucharest. This was his first visit to Romania, although in the six years since he came to power he has visited every other East European country, including Yugoslavia. (He has not, of course, been to Albania.) It is probable that the improvement in Romania's relations with Poland was at least partially conditioned by the RCP's better relations with the USSR.

The most significant indication of the RSR's improved relations with the Soviet Union—again, however, more atmospheric than substantive—was the toning down of the acrimonious polemics over the history of Bessarabia. This dispute, focusing on the ethnic descent of the inhabitants of Bessarabia (or Soviet Moldavia) and the relative merits of Soviet and Romanian historical claims to the area, flared up in early 1975, with Romanian historians vigorously pushing their views on the question with the obvious support of the RCP leadership.[3] Early in June 1976, some two months before his meeting with Brezhnev, Ceausescu signaled the deescalation of these polemics. In a speech to the Congress on Political Education and Socialist Culture, he said that "certain problems" inherited from the bourgeois past must not affect relations with the Soviet Union, and that "Romania has no territorial or other problems" with its northern neighbor.[4] There seems to be little doubt that this disclaimer was in response to strong expressions of Soviet concern delivered by CPSU CC Secretary Katushev and former ambassador Yepishev, both of whom were in Bucharest a few days before Ceausescu delivered his speech.

The most dramatic confirmation of the intention to moderate this historical controversy was the fact that, en route to his meeting with Brezhnev, Ceausescu visited Soviet Moldavia. That he is the first Romanian leader ever to pay an official visit to this Soviet republic added considerable significance to his trip. By accident or design, Ceausescu was in Kishinev on the 36th anniversary of the creation of the Moldavian Soviet Republic—a fact ignored by both Romanian media and Ceausescu but stressed by the Moldavians.

The intensity of the controversy over Bessarabia has always been a barometer of Soviet-Romanian relations rather than a factor in their relationship. Raising the issue has at times been useful to the RSR in connection with domestic politics, and occasionally also from the point of view of its foreign policies. While no doubt finding Romania's claims highly irritating, the Soviet Union clearly has the upper hand in that it possesses Bessarabia and is unquestionably able to back up its claim. Given these circumstances, it was somewhat unusual for Ceausescu to make such concessions to the Soviet Union on the issue, in view of the negative impact his actions must have had on the standing of both himself and the RCP in the eyes of the population at large. This is especially true since the concessions in regard to the Bessarabian polemics appear to be primarily Romanian; equivalent concessions on the part of the Soviets have not yet become apparent. At the same time, it should be noted that Romania has never advanced territorial claims, and in fact in several documents (including the 1966 Warsaw Pact Declaration and the 1975 Helsinki Final Act) has specifically denied any territorial claims in general terms. Though apparently Ceausescu has quieted the Bessarabian controversy for the present, the issue is a real one that can be revived again at any time should the occasion require.

The suggestion has been made by a Western correspondent, citing unnamed "high-ranking Romanian authorities," that the main purpose of Ceausescu's visit to the Soviet Union was to establish contact between the RSR and the Romanians living in Soviet Moldavia,[5] and during the visit he mentioned an agreement "to intensify our contacts with your republic within the framework of the general contacts between the Soviet Union and Romania."[6] While this may be true, it is difficult to see how it represents any concession on the part of the Soviets. The first of the reciprocal visits envisaged took place in December 1976—shortly after Brezhnev had come to Bucharest—with the visit to Romania of Moldavian party leader Ivan I. Bodyul.

ORTHODOXY AND HETERODOXY IN IDEOLOGY
AND INTERPARTY RELATIONS

Since it is doubtful whether much was agreed upon regarding the substance of the Bessarabian conflict, one should probably look for other areas in which Brezhnev and Ceausescu may have reached accord. Ideology would seem to offer some hope in this regard, since Romania has in some ways (though not in all) been "more Catholic than the pope." The campaign to "ideologize" the population has been given an emphasis unmatched in the Soviet Union or any other of the orthodox states of Eastern Europe.

But differences in the doctrinal sphere do exist with regard to the content of communist ideology. While there is a broad area of agreement, there are certain matters on which serious differences exist. Most important in this connection is Romania's insistence upon the right and responsibility of each party to determine its own strategy and tactics in keeping with the specific conditions under which it operates. This has led the Romanians to emphasize national elements and peculiarities, whereas the CPSU stresses the universal applicability of general (that is, Soviet) principles and interpretations of Marxism-Leninism.

A closely related area is that of interparty relations, particularly since the June 1976 East Berlin conference of European communist parties at least temporarily laid to rest one of the issues on which the two parties differed, and since Ceausescu and Brezhnev agreed to "deepen the relations between the two parties."

The apparent rapprochement between Ceausescu's views and those held by Brezhnev on "questions of the world communist movement" seems to reflect a certain narrowing of differences, although divergent positions remain in some important regards. The use of the term "proletarian internationalism" in the reports on the two recent Ceausescu-Brezhnev meetings (and on other occasions involving Ceausescu) likewise obscures the fact that the Romanians continue to attribute to the term a meaning quite different from that given by their orthodox Warsaw Pact allies. At the same time, however, the Romanians have lately shown a greater willingness to use the term.

Although the final document approved by the East Berlin European conference made no mention of "proletarian internationalism"—as a concession to the Yugoslav, Italian, French, Romanian, and other "autonomist" parties—the USSR has since emphasized that it considers the concept to be relevant still.[7] The Romanians, on the other hand, continue to interpret the conference and the concept of "proletarian internationalism" quite differently, and their previous views on interparty relations have changed little, if at all. In contrast to Brezhnev in East Berlin, Ceausescu used the term "internationalism" (without prefixing it with the word "proletarian"), and for a few weeks after the conference Romanian news media favored "international solidarity." But even before Ceausescu met with Brezhnev in the Crimea, the Romanians resumed use of the term "proletarian internationalism" (most prominently in a joint communique on a Ceausescu visit to Bulgaria for talks with Zhivkov in July).

In April 1976, before there were any signs of Soviet-Romanian rapprochement, Ceausescu reiterated in the strongest terms he had used for some time the relevance of national independence and sovereignty, and criticized unnamed Marxist theoreticians for denigrating the importance of the nation. These sentiments were echoed in a series of Romanian statements defending sovereignty, independence, and the nation, and represented the Romanian contribution to the interparty debate on proletarian internationalism that was raging at that time between the Soviet party on the one hand and the Yugoslav, Italian, French, and certain other West European parties on the other.[8] After Ceausescu's visit to the Crimea, Romanian news media reiterated the RCP's position on interparty relations, sovereignty, independence, the role of the nation, and related topics to show that the position has not changed.[9]

Thus one is left with the impression that, in the sphere of interparty relations, past differences between the Soviet and Romanian parties persist, but again there is a hint that the Romanians are being less abrasive and that they have been willing to compromise at least to the extent of returning "proletarian internationalism" to their vocabulary.

MILITARY COOPERATION AND THE
WARSAW PACT

Military relations and cooperation within the Warsaw Pact are another area of past Soviet-Romanian differences where changes would be apparent if substantial improvement in their relations were in the offing. Some Western correspondents have suggested that its improved relationship with the USSR is a factor behind Romania's participation in and playing host to the November 1976 Warsaw Pact summit, but this should not ipso facto be interpreted as indicating any alteration in the RSR's position regarding military cooperation or the Warsaw Pact, since it has always participated in such gatherings in the past.

The results of the November 1976 meeting of the Political Consultative Committee do not reflect major concessions on the part of the Romanians. The structural changes decided upon include the

establishment of a permanent Warsaw Pact secretariat and a Committee of Foreign Ministers. Both measures indicate an effort to
stress the political role of the treaty, a policy Romania is known to
favor. Both are intended to achieve greater coordination and perhaps
integration in foreign policy, but both new institutions are clearly
subordinate to the Political Consultative Committee. Final judgment
on the impact of these structural innovations will have to await their
evolution, but by early 1977 Romanian officials were minimizing their
significance in "leaks" to Western correspondents.

An important official Romanian statement on the eve of the Warsaw Pact summit was rather ambiguous, leaving open the possibility
of a continuation of past policies or a shift toward a more accommo-
dating stance. In one passage of a speech Ceausescu delivered to the
party aktif of the Ministry of National Defense at the beginning of
October,[10] he dealt with the need for the Romanian army to participate
actively in carrying out the international policy of the RCP, noting
that "it is necessary to continue to develop collaboration between our
army and units and those of the countries of the Warsaw Pact, and
to keep up the practice of joint instruction." In the past the Romanians
have participated in joint Warsaw Pact staff exercises in Romania
and elsewhere, but they have not permitted Romanian troops to participate in actual maneuvers in other states nor have they allowed foreign
troops to engage in maneuvers on their own territory.[11] But exactly
what Ceausescu's statement may mean will only be clarified by the
level at which Romanian forces participate in joint exercises in the
future.

Essentially, Ceausescu's other comments on the Warsaw Pact
represent the familiar Romanian balancing act. On the one hand,
he noted—as he had in the past—that "we should always bear in mind
that when we see the concomitant abolition of NATO and the Warsaw
Pact, our army will continue to collaborate with the armies of the
neighboring socialist countries in the spirit of our treaties of friendship, collaboration, and mutual assistance." At the same time,
however, he said that military capability is national—that is, a component of the socialist development of every country: "We lay stress
on the development of each national army, on the fact that the army
is against no one and has pledged good relations with the armies of
socialist countries outside the Warsaw Pact and with the armies of
other friendly countries." Romania will fight only for its own independence and sovereignty and against any attempt at domination or
oppression, he said, thus ensuring the nation its right to build a
socialist and communist society freely in cooperation with other
socialist countries. At the same time, Romanian troops will not
cross the country's borders "except to observe the international
commitments" made in the Warsaw Pact. This carefully balanced

assessment of Romania's links with the Warsaw Pact is in a number
of respects somewhat ambiguous. While many of its accents are
similar to statements in the past, 12 it leaves open the possibility of
compromise.

ECONOMIC RELATIONS AND THE POTENTIAL
FOR THEIR EXPANSION

Another area in which there is a possibility of improved relations
is the economic sphere, and here there have been some signs of
Romanian interest, although no concrete indications of progress have
emerged thus far. A protocol on scientific and technological cooperation signed by Soviet and Romanian representatives at the end of
September was nothing unusual, 13 but two weeks before Ceausescu
saw Brezhnev in the Crimea the Soviet-Romanian Intergovernmental
Commission on Economic Cooperation met in special session. That
this meeting had more than routine significance is suggested by the
size of the delegations and their rank—the Romanian side was headed
by Deputy Prime Minister Gheorghe Radulescu and included four
ministers and other high-ranking officials, while the Soviet side was
headed by Deputy Premier Mikhail A. Lesechko and included nine
full ministers in addition to other officials. The meeting also took
place "in accordance with what had been discussed recently at the
[East] Berlin meeting of Comrades Leonid Brezhnev and Nicolae
Ceausescu."14 Furthermore, the discussions dealt with the possibility of increasing trade between the two countries in the 1977–80 period.
Since the economic agreements for the 1976–80 plan period were signed
at the end of 1975, the talks were clearly intended to consider expanding economic relations beyond the limits envisaged in the original
agreement. The results of the session have not been extensively
discussed in the mass media of either country. Although 14 protocols
were reportedly concluded, it would appear that little progress was
made at this session.

Further evidence that the Romanians are pursuing the expansion
of economic relations with the Soviets, however, is provided by the
fact that the day after Ceausescu met with Brezhnev in the Crimea,
Romania's Deputy Prime Minister and Minister of Foreign Trade
and International Economic Cooperation Ion Patan held talks in Moscow
with Soviet planning chief Nikolai Baibakov, to examine "certain
current and future problems pertaining to the development of trade
exchanges and economic cooperation."15 Again, however, there
has been no indication thus far that concrete results were achieved.

There are a number of reasons why Romania may be interested
in increasing trade and economic cooperation with the Soviet Union

and the other Comecon states. The proportion of such trade has consistently declined since Romania began to pursue its independent foreign policy in the early 1960s, as Table 3.1 shows. Trade with the developed industrial countries in 1975 may be somewhat out of proportion because figures on the value of goods traded were affected by the price increases that took place owing to inflation in the 1970s. Prices within Comecon tend to be rather slow in responding to changes in world prices. The picture, however, is one of a rather dramatic decline in the share of trade with the Comecon states and the Soviet Union. Preliminary indications for 1976 show only minor changes.

Not only have past figures on Romanian-Soviet trade shown a proportional decline, but initial plans for trade in the 1976–80 period were rather modest in comparison with what was envisaged for the other states of Eastern Europe (although imports of Soviet oil, the price of which increased significantly, by all East European states except Romania would tend to explain some of the differences; see Table 3.2).

The smaller relative growth in the value of trade with the USSR and its decline as a proportion of Romania's total trade was probably seen in Moscow as something of a cause for concern. No doubt the Soviet leaders would like to see a higher level of economic relations with Romania, primarily for political reasons. The Romanians, also on political grounds, made an initial decision to reduce their economic dependence on the Soviet Union in order to better pursue their autonomous foreign policy. Now, however, compelling economic factors would seem to be encouraging economic cooperation with the Soviet Union and the other Comecon states.

TABLE 3.1

Romania's Trade with Various Groups
of Countries
(in percent)

Year	European Members of Comecon	Of Which: with USSR	Other Communist States	Developing Countries	"Developed Capitalist States"
1960	66.6	40.1	6.4	4.7	22.2
1965	60.4	38.8	4.6	6.0	28.9
1970	48.9	27.0	6.9	8.1	35.7
1975	37.5	18.6	7.3	15.5	38.1

Source: Official foreign trade data from Anuarul Statistic al RSR (Bucharest, 1970 and 1976).

TABLE 3.2

Value of Five-Year Trade Agreements
between the Soviet Union and the
Warsaw Pact States

Country	1971–75 1976–80 (in 1,000 million rubles)		Percentage Increase 1976–80/1971–75
GDR	22.0	31.5	43
Czechoslovakia	13.5	25.0	85
Poland	13.0	28.0	115
Bulgaria	12.0	21.0	75
Hungary	9.0	17.0	89
Romania	5.3	9.0	70

Source: Romanian Situation Report/24, Radio Free Europe Research, 22 July 1976, Item 3.

The Romanians, who initially avoided joint Comecon ventures, have likewise made certain adjustments in the face of economic realities. While press commentaries have continued to emphasize national economic sovereignty, the Romanians have agreed to partici- pate in a number of cooperative ventures. In agreements to be imple- mented under the current five-year plan, the Soviets will assist in the expansion of Romanian metallurgical combines, and joint plants will be built in Romania for the production of high-pressure polyethy- lene, caustic soda, butyl rubber, and pulp and paper. Romania is also participating in the Orenburg pipeline, the Ust-Ilimsk pulp and paper mill, and other projects in the Soviet Union. It is reported that 18 separate agreements on cooperation in production have been concluded, involving some 23 Soviet and 13 Romanian ministries and departments.[16] Despite this, economic cooperation between Romania and the Soviet Union is below that now under way between the USSR and the other members of Comecon. Considerably greater opportuni- ties exist in this area.

Initially, as it sought to reduce economic dependence on its communist allies, Bucharest attempted to expand trade with the developed industrial states, which—again for essentially political reasons—were willing to grant extensive credits in order to encourage Romania's foreign policy. The Western states' policy of detente with the Soviet Union has lessened the political significance of Romania's autonomous foreign policy, and the general increase in East-West trade has resulted in the placing of such relations in a more exclusively economic, rather than political, context. Growing concern about Comecon indebtedness has also raised problems. Romania has a Western debt estimated at $3 billion, and its current creditworthiness—as measured by debt service as a percentage of hard currency earnings for exports—is twice the generally acceptable limit.[17] As a result, Romania has been forced to pay much closer attention to balancing its trade with the West, and considerable emphasis has been given to a two-pronged program aimed at expanding exports to the West and simultaneously reducing imports that must be paid for in hard currency. Some success was achieved in this program, but only at the cost of a slower rate of increase. In 1974, Romania's balance of trade deficit totaled $200 million, but in 1975 exports and imports were more evenly balanced. In the latter year, however, foreign trade increased by only 6.6 percent while plan provisions had called for a growth of 21.8 percent.[18] The problems involved in trying to balance its trade with the developed industrial states have been complicated by the general economic slowdown.

Problems in trade with the industrialized Western states and the need for raw materials were major economic factors behind the RSR's effort to expand trade with the developing countries, although political considerations were important in this regard as well. The proportion of trade with this group of states in the past was modest (ranging from 6 to 8 percent of the total) until 1974, when it jumped to 12 percent, and in 1975 it reached 15.5 percent. The 1976-80 five-year plan calls for an increase to 30 percent by 1980, and preliminary figures for 1976 show progress in this direction. Although the developing countries have raw materials which the Romanian economy requires, they are less reliable as trading partners than other nations, and their technological level limits the products they can export. In fact, Romania has run a consistent trade surplus with these states. Thus, although trade with the developing countries will continue to grow, it can never supply certain needed products, which are only secured through trade with developed industrialized states.

In light of these difficulties, Romania's best hope of expanding trade and at the same time securing raw materials and machinery for its own ambitious industrialization programs lies in an expansion of economic relations with the Soviet Union and the East European members of Comecon. Since these countries have similar state trading monopolies, it is easier for officials to negotiate unified contracts for both exports and imports. There is less need to "market" products in the East than there is in the unfamiliar and fragmented markets of the West, and although the Soviets and East Europeans have become increasingly concerned about the quality of their products, it is doubtful whether standards are yet as high as they are in the West.

These advantages are certainly important factors behind what appears
to be a growing Romanian interest in trade with the Soviet Union and
Comecon countries.

The RSR is already quite dependent on the Soviet Union for many
of its raw materials. The general reliability of Soviet supplies and
the use of the five-year moving average, which reduces wide price
swings within Comecon, make the USSR look even more attractive in
light of the world price fluctuations and the difficulty and uncertainty
of developing third-world sources of supply. A Radio Moscow broadcast[19] said that "in the last few years the Soviet Union has provided
50 percent of the iron ore, coal, ferrous rolled goods, and cast iron
imported by Romania, as well as considerable quantities of cotton,
potassium fertilizers, and phosphorus." There have been indications
that Romania is interested in importing Soviet oil, though there has
been no evidence that the Soviets have yet agreed to this. In 1973,
a Romanian economic publication[20] reported that "some 6,000,000
tons of oil will have to be imported by 1975, and Romania is interested
in having the major portion of this amount guaranteed by cooperation
with the Soviet Union." (In fact, Romanian oil imports amounted to
6 million tons in 1974.) On the other hand, Romanian officials at
the United Nations were quoted in 1975 as saying that "Romania gets
the extra oil it needs from various Arab countries" and that it buys
no oil from the Soviet Union.[21] The Soviet-Romanian trade protocols
for 1975 and 1976 did not mention oil. Since the Arab oil-producing
countries are becoming more and more reluctant to supply oil on a
barter basis,[22] it is probable that Romania approached the Soviet
Union with regard to crude oil deliveries. This is also suggested
by the fact that during a visit by Prime Minister Manea Manescu to
Moscow for economic talks in August 1975, the Minister of Mines,
Petroleum, and Geology accompanied him and met with his Soviet
counterpart.[23]

THE SIGNIFICANCE OF BREZHNEV'S
"FRIENDSHIP" VISIT TO ROMANIA

The climax thus far in Soviet-Romanian relations was the trip
to Bucharest of Brezhnev at the end of November 1976. The occasion
assumed added significance since it was the Soviet party leader's first
formal visit to Romania for over a decade. It also provides an appropriate milestone for assessing the Bucharest-Moscow rapprochement
six months after it was initiated.

The visit confirmed that relations between the two countries were
indeed improving as a result of accommodations on both sides, but
at the same time certain differences remained, as evidenced by the

fact that the final statement noted the satisfaction of both parties with
the talks but made no reference to unanimity of views.24 Also, in
his toast Brezhnev stated that there were no "important" unresolved
problems between the two countries, while Ceausescu observed that
"differences of opinion on some nonessential questions" should not
hamper cooperation.

Despite the generally positive tone of the speeches given during
the visit, Brezhnev did needle the Romanians on occasion for their
emphasis on the importance of national efforts and their denigration
of international solidarity. In referring to the Soviet party's policy,
he observed (in similar terms to those used at the 25th CPSU congress
in February 1976): "Concomitantly with the national efforts, an important component part of our success is fraternal cooperation, the
natural wish to take into account not only our own interests but also
those of our socialist friends." He also noted: "We highly appreciate
collaboration with the Socialist Republic of Romania on matters of
international politics when it exists" (emphasis added). And in his
rally speech he observed: "Our class opponents . . . try assiduously
to exploit any difficulty in relations among socialist states, and strive
in every way to provoke complications and sow suspicion and mutual
distrust." The proper response to such conduct, he continued, was
a deepening of cooperation and more intense efforts to achieve cohesion, and he saw his Romanian visit as part of such a campaign.
Along this same line he remarked:

> Communists in the countries of socialism are justifiably
> proud that they have shown in practice an example of state
> relations freed from national egoism and filled with
> attentiveness to the interests of friends abroad and com-
> rades in the fight for Marxist-Leninist ideals.

Despite the carefully weighed wording, indicating persisting
differences, there are signs that some concrete action has been taken
to improve relations between the two countries and parties as a result
of the visit. The primary Soviet objective was to secure greater
cohesion, and there were indications that some progress was achieved
in this regard. The statement noted that the two parties "believe it
necessary to expand the practice of exchanging information and holding consultations on the most important questions of the development
of Soviet-Romanian relations and on international problems of common
interest with the aim of coordinating their positions." Another area
marked out for closer links is the cultural and ideological field. The
two leaders agreed to expand cooperation and contacts between ideological, cultural, artistic, journalistic, and other such institutions
and individuals. The mass media of the two countries are to coop-

erate more closely in deepening the ties of friendship between them, and it was decided to study the feasibility of creating a joint governmental commission on cultural cooperation.

It would appear that Romania made more political concessions than it received. But since there are indications that Bucharest's principal concern in improving relations with Moscow has been to secure economic advantages, this would seem to be a quid pro quo. The information so far released on economic cooperation, however, does not appear to reflect any substantial improvement. The statement merely noted that

> the appropriate organs of both countries will ensure the fulfillment, and will strive for the overfulfillment of the five-year trade agreement for 1976-80, and will start the drafting of a long-term program of economic cooperation for the post-1980 period so as to ensure its substantial expansion.

It is possible that the party leaders have established a framework within which government officials will later work out the details of an expansion of economic relations, but the statement is vague on this point and suggests only a limited economic improvement up to 1980.

Perhaps the key to the results of the present visit was a statement made by Brezhnev in his toast during the dinner given in his honor by Ceausescu: "There are premises for broadening Soviet-Romanian collaboration. The decisive role is naturally played by the strengthening of the links between the Communist Party of the Soviet Union and the Romanian Communist Party." In his speech on November 24, Brezhnev said much the same thing: "Our talks broadened mutual understanding between our parties and strengthened the atmosphere of trust that is so important for further consolidation of our fraternal relations." Pravda[25] in its commentary on the visit said that it "had strengthened the confidence necessary for future ties."

In other words, conditions exist for expanding relations in many areas, including the economic field, but whether such expansion does in fact take place will depend on the further development of relations between the two parties. Thus, it would seem that expansion of economic relations will be determined by political conditions. The Romanians have made some concessions in this sphere, but the Soviets apparently wish to test their sincerity. Brezhnev's visit to Bucharest confirms the willingness of both sides to continue the dialogue and the invitation extended to Ceausescu to visit Moscow will provide an opportunity for this.

THE FUTURE COURSE OF RELATIONS

The current status of Romanian-Soviet relations is far from clear, as the present survey has shown. There are many unknowns that only time can clarify. Nevertheless, certain things seem to be fairly well established. Since Ceausescu's adoption of a warmer tone toward the Soviet Union in June 1976, and particularly since his visit to the USSR in August and Brezhnev's to Bucharest in November, there have been unmistakable signs of lessening of friction in Soviet-Romanian relations. Closer examination, however, indicates that what has improved thus far is primarily the atmosphere—the two countries and their leaders are saying friendlier things about each other now than was the case in the past. Greater restraint is being exercised with regard to treatment of the history of Bessarabia, and Ceausescu joined his East European counterparts in Moscow in December for the celebration of Brezhnev's birthday.

A closer look at some of the basic questions that have led to strain in the past—ideological issues, interparty relations, and links with the Warsaw Pact—shows no fundamental concessions on either side, but the Romanians appear to be avoiding antagonizing the Soviets, and there are hints of a certain willingness to be more cooperative. In the area of trade and economic cooperation there is a possibility of expanded relations, and the Romanians have indicated a definite interest in such an expansion. The fact that Romania has intensified its cooperation with Bulgaria and that preliminary steps have been taken to do the same with Poland and Hungary would seem further to confirm Bucharest's interest in closer ties in this regard.

Disappointment thus far with non-Comecon trade, the growing demand for certain raw materials, and the consequences of some internal Romanian economic decisions are pushing Romania economically toward the Soviet Union. Since there appears to be no fundamental shift in the basic Romanian foreign policy, however, it would seem likely that Bucharest will seek to balance this necessity with greater efforts to strengthen and maintain the various political and economic contacts with individual, and groups of, non-Comecon states. At the same time, Moscow is no doubt anxious to draw Romania away from these other extensive contacts. If the Soviets feel that they have the stronger hand economically, they may well seek to pressure Romania to adopt a less active and extended foreign policy. If such indeed is the case, the potential for renewed friction between the two countries remains.

Whether the improvement in atmosphere between Romania and the Soviet Union will be transformed into more concrete measures remains to be seen. Nevertheless, thus far the Romanian leaders have not deviated in any fundamental way in their relationship with the USSR from the careful but ambiguous balance they have maintained with such consummate skill for the last decade and a half. Soviet-Romanian relations indeed appear to be under review in Bucharest and Moscow, but the final results of this assessment are not yet apparent on either side. Nor might they be for some time to come.

NOTES

1. See, for example, Robert R. King, "Romania and the Soviet Union: Disharmony in a Low Key," Romanian Background Report/12, Radio Free Europe Research, 31 July 1974; and Robert R. King, "Romania and the Block: The Extent of Normalization," Romanian Background Report/8, Radio Free Europe Research, 17 March 1971.

2. The announcement was made by Agerpres and Radio Moscow, 3 August 1976, in nearly identical terms. See also Romanian Situation Report/27, Radio Free Europe Research, 12 August 1976, Item 1.

3. See Robert R. King, "The Escalation of Romanian-Soviet Historical Polemics over Bessarabia," RAD Background Report/38, Radio Free Europe Research, 12 February 1976; and Robert R. King and Romanian Unit, "Debate Between Romanian and Soviet Historians over Bessarabia Continues," RAD Background Report/137, Radio Free Europe Research, 15 June 1976.

4. Scinteia (Bucharest), 3 June 1976.

5. David Binder, New York Times News Service/Washington, 10 October 1976.

6. Scinteia, 3 August 1976.

7. See F. Stephen Larrabee, "Moscow and the 'Autonomous' Communist Parties After East Berlin: How Much Compromise?" RL 422/76, Radio Liberty Research, 27 September 1976.

8. See Scinteia, 24 and 27 April 1976; and Alexandru Tanase, "The Permanence of the Nation and the Real Significance of Internationalism," Lumea (Bucharest), 1 April 1976. See also Robert R. King, "Ceausescu Reasserts Position on National Independence and Sovereignty," RAD Background Report/94, Radio Free Europe Research, 28 April 1976.

9. See Nicolae Chilie, "The Application of the Norms of International Legality: Demand for a New International Economic and Political Order," Lumea, 2 September 1976; Stefan Andrei's introduction to a volume on the new international order, Agerpres, 13 August 1976; Stefan Nastasescu, "Sovereignty, Security, and International Cooperation," Era Socialista (Bucharest), no. 17, September 1976; and Romanian Situation Reports/31 and 33, Radio Free Europe Research, 10 and 23 September 1976, Items 5 and 1, respectively.

10. Scinteia, 2 October 1976.

11. See Romanian Situation Report/9, Radio Free Europe Research, 27 February 1974, Item 2.

12. For earlier statements see Robert R. King, "Ceausescu Assesses Foreign Policy in Speech to Grand National Assembly," RAD Background Report/3, Radio Free Europe Research, 13 January 1976; and Romanian Situation Report/49, Radio Free Europe Research, 19 December 1975, Item 5.

13. See Romanian Situation Report/34, Radio Free Europe Research, 1 October 1976, Item 6.

14. Laurentiu Duta, "Special Session of the Romanian-Soviet Intergovernmental Commission on Economic Cooperation," Lumea, 22 July 1976; see also Romanian Situation Reports/2 and 24, Radio Free Europe Research, 20 January and 22 July 1976, Item 3 in both cases.

15. Radio Bucharest, 4 August 1976.

16. Socialisticheskaya industriya (Moscow), 7 July 1976; Radio Moscow, 30 July 1976; and Ekonomicheskaya Gazeta (Moscow), no. 34, 16 August 1976.

17. Washington Post, 18 October 1976.

18. See Romanian Situation Reports/7 and 5, Radio Free Europe Research, 21 February 1975 and 18 February 1976, Items 1 and 2, respectively.

19. 21 August 1975.

20. Viata Economica (Bucharest), 23 February 1973.

21. Radio Free Europe Special/New York, 7 February 1975.

22. See the case of Kuwait, discussed in Romanian Situation Report/32, Radio Free Europe Research, 21 August 1975, Item 6b.

23. See Romanian Situation Report/33, Radio Free Europe Research, 29 August 1975, Item 2.

24. The statement was published in Scinteia, 25 November 1976, and the dinner toasts and friendship rally speeches are to be found in ibid., 23 and 25 November 1976.

25. (Moscow), 25 November 1976.

4

YUGOSLAV-SOVIET
RELATIONS
Slobodan Stankovic

Yugoslav-Soviet relations have regularly alternated between
"hot" and "cold." At times they have been visibly strained (although
in recent years the vehemence of the 1950s and early 1960s has not
been apparent), while at others they have been described as "very
friendly" and anything to the contrary has been branded wishful thinking by the enemies of both countries.[1] Not only have relations varied
from hot to cold, however; one also gets the distinct impression that
each country is pursuing a dual policy toward the other, which results
in a curious counterpoint, with official expressions of warm praise
balanced by rumblings in the press regarding important differences.
In 1976, the fluctuations seemed to become more rapid and the contradictions more numerous. The most probable reason for this is the
instability in Yugoslavia portended by the succession crisis that will
come into full flower when the aging party leader, President Josip
Broz-Tito, leaves the scene.

After Soviet party leader Leonid Brezhnev's visit to Belgrade
in November 1976, Yugoslav media began—usually indirectly—to repeat
the claim that the Soviet Union was trying to undermine Yugoslavia's
independence by supporting pro-Soviet groups ("Cominformists")
within the League of Communists of Yugoslavia (LCY), which could
play a role after the death of Tito. As support for the claim that
Moscow had shown hostility to Yugoslavia, they cited Soviet books
and articles in which the existence of "various roads to socialism"

===

This chapter is based on Slobodan Stankovic, "Yugoslav-Soviet
Relations Following Brezhnev's Visit," RAD Background Report/43,
Radio Free Europe Research, 28 February 1977.

was denied, or which referred to the Yugoslav party program as the "ideology of revisionism."

Only three weeks after Brezhnev's departure from Belgrade, where a joint communique was signed stressing "full satisfaction with the results achieved" during his visit,[2] the Yugoslavs began complaining about Soviet reports (particularly in the periodicals Partiinaya Zhizn and Za Rubezhom) "in which the Tito-Brezhnev meeting was twisted in an unrealistic fashion."[3]

Yet on 9 December 1976 the LCY Central Committee Presidium headed by Tito appraised Brezhnev's visit "positively" and stressed its "significance and usefulness in the development of relations and cooperation between socialist, self-managing, nonaligned Yugoslavia and the Soviet Union." It was also said that relations were "developing favorably and in the interests of both countries."[4] A similar view was taken by the CPSU Politburo, which emphasized the "extraordinary significance of the recent Soviet-Yugoslav meeting."[5] In this connection "observers in Moscow" were said to have noted that the Politburo held the view that "communism is the common Yugoslav-Soviet goal," and therefore "in their march toward that goal the people of both countries may follow their freely chosen roads."[6]

Thus while official documents and statements gave the impression that relations were good, at least some of the information media in each country indicated that they were not as friendly and harmonious as officially described. Although at the signing of the joint communique on his visit to Belgrade Brezhnev said that "what will follow this good document will be even more significant than its contents,"[7] new strains became evident in the relations between the two countries within a matter of weeks.

The day after the Yugoslav Presidium officially released its optimistic appraisal of the Tito-Brezhnev summit, Yugoslav journalists began to leak to their Western colleagues in Belgrade reports that the atmosphere of the meeting had not been particularly friendly. In fact, Brezhnev was said to have attempted to pressure Tito by presenting demands incompatible with Yugoslavia's nonaligned status and its independent road to communism. According to intentionally leaked information from "highly placed Yugoslav sources,"[8] Brezhnev submitted nine demands to Tito—to wit, that Yugoslavia:

1. Increase the services available to Soviet surface warships and submarines in its ports;
2. Cooperate more closely with Comecon (Yugoslavia is more than an observer but less than a full member);
3. Participate in Warsaw Pact ideological activity;
4. Agree to closer coordination of foreign policy;
5. Establish a Yugoslav-Soviet association;

6. Adopt a more pro-Soviet nonaligned stance (more like that of Cuba and Vietnam);

7. Cease to accuse the Soviet Union of supporting Yugoslav Stalinists ("Cominformists") in the USSR and elsewhere;

8. Stop spreading anti-Soviet propaganda in Yugoslav information media; and

9. Stop claiming that the Soviet Union has anything to do with relations between Yugoslavia and Bulgaria (the latter being Moscow's most loyal ally).

These demands—neither confirmed nor denied by Moscow—were said to have been "resolutely" rejected by Tito.[9] A spokesman for the Yugoslav Foreign Ministry denied the report several days later, but his tone was far from convincing, and in some regards he even seemed indirectly to confirm the Western accounts of the meeting. In rejecting them he referred to the LCY Presidium's "positive appraisal" of the Tito-Brezhnev meeting and added that "all interpretations that go beyond its context are arbitrary and tendentious guesses, obviously not designed to serve the interests of international cooperation and understanding."[10]

The nine demands constitute a plausible list that may well have served as a starting point in Brezhnev's discussion with Tito. They could probably be reduced to three major issues over which Belgrade and Moscow have been quarreling since 1948: "the crisis of capitalism" and how it should be dealt with—an ideological issue involving the practical question of relations with "capitalist" Western governments that has come to include the problem of Eurocommunism; the concept of various roads to socialism and whether Yugoslavia's self-managing socialism can serve as a model for other countries; the meaning of nonalignment in general and of Yugoslavia's role in it in particular.

THE "CRISIS OF CAPITALISM" AND THE
PROBLEM OF EUROCOMMUNISM

Yugoslav and Soviet Communists generally agree that capitalism is passing through a serious crisis that will ultimately result in its demise. They have disagreed, however, about the "quality" of this crisis and the methods that should be used to accelerate the disintegration of the capitalist system. For instance, there was a clash of views at a symposium that took place in the Adriatic resort of Cavtat on 27 September-2 October 1976. Soviet party theoretician Yuri Krasin argued that capitalism "is ripe—or indeed overripe—for transition to socialism. . . . Traditional contradictions of capitalism connected with the problems of employment, the high cost of living, material difficulties, and deprivation of the masses have by no means disappeared."11 Similar views can be found in the program approved at the LCY's seventh congress in April 1958, but although that program is still valid, Yugoslav leaders have revised their views regarding the "crisis of capitalism." Practical considerations rather than questions of principle motivated this change—a million Yugoslavs (so-called Gastarbeiter) were working in capitalist Western Europe earning several billion dollars annually and thus making a substantial contribution to Yugoslavia's economic development. Any acceleration of the disintegration of capitalism would therefore have adverse consequences domestically, particularly since there was considerable unemployment in Yugoslavia despite the Gastarbeiter working elsewhere. Thus, though Yugoslav theoreticians continued to accept the idea of a "crisis of capitalism," they adopted a different position regarding both its "quality" and the time of its demise. The Yugoslavs and Russians disagreed in particular over whether a revolutionary or an evolutionary course should be taken in helping capitalism to disintegrate—the Yugoslavs opting for evolution.

At the symposium in Cavtat, Aleksandar Grlickov, LCY Presidium Executive Committee secretary responsible for relations with other communist parties, proclaimed the latest version of the official Yugoslav thesis on the "crisis of capitalism." After stating that difficulties throughout the world were attributable to "a deep crisis in capitalism and hitches in the development of socialist society," he continued:

> The nature of the crisis of capitalism is significant for the strategy of socialism. There is evidence to suggest that this crisis is not merely an economic one. . . . The current crisis of capitalism will not lead to capitalist economic catastrophe, as some people think. On the contrary, there are signs that capitalism is extending its economic boundaries. . . . The crisis has to a great extent been a structural and social one, and no less a moral and psychological one. It is precisely the latter aspect of the crisis that can accelerate the first. The interpenetration and interaction of these two aspects must be made the subject of an analysis on the basis of which the strategy of the socialist forces should be worked out. . . . It is also significant for this socialist strategy that the crisis of capitalism has gone beyond the borders of individual countries. It involves the capitalist system as a whole and the structure of international political and economic relations, as well as the world economic system.12

Unlike Krasin, who saw difficulties only in the capitalist world, Grlickov related the crisis of capitalism to the difficulties plaguing communist countries. The fact that socialism has been victorious in industrially underdeveloped states "has fundamentally influenced the methods and means used in the construction of socialism" in general, and "socialism has developed painstakingly in the socialist countries, often taking a wrong road, at times even suffering dramatic convulsions." It "has not been and will not be able to resolve its own contradictions easily."

Consequently, capitalism has survived and various roads to socialism have been opened up. According to Grlickov, this requires intensification of the struggle not only within capitalism, which is doomed to die, but also within socialism, which history has ordained to replace it. Grlickov maintained that "conflicts" will continue to beset "socialist forces," and in this context mentioned "the new strategies of the communist parties in Italy, Spain, France, Belgium, Sweden, and elsewhere," which regard the efforts to put an end to capitalism and achieve a "democratic transformation," "not as a strategy of war but rather as a form of the class struggle."

Despite expectations of the "final death" of capitalism, the Yugoslavs feel the system will continue to exist for some time (and may even survive indefinitely in modified form). Therefore an important role can be played by Eurocommunism. Although Grlickov did not use the term, he was obviously referring to it and to the negative Soviet attitude toward it when he said:

> Revolutions carried out by violent means in the past and
> those that will follow this path in the future have no
> grounds for ignoring the efforts made by one section
> of the Marxist and socialist forces to devise new strate-
> gies. On the contrary. The failure of the Chilean
> revolution is by no means an argument for opposing
> [nonviolent] revolution. Even violent revolutions have
> had their failures.

"Differing strategies" should be adopted, he said, depending on "specific social conditions, both domestic and international."

Other Yugoslav theoreticians have elaborated on these views. At the Cavtat symposium, Professor Vjekoslav Mikecin said that, since the Russian revolution, the workers' movement had been "passing through a serious crisis" because there was no "coherent theory of revolution adapted to existing situations." Social-democratic parties propagated an "opportunistic theory of revolution," while "numerous communist parties" insisted on a "dogmatic, quasi-apocalyptic theory of revolution." Therefore the socialist forces in capitalist countries had not yet succeeded in transforming capitalist into socialist society.13

These theoretical arguments were particularly relevant to the practical question of Eurocommunism. The official Yugoslav attitude was complicated. On the one hand, Belgrade was a vigorous partisan of "various roads to socialism," which implied acceptance of a "special road" for the Italian, French, or Spanish CPs. On the other, the Yugoslavs were afraid the concept of Eurocommunism was an attempt "to dress the communist movement in Western Europe in a uniform, or to use it to mark out a new center for these parties."14 Thus they did not like the term Eurocommunism, which, they claimed, "originated in the vocabulary of bourgeois circles."15 (They had a similar aversion to the term "national communism," which had been used in the West to describe the Yugoslav system.) But they definitely welcomed the phenomenon of Eurocommunism as yet another road to socialism which "differs from the Soviet one" and as "a different approach by the parties in these [West European] countries to the CPSU."16

Although for the Yugoslavs Eurocommunism was an ally in their struggle against Soviet attempts to establish hegemony, they did not conceal their fear that its views in regard to a pluralistic system might have a detrimental effect on party authority within Yugoslavia. In this respect, Belgrade to a certain extent shared Moscow's interest in combating internal forces that might favor the introduction of such pluralism. Yugoslav theoreticians rationalized away the contradiction by arguing that "the introduction of a pluralistic system in countries from which it has already disappeared and in which it had practically no tradition cannot be considered." At issue, of course, was freedom under socialism, "which can and should be cultivated in a way that suits the sociohistorical conditions of every country."17

The Yugoslavs were willing to allow the Eurocommunist parties, which were in the initial phase of constructing socialism, to perpetuate pluralism by entering into coalitions with various noncommunist parties and groups. But the ideas of the Eurocommunists, they felt, were valid only in capitalist countries and could not be accepted in countries already ruled by communist parties. At the level of interparty relations, nevertheless, the Eurocommunists were regarded as useful allies in opposing Soviet hegemony over the international communist movement. The Yugoslav approach to Eurocommunism was also linked with the attitude toward the "crisis of capitalism." Moscow's plan for the "violent" overthrow of capitalism was rejected in favor of the "nonviolent" approach also advocated by the Eurocommunists. For only capitalism's gradual disappearance, through internal transition rather than violence, could ensure that Yugoslavia's specific road to socialism would not fall prey to Soviet hegemony.

VARIOUS ROADS TO SOCIALISM AND
SELF-MANAGING SOCIALISM AS A MODEL

Yugoslavia's specific road to socialism, which differs in a number of important respects from the Soviet model, has also been a
source of discord in relations between Moscow and Belgrade. This
issue is very closely related to the differing views on the "crisis of
capitalism" and Eurocommunism. In his speech at the special session
of the Yugoslav Central Committee on 28 December 1976 commemo-
rating the 30th anniversary of Tito's selection as head of the Yugoslav
party, CC Presidium member Edvard Kardelj described the Yugoslav
leader's conflict with Stalin as "a conflict between two concepts of
the role, policy, and methods of work of the party and state authority
under conditions of socialism."[18] The last edition of the History of
the LCY: A Short Survey [19] admits that "by the end of 1947" the Soviet
leaders wanted to achieve full domination over Yugoslavia, although
"the whole world knew that Yugoslavia was the sincerest and most
loyal ally of the Soviet Union." Yet on 28 June 1948 Yugoslavia was
excommunicated from the Cominform. During the Cominform session
at which this action was taken, Soviet delegate Andrei Zhdanov said:
"We are in possession of information that Tito is an imperialist spy."[20]
Tito's real "sin," however, was that he allowed his country to refuse
to follow Soviet directives and to insist on determining its own policies.
The Cominform resolution expelling Yugoslavia from membership
admitted this:

> Considerably overestimating the influence of internal
> and national forces, the leaders of Yugoslavia think
> they can maintain their country's independence and
> build socialism without the support of the communist
> parties of other countries, without the support of the
> Soviet Union. They think the new Yugoslavia can do
> without the help of these revolutionary forces.[21]

The expulsion of the Yugoslav party brought to the fore a conflict that
had been developing behind the scenes even during the war. The
ideological issue came into the open when Tito and his colleagues
wrote that they had used the Soviet Union as a model in developing
socialism, but "we . . . are developing socialism in a somewhat
different form in this country."[22]

Thus Yugoslavia's "national communism" was born not only of
the conviction that every communist state should pursue its own
independent course but also of necessity, since the Yugoslav party
was forced—often against its will—to be independent. Circumstances
after 1948 required the LCY to develop new theories to replace orth-

odox interpretations of Marx, Engels, and Lenin that did not suit
Yugoslav conditions. Having their own "creatively developed" ideological views, the Yugoslavs began an assault against some of those
held by the Soviet and "loyal" East European parties. Belgrade proclaimed that the USSR was a country with a "state capitalist" system
and affirmed that the only way to remain independent would be to
abandon completely the Soviet theory of "ideological units," thus
rejecting Kremlin tutelage in ideological matters.

One of the most important Yugoslav innovations was the system
of workers' self-management, called a kind of "democratic humanistic
socialist model," which was introduced in June 1950. From this
concept evolved the idea of the eventual "withering away of the state,"
and this in turn gave birth to the idea of the "withering away of the
party." This was a logical development, because if the self-
management system really prevailed, then it must produce a corresponding political system in which the leading role in society must be
played by the workers, with the state and party becoming less and
less important. By the beginning of the 1970s the idea of the party
"withering away" was revised, although it was still emphasized that
it "cannot be an agency outside self-management, a commander
commanding other people, merely issuing resolutions which everyone
must listen to and implement."[23] At the same time, the party must
unquestionably remain the "leading force" in the country.

The self-management system and the unique ideological concepts
associated with it were officially enshrined in the LCY program
adopted at the seventh party congress in April 1958. Although Stalin
had died some five years previously and his successors had initiated
a rapprochement with the Yugoslavs, the Yugoslav party and its
program were stigmatized by the Soviets as "revisionist." The program adopted at the 22d CPSU congress in October 1961 specified:

> Revisionism—rightist opportunism—which is a reflection
> of bourgeois influence, is the chief danger within the
> communist movement. The revisionists, who mask their
> renunciation of Marxism with talk about the need to take
> into account the latest developments in society and the
> class struggle, in effect play the role of peddlers of
> bourgeois-reformist ideology within the communist
> movement. . . . The revisionists deny the historical
> necessity of the socialist revolution and the dictatorship
> of the proletariat. They deny the leading role of the
> Marxist-Leninist party, undermine the foundations of
> proletarian internationalism, and drift toward national-
> ism. The ideology of revisionism is most fully embodied
> in the program of the League of Communists of Yugo-
> slavia.[24]

One should not forget that this program is still valid, and articles against revisionism in the Soviet press still hark back to the ideas expressed in it.

Yugoslav-Soviet relations continue to be affected by these events of the past. In order to maintain its legitimacy in and hegemony over its client states in Eastern Europe, the Soviet Union must insist on the universal validity of its own path to socialist development. Any meaningful admission that alternative roads are consistent with Marxist-Leninist laws would open up a Pandora's box. Attempts to put across the idea that the Yugoslav model is valid in Yugoslavia only and the Soviet one must be followed elsewhere (particularly in Eastern Europe) have not been successful. The Yugoslav party, on the other hand, cannot admit the validity of the Soviet model with regard to its own situation, for to do so would undermine the legitimacy and raison d'être of the LCY. Thus it has no alternative but to insist that there are various roads to socialism. Since the May 1955 "reconciliation," repeated efforts have been made by the two parties to establish a lasting rapprochement; in every case, however, the effort has been confounded by the incompatibility of their respective positions regarding the existence of different models of socialism. There has been nothing thus far to indicate that Belgrade and Moscow have come to grips with this dilemma, and hence it is unlikely that any fundamental change will come about.

SOVIET-YUGOSLAV DIFFERENCES OVER NONALIGNMENT

Another issue over which Belgrade and Moscow have been at odds for years is nonalignment. The Yugoslavs were therefore plainly gratified when the Soviets accepted their thesis and permitted the claim that nonalignment was "one of the most significant factors in world politics" to be included in the closing resolution of the June 1976 conference of European CPs in East Berlin. Moreover, the nonaligned countries were listed along with the socialist countries as "revolutionary and progressive forces in the developing countries and in all workers' and democratic movements fighting to establish new international political and economic relations."[25] Moscow's change of mind was gradual, however. Its hostility to nonalignment was particularly strong after the August 1968 invasion of Czechoslovakia, which Yugoslavia criticized. At that time a Soviet newspaper[26] claimed that Yugoslavia's policy of nonalignment was actually "a policy of alignment, not with socialism but rather with antisocialist forces in Czechoslovakia and the whole imperialist chorus." In March 1970, an article in a Yugoslav journal criticized certain Polish writers

for referring to "the so-called policy" of nonalignment and citing
Tito's attitude toward the Warsaw Pact invasion of Czechoslovakia
as evidence that Yugoslavia was not a truly nonaligned country; it
charged the Warsaw critics with claiming that such nations "can play
the game of nonalignment thanks only to the existence of the Warsaw
Pact forces."[27]

In meetings with Tito the Soviets gradually took a more diplomatic
position in regard to Yugoslavia's nonalignment. After meeting with
Brezhnev in 1973, Tito reported that the CPSU leader "completely
agreed with the principle of nonalignment, [and admitted] that such
a policy had been useful in the struggle to counter imperialism and
various attempts at aggression." When reminded that initially the
Soviets had taken a hostile stand in regard to nonalignment, Tito
replied that they had obviously "needed a little time":

> Today there is no difference in our attitudes toward
> nonalignment. The Soviet leaders consider this policy
> useful, and realize that it is praiseworthy that Yugo-
> slavia is among the nonaligned countries; they recog-
> nize that Yugoslavia has been conducting an unselfish
> policy.[28]

Tito was clearly overoptimistic at this time, and subsequent
events showed that the Soviets' support was conditioned by their
realization that nonalignment served their own interests. Only three
months before the nonalignment clause was included in the June 1976
CP conference resolution, a Yugoslav correspondent in Moscow complained that although the Soviet leaders had changed their negative
attitude toward nonalignment they nonetheless expected Yugoslavia
and other nonaligned countries to "support Soviet foreign policy."[29]

Naturally, the East Berlin conference's acceptance of nonalignment involved Yugoslav concessions, the most important being agreement that nonalignment was a path that led ultimately to socialism.
At the end of 1975, the LCY party weekly Komunist[30] said that nonalignment leads to the destruction of capitalism and the introduction
of socialism, and the essential characteristics of its policy are that
it ensures independence for the people and militates for "the transformation of the world, for a new international political and economic
order." The article went on:

> The class content of the anti-imperialist policy of non-
> alignment therefore has at least two dimensions: first,
> nonalignment rejects the basic elements of capitalism
> as a world system based on domination, and does this
> in the name of relationships (independence, equality,

etc.) that are the starting point for all socialist international links; secondly, in the proportion in which such
international relations are created the basic preconditions
for socioeconomic development and progressive social
change in large areas of the world (which until recently
were "outside history") are brought into being. . . .
Briefly, nonalignment (as a doctrine, movement, or
political action) is a component part of socialism as a
world process rather than a mere "parallel" category
with only an "outward" connection.

The Yugoslav theory that the nonaligned countries are pursuing
an antiimperialist policy with a class content that leads to socialism
differs from the political yardstick used to determine whether a
country is nonaligned. As formulated in Cairo by Tito, Nasser,
Sukarno, and Nehru in July 1961, during the preparations for the
first nonaligned summit in Belgrade, a country preparing to join the
nonaligned group had to (1) follow an independent policy based on
peaceful coexistence; (2) support the struggle for national liberation;
(3) abjure membership in all military pacts; (4) refrain from entering
into a bilateral alliance with a great power; and (5) forbid the establishment of foreign military bases on its territory.[31] (This political
yardstick was violated, however, when countries like communist
Cuba were accepted as nonaligned and when Romania, with Yugoslav
backing, was given permanent observer status at the August 1976
nonaligned summit in Colombo despite its membership in the Warsaw
Pact.)
    The concession to Moscow that nonalignment leads to socialism,
however, is a two-edged sword, since Tito's brand of socialism is
obviously not the same as Brezhnev's. Nevertheless, for the time
being Moscow seems ready at least to tolerate Yugoslavia's propaga-
tion of self-managing socialism among the nonaligned countries.
Thus, although Belgrade and Moscow agree in principle that nonalignment leads to socialism, they disagree about how this happens and
what kind of socialism will emerge. In December 1976, the Yugoslavs accused Moscow of trying to "divide the nonaligned movement
by attributing to some of its members more and to others less positive
significance."[32]
    A similar claim was made by Grlickov, who said that attempts
to divide the nonaligned countries "are often due to failure to understand the essence and goals of the movement."[33] He also stressed
that not all nonaligned countries "are inclined to undertake exclusively
socialist transformation." In sum, the Yugoslavs are afraid that
Moscow's efforts to win over individual nonaligned countries that
are striving to achieve a "socialist transformation" will be success-

ful, and they keep stressing that there are various roads to socialism and that this has particular relevance for the nonaligned.

Grlickov pointed out at the Cavtat symposium, for instance, that there are marked differences between the economic and social systems in the Soviet bloc countries and those in, say, Yugoslavia or Tanzania, and on these grounds he rejected the Soviet theory with the observation that "socialism as a world process is not a linear function, nor is it the extended arm of the existing socialist countries."[34] Rather, it is "a function of the struggle of the working class in the capitalist countries and the peoples of the developing countries to achieve political and economic emancipation." Therefore the nonaligned countries, because of their political-ideological idiosyncrasies, "are emerging on the world stage with their own political and economic programs," which will "bring about substantial changes in international political and economic relations." Grlickov capped these remarks with the following statement:

> This is one of the important factors of contemporary revolutionary conditions in the world, of the strategy of socialism. That is why we may rightly say that the policy of nonalignment constitutes the political framework of the contemporary class struggle on a global scale or, as somebody figuratively put it, the arena in which two worlds collide.

The role the socialist countries should play in helping nonaligned countries is, according to Yugoslav theoreticians, the same as the one that the Soviet Union and its East European allies should play vis-a-vis Western capitalist countries. As Professor Mikecin put it at Cavtat: "They can best do this by steadfastly putting into practice in their own countries the principles stemming from Marxist teaching. Among other things, this means that they should uphold the premise that democracy is inseparable from socialism."[35] Yugoslav theoreticians maintain that the Soviet road to socialism is not suitable for nonaligned countries in Africa, Asia, and Latin America. The Soviets advocate a "violent" road to socialism, which is good neither for these countries nor for socialism. As Todo Kurtovic, a member of the Yugoslav Executive Committee, said in an interview with Borba,[36]

> If we were to analyze the experience of some countries in Asia and Africa—i.e., the attempts made by the communist parties in these countries to take power in a violent manner— we would see both how unrealistic they were and how such misplaced revolutionary zeal impeded revolutionary processes.

Instead of defending the national interests of their countries, these parties "have fallen prey to radical phrases" which conflict with the nation's real interests.

The Soviet attitude toward and propaganda on internationalism and the national interests of the individual nonaligned states cannot but produce sharp differences. One Yugoslav writer[37] put it this way: "No socialist revolution can be carried out if national interests are ignored," and went on to stress again the familiar Yugoslav thesis that "class interests should not be identified with international (general) interests but must be linked with national interests; in other words, class interests must remain chiefly within the framework of national interests and only in this context can they lead to international interests." Therefore, "relations among nations cannot be identified with relations among classes." At the same time, however, "no theoretical view preaching the absolutization of any individual road to and form of socialism can be accepted in principle."

The Soviet theory regarding "national interests" and "international interests" is quite opposite. A Soviet party history journal[38] claimed that "international interests" must be given priority over "national interests" and that the only dangers to the unity of the international communist movement in the postwar period have been nationalism and "the absolutization of one's own experience." The article attacked both "rightist" and "leftist" revisionism and in this context mentioned the case of the Yugoslav communist party.

AND AFTER TITO, WHAT?

The Soviets are aware that as long as Tito is in power there will be no change in the Yugoslav attitude toward these important issues. At the same time, however, Moscow has made attempts to improve relations with Tito without making concessions on its basic positions. This has been coupled with efforts to increase Soviet influence among the possible successors to the aging Yugoslav president, in the expectation that post-Tito Yugoslavia will have a different aspect.

Soviet hopes are based on the belief that there will be less opposition to rapprochement after Tito goes. Although some Yugoslavs would not object to "fraternal" Soviet help, the vast majority (including the younger generation) are still influenced by the break with the Soviet Union in 1948 and committed to the Yugoslav course that has evolved since that time. Any Soviet attempts to use pressure against Yugoslavia would probably unite all factions in the country. The Kremlin, however, has followed a more subtle policy, seeking to take advantage of internal dissension, particularly between Serbs and Croats. In many regards the question of external Soviet pressure is less of a threat than internal strife. As Presidium Secretary Stane Dolanc phrased it in a question he did not answer: "What will happen if no one attacks Yugoslavia?"[39] The future course of relations between Belgrade and Moscow will depend on the evolution of the internal situation. An internally strong Yugoslavia will certainly be able to resist Soviet pressure even without Tito. An internally disrupted Yugoslavia would have considerable difficulty in doing so.

NOTES

1. The latter statement is from Tito's short farewell to Brezhnev, as published in Borba (Belgrade), 18 November 1976.

2. Ibid.

3. See, for instance, Politika (Belgrade), 4 December 1976.

4. Borba, 10 December 1976.

5. Politika, 4 December 1976.

6. Ibid.

7. Borba, 18 November 1976.

8. Reuter, 26 January 1977; Olaf Ihlau in the Sueddeutsche Zeitung (Munich), 14 December 1976.

9. United Press International (UPI) in a dispatch from Belgrade, 11 December 1976.

10. Borba, 17 December 1976.

11. Socijalizam (Belgrade) no. 11, November 1976, pp. 1638-39.

12. Ibid., pp. 1724-25.

13. Ibid., p. 1732.

14. Borba, 16 January 1977.

15. Ibid.

16. Vus (Zagreb), 22 January 1977.

17. Nedeljne informativne novine (Belgradc), 23 January 1977.

18. Edvard Kardelj and Miroslav Krleza, Tito i Savez komunista Jugoslavije (Tito and the League of Communists of Yugoslavia) (Belgrade: Radnicka stampa, 1975), p. 66.

19. Istorija Saveza komunista Jugoslavije, kratak pregled (Belgrade: Rad, 1976), p. 203.

20. Vladimir Dedijer, Tito Speaks (London: Weidenfeld and Nicolson, 1953), p. 370.

21. Borba, 30 June 1948.

22. The Soviet-Yugoslav Dispute (London: Royal Institute of International Affairs, 1948), p. 27.

23. Stane Dolanc, in an interview with the Ljubljana daily Delo, 31 December 1976-2 January 1977.

24. Program of the Communist Party of the Soviet Union (Moscow: Foreign Languages Publishing House, 1961), p. 41; emphasis added.

25. Borba, 3 July 1976.

26. Pravda Ukrainy (Kiev), 4 October 1968.

27. Komunist (Belgrade), 26 March 1970. The party weekly was quoting the Polish Mala Encyklopedia Powszechna (Small General Encyclopedia).

28. Vjesnik (Zagreb), 23 February 1973.

29. Ibid., 3 April 1976.

30. 15 December 1975.

31. Review of International Affairs (Belgrade), 5 September 1975.

32. Borba, 28 December 1976.

33. Ibid., 17 February 1977.

34. As quoted in Socijalizam, no. 11, November 1976, p. 1725.

35. Ibid., p. 1736.

36. 13 February 1977.

37. Stanislav Stojanovic, writing in Komunist, 14 February 1977.

38. Voprosy Istorii KPSS, quoted in Borba, 17 February 1977. (In the first issue of the magazine Rabochii klass i sovremenny mir, however, Vadim Zagladin, first deputy head of the International Department of the CPSU Central Committee, said every communist party was entitled to define "internationalism" in its own way. Zagladin's article was summarized by TASS on 18 February 1977.)

39. Borba, 31 January 1973.

5

ALBANIAN FOREIGN POLICY IN THE WAKE OF THE SEVENTH PARTY CONGRESS

Louis Zanga

Albania enjoyed considerable limelight from the beginning of its rift with the Soviet Union, which became evident in 1959, to Khrushchev's open denunciation of the Hoxha leadership at the 22d CPSU congress in 1961. Thereafter, however, it settled into the obscure role of a Chinese client. The Albanian leadership's fear of intercourse with the West, the country's very low socioeconomic level, the (limited) assistance received from China, and the fact that the leadership did not need to concern itself about the opinion or aspirations of the population have been the major reasons why Albania has survived as a Balkan backwater of Stalinism for well over a decade. Its political institutions have undergone little change, the country is still ruled by an iron hand, and such development as its economy has recorded—and its basic extractive industries in particular have achieved a relative degree of sophistication—can be attributed to Chinese aid.

The truth is that Albania is noticed only when it plays a role in diplomatic combinations or permutations that may affect the international status quo. As an ally first of the Soviet Union and later of China, it has attracted world attention only when its adherence to one or the other appeared to be in question. Since the American attempts at rapprochement with China, which began in 1971, there has been speculation about the future of the Sino-Albanian alliance,

This chapter is a shortened and updated version of the following Radio Free Europe Research papers by Louis Zanga: "On the Forthcoming Albanian Party Congress," RAD Background Report/220, 28 October 1976; "The Congress of the Great Purge," RAD Background Report/230, 9 November 1976; and "Albania's Unique Foreign Policy," RAD Background Report/234, 15 November 1976.

however, and it is on this account that there has been a slight increase
in Western interest in Albania.

THE GREAT PURGE AND PARTY UNITY

In the last few years it has become obvious that uncertainties
over the future of Albania's position in the world have tended to cause
rifts in the country's leadership. The clearest reflection of the scope
of the problem is to be found in the changes that took place during
the five-year interval (1971-76) between the sixth and seventh congresses of the Albanian Party of Labor (PPSh). The purge began in
the cultural sector in 1973, spread to the army in 1974, and engulfed
the economic field in 1975. The sanctioning of these changes by the
seventh congress and the additional alterations resulting from the
elections with which it concluded its work, as well as the almost
entirely new look of the Central Committee, indicate continuing
turbulence within the leadership.

The congress ended its seven-day session on 7 November 1976
with the reelection of Enver Hoxha as party first secretary, a post
he has held since 8 November 1941, when the party was founded.
The Politburo remained unchanged. All 12 members were reelected,
including two relative newcomers who had been catapulted into sudden
prominence when they were elected to that body in the summer of
1975. The rest of the Politburo members are old-timers whose
careers go back to wartime days, and their "reliability" enabled
Hoxha to bring about the leadership changes that took place in 1976.

The real surprises of the elections in terms of membership
changes came below the Politburo level. Five persons were elected
to candidate Politburo membership, the same number as at the last
party congress. With the exception of that perennial candidate Pilo
Peristeri (Hoxha's earliest associate in the city of Korce in 1939),
the other four were either fairly recent arrivals or brand new: Two
had been promoted in 1975, and nothing is known about the other two
except that they belong to the new generation that has achieved sudden
prominence.

Most surprising, however, was the composition of the new Central
Committee. The old membership was almost completely decimated.
The new CC was composed of 77 members, an increase of 6, of whom
43 were newly elected—an unprecedentedly large turnover. Moreover,
excluding the 12 Politburo members in the CC and the wives of the
three top leaders (who have been CC members for some time), fewer
than 20 of the members elected at the 1971 congress were retained.
Former CC members with a military background appear to have fared
poorly, but so did others with economic or cultural expertise. Most

of the newcomers were practically unknown, and many rose from the
rank of candidate CC member to which they had been elevated at the
1971 congress. The 1976 congress elected 38 candidate CC members
(one less than in 1971), including seven who were demoted from full
membership. There were many new faces among the candidates—
18 out of 38. This body of young aspirants is worth watching, for it
appears to be the reservoir from which Hoxha draws the future leaders
of the country. (This was certainly the case during the period span-
ning the two party congresses.)

In his speech to the congress,[1] Hoxha's treatment of the purge
was disappointing; he dealt with it only in general terms, thus leaving
the outside world uncertain about what actually happened in the upper
ranks of the Albanian leadership during the past few years. The
allegations he made during a 13.5-hour speech were nonetheless of
an extremely grave nature and all-encompassing. He charged that
"the internal and external class enemy" had shown its hand in all
spheres of Albanian life—in culture and ideology, in the armed forces,
in industry, planning, and trade. In this context, he named the (purged)
leaders of these sectors.[2]

Hoxha's comments on the "military plotters," however, were
the most significant. The incidents involving the armed forces came
to light during 1974. They revolved around the personality of Minister
of Defense Beqir Balluku, a Politburo member, who disappeared from
public view during the summer and was officially replaced as minister
in October by Mehmet Shehu, who retained his post as prime minister.
At the same time, there was considerable reshuffling at the Ministry
of Defense and in the top echelons of the army. Apparently the intention in having Shehu, the regime's no. 2 "strong man," take over the
ministry (at least temporarily) was to restore order and obedience
to the official Hoxha line.

There was considerable speculation about the reasons behind
General Balluku's disappearance. Some Western observers believed
he had urged a shift in Albania's alliances back to closer, or at least
"normalized," relations with the Soviet Union—in fact, some considered him an Albanian Peng Teh-huai or even Lin Piao. There
was no direct evidence for this—merely strong circumstantial pre-
sumption. The possibilities of total Albanian isolation because of
changes in Chinese foreign policy and increasing instability in the
Balkans, the Eastern Mediterranean, and Middle East raised questions
that seriously affected the military establishment of which Balluku
was the head. If, as was quite possible, they were accompanied by
concern about China's ability to supply the Albanians with modern
armaments, it is not difficult to see why disaffection should have
centered in the armed forces. But whatever the reasons, the Albanian regime acknowledged its first serious disunity since the early

1960s. The disappearance of Balluku was accompanied by strong
attacks on the Soviet Union by Hoxha, Shehu, and others, along with
indirect hints of Soviet interference (though at the time Balluku himself was never criticized or even mentioned). The alliance with China
was vehemently reaffirmed and any fears that the Hoxha-Shehu leadership was wavering in its alliance commitments were dispelled.

In his speech to the seventh party congress, Hoxha leveled grave
charges against the "military plotters" but supplied few details of
their actual deeds:

> The treasonable group consisting of Beqir Balluku,
> Petrit Dume, and Hito Cako formed a faction at the
> head of the armed forces, a group that planned to over-
> throw the Albanian Central Committee by an armed
> coup in order to destroy the Albanian Workers' Party
> and the dictatorship of the proletariat. To bring this
> about they intended to rely on foreign military inter-
> vention.

He did not describe the activities of the purged men nor did he
say anything further about the planned "foreign military intervention"
but merely stated that the "unmasked antiparty group" had been thrown
upon the garbage dump where all traitors to the revolution properly
belonged. (These grave allegations, and in particular those made
against Balluku, Dume, and Cako, gave rise to a wide range of
speculation about their fates; it has been rumored that they were
summarily executed.) Nor was Hoxha any more specific about the
"external enemy." In the spring of 1976 he went so far as to charge
that those named above "had wanted to bind their country to the Soviet
revisionists." At the congress, however, he made no reference to
the Soviet Union in this context but merely mentioned "certain revisionist countries."

Hoxha's treatment of the antiparty group is reminiscent of the
trumped-up charges of the Stalin era, and the great purge was a clear
sign of intense strife within Albania and of a power struggle raging
within the leadership triggered by the approaching end of Hoxha's
remarkably long reign—a struggle influenced by strong demands for
more reasonable economic policies and a lessening of the country's
extreme isolationism—and the unrest is aggravated by strains in the
once untroubled Sino-Albanian alliance.

UNCERTAINTIES SURROUNDING THE
CHINESE CONNECTION

The seventh congress provided further evidence of stress in
Sino-Albanian relations. Following the precedent set at the sixth

congress in 1971, the Chinese did not attend the gathering, and nothing was said on this sensitive question by either side. The CCP did send a warm message to the assembly signed by Hua Kuo-feng, which stated that socialist Albania was "the citadel of revolution towering over Europe," and praised Sino-Albanian friendship. The message did not mention the two superpowers by name in its criticism of "imperialism, social imperialism, and modern revisionism"—a fact that can hardly have been pleasing to Hoxha.

The China connection was a muted issue at the seventh congress—in contrast to the treatment accorded it at the sixth. Hoxha devoted a mere seven minutes or so of his marathon speech to relations with that People's Republic, touching only upon the highlights of the friendship between the two countries. He mentioned the "smashing of the counterrevolutionary plots of Liu Shao-chi, Lin Piao, and Teng Hsiao-ping," but had nothing to say about the downfall of the leftist antiparty group. He said, indeed, the irreducible minimum about China, and completely ignored important matters like Chinese credits for Albania's 1976-80 plan period or the two countries' common political and ideological policies in the international arena.

More light was thrown on the state of relations between China and Albania by Prime Minister Shehu in his speech to the congress.[3] He did at least mention the economic aid the PRC is providing in the current plan period, though he did not do so at any length. In the past it was always Hoxha who went into detail about Chinese aid, using both past and future tenses, but in his speech to the 1976 congress he limited himself to thanking Peking for its help and made no specific mention of future support. Shehu, for his part, had the following to say:

> In defining the tasks of the sixth five-year plan we have taken into consideration the internationalist aid extended by the People's Republic of China [and] the credits it has accorded the People's Republic of Albania in accordance with the official agreements signed between the governments of the two countries. We are grateful to the People's Republic of China which, thanks to the solicitude and recommendations of Mao Tse-tung, has given and is giving internationalist aid to our country to help in its socialist construction and the strengthening of its defensive capability.

The striking point about this statement is its extremely formal wording, which was in strong contrast to past Albanian statements of this kind. The credit agreement referred to was signed in Peking in the summer of 1975, but no details were released by either side, nor did Shehu provide them in his report to the congress, although in the past both he and Hoxha used to dwell at length on the projects to be built with Chinese aid. It is the omission since 1975 of any reference to industrial projects to be built during 1976-80 that gives rise to speculation as to whether Chinese aid will be forthcoming. Shehu chose to lay unprecedented stress on the formal nature of the accords by pointing out that they were "official agreements signed between the two governments," as though he wished to remind Peking that such documents are binding. Even more significant was the fact that in thanking China for its aid he went out of his way to mention the solicitude shown by Mao Tse-tung.

Hoxha also went out of his way to praise the late Chairman Mao, but said nothing complimentary about the new CCP chairman. One is reminded of the early stages of the Soviet-Albanian split, when anything favorable to the Soviet Union said in Albania was always carefully related to the name of Stalin. In view of Sino-Albanian divergencies and the possibility of further deterioration in relations between the two countries, the contrast in the treatment accorded Mao and that given to the new Chinese leadership at the congress may be a veiled warning to Peking to avoid the errors made by the Soviets when the Albanians began to disagree with Khrushchev.

Thus the PPSh congress further confirmed the existence of Albanian-Chinese divergencies, which, as noted above, began to appear in 1971. China and Albania were mainly of use to each other while both enjoyed self-inflicted isolation from the two most powerful international alliances of the day. China's usefulness to Albania was obvious; Albania's potential usefulness to China was as a foothold in Eastern Europe that could be used in countering Soviet domination. Although Albania did not prove to be the bridgehead the Chinese seem originally to have hoped for, it still retained symbolic value as long as the Chinese were determined to operate outside the established perimeters of world diplomacy. Once they began to cultivate normal relations with the American and other Western governments, however, it was natural that the durability of the once special relationship between Peking and Tirana should be questioned.

Most of the questions must have come from the Albanian rather than the Chinese side. Though much less important than before, Albania still had symbolic, propaganda, prestige, and psychological importance for the Chinese. Its return to Soviet domination would represent a considerable defeat for China. The cost of patronage was by no means inconsiderable, but in Peking political considerations apparently carried more weight than cost-accounting, at least as far as Albania was concerned.

The question the Albanians were asking must have centered precisely on whether this patronage would continue. Albania's misfortune is that it is, by definition, a client state. Its brief 20th-century history as a separate nation has seen it under the tutelage first of Austria, then of Yugoslavia, Italy, Germany, Yugoslavia again, the Soviet Union, and China. If set adrift by China, it would sooner or later have to seek economic and diplomatic support elsewhere. The Albanian leadership obviously disapproved of China's diplomatic maneuvering with the United States. It did not openly say so, but in 1972 the Sino-Albanian relationship began to cool; attacks on the United States in the Albanian media continued unabated, and U.S. overtures were ignored.

Nevertheless the Sino-Albanian alliance remained intact. In fact, the small, closely knit group at the head of the Albanian regime had little option but to continue to adhere to its relatively long-standing policies. The danger lay in the increasing pressure for change from the echelon below, and that accounted for the great purge of the leadership in recent years. But the uncertainties inherent in continued reliance on Peking caused some movement in other areas of Albanian foreign policy, particularly in regard to relations with neighboring Yugoslavia and Greece, its two traditional enemies. At the same time, however, there was no evidence that the possibility of improving relations with the Soviet Union was being considered, despite overtures from Moscow. The seventh party congress highlighted all this.

RELATIONS WITH THE SOVIET UNION

In his report to the congress, Hoxha said bluntly that Albania refused to maintain relations with the "Moscow social-imperialists" and that its attitude toward "the revisionist Soviet Union, the enemy of Albania, of socialism, and of the freedom and independence of all peoples, remains unchanged." If Hoxha provided the ideological directives, his second in command, Mehmet Shehu, was ready to put them into practice, as he did in a speech marking the 35th anniversary of the founding of the PPSh.[4] He rejected the overtures made by Brezhnev during the October 1976 CPSU CC plenum[5] in the following terms:

> The present tsar in the Kremlin, the archrevisionist Brezhnev, with the shamelessness that characterizes all revisionists, declared a few days ago that "there is no objective factor" now hindering the restoration of relations between the Soviet Union and Albania. These renegades believe that our party can be turned whichever way the wind blows. Once again, they are gravely mistaken. There is not and never will be a wind or storm that will change the course of our ship,

which is always correctly steered by the unerring compass
of Marxism-Leninism.

There is a significant difference between this overture by Brezhnev and earlier Soviet advances. At the 25th CPSU congress in February 1976, in a departure from past practice, no reference was made
to Albania, but in his report to the October plenum mentioned above
Brezhnev extended a tentative hand of friendship. The change in the
Soviet attitude can be explained by the momentous developments that
took place in China during the period between the Soviet congress and
the October plenum—the death of Mao Tse-tung, his replacement by
Hua Kuo-feng, and the downfall of the leftist faction. These events
and their repercussions in Albania may well have led Moscow to probe
the firmness of the Sino-Albanian relationship, which was already
known to be less strong than it had been in the past.

The flowery, Chinese-style wording of Shehu's rejection was a
clear indication of Albania's awareness of Brezhnev's effort to drive
a wedge between Tirana and Peking. At the same time, Shehu seemed
to be addressing himself to the Chinese, to be saying in effect: "You
may compromise, but we shall never betray our principles."

Hoxha charged that the East European countries oriented toward
Moscow were taking orders from the Soviets and that they followed a
policy hostile to Albania. There would be no change in Albania's
relations with these countries, he said, "as long as they follow this
road." His comments on Bulgaria were particularly harsh, although
he was generally quite diplomatic in speaking about Albania's other
Balkan neighbors. It was undoubtedly Bulgaria's especially close
relationship with the Soviet Union and the fact that it is the closest
to Albania of the loyal Warsaw Pact states that prompted Hoxha's
diatribe.

Albania "has not the slightest trust in Bulgaria's present leadership," he said, since Bulgaria had shown itself hostile to Albania and
had become "an instrument in the hands of Soviet social imperialism."
He also claimed Bulgaria had become a country that staged "plots"
and "blackmailed" some of its neighbors—Yugoslavia, Turkey, Greece,
and Albania. Finally, he alleged that, with the support of the Soviet
Union, Bulgaria "is ready at an opportune moment to seize the
Dardanelles and thus revive the Treaty of San Stefano." For this
reason Albania wanted to see an improvement of relations between
Greece and Turkey. The objective of the Albanian leader's attack
was no doubt to focus attention upon Moscow's dark intentions in the
Balkans, and one of his tactics was to point to the direct link between
the Soviet Union and Bulgaria, Moscow's only reliable ally in the
region.

RELATIONS WITH OTHER BALKAN STATES

For the rest of Albania's Balkan neighbors, however, the improvement in atmosphere that was becoming increasingly apparent was further confirmed by Hoxha's speech at the congress. This was particularly true with regard to Yugoslavia and Greece, but this must not be interpreted as indicating a more friendly attitude toward Western countries. As the party leader made clear, Albania's isolation from the West is apparently immutable.

Hoxha's treatment of the Yugoslav question made up a chapter in itself, but he broke no new ground at the congress. The only major change was one of stress. As he had done in the period following the Warsaw Pact countries' invasion of Czechoslovakia, he expressed readiness for good-neighborly relations with Belgrade and solidarity with a "militarily threatened" Yugoslavia, but from the ideological angle, and in some ways from the political one as well, he took a surprisingly hard-line approach. In fact, not since Tirana and Belgrade were set on converging courses by the invasion and the subsequent enunciation of the Brezhnev Doctrine had Hoxha shown such ideological intransigence toward Yugoslavia as he did at the seventh congress. Despite his remarks about good-neighborliness and his advocacy of an increase in trade and cultural exchanges, in matters of ideology he was uncompromising. In the section of his speech dealing with "the Marxist-Leninist movement and the struggle against modern revisionism," he devoted an entire chapter to blasting Yugoslavia's "revisionist" policies, including its attitude to the nonaligned world and its self-management system, ending by affirming that "the Albanian party will continue to expose the deceptive nature of the Yugoslav variety of revisionism and the danger it represents."

This return to public ideological polemics can be attributed partly to the hardening of the general political line in Albania and partly to Hoxha's obvious desire to assume the leadership of the "international Marxist-Leninist movement"–that is, the radical anti-Soviet splinter parties. Domestic considerations, however, also appear to have been involved, since it was around the middle of 1973, during the early stages of the internal political unrest that eventually led to the great purge, that Tirana first applied the brakes to the process of rapprochement with Belgrade.[6] The renewed campaign mounted by Hoxha against Yugoslav "revisionism" suggested that Albania feared further ideological infiltration from its northern neighbor.

Hoxha said this policy

does not mean that for the sake of these relations, or of good-neighborliness with bordering states, or of the policy of noninterference in internal affairs, the Albanian

state should be silent about its views on international
policy in general and on the ideological and political
attitudes of these countries.

At the same time, however, he declared that "these attitudes should
not hinder economic, cultural, and political relations in the fields
in which we have common interests."

The Albanian leader's remarks about bilateral relations were a
mixture of flattery and covert warning. Albania, he said, was convinced that Yugoslavia would never permit Soviet tanks to enter its
territory or allow the country to become "another Czechoslovakia"
and reiterated his promise that Albania would side with Yugoslavia
in the event of a Soviet attack. But, he added, the Yugoslavs must
respond with "just and correct actions" toward Albania. He regretted
that Belgrade had seen fit to admit Soviet naval units to its ports and
to provide them with facilities—an act he termed "detrimental to good-
neighborliness" between the two countries. (This may have been an
oblique indication that further improvement in Yugoslav-Albanian
relations depends on the denial of permanent Adriatic bases for the
Soviet fleet.)

Hoxha then came to the heart of the matter—namely, the situation
of the large Albanian ethnic minority in Yugoslavia. It was certainly
not "interference" for Albanians to concern themselves with the fate
of their brethren across the border; this was warranted by "fraternal
ties of blood and language, ties of tradition and national custom" with
the 1.5 million Albanians in Kosovo, Macedonia, and Montenegro.
He went on to say that "the ugly policies and deeds of the Rankovic
era must never be repeated," and that the "Albanian minority must
not be persecuted, left in poverty, or discriminated against on the
political, economic, or cultural levels."

Belgrade's reaction to Hoxha's remarks can be described as mild
and considerate, and the Yugoslavs reiterated their willingness to
normalize relations.[7] The response from Yugoslav-Albanian officials
in Kosovo was more interesting; they were more outspoken in their
criticism of Hoxha's attacks on Yugoslavia and came more readily
to its defense but also expressed interest in improved relations.[8]

Hoxha's comments on relations with Greece were exceptionally
warm. His amiability was marred only by an attack on the "monarcho-
fascists" and what he termed "the crazy self-styled northern Epirots"
for trying to create a tense atmosphere in relations between the two
countries by their "absurd claims"—a reference to complaints in some
Greek quarters about suppression of the rights of the Greek minority
in Albania, which numbers between 30,000 and 50,000. In dealing
with state-to-state relations the first secretary's message of friendship for and solidarity with "capitalist" Greece surpassed in warmth
his words to socialist Yugoslavia:

We wish to live in friendship with the fraternal Greek
people, and have made and will continue to make every
effort to ensure that the ties linking our two countries
become ever stronger. The present Greek government
has sought and continues to maintain a friendly stand
toward us. This is in the interest of our two countries
and to the detriment of our common enemies.

As for Albania's other neighbors, Hoxha said there were "no
obstacles" in relations with Turkey, and that Albania wanted to maintain good relations with Romania and even to expand them. His
message to the latter, however, was cool by any standards and may
have reflected uneasiness about Romania's role in the Warsaw Pact.[9]

THE UNCERTAIN FUTURE OF
A CLIENT STATE

The improvement in Albania's relations with its Balkan neighbors
represents in large part a hedge against the consequences of growing
differences with China. At present these differences are manageable;
no reorientation has taken place in Albanian foreign policy and the
Chinese connection remains the key to Tirana's external relations.
The most probable future development, however, will be a steady
erosion of that alliance. Much will depend on the stability of the
leaderships in both China and Albania. For their part, the Albanians
must be watching more closely than most the factionalism in the
Chinese leadership, strongly hoping that it will produce a reversion
to the anti-Western obduracy of the 1960s as well as maintaining an
implacable anti-Sovietism. The course of events in China, however,
appears to be taking a somewhat different direction.
    Until the Albanian leadership changes, there seems little prospect
of an end to the inward-looking, paranoid ferocity that has characterized it for over 30 years. But both Secretary Hoxha and Prime Minister Shehu are well over 60 and the state of their health is dubious.
Whatever its concern about the CCP's policy, the present leadership
will presumably cling to the Chinese connection as long as it can.
It could hardly return to Moscow, and it could never embrace
Yugoslavia—two previous patrons it has known. There have been
indications since 1973 of some readiness to expand relations with
Western Europe, especially Italy, France, and Austria. But it is
very difficult to see the Hoxha leadership countenancing the kind of
rapprochement with the West that would open up Albania to Western
influences and contacts.
    If a new leadership appears in Tirana as the link with Peking is
eroded, a new situation may emerge. The end of the Hoxha era could

well usher in a period of domestic instability, with clan and regional
politics reassuming their traditionally important roles. But it could
also lead to diplomatic alignments with as many factions as there
are actual or potential international patrons. A faction demanding
the reinvigorating of the Chinese alliance would almost certainly be
present; a group demanding a return to Moscow could emerge; the
Yugoslavs would almost certainly see to it that they too had their
champions; there might also be a group, impressed by the Yugoslav
and Romanian examples, urging closer political and economic ties
with the West as the best way of engineering at least some national
autonomy.

When Albania opted for China some 15 years ago, its action
was regarded as a diplomatic sensation fraught with the most explosive
implications. Now, if any new leadership in Albania chose to continue
that option, it would be regarded as a stabilizing factor of considerable
importance on the international scene. Any other choice would certainly have destabilizing tendencies. The least destabilizing, at least
internationally, would be the Western option, provided it were pursued
with restraint. (Internally, of course, this could prove very destabilizing.) The predominance of a Yugoslav faction in Tirana—which,
considering Albanian hatred and fear of the Serbs, is perhaps the
least likely outcome—would produce serious strain with the Soviet
Union. It might also produce instability in Yugoslavia itself, where
the Albanians in Kosovo might seek to use Tirana to win further concessions from Belgrade. Moreover, such a development could only
worsen Yugoslavia's relations with Italy. In the unlikely event of
the Yugoslav option ever coming up, therefore, the chances are that
it would not remain in the ascendant for long.

It is the Soviet option, of course, that would constitute the most
destabilizing factor, and the result would benefit the Soviet Union
without entailing the penalties that would be inflicted by either China
or the United States in the case of military occupation. Neither could
retaliate militarily or diplomatically if a new Albanian leadership
itself chose to reforge its links with Moscow. On the other hand, a
prolonged period of leadership instability in Tirana in which no faction
held the decisive advantage could also lead to a dangerous situation,
with opportunities for miscalculation and mischief all too numerous.
As a country whose potential international significance is in inverse
ratio to its size and intrinsic importance, Albania is well worth
watching. Most observers see possible future instability in the
Balkans as coming from Yugoslavia. They may be right, but they
should not neglect Albania's potential in this respect.

NOTES

1. Zeri i popullit (Tirana), 2 November 1976.

2. On these purges and their implications, see Louis Zanga, "Changes in Albanian Leadership Signify Struggle for Succession to Power," RAD Background Report/161, Radio Free Europe Research, 24 November 1975, and "Whither Albania?" RAD Background Report/112, Radio Free Europe Research, 18 May 1976.

3. Zeri i popullit, 5 November 1976.

4. Albanian Telegraph Agency (ATA), 9 November 1976.

5. Pravda (Moscow), 26 October 1976.

6. See Louis Zanga, "Irredentism in Kosovo as Tirana's Policy Toward Belgrade Hardens," RAD Background Report/166, Radio Free Europe Research, 2 December 1975.

7. Borba (Belgrade), 9 November 1976.

8. Rilindja (Pristina), 4, 22, and 28–30 November 1976.

9. See Chapter 3.

PART

II

**FOREIGN ECONOMIC
RELATIONS**

In Eastern Europe, perhaps more than elsewhere, economics is very much a question of politics. While this is particularly true of domestic economic issues, it is also the case with regard to foreign economic relations. The Soviet Union is anxious to foster closer ties with Eastern Europe and among the East European states as a means of strengthening the political cohesion of the Warsaw Pact and buttressing its own political and military influence. Thus economic relations with the United States and Western Europe also take on a distinctly political flavor, and the USSR is anxious to control and channel such relations.

For the countries of Eastern Europe, international economics is particularly important because the individual economies are not strong and the countries have only limited supplies of natural resources. Thus there is considerable economic advantage to be gained from trade and international cooperation. Other important advantages, particularly in terms of Western technology, can also result from greater East-West trade. Recognizing the benefits of such trade, the Soviet Union is anxious to foster it while at the same time controlling its political consequences.

Thus a major Soviet priority since 1960 has been to encourage greater economic similarity, more trade exchanges, joint economic operations, and closer integration of the economies of Eastern Europe and the Soviet Union. The principal instrument through which this effort has been channeled is the economic organization known as Comecon (the Council for Mutual Economic Assistance). Chapter 6 reviews the current status of this organization and assesses its success in achieving East European economic cohesion. While progress has been made in a number of areas, many important problems remain to be solved, including inter-Comecon price determination practices, monetary, financial, and banking issues, plan coordination, and joint planning.

In an effort to avoid competition for Western trade and maintain Eastern cohesion, the Soviet Union has also sought to channel relations with the members of the European Economic Community through Comecon. Since the EEC institutions play a growing role in the external economic relations of the community and individual states a smaller one, the Soviet Union has argued that Comecon institutions are the appropriate counterpart to the EEC. While a unified Comecon approach is more likely to secure better terms for all from the Com-

mon Market than can the individual states acting alone, there is also
a possibility that specific East European needs would be overlooked
in a general approach. Chapter 7 deals with this question. Comecon's
proposed framework for relations with the EEC highlights differences
in organizational and trading practice between those two economic
groupings that make the establishment of institutional ties difficult.

Another important question that has come to the fore since 1973
is the indebtedness of the Soviet Union and Eastern Europe to Western
creditors. The aggregate sum of such loans was over $30 billion by
the end of 1975, and it increased considerably during 1976. Poland
and the USSR have been the largest borrowers. In evaluating this
debt burden, however, criteria different from those applied to the
foreign debts of market economies must be used, since several factors
specific to communist economies must be taken into consideration.
Should the West decide to impose credit restrictions in view of the
size of the debts that have accumulated, the Comecon countries have
a number of alternatives open to them.

A desire to expand economic relations with Western states, not
only by increasing trade exchanges but—more significantly—by various
forms of economic cooperation, has been evident in both the Soviet
Union and the East European states. Western countries have expressed
similar interest and, in fact, committed themselves to such a policy
at the Helsinki Conference on Security and Cooperation in Europe.
The extent to which such desires are realized, however, will be in
large part conditioned by the considerations raised in these chapters—
economic cooperation within Comecon, relations with the Common
Market, and Soviet and East European indebtedness to the West.

6

ECONOMIC INTEGRATION
AND PLAN COORDINATION
UNDER COMECON
Harry Trend

The reasons for and circumstances of the creation of the Council for Mutual Economic Assistance (Comecon) in January 1949 are unclear. Nor, for that matter, is there unanimity in Eastern Europe as to the exact date of its birth. The first ten years of its existence were uneventful, and the organization was "of marginal relevance to the economic development of member countries in the early 1950s."[1] In the last 15 or so years, however, Comecon has been transformed by its members into an instrument with which they hope to give considerable impetus to the process of economic cooperation and integration within this communist economic grouping.

With the expansion of Comecon's economic activities came a rapid growth in its organizational structure and a proliferation of its agencies.[2] The personnel directly involved in carrying out its functions also expanded and today must exceed 100,000.

MEMBERSHIP AND AFFILIATION

There are four degrees of attachment to Comecon open to individual countries: full membership, limited participation, observer status, and nonsocialist cooperating status.

There are now nine full members: Bulgaria, Cuba, Czechoslovakia, the GDR, Hungary, Mongolia, Poland, Romania, and the Soviet Union. Albania, which joined the group in February 1949, has taken no part

This chapter is a shortened version of Harry Trend, "Comecon at the Beginning of 1977," RAD Background Report/65, Radio Free Europe Research, 25 March 1977.

in its activities since 1961. Under the organization's charter, full members must favor "the development of socialist integration, the planned development of their national economies," accept the "aims and principles [of Comecon] and agree to accept the obligations contained" in the charter. Members may participate in specific Comecon programs or stand aloof, as they choose. This is permitted by the now famous "interested party" provision of the charter.

Yugoslavia is the only "limited participant," cooperating in the work of a majority of the organization's permanent commissions and with a number of other Comecon agencies.

North Korea and Vietnam have from time to time attended Comecon Council and other sessions as observers, and Angola sent an observer to the 30th council session held in July of 1976. China also accepted this status many years ago, but since the Sino-Soviet split has broken all links with the organization and is now (along with Albania) one of its severest critics.

Finland was the first nonsocialist country to become a "cooperant," which it did on 16 May 1973. Iraq and Mexico followed suit in 1976, and many other states expressed interest in doing the same: they included Egypt, the People's Democratic Republic of Yemen, Argentina, Peru, Allende's Chile, Colombia, Bangladesh, Angola, Jamaica, and Guyana. At the 79th Executive Committee session, Desmond Hoyte, Guyanese economic development minister, stated that his country had requested a formal association with Comecon,[3] probably on the Finnish pattern.

Nonsocialist countries with this type of relationship act through a Joint Committee on Cooperation in which their representatives and interested Comecon member states participate.

PINNACLE ORGANIZATIONS

The Comecon Council is the organization's supreme policy-making body and meets about once a year. The Executive Committee acts in its stead between council sessions, while the Secretariat carries on the day-to-day work of the organization.

1. The Comecon Council. This supreme deliberative body comprises permanent representatives selected by each member country, usually of deputy premier rank, and each state has one vote. Sessions dealing with major matters of principle are usually attended by party first secretaries.

The council can only adopt recommendations, which have then to be approved individually by each country and can only be implemented through bilateral and multilateral treaties or other types of agreement.

2. <u>The Executive Committee</u>. The main organization entrusted with making policy recommendations and overseeing their implementation between council sessions is the Executive Committee. The chairmanship of this body is rotated after each council session, and the person thus selected also acts as chairman of the council meeting.

3. <u>The Secretariat</u>. Day-to-day operations are entrusted to a Secretariat based in Moscow, headed by a citizen of the USSR.

The Secretariat has departments that in general correspond in number to the branch permanent commissions, and several other agencies that undertake much of the preparatory and staff work connected with policy recommendations and their implementation.

These subdivisions of the Secretariat are also responsible for much of the preparatory staff work necessary before the branch permanent commissions can begin to deal effectively with the numerous problems of common interest that fall within their purview.

LINE ORGANIZATIONS

Of the large assortment of special-purpose organizations that perform line functions within Comecon only the council committees and permanent commissions are mentioned specifically in the charter; the others are covered by the general provisions that authorize the council "to establish those organs that it considers necessary for the fulfillment of the council's functions" and permit the Executive Committee to "establish any auxiliary agencies it considers necessary to discharge its responsibilities."

Council Committees

Council committees were first established in 1971 but were not mentioned in the charter until the adoption of the 1974 revised version. The jurisdiction and prerogatives of the committees are wider than those normally given to the permanent commissions. They have the right to "influence" the work of council organizations and agencies in accordance with prescribed uniform principles and methods. More important, they are also empowered to "assign priorities" in whose light the work of the council and its agencies must be oriented.

Only three council committees have been created: (1) the Committee on Cooperation in Planning, (2) the Committee on Scientific-Technological Cooperation, and (3) the Committee on Cooperation in Material and Technical Supply.

The Committee on Cooperation in Planning is perhaps the most important and influential of the three—or, for that matter, of all line organizations. Since its members are chairmen of the economically very powerful central planning agencies of their respective countries, the committee's decisions carry considerable weight. Indeed, it comes close to being a supranational planning agency for handling specific economic problems, a target that has long been in the sights of the Soviet party leaders. In the field of plan coordination, before the five-year and long-term plans of the various member nations take their final shape, the work of this committee provides a new dimension to the plan synchronization process.

The vice-chairmen of the various central planning agencies form the permanent operating body of the Committee on Cooperation in Planning and carry out much of the work underlying the coordination of major goals set within the Comecon framework.

A list of the committee's main tasks provides ample indication of its vast scope: (1) the elaboration of forecasts for the most important areas of the national economies, and for science and technology; (2) the coordination of long-term plans for the main economic branches and major production and technical problems; (3) the coordination of national five-year economic plans; (4) joint planning for certain industrial branches and production by "interested parties"; and (5) the exchange of experience relevant to improving national economic planning and management.

Of particular interest to this committee are problems of the fuel-energy balance, for which a special permanent working group has been set up. It prepared much of the material included in the 1971 Comprehensive Program for Economic Cooperation and Integration—an ambitious program that outlined the 10- to 15-year major economic objectives of Comecon.

The Committee on Scientific-Technological Cooperation has proved Comecon's most active committee. Almost 50 coordinating centers have been established to handle the coordination and application of scientific-technological research by "interested parties" with Comecon.

Collaborating organizations in the participating countries divide up among themselves the various aspects of a particular scientific-technological problem.

The Committee on Cooperation in Material and Technical Supply, in whose activities Yugoslavia participates, deals with problems associated with supplies of materials needed by various production units and with those related to the management, packaging, and handling of resources and materials in short supply.

The Permanent Commissions

These are among the oldest Comecon agencies and are generally organized along branch lines. In recent times others have been added to handle questions that cross branch lines—for example, the Health Affairs and Environmental Protection Commissions. Older agencies of this type are the Statistics, Standardization, and Currency and Financial Problems Commissions.

Most of the commissions have established permanent working groups falling within their jurisdiction.

Other Major Comecon Organizations

The broad spectrum of organizations to which Comecon has given birth include (1) informal interstate conferences at which representatives of member countries discuss specific issues and problems, sharing their experiences, consulting, and coordinating their activities; (2) scientific institutes that provide a formal framework to cover specific areas of scientific-technological research and the application of research findings to practical problems; (3) specialized economic organizations of a multinational character, such as the international economic associations and interstate economic organizations; (4) intergovernmental ad hoc commissions dealing with special problems such as water conservation and flood control; (5) financial institutions such as the International Bank for Economic Cooperation and the International Investment Bank; and (6) a large number of conferences of nongovernmental organizations possessing loose ties with Comecon agencies.

Figure 6.1 shows the major Comecon agencies as of 1975.

ECONOMIC INTEGRATION IN THE 1970s
AND BEYOND

The methods and instruments used to further economic cooperation and integration within the grouping add their quota to the problems arising from the implementation of major objectives and from the substantive questions facing Comecon in the present decade and the years beyond. The intra-Comecon price system is certainly one of the most conspicuous trade instruments in this category.

Intra-Comecon Foreign Trade Price
Determination

When there were as many domestic price determination systems as countries, the East European states found it difficult to arrive at intra-Comecon foreign trade prices that were uniform for identical

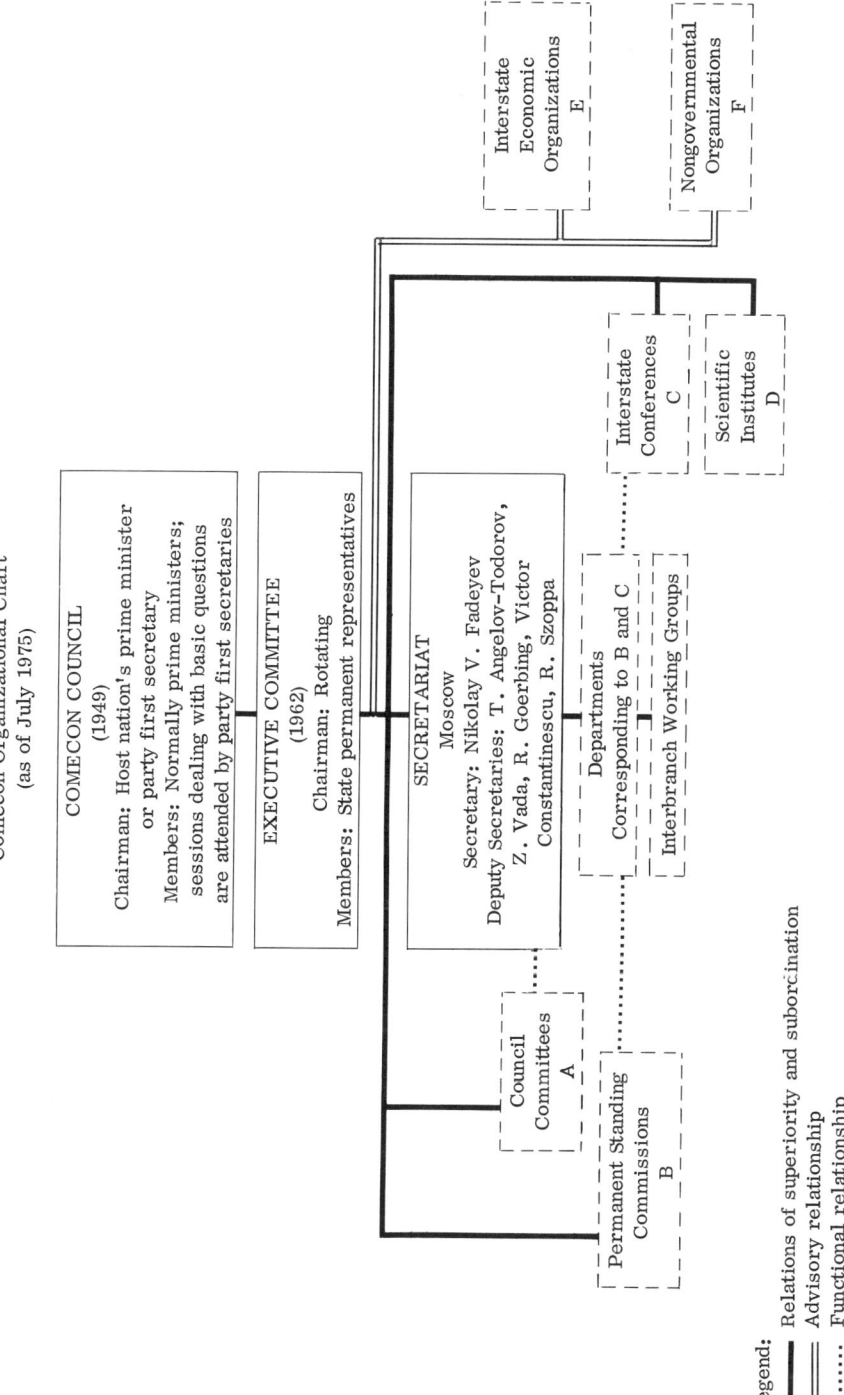

FIGURE 6.1

Comecon Organizational Chart
(as of July 1975)

COMECON COUNCIL
(1949)

Chairman: Host nation's prime minister
or party first secretary
Members: Normally prime ministers;
sessions dealing with basic questions
are attended by party first secretaries

EXECUTIVE COMMITTEE
(1962)

Chairman: Rotating

Members: State permanent representatives

SECRETARIAT

Moscow

Secretary: Nikolay V. Fadeyev
Deputy Secretaries: T. Angelov-Todorov,
Z. Vada, R. Goerbing, Victor
Constantinescu, R. Szoppa

Council
Committees
A

Permanent Standing
Commissions
B

Departments
Corresponding to B and C

Interbranch Working Groups

Interstate
Conferences
C

Scientific
Institutes
D

Interstate
Economic
Organizations
E

Nongovernmental
Organizations
F

Legend:

Relations of superiority and subordination
Advisory relationship
Functional relationship

101

products. Before Comecon was formed, they had begun to use world market prices in their trade with one another, but from 1949 onward they were able to agree basically on a uniform system of fixed-price determination for intra-Comecon trade. In 1950 these prices were tied to "historical" world market prices and set for a given time period—that is, they were fixed in terms of past prices of products traded in nonsocialist world markets.

Since 1945 the pricing systems employed by the East European countries and then by Comecon have passed through a number of stages—from a system based on a single year with a one-year lag, to one with historical fixed prices* based on a single year but valid for several years, to fixed prices based on an average of historical world prices over a five-year period, and (most recently) to a system using a movable average of historical world prices. The result has been that intra-Comecon prices have been changed annually—for a single year (1975) they were based on a three-year average, and in the current five-year plan period they are based on a moving (sliding) five-year average of historical world market prices. See Table 6.1.

For a few years after World War II, foreign trade transactions took place in dollars at prices quoted daily. Soon the trading parties shifted to a fixed price system for the more important commodities, based on world market prices for the preceding year.

During the 1949–50 period, Comecon switched to the use of the clearing ruble and used third-quarter 1950 prices. These prices were frozen for the period 1951–57, except for products whose prices fluctuated widely as a result of the Korean war; these were determined bilaterally.

The Comecon Council at its ninth session held in Bucharest in 1958 adopted what was to be known as the "Bucharest price formula." This formula, with some modifications, is still being used today.

The Bucharest Price Formula

The main features of the Bucharest price formula can be outlined as follows: (1) stability of prices, except in those situations where modifications were necessary to reflect established price trends on the world market; (2) listing of commodities that the parties agreed would be subject to the formula; (3) conditions defined under which prices could be adjusted; (4) bilateral negotiations of specific prices provided for, subject only to general requirements; and (5) inclusion

---

*In Eastern Europe the fixed prices applied to intra-Comecon dealings have also been called "contract" and "stop" prices.

TABLE 6.1

Price Determination Stages for
Intra-Comecon Trade

Stage	Period of Historical World Prices Chosen as a Basis	Period to Which Fixed Prices Applied
1	(Current) prices in the preceding year	1945–1950
2	1950, 3d quarter[a] (products with widely fluctuating prices—negotiated bilaterally)	1951–57[a]
3	1957[b] (Bucharest price formula)	1958–64[b] (Bulgaria, Hungary, and Mongolia: 1959–65)
4	Average of 1960–64 period	1965–70 (Bulgaria, Hungary, and Mongolia: 1966–70)
5	Average of 1965–69 period	1971–75[c]
6	Moving multiple year: (a) 1972–74 average	1975[c]
	(b) 5-year average changed annually	1976–80

[a]Marszalek gives a 1949–50 base period as applicable during 1951–57; Penkova agrees on the base period but says it is applicable during 1951–58.

[b]Penkova lists a 1958 price base period applicable during 1959–64.

[c]With the exception of the GDR and Mongolia in their trade with the USSR, the other members terminated this stage at the end of 1974 and adopted a three-year average system (1972–74 price level) for some commodities in 1975.

Sources: Jaromir Penkova, "Improvement of Price Formation During the Socialist Economic Integration of the Comecon Countries," Finance a Uver (Prague), October 1975; Herwig Haase, "The Foreign Trade Pricing System of Comecon," Osteuropa (Stuttgart), September 1975; Antoni Marszalek, "The World Price as a Category for Balancing Exchange Ratios on the International Market," Gospodarka Planowa (Warsaw), February 1976; Andrzej J. Klawe, "Prices in Comecon Countries' International Trade," Sprawy Miedzynarodowe (Warsaw), February 1976; and Istvan Garamvolgyi, "New Prices in Socialist Foreign Trade," Figyelo (Budapest), 5 March 1975.

of a "phantom" charge for hypothetical movement to the importer's border, equivalent to 50 percent of the freight cost had the commodity concerned been bought in a recognized world market center.

The Bucharest agreement did not specify the period during which the prices agreed upon would be applicable to intra-Comecon trade; nor did it ensure price uniformity for the same product to all training partners; nor did it guarantee the establishment of harmony—or even a close relationship—between intra-Comecon and current world prices. It did, however, permit either party to request price adjustments, provided the case could be supported with arguments based on economic evidence. This option was rarely exercised during a given five-year plan period, but it was used by the Soviet Union when the latter terminated the five-year fixed price system one year ahead of schedule during the 1971-75 plan period.[4]

At the 70th Comecon Executive Committee session in January 1975, the Soviet Union pressed for and obtained general agreement to this change, thus enabling it to take advantage of the rapid price increases on world commodity markets during 1973 and 1974 and to shift the terms of trade in its favor. Had the price determination system under which five-year average prices were fixed for five-year plan periods remained in use until then, prices for 1976-80 would have been based on average free market prices for 1970-75 and would have conferred much less benefit on Comecon's principal raw material supplier. In the event, the USSR obtained agreement on the use of a three-year average basis (1972-74) for 1975 prices, thereby allowing it to take advantage of two high-price years in world markets. Anticipating that continued increases in world prices of raw materials would bolster up the moving five-year average under which prices are changed annually during 1976-80, the Soviet Union thus reinforced its terms-of-trade advantage for the whole of that period.

Bilateral negotiation of specific prices has, however, led to differentiation ("discrimination") in prices charged for identical products between trade partners, a practice criticized on several occasions by the Romanians.[5] This lack of uniformity has had the effect of modifying exchange rates.

Intra-Comecon foreign trade prices are in no way related to domestic production costs or domestic prices. As a result, exports have frequently had to be subsidized, directly by the payment of subsidies or indirectly by modifying the exchange rates used for domestic accounting purposes, reducing taxes and other contributions to the state, and so on. More frequently, a combination of the two methods has been used.

Problems of Intra-Comecon Pricing Methods

In the past a rough equivalence between intra-Comecon and world price movements has depended on the maintenance of stability in the latter. Whenever the two sets of prices have deviated significantly, one of the partners in bilateral trade has taken advantage of the differential by shifting its commerce to world markets, thereby destabilizing trade flows within Comecon.

Fixed prices also tended to discourage the upgrading of commodities sold on intra-Comecon markets, thereby ensuring the continued output of obsolete products.

Pricing of components, subassemblies, and semifinished commodities proved to be troublesome. The lack of comparable world market prices in many cases, coupled with the absence of a uniform internal cost methodology, did not help trading parties in their search for a solution. Special contract prices were devised in each case on an ad hoc basis. Ironically enough, cooperative production arrangements of this type frequently entail the sale of some of the goods produced on world markets. So these special prices cannot ignore world prices entirely.

Similar price problems reared their heads in one form or another in all production cooperation and specialization schemes, which rapidly increased in volume. On 1 June 1972 the Permanent Commission on Foreign Trade issued guidelines based on the principles underlying the Bucharest price formula,[6] which brought with them many of the formula's familiar problems and some new ones. For example, dependence on world market prices as a basis meant that resultant prices were not linked with changing production conditions; nor did the system allow for large-quantity discounts. Yet the solution of price and monetary questions was a desideratum of fostering economic cooperation and integration.[7]

At a conference held in Bucharest in mid-1976, two Poles put forward the view that prices should cease to be a passive factor and should instead contribute to the directing of inputs and as a viable source of information for decision making. They also recognized the need to bring lower levels of management (that is, associations and combines) more directly into the latter process.[8]

Comecon's international economic organizations have been inhibited from expanding their activities by the lack of agreement concerning commodity-monetary relationships.[9] Questions that still remain unsolved include the following: (1) how should the foreign trade and domestic prices used be recalculated to take account of supplies bought on Western markets that are included in the production process? (2) how can one ensure the production of goods of a quality

comparable with that found on world markets and, if they differ, how
far are these differences to be taken into consideration when prices
are being determined? and (3) "by whom, when, and how are prices . . .
to be set, approved, adjusted, or changed?"[10]

Some Suggested Solutions

A large number of solutions were put forward to the problems
raised by pricing policy. They include the following: (1) the establishment of multiple prices for international economic organizations[11]
and the adoption of "regional prices" for Comecon, based on the
member countries' production, demand, and supply conditions;[12]
(2) the enforcement of binding principles for the selection of the main
world commodity markets, because the use of main exporter markets
must of necessity introduce into the calculations monopoly market
influences in world markets, which the Comecon price-setting process
"attempts" to screen (it has also been noted that more and more world
prices are being set by big importers and big exporters in long-term
agreements that make such prices "more authoritative");[13] (3) use
of differing base periods for various commodities;[14] (4) improved
price flexibility;[15] (5) multilateral determination of prices and price
analysis to replace bilateral negotiations;[16] (6) the establishment of
special intra-Comecon prices based on domestic wholesale prices in
the USSR;[17] and (7) the liberalization of trade, particularly for those
products that "are characterized by high competitiveness of foreign
markets."[18]

While the modifications made to the Bucharest price formula
have improved price flexibility, reduced the more erratic price swings
between five-year plan periods, and narrowed some of the major price
differences between intra-Comecon and world commodity market
prices, the changes made in the formula have not resolved the more
fundamental questions of the Comecon price formation process, and
this failure is an obstacle to the continued expansion of economic
cooperation and integration.

Currency and Finance Within Comecon

As long as the East European countries traded in terms of dollar
values on the basis of current world market prices, as they did
immediately after World War II, many objections now levied at the
economically irrational "commodity and currency relationships" did
not raise their heads. The switch to historical prices and a turning
away from dollar transactions to a settlement system based on a

clearing ruble brought in their train a number of problems that have
failed to yield to the partial solutions applied by Comecon members.

The clearing ruble was later replaced by the transferable ruble,
but here too the practice of "price discrimination" in Comecon markets led to variations in the measure of value of the settlement medium,
which changed from one commodity to another.

The Transferable Ruble

Since January 1964 Comecon has been operating on a clearing
system based on the transferable ruble (TR), which was introduced
in that year. It is used as an accounting unit to measure exchange
values arising from economic activities among members and to draw
up payment balances. It is not convertible into other currencies,
whether of member or nonmember states. Nor, generally speaking,
are trade deficits or surpluses among members; such adjustments
are usually made by commodity deliveries or, if the parties agree,
through the supply of services. As Hungarian Deputy Minister of
Finance Imre Vincze put it: "A member nation with assets (credit
balances) in the form of transferable rubles may not use these assets
at any time to buy the commodities it needs."[19]

Commodity exchanges covered by bilateral agreements between
Comecon members are planned for a five-year period and confirmed
in detail in annual trade protocols, so either imbalances are planned
and provision is made for their settlement in goods or services in
subsequent trade periods, or else "accidental" imbalances arise
because of nonfulfillment or overfulfillment of delivery pledges by
one of the parties in a particular year. The amounts involved are
very small compared with the over-all level of trade: For several
years, annual net balances for Comecon as a whole have been running
between 400 million and 800 million TRs.[20]

When the settlement of a trade surplus has not been provided
for in the appropriate bilateral agreements, the parties make provision for it in the subsequent annual trade protocol. The settlement
of a deficit of this kind usually takes the form of higher exports by
the debtor or lower imports by the creditor in the next trade period.
During the period between the appearance of a surplus deficit and its
correction, credits may be extended by the creditor partner or a
loan may be obtained from the Comecon International Bank for Economic Cooperation for a period of up to three years, at a rate of
interest varying according to the term of the credit.

It is possible for one of the partners to have a negative net trade
balance with another Comecon member and a trade surplus with a
third. The surplus, measured in TRs, cannot be used automatically

in settlement of the deficit; prior agreement by all three parties involved is necessary before this can be done. In the event, few such multilateral settlements occur, and one cannot legitimately describe the Comecon TR clearing system as multilateral: The epithet is justified only on the few occasions when tripartite agreement is achieved.

For commercial trade accounting purposes the value of the TR was at first determined by the declared content of 0.987412 of a gram of pure gold, and its value in terms of convertible (noncommunist) currencies was established on a basis of the ratios of relative gold content for each currency. When convertible currencies were permitted to float, the relative value of the TR was—and still is—adjusted accordingly on a monthly basis.

The commercial exchange rates in terms of the TR that have been established for convertible (noncommunist) currencies on the basis of world money markets and for nonconvertible (communist) currencies on the basis of agreements are employed in recalculating the costs incurred in various currencies associated with Comecon joint investment projects and in assessing, in a common currency, the value of the trade exchanges transacted by Comecon members throughout the world.

Comecon noncommercial transactions are accounted with the help of a different set of exchange rates from those associated with normal intra-Comecon trade. Noncommercial exchange rates are based on a so-called market basket of consumer goods. The standard is set in rubles and uses Soviet consumer prices; the same basket is then valued by each country in its national currency using its own domestic retail prices. These are converted into ruble values and then into TRs. The ratio of values (based on prices in the Soviet Union and in the particular country in question) determines the noncommercial exchange rate in TRs.

Initially, noncommercial rates were mainly applied to intra-Comecon travel, the cost of consular services, transport, expenditure incurred during conferences and exhibitions, settlement of social security payments, transfers of royalties earned by writers, and so on. More recently, the expansion of the flow of workers across national boundaries and the establishment of interstate enterprises, international economic associations, and organizations have been reflected in the growing proportion of transactions to which noncommercial exchange rates have been applied. Table 6.2 lists the commercial and noncommercial exchange rates of Comecon members' national currencies in terms of the TR.

In practice, the application of TR commercial and noncommercial exchange rates has produced some serious difficulties.[21] Several articles appearing in East European economic journals have proposed

TABLE 6.2

Commercial and Noncommercial Exchange Rates
of National Currencies of Comecon
Member Countries

Country	National Currency	National Currency Units per TR	
		Commercial	Noncommercial
Bulgaria	lev	1.30	0.88
Cuba	peso	1.11	1.11
Czechoslovakia	Kcs	8.00	10.00
GDR	mark	2.47	3.20
Hungary	forint	13.04	14.75
Poland	zloty	4.44	19.70
Romania	leu	6.67	8.30

Source: "Toward More Conversion in the Comecon Foreign
Exchange System," Svet Hospodarstvi (Prague) no. 153, 23 December
1976 (translated in RAD Background Report/4, Radio Free Europe
Research, 4 January 1977).

a number of partial solutions to this problem, but none of them has
been adopted by Comecon.

Comecon International Banks

Comecon has two international banks: the International Bank
for Economic Cooperation (IBEC) and the International Investment
Bank (IIB).[22] The function of the former, which started operations
in 1964, is to facilitate the creation of a multilateral settlements
system for payments arising as a result of intra-Comecon foreign
trade; the role of the latter, which dates from 1971, is to help finance
investments in which two or more member countries are interested.

The IBEC conducts clearing operations in TRs, provides short-
and medium-term credits, acts as a depositary for idle TRs, and
engages in money market activities involving gold and convertible
and other currencies. It was set up with an authorized capital of
300 million TRs, members' contributions being proportional to the
volume of their intra-Comecon export trade. It has borrowed dollars
on the Euromarket and offers revolving and medium-term credits to
its members at rates that are determined by the type of loan and its
term: The spread is between 2 and 6 percent, but charges for convertible currency are related to prevailing international rates. The

credits granted to members up to 1975 totaled over 29,000 million TRs, with Bulgaria the main recipient.[23] Loans are also available to nonmember countries, although the lack of convertibility of the TR hampers the IBEC's operations in the third world. The bank pays interest at between 1.5 and 4 percent on deposits, and the volume of these rose by 50 percent between 1972 and 1974 to a total of 1.5 billion TRs.[24]

The IBEC has links with over 300 banking institutions in many parts of the world, and its operations on international money markets are likely to expand greatly in the next decade.

All nine Comecon countries are members of the IBEC's sister organization, the International Investment Bank, and each, regardless of its contribution to capitalization, has one vote in the conduct of the bank's affairs. IIB Council sessions are normally attended by a sprinkling of nonsocialist banks with observer status, and the organization has contacts with 191 banks throughout the world.

It was established with a capitalization of 1 billion TRs, and quota contributions are related to foreign trade turnover. Like the IBEC, it borrows on the Eurodollar market, and its members often use such funds to buy equipment in the West for Comecon joint investment projects.

As already noted, the IIB's main raison d'être is to help finance Comecon joint investment projects, which are monitored by the bank from inception until repayment is complete. TR credits run for up to 15 years and carry interest rates of 3 to 5 percent per annum; Mongolia, exceptionally, pays only 1.5 percent. As is the case of the IBEC, loans made in convertible currency vary with world market rates. The fuel and power industry is by far the greatest beneficiary of IIB credits, and most of the money goes on joint investment projects in the Soviet Union.[25]

The bank has set up a loan fund intended to help the economies of the developing countries, but no grants from it have been publicly announced to date.

The IBEC and the IIB are now firmly established on the Comecon and international banking scene, and there have been reports that a third institution of the same kind might be created at a later date. The Polish monthly Sprawy Miedzynarodowe[26] suggested the creation of a special fund within the IIB for financing scientific-technological ventures "and later perhaps even a special Comecon Bank."

PLAN COORDINATION AND JOINT PLANNING

We now turn from an examination of Comecon's prices policy and finance to consider the organization's function in plan coordination and joint planning.

Improved methods of international plan coordination have enabled Comecon members to make progress in their attempt to reconcile with each other their national production and development plans, notably in the main economic branches and for selective commodity groups, together with transportation. By more efficient coordination of national plans, it was hoped to achieve a more rational distribution of resources within the economic region as a whole and a more efficient utilization of available resources in production.

The international coordination of planning has never encompassed all plan indicators. The process even at its widest has been confined to those aspects of production, investments, and exchange that are directly related to international economic cooperation within Comecon. It has not normally covered joint planning of production and distribution, and each member has drafted its own national economic plans independently. It has only been through the conclusion of bilateral- and more recently, a few multilateral—trade and other agreements that an international reconciliation of plans has been effected.

Plan Coordination Stages

The period since the establishment of Comecon in 1949 can be subdivided into four stages of plan coordination eras:[27] (1) era of the foreign trade model (1949-54); (2) era of balancing physical units model (1955-61); (3) era of joint planning conflict and economic reform (1962-75); and (4) era of strategic integration and selected joint planning (1976 onward).

The Foreign Trade Model

Between 1949 and 1954, the Comecon member countries reconciled the foreign trade plans included in their medium-term (five- or seven-year) national economic plans. This reconciliation was followed by the conclusion of medium-term foreign trade agreements on a bilateral basis. Such coordination did not, however, lead to a balanced development of the raw material bases of industry and manufacturing, and raw material shortages within Comecon remained a chronic problem. Nor, for that matter, did it put an end to wasteful duplication of productive facilities. A slowing down of economic growth began to appear before the end of this period, and the extension of the "socialist international division of labor" was impeded.

The Balancing-of-Physical-Units Model

After 1955, Comecon's member states began to switch from foreign trade plan coordination to the coordination of targets in production plans. Comecon established permanent standing commissions for selected branches in which this was to be attempted; several rounds of negotiations were usually needed to bring about, for the first time, a degree of international specialization of production within the organization.

Each branch committee assembled information on the production of specific commodities within its sphere of competence, aggregated production and projected consumption data and foreign trade projections, and arrived at net balances for each commodity, thus identifying potential shortages or surpluses. The collected data were presented in terms of physical units rather than values; intra-Comecon price and currency anomalies made it impracticable to attempt the coordination of national plans on a basis of economic values.

Whenever overall shortages appeared likely, the committee tried to encourage an expansion of production in the spheres affected. The work done by the various branch committees was not coordinated, however, and they were unaware of overall problems related to the question of trade and payments balances—or of the availability of investment resources within Comecon that could be directed toward an expansion of production capacities.

By the end of the period, discussions of these problems began to turn to the question of the need for the establishment of an international central planning agency within Comecon. The increasing difficulties of carrying out international coordination of plans on the basis of physical units in turn focused the attention of some critics on the need to expand the use of commodity-money relationships.

The Comprehensive-Joint-Planning Model and the Period of Economic Reform

It was during the early years of the 1962-75 period (the third stage) that the conflict over the substitution of international joint planning for plan coordination reached its climax.

In 1962 a number of Comecon countries, led by the Soviet Union, suggested that international joint planning could solve Comecon's economic integration problems. Although details of the proposal were not fully developed by its proponents, the latter favored the concentration and redistribution of economic resources under national control for the benefit of those economic branches where they were most needed and where economic conditions were thought to exist for the most effective utilization of the resources to be transferred from national control. A centrally controlled joint planning agency should be given authority to issue orders and to determine the types, level, and sectors to receive centrally directed investment resources.

A group of members, of which Romania was the most visible and vocal, declined this Khrushchev-inspired gambit.

Summarizing the reasons for the Soviets' failure to achieve their goal, a Hungarian economic specialist wrote:[28]

> The joint-planning concept proved unrealistic, not only because it was cumbersome technically and methodologically, but also in terms of its economic and political thinking. It forgot that the perfection of multilateral coordination—from the developed information systems through the designation of a feasible methodology to the multilateral solution of the planning problem—did not depend simply on improving methods but was primarily a question of self-interest. The joint-planning concept disregarded actual production conditions in the socialist countries and the objective necessity of maintaining their economic independence. . . . The joint-planning concept was based on false theoretical considerations and was a direct result of attempts to perfect international coordination of planning by relegating market and value and price relations to the background.

The physical—unit—balance method was retained, but with some modifications. Comecon-wide balances, listing 233 industrial and agricultural commodities, were prepared for the 1966–70 plans, and a series of sessions was organized to enable members to inform each other about major investment projects. Tertiary economic areas, such as transportation and the interconnection of power systems, were also included. A few selected economic subsections were earmarked for the introduction of specialization programs and the expansion of production.

In their search for greater economic rationalization within their economies during this period, a number of East European countries initiated programs for reforming their economic management systems; these emphasized the introduction of indirect methods of influencing economic activities, including greater reliance on the market and increased decentralization of the decision-making process. Toward the end of the period, some disillusionment became evident in the East European countries about the efficacy of such reforms in solving the various problems facing their national economies.

At the very beginning of the 1971–75 plan period, the Comprehensive Program for Economic Cooperation and Integration was accepted, and this determined much of what went into Comecon's 15- to 20-year long-term program. The adoption of the Comprehensive Program obviously implied a need for change, but the old (if partially modified) system of international plan coordination, which relied largely on the reconciliation of national plans on the basis of commodity physical units, continued to be used.

Developments Leading up to the Fourth Stage

The preparatory ground work for the current stage (1976 and beyond) of international plan coordination within Comecon began in effect with the 1971 Comprehensive Program. In an attempt to help coordinate and supervise the planning work entailed by this program Comecon authorized in 1971 the creation of a Committee on Cooperation in Planning with its headquarters in Moscow.

The 26th Comecon Council session in Moscow (10-12 July 1972) instructed the planning committee to produce a detailed work program for coordinating the plans for 1976-80 and for longer periods, and to draw up a list of problems whose solutions were to be coordinated by the members.[29] The 27th session, held in Prague in June 1973, decided to use the Coordinated Five-Year Plan of Multilateral Integration Measures (COPMIM; or SOPMIM in Russian—Soglasovanye piatiletnii plan mnogostronnikh integratsionnyhk meropriatii) as a basis for implementing the 1971 Comprehensive Program. Party leaders from member countries met in the Crimea during July 1973 and agreed to include a special section in their national plans for 1976-80 that would outline economic integration measures leading to closer coordination of national systems of economic planning and management in line with the methods given in COPMIM.

In their 1974 plans, the Soviet Union[30] and the GDR[31] included special economic integration sections for the first time. All Comecon countries did so in their 1976-80 plans—the first time integration was reflected in them.

Integration in the Five-Year Plans

These special sections consist of two parts:[32] (1) a breakdown of resources allocated for the construction of joint projects that create new industrial capacities or expand existing facilities, and of reciprocal deliveries of commodities produced by these increased capacities; and (2) a breakdown of resources directed to specialization and production integration programs and reciprocal deliveries.

The joint investment subsections* provide data in terms of physical volume and value for (a) exports and imports of investment com-

---

*The breakdown given for specialization and joint production lists reciprocal deliveries of investment goods for which joint production

modities; (b) labor resources invested in the joint project; and (c) reciprocal barter deliveries flowing from the productive facilities made possible by the scheme in question. Each of these three is broken down further by (a) totals, (b) industrial branches, (c) nation-agreement-commodity, and (d) the countries involved—again expressed in both value and volume. These figures are subsequently still further subdivided according to individual years within the national five-year plans.

Preparations are scheduled to begin in 1977 for the draft coordination plan covering integration during the period 1981-85, and the Comecon planning committee and the national planning agencies have already started work on long-term target programs for the period up to 1990 and beyond.[33]

Agencies Involved in International
Plan Coordination

In addition to the Comecon planning committee, the following agencies are involved in the work of plan coordination: two other Comecon committees (scientific-technological cooperation, and material-technical supply); the branch and interbranch commissions; the Secretariat's departments and interbranch working groups; the two Comecon banks; and the organization's international economic enterprises and associations. Joint intergovernmental committees and the national agencies of the various interested parties also participate in the work at several levels.[34]

Member countries coordinate their national economic plans on two levels simultaneously:[35] On the sectoral level, consultations are held by ministries and departments, with the participation of national central planning agencies, on specialization and production cooperation, including research; on the national level, member country planning agencies, sectoral ministries, and foreign trade agencies arrive at joint decisions on areas of cooperation and their boundaries, including the balancing of trade and payments. Decisions made on the national level are spelled out in a protocol signed by the countries involved.

In 1975, before the effects of using COPMIM had been fully evaluated and the results incorporated in the current five-year plans

---

and specialization programs are not formalized by agreements, and mutual deliveries of commodities produced on the basis of these specialization and joint production programs. A further breakdown given is similar to that for joint investment projects in terms of value units.

of the member countries, USSR State Planning Committee Chairman
Nikolai Baibakov was talking about the need to improve the structure
and organization of Comecon agencies participating in the work:[36]

> First we have to increase the part played by the com-
> mittee in coordinating the work of Comecon's branch
> and operational units. Secondly, we must create more
> flexible organizational forms to implement the compre-
> hensive interbranch programs by setting up various
> coordinating councils. And it is unavoidable that the
> committee's activity must become permanently opera-
> tive in character.

At the 30th session of the Comecon Council held in July 1976,
the Executive Committee was instructed "to prepare concrete proposals" for improving its effectiveness and "the style and methods
of the Comecon organs' work."[37] Its recommendations were to be
presented to the 31st session in 1977. In his speech at the 30th
session, Romanian Premier Manea Manescu expressed a measure
of uneasiness about what was in store as a result of all this reorganization and expansion of responsibilities.[38]

Joint Planning: An Aspect of Plan Coordination

As noted above, during the 1962 intra-Comecon conflict international joint planning was suggested by Khrushchev as an alternative
to international plan coordination. Following pressure from other
members, the Soviet Union withdrew its proposal, and since then
joint planning has been very restricted in scope; for the most part
it is now limited to a few branches and types of production. Within
these very narrow sectors joint planning in its widest form has been
visualized as encompassing "scientific research, project and design
work, investment construction, development of international specialization and cooperation in production within branches . . . the realization of production,"[39] and marketing—that is, the whole spectrum of
a commodity's life from its inception to its sale.

As long ago as 1972 agreements were signed covering the multilateral joint planning of a container transportation system.[40] Other
areas in which joint planning experiments are under way include the
production of (1) certain classes of machine tools, particularly numer-
ical control types; (2) electronic computers; and (3) multipurpose
metal sheets, tubes, and so on.[41]

A number of Comecon-sponsored international economic enterprises and associations that employ joint planning in some aspects

FIGURE 6.2

Schematic Representation of Flow of Substantive Matters
Relating to Multilateral Integration Measures Plan (1976-80)

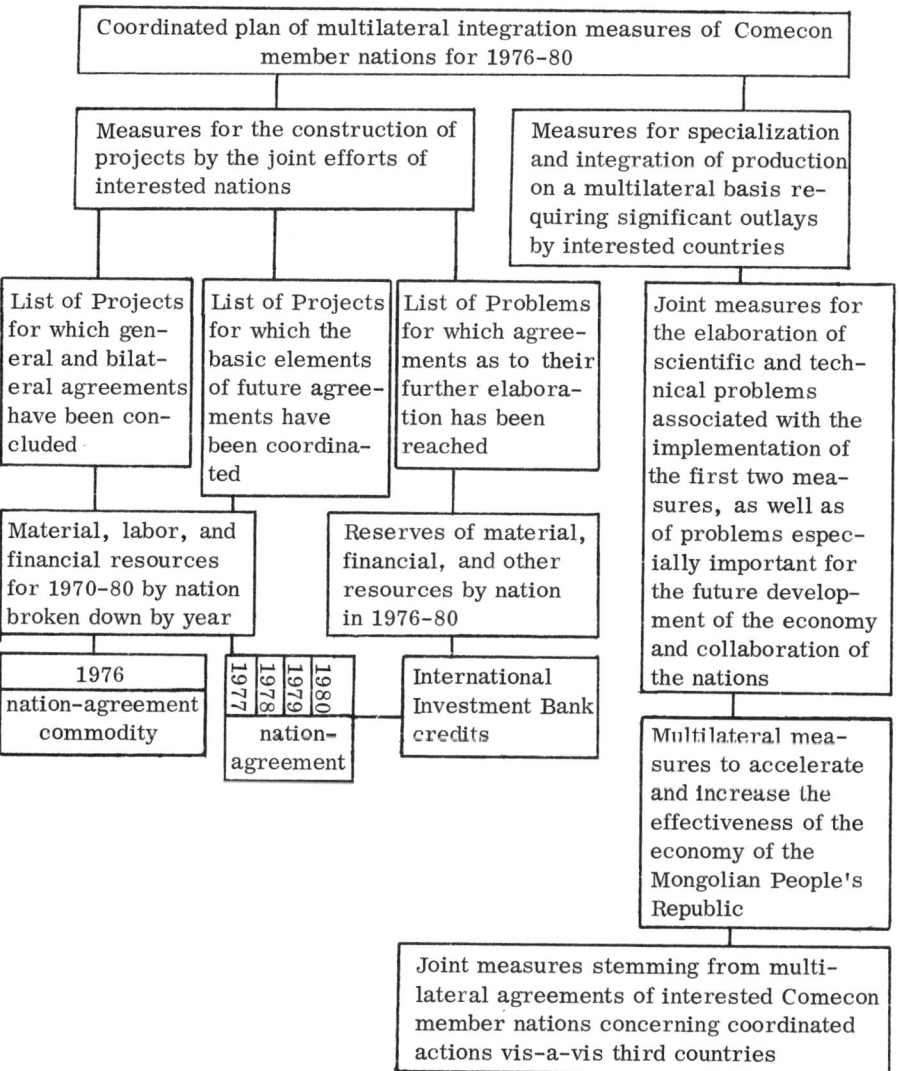

Source: This chart originally appeared in O. Ryabakov and N. Khmeleskii, "Certain Methodological Aspects in the Planning of Integrative Measures," Planovoye Khozyaistvo (Moscow) no. 1, 1974, as translated in Problems of Economics (White Plains, N.Y.) no. 5, September 1974.

of economic cooperation have been set up. In one case a bilaterally established association (Assophoto), created by the GDR and the USSR in 1975, is applying joint planning on an industrywide scale.[42] A few joint-production enterprises involving some use of joint planning such as Haldex (Hungary and Poland) and a cotton textile mill located in Poland (Poland and the GDR), have also come on stream.

It has been suggested that there are minimum periods during which joint planning should be allowed to operate and that the length of these periods should vary, depending on "specific problems and the branch of industry or type of production concerned."[43] The period needed to recover the capital outlay could serve as a guide in determining these minima in particular instances.

Joint planning has the potential to become "the core of joint management,"[44] but it is not without its own difficulties:

> The effective management of integration planning is a complicated process. Many problems remain unresolved. The effectiveness of joint planning within the framework of Comecon will depend mainly on how successful we are— in the projects and processes that are to be planned jointly— in achieving an ever closer harmony between national and international interests. This means that we shall have to meet heavy demands for the indoctrination of cadres with a sense of the inseparable unity between patriotism and internationalism, for rational solutions must be found within the process of joint planning that accord with the interests of all participants.[45]

Target Programs: Examples of Long-Term Plan Coordination

The concept of Comecon target programs was included in the Comprehensive Program, and the 29th Comecon Council session (held in Budapest from 24 to 26 June 1975) instructed the planning committee to assemble the necessary material for work on long-term target programs. As chairman of the planning committee Baibakov submitted a draft program to the 30th session, and the Executive Committee was directed to report on the "formulation of draft long-term, specific cooperation programs";[46] this report is due to be considered at the 31st session, to be held in June 1977 in Warsaw.

The five long-term integrational programs on which work is in train are as follows: energy and raw material supplies; the machine-building industry; agriculture and the food industry; industrial consumer goods; and transportation. The long-term integrative program of multilateral economic cooperation for each sector selected will encompass (1) development of economic and scientific-technological forecasts; (2) coordination of long- and medium-term plans for the main production branches and types; (3) joint planning of production for selected commodities and related branches, including research; and (4) exchanges of planning system experiences. The "interested-party" principle will apply here as in other forms of plan coordination.

The bulk of the preparatory work on the target programs is being done by the Comecon committees and permanent commissions that dealt with the economic branches concerned, the Secretariat, and several international economic organizations created under Comecon auspices. The planning committee is coordinating and supervising the task, and has established several study groups headed by deputy chairmen of national planning agencies. The committee has also organized units similar to general staffs with the participation of senior personnel from these agencies.[47]

It is hoped that this program of economic integration, if extended for a slightly longer period, will complete "the process of approximating and equalizing the levels of economic development of the Comecon states within 15-20 years."[48]

Some Old Issues and Unsolved Problems

The integrative measures approved by Comecon involve a number of changes, some of which were alluded to in the 1971 Comprehensive Program. For the most part, recommendations for such changes, both implied and openly expressed, have yet to be implemented.

On the macroeconomic, national level, the types of integrative measures appropriate to the fourth stage of international plan coordination require the development of more effective plan-conforming economic management, especially in the sphere of investments. The continued tendency to solve economic problems as they arise by directing a larger share of national resources to investment ensures the recurrence of an investment-type business cycle—the planned economies' equivalent of "boom-or-bust."

On the microeconomic level there is a continuing need to improve commodity-money relations and the functioning of markets as well as their involvement in economic processes—that is, a measure of decentralization.

Internationally the establishment of more direct connections between domestic and foreign markets is still required. As long as Comecon member states continue to insulate domestic markets from what is happening on the international scene, ad hoc "solutions," administratively imposed, will have to be applied more often, thereby

increasing the need for further administrative intervention. Expanding the interrelationships of domestic and foreign markets necessitates
an expansion of direct relations between member countries' economic
units, now only in their infancy.

An expansion of foreign trade and international economic cooperation requires the freeing of mutual exchanges of commodities—that is,
the abandonment of traditional practices such as barter-type trade.
This presupposes several other changes: the establishment of convertibility of national currencies and of the transferable ruble; a
synchronization of pricing methods that will help to eliminate the
most important differences in costing practices; the establishment
of realistic price ratios, especially for substitute and complementary
commodities; greater use of indirect economic instruments and a
movement away from dirigistic methods; and a fuller recognition that
supply and demand, commodity-money relations, and other economic
market relations are also a part of international trade.

An almost exclusive reliance on nonmarket economic institutions
and methods and the restriction of market categories are bound to
impede economic integration and cooperation. Dependence on administrative decision making in economic matters makes it difficult to
recognize and assess the advantages of the international division of
labor, encourages a continuation of the off-setting system of trade,
prevents the development of a satisfactory mode of compensation in
joint investments that can be applied generally, and reinforces the
bilateral method of settling payments balances—that is, bilateral
barter.

Plan coordination now covers a very wide range of products, in
a number of instances even more detailed than in the national plans.
This can only increase rigidity and thus stifle intra-Comecon trade.
Since 1960, the ratio of the growth rate of intra-Comecon trade to
that of national income has generally declined, and successive changes
in methods of international plan coordination have failed to reverse
this trend.

With an expansion of integrative measures and economic cooperation, the international coordination process has required a longer
lead time. This has meant that changes in economic factors cannot
always be taken into consideration, and what seemed initially to be
economically rational may prove unacceptable to one or more of the
parties and result in a breakdown in relations on which it seemed
there was agreement at an earlier stage. In a world where significant
technological change is becoming ever more rapid, a system is needed
that ensures rapid response to signals appearing on world and intra-
Comecon markets that necessitate economic policy shifts and new
ways of doing things. This situation—relatively new in Eastern Europe's experience—means that plans previously considered directive

must sometimes be recategorized as indicative. Some partners in economic cooperation and integration projects have resisted this logic and have instead called for a "freezing" of obligations even in the face of changes that obviously demand significant modification of original agreements.

One new problem in Comecon relations is becoming ever more critical: the increasing economic burden imposed by joint investments for the development of the USSR's raw materials sector. In 1975 joint investments within the USSR cost 500 million TRs, half of that amount being provided by the Soviet Union. During the 1976-80 plan period, the total is scheduled to reach between 9 billion and 10 billion TRs and entail heavy hard-currency expenditures by member countries, and the target programs imply even larger joint investments in subsequent medium-term plan periods. Economically less developed economies, and those that are implementing extensive modernization programs or are facing extensive restructuring of their economies, are discovering that the burden imposed by joint investments is restricting their domestic options.

Two old problems reappear whenever programs of economic cooperation, specialization, and integration are discussed. The less developed countries fear that the Comecon program will crystallize existing economic differences among members and confirm the advantage of the lead possessed by the more technically advanced members in new industrial sectors. They foresee themselves being relegated to economic sectors where technology does not change rapidly and where the economic harvest to be reaped from production is sparse.

The second problem that keeps reasserting itself is that of national sovereignty—that is, the possible loss of economic and political independence. Romania is not the only Comecon member country that is deeply sensitive to this insecurity, and concern usually finds expression in discussion of the primary importance of the national plan in international plan coordination and joint planning, insistence on the inclusion in Comecon documents of clauses recognizing the need to safeguard the independence and sovereignty of individual states and to prevent external interference in internal matters, and stress on the right to select the program in which a member state wishes to participate.

NOTES

1. Jozef M. van Brabant, "On the Origins and Tasks of the Council for Mutual Economic Assistance," Osteuropa Wirtschaft (Stuttgart), September 1974.

2. For a full account of Comecon's organization in late 1975, see Harry Trend, "Comecon's Organizational Structure," Part I, RAD Background Report/114, Radio Free Europe Research, 3 July 1975, and Part II, RAD BR/138, 7 October 1975.

3. Radio Havana International Service, 20 January 1977.

4. When reviewing the history of Comecon prices, a number of economic writers in East European countries ignore this premature abrogation (see, for example, Antoni Marszalek in "Prices in Trade Turnover Among Comecon Countries," Przeglad Techniczny–Innowacje, Warsaw, 6 July 1975).

5. See Harry Trend, "An Assessment of the Comecon Council 30th Session," RAD Background Report/183, Radio Free Europe Research, 23 August 1976.

6. Pawel Bozyk, "Economic Integration of Poland with Comecon Nations in the 1970s," Handel Zagraniczny (Warsaw), no. 11, November 1975, pp. 8–12.

7. Jerzy Marciszewski and Jerzy Rutkowski, in a report presented at the 16th Conference of Foreign Trade Research Institutes of the Comecon countries and Yugoslavia held in Bucharest on 14–18 October 1975, ibid., no. 7, July 1976.

8. Ibid.

9. Boris Atanasov, "Methodological Questions of the Setting and Application of Prices in International Socialist Enterprises," Ikonomicheska Missal (Sofia), no. 3, 1975, pp. 3–13.

10. For a Hungarian discussion of the problems common to the Comecon Interatomenergo and other international associations, see Harry Trend, "Comecon International Associations Unable to Function Effectively," RAD Background Report/81, Radio Free Europe Research, 6 April 1976.

11. Ibid.

12. Marszalek, op. cit.

13. Jerzy Basiuk and Jerzy Marciszewski, "Some Aspects of Shaping Contractual Prices in Trade Among Comecon Countries," Handel Zagraniczny, no. 9, September 1975.

14. Ibid.

15. Ibid., and Marszalek, op. cit.

16. Marciszewski and Rutkowski, op. cit.

17. Jaromir Penkova, "Improving Price Formation During the Socialist Economic Integration of the Comecon Countries," Finance A Uver (Prague), October 1975.

18. Marszalek, op. cit. (About 90 percent of socialist foreign trade turnover currently is nonliberalized and in the cases of Bulgaria, Romania, and the Soviet Union this share approaches 100 percent.)

19. "The Role of the Comecon Currency in the Methods and Instruments of Economic Cooperation," Penzugyi Szemle (Budapest), September 1976.

20. Ibid.

21. For a discussion of some of the difficulties encountered in the application of these exchange rates to intra-Comecon economic activities, see Harry Trend, "The Labyrinth of Intra-Comecon Exchange Rates," RAD Background Report/187, Radio Free Europe Research, 30 August 1976.

22. For a full treatment of this subject, the reader is referred to Harry Trend, "Comecon's International Banks," RAD Background Report/61, Radio Free Europe Research, 25 March 1977.

23. Milcho Stoimenov, "The International Banking Institutions of Comecon Member Countries: Practices, Problems, Prospects," Mezhdunarodni Otnoshenia (Sofia), no. 1, 1973.

24. Karl Hercher, "IBEC Fostered Reciprocal Trade," Die Wirtschaft (East Berlin), no. 28, July 1974; Ekonomicheskaya Gazeta (Moscow), no. 19, May 1976.

25. K. Hajek, "In the Common Interest," Hospodarski Noviny (Prague), 7 May 1976.

26. Polska Agencja Prasowa (PAP) in English, 27 September 1976.

27. Patterned, with some modifications, on the suggestive analysis presented by Tibor Kiss, deputy department chief at the Hungarian Institute of Planned Economy, in Kozgazdasagi Szemle (Budapest), no. 6, June 1975.

28. Kiss, op. cit.

29. O. Ryabakov and N. Khmelevskii, "Certain Methodological Aspects in the Planning of Integration Measures," Planovoye Khozyaistvo (Moscow), no. 1, 1974.

30. A. Shabalin, "The Comprehensive Integration Program," International Affairs (Moscow), April 1975.

31. Horst Tschanter, "Further Steps to Strengthen Socialist Economic Integration," Einheit (East Berlin), August 1975.

32. Ryabakov and Khmelevskii, op. cit.

33. Interview with N. K. Baibakov, Freundschaft (Tselinograd), 14 May 1976; also Rabotnichesko Delo (Sofia), 4 June 1976. A discussion of the target programs is included in a subsequent section of this article.

34. I. Ikonnikov, "Move Ahead More Quickly," Sotsialisticheskaya Industria (Moscow), 20 October 1975.

35. K. Kovaltsev, "Socialist Integration and Planning," International Affairs, August 1975.

36. Baibakov interview (see footnote 33).

37. Communique on the 30th Comecon Council session, Izvestia (Moscow), 10 July 1976.

38. Scinteia (Bucharest), 10 July 1976.

39. J. Tyll, "The Principle of Responsibility in Joint Planning," Rude Pravo (Prague), 17 November 1975 (translated in Czechoslovak

Press Survey no. 2551, Radio Free Europe Research, 28 November 1975).

40. TASS in English, 24 December 1976.

41. Tyll, op. cit.

42. Shabalin, op. cit.

43. V. Vasilev, "Joint Planning of Branches of Industry and Types of Production by Comecon Countries," Ekonomicheskie Nauki (Moscow), no. 12, 1974.

44. Gerhard Gruener, Einheit, January 1974.

45. Tschanter, op. cit.

46. Some details on specific target programs are included in Harry Trend, "Some Issues for the 30th Comecon Council Session," RAD Background Report 151, Radio Free Europe Research, 2 July 1976.

47. Baibakov interview (see footnote 33).

48. Romanian Premier Manescu's July 8 speech at the 30th Comecon Council session, Scinteia, 10 July 1976.

CHAPTER

7

COMECON-EEC
COOPERATION
NEGOTIATIONS
Harry Trend

In 1973, members of the Common Market transferred to the EEC Commission authority to negotiate commercial agreements with individual state-trading countries. Existing bilateral trade agreements expired at the end of 1974, and since then the commission has been extending them with some quota modifications. It is this change in trade negotiating practice within the Common Market that prompted the opening of negotiations between Comecon and the EEC on the nature of future economic relationships.

An EEC delegation headed by Edmund Wellenstein, the commission's director-general for external relations, visited Moscow from 4 to 6 February 1975 to pave the way for high-level exploratory discussions concerning Comecon-EEC economic relations. In response to these initial soundings Comecon's Executive Committee chairman, GDR Deputy Premier Gerhard Weiss, delivered the organization's "framework" proposal to the EEC president, Prime Minister Gaston Thorn of Luxembourg, on 6 February 1976.

It was not until November 15 that the EEC foreign ministers approved the reply to this proposal drafted by officials of the Common Market. On November 18 the EEC draft agreement, accompanied by a letter, was handed to Polish Deputy Premier Kazimierz Olszewski (who was serving as chairman of Comecon's Executive Committee) by the Dutch ambassador to Poland, Willi Pelt.

Comecon's "framework" proposal and the Common Market's reply silhouette the differences in organization and trading practices

‗‗‗‗

This chapter is an expanded and updated version of Harry Trend, "Comecon 'Framework' Proposal for Relations with EEC," RAD Background Report/60, <u>Radio Free Europe Research</u>, 12 March 1976.

between the two economic groups. The length of time it took to bring
Comecon-EEC economic relations to the point they reached in 1976
merely reinforced the opinion, held by many, that the differences
will not be easy to resolve and will require ingenuity and a capacity
to compromise on the part of both organizations.

SOME DETAILS OF THE COMECON PROPOSAL

Article 14 of the framework draft agreement[1] proposed an organizational structure that closely paralleled the Committee on Cooperation set up by Comecon and Finland for the purpose of reviewing
policies related to economic interrelationships.[2]

The proposal called for the establishment of a joint Comecon-
EEC Committee on Cooperation, with each of the two groups determining its own membership. This allowed the EEC to designate its
commission as sole representative or to appoint the commission and
its members to the joint body in the proportion considered most suitable. It also suggested establishing a number of standing working
parties to handle questions arising in special areas of economic
cooperation. Such groups are a feature of the Finnish-Comecon
cooperation arrangement; by the beginning of 1975, the Finnish-
Comecon Committee on Cooperation had set up permanent working
parties for foreign trade, machine building, the chemical industry,
transport, and scientific-technological cooperation. A number of
spheres were suggested as areas of joint interest in which this
approach could be applied: protection of the environment; statistics,
information, and economic forecasting; trade; scientific-technological
cooperation; and foreign finance and currency. Ad hoc working parties
could also be established when required.

Article 14 did not suggest the elimination of the joint governmental
commissions on economic and technological-scientific cooperation,
nor did it foresee interference with any other joint organization already
in existence. The powers of the Comecon-EEC Committee, it was
stated, would not affect those of the mixed committees already "existing within the framework of bilateral and multilateral agreements
between the member countries of Comecon and the member states
of the EEC."

Other provisions safeguarded various types of bilateral and
multilateral agreement the parties might wish to conclude. Article
11 said, for instance: "Certain questions of commercial and economic
relations . . . may be settled by bilateral and multilateral agreements between the member countries." The use of the term "certain
questions" implied that other matters would be reserved exclusively
for the joint committee. The following links, however, were safe-

guarded: direct relations between individual members within each of the two groups; Comecon member-EEC organization contacts; EEC member-Comecon organization contacts; and relationships between subunits of the two groups.

It was clearly implied that the "interested party basis for participation in particular programs, which is standard practice within Comecon, would apply to any arrangements with the EEC. Members of both groups would have the option of associating themselves with or dissociating themselves from projects approved by their two organizations. Although the option to participate was preserved, Article 3 called upon both Comecon and the EEC to "encourage and support the development of direct cooperation between member countries of Comecon and the member states of the EEC," particularly in the areas mentioned above, for which joint working parties could be established.

In short, virtually all types of contact would be permitted within the proposed framework: intergroup (that is, between the two central organizations, or between any of their agencies); direct contact between members, or between an individual member country of one organization and the central agencies of the other; and all types of multilateral arrangement. The particular form chosen would presumably depend on the subject matter of the intended agreement and on the wishes of the parties concerned.

Romania's special relationship with the EEC was to be preserved, and similar treatment was proposed for the less economically developed members of Comecon, particularly Cuba (Article 12); Mongolia does not appear to have been specifically designated for special treatment in this context, however. Any existing special arrangements between the EEC and certain trading partners (for example, former colonies of members) would be permitted to continue.

TRADE RESTRICTIONS AND PROTECTION

The methods favored by the Comecon proposal for removing trade restrictions were the granting by both groups of reciprocal most-favored-nation status (Article 6), and pledges to "organize relations on a nondiscriminatory basis" (Article 7). More specifically, an end should be put to all restrictions on the import and export of commodities, unless these were already universally applied to non-member states. There should be no "unilateral" restrictions on trade in agricultural products that do not apply to all nonmembers (Article 9). No new extension of this type of control would be permitted (Article 7). One exception to this rule was implied by Article 8, which required that foreign trade should be conducted "in such a

way that internal markets are not seriously harmed." This general
escape clause apparently allows dumping and other such activities
to be controlled in order to safeguard internal markets.

SPECIAL CONSIDERATION FOR
COMECON MEMBERS

One area of special treatment covered by Article 9 reflected the
interests of Comecon's agricultural exporters (mainly Bulgaria,
Hungary, Poland, and Romania). It called for the establishment of
trade in agricultural commodities on "a stable, equitable, and long-
term basis" and, as noted above, asserted that there should be no
unilateral restrictions on such trade that did not apply to all non-
member countries.

Protection of domestic farmers' markets is a cardinal Common
Market principle, and agricultural imports by EEC countries are
normally tolerated only if they are supplementary. Comecon's proposal that trade in agricultural commodities between the two economic
groups should be on a "stable" and "long-term" basis challenged one
of the basic preconditions for the setting up of the EEC and the community's policy of favoring other countries associated with the Common Market. Comecon's agricultural suppliers could hardly hope to
succeed in a confrontation that would inevitably provoke a domestic
political challenge in most EEC countries, and indeed the second
part of Article 9 seemed to indicate that Comecon would be satisfied
with something less and would be content if (1) the restrictions applied
to its members by the EEC in this field were no greater than those
imposed on other EEC nonmembers, and (2) the Comecon group was
consulted whenever a more discriminatory agricultural trade policy
is contemplated by the Common Market. The first of these positions
would have to be narrowed somewhat in order to accommodate the
Common Market's policy of favoring developing countries, such as
former French colonies.

Article 10 implied that preferential treatment in financial questions be given by both sides when it called for the granting of loans
"on the most favorable conditions possible." This formulation, however, provided a loophole that would enable the EEC to maintain that
its credit policy toward the Comecon countries, which was arrived
at unilaterally, was in fact "the most favorable" possible under current conditions. It seems unlikely that the chief creditor (the EEC)
could realistically be expected to grant more favorable conditions
unless they happened to serve its own purposes rather than primarily
those of the would-be debtor. Further, financial ties with countries
possessing non-centrally planned economies that are not EEC mem-

bers would require three-way negotiations to achieve Comecon's objectives. At best, Western creditors could be expected to get together and formulate a joint credit policy toward the Comecon countries and other state-trading economies.

Article 9 also recognized the EEC's interest in establishing convertibility for Comecon members' currencies, but all that was offered was a promise that the question would be studied.

ASYMMETRY IN THE GRANTING OF
MFN BENEFITS

The removal of trade obstacles and the joint application of most-favored-nation (MFN) benefits would not put an end to certain Comecon methods of enforcing trade discrimination. Comecon members would apparently be able to continue to restrict domestic consumption of imported items by imposing heavy turnover taxes on them, by permitting high domestic profits, which would then be severely taxed, or by restricting imports by exercising state monopoly powers over trade. These techniques would raise prices of goods imported by Comecon or control the level of imports and would therefore in effect restrict trade—particularly in consumer goods sold by EEC members (or in any other product whose import the planners wished to reduce). For example, a selective turnover tax or a discriminatory domestic exchange multiplier could be used to raise the price of machinery imported from the EEC and thus give a competitive edge to commodities produced by enterprises in the Comecon countries.

Insistence on barter-type commercial arrangements is another restrictive trade practice applied within Comecon, as are refusal to allow Western firms to use earnings from trade with one Comecon member to offset debts to another and the prevention of withdrawal of convertible currencies for use in trade outside the group. Comecon would be reluctant to give up these practices and tries to argue that their proscription would amount to intolerable interference in the planning processes of its member countries.

Variable internal foreign currency multipliers can also be used to help manipulate or restrict Western trade with Comecon and to favor the group at the expense of the EEC countries. Acceptance of state monopolies in specific sectors (a cardinal feature of Eastern Europe's economic system) would also have restrictive implications and would force the EEC to permit the creation of similar monopolies by Common Market enterprises in spite of a general ban on them within the organization.

The mere fact that Comecon members tend increasingly to coordinate their production plans for specific commodities on a medium-

and long-term basis—a process that cannot be readily duplicated in
a market economy based largely on private enterprise—would make
a mockery of any MFN treatment accorded by Comecon to EEC member countries. The normal GATT (General Agreement on Tariffs and
Trade) requirement that controlled economies increase their imports
from market economies by an agreed percentage still leaves considerable room for Comecon member countries to determine import structure by applying discriminatory practices to specific commodities
that they wish to exclude or limit.

These are only a few of the restrictive trade practices followed
by Comecon members that would not be eliminated by any MFN
arrangement of the kind envisaged by that organization, and the continuance of the trade practices and regulations currently in force
within that group would tend to give its members greater access to
EEC markets without offering Common Market members' firms a
corresponding freedom of access to those of Comecon.

CONTROL OF DUMPING

Control of dumping and similar undesirable trade practices was
covered by Article 8 of the proposal. It contained a provision similar
to that found in the Helsinki Final Act, which ensures that "trade in
various goods is carried out in such a way that internal markets are
not seriously harmed." The same provision could be used by Comecon
members to restrict the flow of those Western goods that the ordinary
East European consumer generally prefers to the "socialist" alternative.

It is, however, quite difficult to define dumping when the socialist
countries are involved. In Western eyes the term "costs," as defined
in Eastern Europe, has an unfamiliar look about it, and the region's
major exports of identical commodities are handled within Comecon
largely on a "tie-in" basis (virtually the same as barter). Under
these conditions EEC members find it difficult to apply the objective
and uniform standards used in defining dumping of products by market-
type economies. The root of the problem is that Comecon products
are largely traded on markets that are not comparable to those found
in the rest of the world.

INITIAL REACTIONS

The East European countries initially expressed the view that
their proposal took into consideration "existing realities" and made
a significant contribution "to putting into practice the principles of

the Final Act" signed in Helsinki. They also saw the Comecon document as an initial step toward the establishment of "pan-European cooperation."3

The Common Market promised to study the proposal, and EEC Foreign Relations Commissioner Sir Christopher Soames said that "we owe it to ourselves as well as to our Eastern neighbors to set about the task with all seriousness and in a constructive spirit," adding that "it cannot but be a source of satisfaction that, after years of systematically cold-shouldering the community, the countries of Eastern Europe are now prepared to sit down at the negotiating table to explore ways of cooperating."4

THE COMMON MARKET'S REPLY

In its reply to Comecon's proposals, the community did not reject the establishment of cooperative relationships between the two groups. For the most part, however, the answer reaffirmed the Common Market's offer made initially in November 1974, before Wellenstein's visit to Moscow in February 1975, to negotiate separate trade agreements between individual Comecon members and the community. In short, the EEC reply excluded commercial relations on a bloc-to-bloc basis. This meant that problems concerning economic cooperation would be reserved for bilateral discussion. Cooperation between the groups, according to the EEC, would be confined to those areas in which the EEC believed Comecon had authority to act— environmental questions, the exchange of statistical information, and such technical fields as international waterways, power grids, and cooperation on agricultural methods. In effect, the EEC emphasized the importance of links not only with Comecon but also with each individual member state.

The community also expressed its willingness to continue negotiations on the basis of its reply to the Comecon framework proposal. The policy on commercial relations with state-trading countries introduced in 1973 remained unchanged. In that year EEC members transferred to the EEC Commission the right to negotiate commercial agreements on a bilateral basis between the commission and individual members. As noted above, the trade agreements between individual members of the community and Comecon members expired at the end of 1974, and the commission began extending the provisions of the formal trade agreements for 1975. The import quotas were amended for 1976 in December 1975, and the scheduled November 1976 review of the trade quotas applicable to individual Comecon member countries for 1977 was postponed.

Immediately after the 79th session of the Comecon Executive Committee, held in January 1977, a preliminary exchange of views took place concerning the community's reply, and the news media reports on these discussions indicated that no formal response was drawn up,[5] and in fact shortly thereafter a letter that merely acknowledged receipt of the EEC's proposal was dispatched by Comecon.[6]

The EEC Commission continued its bilateral approach to state-trading countries. In October Romania and the EEC, under the auspices of GATT, signed a multifiber agreement for the export of textile goods to EEC markets. This was the first public document bearing the signatures of the commission and a member of Comecon. Poland agreed to open similar negotiations, thereby recognizing the commission's competence in regard to commercial questions.[7] As of the middle of December 1976, Hungary, which is also a contracting party to GATT, had not responded to the commission's invitations to negotiate on the same issue.

The EEC also instituted fishing controls over the area covering its members' coastal waters within a 200-mile limit, and these have applied to the fishing fleets of individual Comecon members. It also negotiated with Yugoslavia, which, while not a Comecon member, cooperates with it very closely, and established a special status for this Balkan communist country. Romania has been recognized by the EEC as an economically developing country, thereby acquiring special benefits in regard to certain of its economic relations with the community.

For their part, Bulgaria and the Soviet Union were critical of those in Western Europe who maintained that Comecon was not competent to deal with the EEC on commercial questions and of the Common Market's continued insistence that its commission is the only agency authorized to handle trade negotiations with Comecon members on an individual country basis.

By expressing its willingness to continue negotiations with Comecon on the basis of its own reply, the Common Market brought to an end the phase of indirect discussion during which each side kept the other at arm's length. It seemed likely that direct negotiations were about to begin.

NOTES

1. See Radio Free Europe Special/Brussels, 25 February 1976, and the Frankfurter Allgemeine Zeitung, 23 February 1976.
2. For details on the Comecon-Finnish agreement see Harry Trend, "Comecon's Organizational Structure," Part II, RAD Background Report/138, Radio Free Europe Research, 7 October 1975,

especially Appendix II, which reproduces the agreement (including supplement). This should not, of course, be confused with "Finland-ization," which is generally taken to mean a situation in which a small country retains apparent freedom of action but only within the limits acceptable to a more powerful neighbor.

3. Interview with Gerhard Weiss, Izvestia (Moscow), 21 February 1976.

4. Reuter, Hamburg, 5 March 1976.

5. Radio Moscow I, 21 January 1977.

6. Viliam Roth in a commentary over Radio Prague, 12 February 1977.

7. David Lascelles in the Financial Times (London), 14 December 1976.

8

**EAST EUROPEAN
INDEBTEDNESS
TO THE WEST**
Harry Trend

The indebtedness of the Soviet Union and the East European
countries to the West has been rising rapidly, particularly since
1973. A number of articles have appeared in the Western press on
this topic, pointing up the concern now widely felt about the rapidity
of its growth and the increasing nervousness in some Western quarters
concerning the ability of the Comecon countries to bear the burden
of servicing and ultimately repaying this ever-expanding debt.

ESTIMATING THE INDEBTEDNESS

Although it seems to be generally agreed that the East European
countries are fast approaching the limits of economically justified
borrowing, there is no agreement about the actual size of their indebtedness. Estimates made at the end of 1975 ranged between $28
billion and $40 billion, and others made a year later envisaged a
total of $37 billion to $38 billion. Table 8.1 gathers together the
latest thinking on the question.

Some of the differences in these estimates are due to variations
in definitions—for example, net versus gross—or to incomplete information. At a 1976 OECD meeting it was decided, in view of the prevailing uncertainty about the size of Eastern Europe's debt to the
West, to conduct a survey of the situation. Until this report appears,

─────

This chapter is an updated version of Harry Trend, "A Suggested
Framework for Analyzing East European Indebtedness," RAD Background Report/202, Radio Free Europe Research, 28 September 1976.

TABLE 8.1

Estimates of Comecon Indebtedness to the West
(in billions of U.S. dollars)

Source of Estimate	Estimated Indebtedness	
	End of 1975	End of 1976
Time (New York), 6 September 1976	32	37[a]
Miriam Karr, EastWest Markets (New York), 26 September 1976	27.9[b]	
A. Vernholes, Le Monde (Paris), 31 August 1976	31	
Hans Friderichs (FRG Economics Minister), dpa 27 August 1976	34[c]	
Craig G. Whitney, New York Times, 16 August 1976	40	38
J. Palmer, Times (London), 30 July 1976	29.75[d]	38.5[d]
Mary Campbell and David Lascelles, Financial Times (London), 29 July 1976	30.8[e]	
E. Hoorna, Die Presse (Vienna), 27 July 1976	31-35.7[f]	
David R. Francis, Christian Science Monitor (Boston), 22 July 1976	32	
Peter Brinkman, Die Welt (Bonn), 7 April 1976	32[g]	

[a]"Latest."

[b]Net, including Comecon bank debt of $1.6 billion.

[c]DM 85 billion (DM 2.50 – $1; FRG share is DM 20 billion).

[d]17 billion and 22 billion pounds sterling, respectively (1 pound sterling = $1.75).

[e]Calculated on the basis of the Bank for International Settlements table of reporting banks' assets and liabilities as of December 1975, plus known government credits and other borrowings but excluding inter-German trade, where the GDR has a debt of about $1 billion in "clearing account units" financed (largely interest-free) by the FRG.

[f]As of 1 July 1976.

[g]$22.3 billion at the end of 1974, plus an estimated increase of about $10 billion during 1975.

it will be difficult for members of the organization to formulate a
common credit policy to govern their dealings with Comecon, and
the differences in thinking that exist among them will not make the
task of coordination any easier.

An attempt was made in the spring of 1976 by the European Economic Community to arrive at a gentlemen's agreement on export
credits during an "experimental stage." France, however, protested
that it could not be made binding for the whole community and rejected
the commission's proposal that the final decision be made before
1 July 1976.[1] Subsequently, in June 1976, Britain, France, West
Germany, Italy, Japan, Canada, and the United States reached agreement on export credit guidelines, and particularly on regulating the
practice that permits debtors to delay repayment during the construction period, often lasting for a number of years. The agreement went
into effect on 1 July 1976, and a review of the new credit policy on
the basis of experience was scheduled for mid-1977.[2]

The West's largest debtors are the Soviet Union and Poland,
followed by the GDR and Romania. (See Table 8.2.)

The East European debt to the Western countries is still growing,
probably at a faster rate than during 1975. An indication of this is

TABLE 8.2

Comecon Debt at the End of 1975
(in billions of U.S. dollars)

Country	Accumulated Debt[a]
Bulgaria	1.8
Czechoslovakia	1.2
GDR	4.5[b]
Hungary	2.3
Poland	6.0
Romania	3.0
Soviet Union	13.0
Comecon Banks	1.6
Total	33.4

[a]Calculated on the basis of BIS table of reporting banks' assets
and liabilities as of December 1975, plus known government credits
and other borrowings.

[b]Includes $1 billion of East German debt in "clearing account
units" financed largely interest-free by West Germany.

Sources: Mary Campbell and David Lascelles, the Financial
Times, 29 July 1976. Comecon bank indebtedness based on estimate
by Miriam Karr, EastWest Markets (New York), 20 September 1976.

TABLE 8.3

Eurocurrency Bank Credits
(in millions of dollars)

Country	1974	1975		1976, 1st half
		Year	2d half	
Poland	509	475	125	356
Soviet Union	100	650	400	250
Other[a]	647	1,472	975	1,183
Total for communist countries	1,238[b]	2,597	1,500	1,789
Global total	22,263	20,992	12,803	13,458

Note: Credits are those publicly announced in listed period.
[a]Includes Comecon institutions.
[b]Apparently incorrect total not explained by source.
Source: Mary Campbell, Financial Times (London), 20 September 1976.

to be found in the available figures for Eurocurrency Bank credits
(Table 8.3).

Comecon members' and institutions' share of the Eurocurrency
Bank credits granted to all countries grew from 5.5 percent in 1974
to 12.37 percent in 1975. The proportion dropped in the second half
of 1975 to 11.7 percent, but jumped to 13.3 percent in the first half
of 1976. Thus Eastern Europe's share is growing not only absolutely,
but also relatively.

MEASURING THE ECONOMIC BURDEN
OF THE DEBT

Various methods for measuring the economic burden the debt
imposes on the East European countries have been proposed in articles
that have appeared in the Western press. The one most favored is
to relate the size of the debt to the volume of East European exports
to the West. Another is to measure the cost of servicing the debt.
The associate editor of EastWest Markets, Miriam Karr, who estimated net East European indebtedness at $27.9 billion at the end of
1975, put the Soviet share at $10.7 billion and Poland's at $7 billion,
and noted that two of Latin America's more developed countries,
Brazil and Mexico, had net external debts of $16.9 billion and $10
billion, respectively. In terms of the debt/hard currency export

ratio, the Soviet Union (1.2) was below Brazil (2). For Poland and
Mexico the ratios were 2 and 3 respectively.[3]

The Soviet Union's largest creditors are France, the FRG, Italy,
Japan, Great Britain, and the United States, in that order. Austria
is seventh and Sweden eighth. Poland's four main creditors are
Great Britain, France, Austria, and the FRG, followed by Japan,
Italy, Sweden, Switzerland, and the United States.

The criteria of relative debt size or level of debt servicing normally applied to trade among Western countries must be modified to
take into account the points on which state-controlled and market-type
economies differ.

One obvious difference is the East European countries' minimal
reliance on risk capital. In making comparison with the indebtedness
of market economies, one should include foreign-sourced risk- and
debt-capital funds before calculating the debt/export ratio. The
average profit rate the East Europeans would have had to pay Western
investors in joint projects would normally have been higher than the
interest paid to service a debt. Refinancing of credits would put
credit capital on a par with risk capital as far as repayment is concerned. Ultimately, of course, risk capital has also to be repaid.

A second point on which modification is necessary is that some
credits are "self-liquidating"—that is, the creditor agrees to accept
in payment the goods or commodities produced by the facility for
which the credit was granted; this is sometimes referred to as
commodity payment credit. In effect these are "barter credits"—
investment goods are exchanged (bartered) against promised deliveries
of whatever the new facility produces. When, therefore, a comparison
is made between the size of the debt and exports to Western countries,
the amount of the credit and the value of future exports specifically
tied to it should perhaps be deducted; "net credits" could then be
compared with "net exports," and the ratio would be considerably
smaller.

A third, and significant, difference concerns the added powers
possessed by a centrally planned economy. The Western democracies
have to take much greater account of public reactions than the socialist countries and have less power to enforce restrictions on the
domestic economy (particularly those that affect personal consumption). The East Europeans can increase exports by selling goods
below cost, whereas in the West such action (usually achieved by
export subsidies) requires the prior approval of legislative bodies
more responsive to public opinion. Again, financial authorities in
the West often require additional legislation before they are in a
position to impose higher taxes or increase internal governmental
indebtedness. Because of the larger number of tools available to
them, the East European planners possess greater flexibility when
it comes to acquiring or meeting international financial obligations.

A number of factors affecting the level of the debt burden are related to the elapsed time between receipt of the credit and its repayment. World price inflation, for example, tends to lessen the burden on the debtor, who benefits from the difference between the cost of buying investor goods and the prices received for the commodities sold in order to earn currencies with which to repay their borrowings. Similarly, currency devaluation, a more frequent occurrence of late, also helps the debtor. On the other hand, revaluations such as those that have affected the West German and Swiss currencies in recent years will naturally have the opposite effect.

ALTERNATIVE METHODS OF FINANCING ECONOMIC DEVELOPMENT

Should Western credits be restricted, a number of alternatives are open to the East European countries. They can obtain access to risk capital by establishing joint enterprises that enable foreign firms to invest directly in their economies—a frequent practice in the West, of course, but so far unknown in the East outside Yugoslavia.

Another alternative is to make greater use of leasing. At a recent East-West meeting, a Soviet official indicated that the existence of foreign-owned property in a socialist country raises certain problems, but the Soviet Union has in fact leased containers from the West since then. The "problems" are probably of less ideological import than those associated with the establishment of joint enterprises.

Finally, a socialist economy can always revert to internal financing. This method requires the allocation of a larger share of the national income to investments, and standards of living are the inevitable losers. Internal financing has often been used in the past to solve economic problems, but the ordinary man in the East European street is less inhibited (in some countries at least) than he once was about expressing his dissatisfaction over reductions in living standards—as the June 1976 events in Poland, for example, clearly demonstrated—and that makes this particular policy subject to a number of political constraints.

During periods of economic recession, however, Western governments are more willing than in times of prosperity to extend credits at low interest rates to the East in order to maintain domestic employment. The FRG, heavily dependent on its exports of capital goods, has followed this policy, and others have not been far behind. To some extent, therefore, Eastern Europe has to depend on economic adversity in the West to produce its credits and, as a corollary, hope for an upswing when repayment has to be made.

Addressing those who are concerned about repayments by the East European countries, Dr. Janos Fekete, deputy chairman of the Hungarian National Bank, said recently: "I can promise the Western banks that they will not lose their money in the East. I cannot guarantee that they will not lose it in Latin America or New York City."[4] Although this observation may be perfectly valid, it is perhaps wise to recall that Fekete hails from a country that is heavily in debt to the West.

NOTES

1. EastWest Fortnightly Bulletin (Brussels), no. 1952, 29 April 1976.

2. Melvin Westlake, "Export Credit Guidelines Redefined," The Times (London), 16 June 1976.

3. EastWest Markets (New York), 20 September 1976.

4. Ibid., 12 July 1976.

III

THE DOMESTIC
ECONOMIC SCENE

Economic development is one of the top priorities of the communist parties of Eastern Europe. From the very beginning, the emphasis has been on industrialization, and this continues to be the main focus of domestic economic policy, with agriculture and consumer goods production clearly second in importance to the production of capital goods and raw materials. After the invasion of Czechoslovakia in 1968 and—particularly—the workers' riots in Poland in 1970, however, a degree of concern with consumer goods became evident in a number of East European countries. During the first half of the 1970s, the living standard rose perceptibly, and on the whole it is today higher than it has ever been in the history of these countries— before or after World War II.

Nevertheless, from 1960 to 1975, only in Hungary did the average annual growth rate for consumer goods production outstrip that of producer goods. Total industrial production has increased in all East European countries, but given the more rapid growth rate of heavy industry, the share attributable to the production of consumer items has declined in all of them except, as noted, Hungary. The 1976-80 plans indicate a continuation of this policy despite statements by the leaders exhorting planners to expand consumer goods production more rapidly. Even at the projected growth rates, however, the planned difference is understated, owing to the fact that, generally speaking, these countries have a net export of consumer goods representing payment for imports of producer goods. Also, pricing practices throughout Eastern Europe tend to overvalue consumer goods, which results in overstatement of their relative gain. Chapter 9 analyzes the growth in consumer goods relative to producer goods production. It also reviews Bulgaria's success in meeting its commitments to raise the living standard. (Since a rather ambitious program was launched in December 1972, some progress has been achieved, but initial estimates appear to have been on the optimistic side, and there has been an evident scaling down of some goals.) The efforts of the East European parties to have their citizens accept the idea of forgoing individual material rewards in exchange for higher general social benefits do not appear to have been successful. A research survey in Hungary, also briefly discussed in Chapter 9, indicates that consumer desires in that country (and by implication in the remainder of Eastern Europe as well) are very similar to those that motivate consumers in the West.

While the economic aspects of so-called consumer communism are important, the psychological and political implications are also significant in terms of the attitude of the population toward the government and with regard to their expectations. Given the increasing problems facing the East European economies as a result of the increase in prices for Soviet and other raw materials, the worldwide economic slowdown, the need to export more in order to repay foreign debts, and domestically caused difficulties, the long-term prospects are for at least a significant slowing down in the improvement of the standard of living. Among the most seriously affected economies is that of Czechoslovakia (Chapter 10). In 1975 and 1976, shortcomings in the economy were criticized in the mass media and by the party leadership. The existence of a disquieting situation in a number of economic sectors was confirmed, and there were suggestions that austerity measures might be necessary. The economic problems of the CSSR are attributable to both external and domestic causes, and, with the exception of a very low foreign indebtedness, they are similar to those facing a number of other East European states.

A more promising economic picture is presented by Yugoslavia's current attempts to come to grips with its economic problems (Chapter 11). Official reports and press comments in late 1976 indicated that the economy had experienced a partial revival: The foreign trade deficit had been reduced, the imbalance in payments had been narrowed, the inflation rate had declined, and the problem of providing adequate domestic liquidity was being dealt with. Much of this had been achieved by strengthening commercial relations among domestic enterprises and reducing state intervention and controls. Moreover, during a difficult period, Yugoslavia had continued to develop its self-management and socialist market economy system. In assessing these developments, Yugoslav commentators have shown increasing self-confidence, interpreting the latest results as confirmation of the viability of self-managing socialism, but at the same time recognizing that much has yet to be done to bring about the desired rate of economic development under stable conditions.

While industry remains the principle focus of the East European planners, agriculture remains the Achilles' heel of their economies (Chapter 12). Future progress in increasing agricultural production is threatened by persistent technical problems, a declining agricultural labor force, and a number of changes—which may have become permanent—in behavioral patterns that are inimical to the attainment of higher production levels. These hindrances include changing attitudes toward work; specialization-induced diversity of interests; restrictive organizational relationships; unresponsive management and the shackling effects of the economic control system; inadequate agricultural investments; and a shortage of the skilled technicians needed to operate an "industrialized" agriculture effectively.

While problems of this general nature are to be found in agriculture throughout the region, there are striking divergencies among the individual states. In Bulgaria, agriculture is organized into huge agro-industrial complexes managed by a single national administration in a given sector. Vertical and horizontal integration on a national scale has progressed further in Bulgaria than elsewhere in Eastern Europe. Since the system was introduced in 1970, individual agro-industrial complexes have gradually undergone internal transformation leading toward vertical integration with industry, and a variety of new organizational forms have been introduced. The complexes are still far from problem-free, however, and there is an urgent need for continued agricultural mechanization and "industrialization." Nonetheless, great efforts have been made, and performance in the agricultural sector appears to be showing some improvement, reflecting past increases in agricultural resources. Other East European countries seem to be adopting some aspects of the Bulgarian model.

Poland is at the other end of the spectrum, with over 70 percent of its arable land still in private hands and worked by peasants with small individual holdings. The government is caught in a dilemma: It needs the agricultural output of the private farms to meet the increasing demands of its growing urban population, but at the same time it is ideologically and politically committed to more rapid growth of the relatively small socialist sector of agriculture. The exodus from the countryside has been extensive since 1945 and will continue for the foreseeable future, but it is not certain whether the authorities will allow the private sector to benefit from this by permitting individual farmers to buy tractors in greater numbers and to acquire an appropriately larger share of the available land. So far, when such concessions are made, they are made to those individual farmers who cooperate with the socialist sector or to those who have signed state procurement contracts. It is feared that any overt support of an "unadulterated" individual sector would seriously retard the socialization of agriculture. The factor that perhaps circumscribes the authorities' freedom of movement toward greater socialization most rigidly is the fear that too rapid an advance toward the "gradual transformation of agriculture" may disrupt the vital food-production process for the immediate future. Nevertheless, both party and government are firmly committed to a policy of extending the socialized sector to the limits possible within the pragmatic context of their more short-term needs. Although Poland is the only Comecon state in which agriculture is dominated by private peasants, throughout Eastern Europe private plots (or "personal plots" as most governments prefer to call them) still play a significant role in filling gaps in the consumer market, particularly those caused by shortages of the high-value products on which more and more of the family budget is spent as personal incomes increase.

9

"CONSUMER COMMUNISM": MYTH OR REALITY?

Harry Trend
Rada Nikolaev
The Hungarian Research Unit

The Western press has often characterized the post-Stalin period in Eastern Europe as "goulash communism." The stated economic policy of almost every East European leader has been to favor narrowing the large gap in production growth rates between industrial producer and consumer goods—or as official literature prefers to call these industrial sectors, Groups A and B production, respectively. The situation over the 15 years from 1960 to 1975 and the stated objectives in this connection during the current five-year plan period (1976-80) are discussed below.

Western journalists freely admit that there has been a marked improvement in consumption levels in every East European country, but they are quick to add that the newly attained levels are still below those prevailing in the economically developed West European countries. The issue, however, is not whether consumption levels have increased in Eastern Europe or whether the living standard of the average inhabitant in these countries has matched or surpassed that of most of the rest of Europe; an improvement in the living standard has been characteristic of a good part of the world over the last ten years. It would have been more surprising if the East European levels had remained relatively constant. On the other hand, it be-

---

This chapter is a shortened and updated version of the following Radio Free Europe Research Background Reports: Harry Trend, "'Consumer Communism': Myth or Reality?" RAD Background Report/143, 23 June 1976; R. N. (Bulgarian Unit), "The Bulgarian Party Theses on the Standard of Living," RAD Background Report/59, 11 March 1976; and Hungarian Unit, "Hungarian Families' Incomes, Expenditures, and Attitudes," RAD Background Report/101, 5 May 1976.

came clear some time ago that Khrushchev's boast that the East European standard of living would match or surpass that of the West has remained just that—a boast. His successors have not made the mistake of repeating his "prophecy."

THE PAST RECORD IN EASTERN EUROPE

An analysis of what has happened to the relationship between the growth rates for industrial producer and consumer production in

TABLE 9.1

Average Annual Industrial Production Growth
Rates by Production Group,
Comecon States, 1961-74
(in percent; production valued at
constant prices in each country)

Country	Production Group*	Plan Period		
		1961-65	1966-70	1971-74
Bulgaria	T	11.7	10.9	8.9
	A	14.1	11.9	10.1
	B	9.4	9.8	7.2
Czechoslovakia	T	5.2	6.7	6.6
	A	5.7	7.1	7.0
	B	4.6	6.2	6.2
East Germany	T	5.8	6.5	6.4
	A	6.3	7.3	6.8
	B	4.9	4.6	6.0
Hungary	T	7.8	6.3	6.8
	A	7.7	5.8	6.8
	B	8.5	7.2	7.2
Poland	T	8.6	8.4	10.4
	A	9.8	9.4	10.6
	B	6.6	6.6	10.1
Romania	T	13.8	11.9	13.2
	A	15.7	13.0	13.7
	B	10.5	9.5	12.3
Soviet Union	T	8.6	8.5	7.4
	A	9.6	8.6	7.8
	B	6.3	8.4	6.6

*T = Total; A = Producer Goods; B = Consumer Goods.
Source: Stanlislaw Paradysz, "Relative Growth of Producer and Consumer Goods," Nowe Drogi (Warsaw), March 1976.

TABLE 9.2

Average Growth Rate of Consumer Goods as
Percent of Growth Rate of Producer Goods:
Comecon States, 1961-74

Country	Plan Period		
	1961-65	1966-70	1971-74
Bulgaria	66.7	82.4	71.3
Czechoslovakia	80.7	87.3	88.6
East Germany	77.8	63.0	88.2
Hungary	110.4	124.1	105.9
Poland	67.3	70.2	95.3
Romania	66.9	73.1	89.8
Soviet Union	65.6	97.7	84.6

Source: Calculated on the basis of figures in Table 9.1.

Eastern Europe should provide at least a basis for determining the
East European economic policy on this issue in the past few years.
Table 9.1 gives a picture of developments during the last three five-
year plan periods. (It will be noted that in this and the next two
tables, the figures for the last five-year plan are confined to its first
four years. No comparable data appear to have been produced for
1975, but all the evidence suggests that there were no significant
changes in that year.)

As can be seen, the annual average growth rate of overall industrial production has tended to decline in Bulgaria and the Soviet Union;
in Czechoslovakia and East Germany it has largely risen, and in the
other East European countries it has seesawed. Of greater interest
for the purpose at hand, however, is the relative growth rate of
industrial and consumer goods production. Table 9.2 presents these
ratios for the years 1961-74.

A comparison of the initial two five-year periods indicates that
only for East Germany did the relative difference in the growth rate
widen in favor of producer goods production. The growth rate for
producer goods continued to outstrip that of the industrial consumer
goods sector in All East European countries except Hungary, where
the growth rate for the consumer goods industry consistently surpassed that for Group A industries.

The tendency to narrow the differences in growth rates between
the two industrial sectors continued, but the greater emphasis on
producer goods output was maintained into the recently completed
quinquennium in Czechoslovakia, Poland, and Romania, and resumed

in the case of East Germany. For the Soviet Union, where the average growth rates of the two sectors almost matched each other during the 1966-70 period, some slippage appeared for Group B even before the near disastrous grain harvest of 1975, which had such an adverse effect on canning and processing. This slippage also occurred in Bulgaria during 1971-74. In Hungary, even though the average growth rate continued to favor Group B production over producer goods, the difference between the two indexes narrowed considerably in comparison to the average for 1966-70.

All East European countries except Hungary continued to favor producer goods over industrial consumer goods, and the effect of this policy on the respective shares of overall industrial production is clear—a smaller share was represented by commodities classified in Group B and, conversely, a continually larger proportion was accounted for by Group A.

The country in which the lowest share of industrial production was represented by the consumer commodity sector was the Soviet Union, closely followed by East Germany and Romania. Bulgaria had the highest proportion of industrial consumer goods, reaching over 50 percent in 1960, but here too the consumer share has been declining rapidly, falling to below 42 percent in 1974. Hungary is the only country where the industrial consumer goods production ratio has been improving, and in 1974 it stood at 35.4 percent of total industrial production. Despite the improvement, however, it still remains below the levels in Bulgaria and Czechoslovakia.

PROSPECTS FOR THE FUTURE

Public statements by East European officials continue to emphasize the importance of developing the consumer sector during the current quinquennium, but only in the Soviet Union are specific figures on the relative proportion of industrial producer and consumer goods production to be found. In the other countries they can only be estimated from information released on the light and food industries.

In his report to the 25th CPSU congress,[1] Soviet CP Secretary-General Leonid Brezhnev criticized shortages of consumer goods and services and blamed central planning and economic organizations for showing "insufficient concern for the light and food industries and the services sector." He added, "We have not been able to stop treating consumer goods production as something of secondary importance or as a side issue," and specified that the plan tasks for Group B industries must be considered as a minimum goal. At the same time, however, Section III of the "Main Directions of the Development of the USSR National Economy in 1976-1980" adopted at the 25th

TABLE 9.3

Share of Industrial Production by Production
Group: Comecon States, 1960-74
(in percent; production valued at constant
prices in each country)

Country	Production Group*	1960	1965	1970	1974
Bulgaria	T	100.0	100.0	100.0	100.0
	A	47.2	52.3	54.7	58.3
	B	52.8	47.7	45.3	41.7
Czechoslovakia	T	100.0	100.0	100.0	100.0
	A	59.2	60.6	61.6	63.9
	B	40.8	39.4	38.4	36.1
East Germany	T	100.0	100.0	100.0	100.0
	A	66.5	68,1	70.2	71.1
	B	33.5	31.9	29.8	28.9
Hungary	T	100.0	100.0	100.0	100.0
	A	66.0	65.4	65.1	64.6
	B	34.0	34.6	34.9	35.4
Poland	T	100.0	100.0	100.0	100.0
	A	57.5	60.9	65.0	65.4
	B	42.5	39.1	35.0	34.6
Romania	T	100.0	100.0	100.0	100.0
	A	62.8	67.3	70.4	70.9
	B	37.2	32.7	29.6	29.1
Soviet Union	T	100.0	100.0	100.0	100.0
	A	72.5	74.1	73.4	73.8
	B	27.5	25.9	26.6	26.2

*T = Total; A = Producer Goods; B = Consumer Goods.

Source: Stanislaw Paradysz, "Relative Growth of Producer and
Consumer Goods," Nowe Drogi (Warsaw), March 1976.

CPSU congress on March 3 stipulates the growth level of industrial
production as follows: "Industrial production is to be increased by
35-37 percent, including 38-42 percent for the means of production
and 30-32 percent for consumer goods."[2]

For 1976-80 an average annual growth rate of 6.2 to 6.5 percent
has been set for overall industrial production, 6.7 to 7.3 percent for
producer goods production, and 5.4 to 5.7 percent as the "minimum"
for industrial consumer commodity production. Since the relationship
between the planned average growth rates of consumer and producer

goods is to range between 78 and 80 percent, the share represented by consumer goods will continue to decline during the next five years, and producer goods production will retain its priority position in the eyes of the Soviet Union's policy-makers.

According to the basic draft directives on the socioeconomic development of the Bulgarian People's Republic during the seventh five-year plan adopted by the BCP CC in February 1976, Bulgaria is to increase its overall industrial production by 55 to 60 percent, its light industrial production by "approximately" 45 percent; its industrial food production "must" increase by 40 percent.[3] This comes to a planned annual average growth rate for 1976-80 of 9.2 to 9.9 percent for overall industrial production, 7.7 percent for light industry, and 7 percent for the food industry. These figures make it clear that during the current five-year plan producer goods production will continue to expand more rapidly than consumer goods production.

Czechoslovakia foresees an industrial production increase of 32 to 34 percent during this medium-term period. The consumer goods industry is to expand by "roughly" one-quarter and industrial food production by 20 to 21 percent.[4] On an annual basis this means 5.7 to 6.0 percent, 4.6 percent, and 3.7 to 3.9 percent, respectively. The Czechoslovak planners also continue to favor producer over consumer industrial goods production. The share of overall industrial production attributable to the consumer industrial sector will continue to decline.

According to the Draft Directives, East Germany's growth rates for the current quinquennium have been set at 40 to 42 percent for overall industrial production, "at least" 23 percent for light industry, and 18 to 19 percent for industrial food production.[5] On an annual basis, the respective figures are 7.0 to 7.3 percent, 4.2 percent, and 3.3 to 3.5 percent. Thus the GDR is also falling into line with those who continue to favor Group A production over industrial consumer commodity production, and by a considerable margin.

For Hungary only, the target for total industrial production is available. This has been set at 33 to 35 percent, or an annual rate of about 5.9 to 6.2 percent.[6] With only this figure available, no comment can be made at this time concerning the relative growth rates for producer and consumer goods production.

Poland has tentatively set its total industrial output target at 45 to 48 percent, its light industrial output at 41 to 43 percent, and its food industry output at a minimum of 35 percent.[7] On an annual basis, the growth rates come to 8.2-8.4 percent, 7.1-7.4, and at least 6.2 percent, respectively. Since both light and food production growth rates are below that set for overall industrial production, the growth target set for producer goods production is at a higher annual average rate than that for consumer goods. It also appears

that the planned gap is to be greater than during 1971-74. This por-
tends a further shrinking of the share of total industrial production
attributable to the industrial consumer sector.

The Romanian 1976-80 plan[8] calls for total industrial production
to increase at an average annual rate of 10.2-11.2 percent. For
important industrial sectors, the rates are above this average, but
the growth rate of the consumer goods industry is to be much more
modest with an average annual rate of about 9 percent. Although the
light and food industries are scheduled to grow far more slowly than
the main industrial sectors, it is noteworthy that the planned annual
production of the food industry has been raised significantly from a
maximum average annual increase of 7.3 percent to one of 9.1 percent. Since the average growth rate gap between overall industrial
and consumer goods production is wider than for 1971-74, there will
be a reversal of the tendency noted during the last three five-year
plan periods for Group B production to catch up to the Group A level
(see Table 9.2). Producer goods production has to some extent
regained its favored position.

Even though living standards in Eastern Europe have been improving and can be expected to become better, the available information concerning 1976-80 growth rate targets would indicate that
"consumer communism" has an aura more of myth than of reality.
This conclusion, as indicated above, is but a first approximation,
and two caveats should be voiced concerning interbranch and intercountry comparisons of the growth rate figures discussed and some
of the derivative data.

First, there is a general tendency throughout Eastern Europe
to load industrial consumer goods with a heavier burden of profit
taxes and other charges than is the case with producer goods, adding
more in the way of costs to the price of consumer goods. As a
consequence of this practice, a percentage point change in the overall value of consumer goods production represents a smaller absolute
change in comparable values than it does for producer goods production. This is true also because the share of Group A production is
about twice that of consumer goods in absolute terms. A given percentage for the former provides an absolute change double in value
for a like percentage change for consumer goods production. Therefore allowances should be made for this, and the stated value of
consumer goods should be discounted in each country, depending on
the differences in "loading," before making interbranch comparisons
of growth rates, and in making comparisons one must remember
that all percentage point differences do not have identical absolute
values.

The second caveat concerns the use made of the industrial
consumer items produced. For example, in Bulgaria and Romania

TABLE 9.4

Net Trade Balance for Consumer Goods
(in millions of current dollars)

Country	1971	1972	1973
Soviet Union	-2,109	-2,510	-2,915
Other East European	2,419	2,826	3,412

Note: Figures exclude foodstuffs. For 1972, the Soviet Union had a net deficit of $2.51 billion in its trade balance for consumer goods. All the other East European countries had a net surplus for this trade sector: Bulgaria, $173 million; Czechoslovakia, $558 million; East Germany (including food) only $18 million; Hungary, $460 million; Poland, $381 million; and Romania, $357 million. The difference between this total and that given in the table is due to the inclusion of the very high negative trade balance for the GDR's food sector.

Sources: "Recent Change in Europe's Trade," UN Economic Bulletin for Europe (Geneva), vol. 26, no. 1, p. 23; and UN Economic Bulletin for Europe, vol. 25, Table 14, p. 26.

a significant amount of the consumer goods output is used to pay for imports of producer goods (see Table 9.4). The quantity of consumer goods exported should for all practical purposes be counted as a segment of producer goods production. For the Soviet Union the opposite is the case, however, because it is a net importer of consumer goods.

More recently it has become simpler to sell various types of consumer goods to the West, particularly those requiring large quantities of labor input. These consumer goods are becoming a favorite East European export item, and as the Western economies improve, the opportunities for such sales will be enhanced. Proceeds from them will be used largely to buy additional capital goods in the West or to pay off international debts incurred in the past. To the extent that this situation obtains, the net export (or conversely, the net import) of consumer goods should be taken into account before making interbranch or intercountry comparisons of growth rates for various branches of industrial production.

BULGARIA'S PROGRAM FOR RAISING THE STANDARD OF LIVING

Bulgaria's handling of the problem of providing consumer goods is in many regards typical of the situation in the rest of Eastern

Europe, although there are variations from country to country. At the end of December 1972 the Bulgarian CP's Central Committee devoted a three-day plenum to the discussion of a vast program for raising the standard of living. The lengthy report by party leader Todor Zhivkov and the documents adopted at the session announced far-reaching reforms and immediate and long-term improvements. The plenum was seen at the time as demonstrating a new approach and a new spirit in party policy.[9]

In preparation for the party's 11th congress in March 1976, the CC adopted a document entitled "Theses on the Further Fulfillment of the December [1972] Program to Raise the Standard of Living During the Seventh Five-Year Plan [1976-1980] and up to 1990."[10] The December Program remains the basic policy statement, however, and the Theses are intended merely to update and supplement its targets. Nevertheless, they do provide direct and indirect indications of the results of the December Program some three years after it was adopted, and the modifications introduced reflect shifts in emphasis.

Thanks to the impetus of the December Program, many of the targets set in 1971 for the 1971-75 period were overfulfilled. By 1975, real income had increased by 32.4 percent over 1970, instead of the planned 25 to 30 percent; in 1973 the minimum monthly salary rose from 65 to 80 leva, instead of the planned 70 leva; by 1975 annual average per capita public consumption funds increased to 410 leva (the 1970 figure was 285), and retail goods turnover increased by about 47 percent, instead of the planned 38 to 40 percent. At the same time, however, the Theses noted that "despite the achievements certain unresolved problems still exist. They arise mainly because in the last few years the purchasing power of the population has been running ahead of the ability to satisfy the demand for goods and services."

The Theses contain data, similar to those issued at the December plenum, on the consumption of some of the main food items and consumer goods. Table 9.5 lists the two sets of figures. Almost none of the 1975 targets for food items set in 1972 were met, but those for nonfood items were slightly surpassed. In a large number of cases, the 1980 targets have been set somewhat lower, probably because it was realized that progress cannot be achieved as rapidly as need would dictate. This means, however, that the "scientific consumption norms"—that is, scientifically set minimum standards that ought to be achieved—will not be reached even by 1980.[11]

It is interesting that, despite the initial claim that the purchasing power of the population is running ahead of supply (a statement generally believed to be correct), the Theses ask for conditions to be created that will permit "including in the turnover not only the current purchasing fund but also some of the population's savings." To this

TABLE 9.5

Bulgarian Consumption of Certain Food Items and Consumer Products

Product	Unit of Measure	Scientific Norm	Actual Figure 1970	December [1972] Plenum Goal for 1975	Actual Figure 1975	December [1972] Goal for 1980	Theses [1976] Goal for 1980
Meat and meat products	kg. per capita	80.0	41.4	55.0	57.0	75.0	70.0
Fresh and canned fish	kg. per capita	12.0	5.5	8.0	6.2	10.0	8.0
Milk	liters per capita	260.0	152.0	196.0	174.0	250.0	220.0
Eggs	per capita	265.0	122.0	159.0	145.0	250.0	200.0
Flour	kg. per capita	135.0	170.0	182.0	157.0	150.0	150.0
Vegetable oils	kg. per capita	13.0	12.5	13.9	13.8	14.0	14.0
Sugar and sugar products	kg. per capita	32.0	32.9	37.0	34.0	36.0	36.0
Vegetables	kg. per capita	180.0	89.0	136.0	94.0	160.0	150.0
Fruit	kg. per capita	200.0	148.0	179.0	118.0	200.0	190.0
Cotton fabrics	meters per capita	36.0	22.2	24.7	26.5	33.0	30.0
Wool fabrics	meters per capita	7.0	3.8	4.7	4.9	6.0	6.0
Shoes	pairs per capita	4.0	1.7	2.1	2.1	3.0	2.2
Radio sets	per 100 families	130.0	100.8	104.0	106.9	100.0	130.0
TV sets	per 100 families	105.0	42.0	53.0	60.3	80.0	80.0
Washing machines	per 100 families	70.0	50.0	50.0	50.0	60.0	65.0
Refrigerators	per 100 families	100.0	29.0	59.0	61.0	90.0	90.0
Automobiles	per 100 families	40.0	6.0	13.5	16.0	30.0	26.0

Sources: Bulgarian Communist Party Central Committee, December 1972 Program, and Theses on the Standard of Living, 1976.

end, new opportunities should be created to spend money on "non-market" undertakings such as individual and cooperative housing construction, individual transport, winter sports, trips abroad, and domestic tourism. It seems that, despite the constant propaganda in favor of saving, there is also some concern about the large amounts kept in savings accounts.*

The share of imported goods on the Bulgarian market is to continue to increase, but the target set in the Theses seems to be somewhat lower than that in the December Program. At that time it was said that imported goods accounted for 6 to 8 percent of the total turnover on the domestic market and that this figure should increase to 10 percent in 1973, 15 percent in 1975, and 20 to 25 percent during the 1976-80 period. The Theses say the share of imported goods should be about 20 percent during the 1976-80 period and 25 to 30 percent between then and 1990. No information is available on the actual increase in the share of imported goods, but such imports are known to depend mainly on agreements regarding exchanges of consumer goods among the Comecon countries, and the volume of exchanges under these agreements has been increasing.

HUNGARIAN ANALYSIS OF CONSUMER EXPENDITURES

A survey undertaken by a Budapest university research team in 1976 gives an interesting picture of the expenditures of Hungarian families, which although unique to Hungary is generally indicative of the situation in Eastern Europe.[12] The study team divided family expenditure into five categories: (1) overhead expenses such as rent, heating, electricity, gas, television and radio, and telephone; (2) food, detergents, laundry, cosmetics, and so on; (3) car maintenance, spending on other consumer durables, and purchases on the installment plan; (4) miscellaneous items, such as clothing, cultural activities, and all cash purchases; and (5) savings (mainly intended for later purchases of costly objects such as houses). The percentage breakdown of these categories was as follows:

---

*According to the latest statistics, the number of savings accounts remained relatively stable between 1965 and 1972, only decreasing from 7,985,000 to 7,952,000; the number increased to 8,338,000 in 1973, however, and the amounts on deposit have constantly risen—from 1,494 million leva in 1965 to 3,139 million in 1970, 4,106 million in 1972, and 4,773 million in 1973 (Statisticheski Godishnik [Sofia, 1974], p. 74).

Rent, utilities, radio and television, telephone	20
Food, detergents, cosmetics	42
Cars, consumer durables, installments	7
Miscellaneous cash purchases	15
Savings	16
	100

The team then enumerated the factors that influence decisions on expenditure within individual households, such as price changes, advertising, and installment plan offers. They concluded that many household budgets are strongly influenced by fashion and social prestige, but found that proportional spending varied widely according to type of household. Similar disparities were noted in savings habits: 57 percent of families save regularly, but the proportion of income thus allocated varies from 2 to 18 percent. One interesting finding was that households spend an average of 245 forint a month on impulse buying—largely triggered off by advertising—chiefly of "cultural goods," theater tickets, food delicacies, and so on.

The survey found that 12 percent of the families studied possessed automobiles (this particular figure relates to the year 1972). Some 5 percent of planned expenditure in 1973 was earmarked for the purchase of a car, and the rising trend in car ownership suggests that the proportion of households owning an automobile will grow by 2.3 percent annually. On 31 December 1972, there were 340,202 privately owned vehicles in Hungary, and the figure for 1985 is expected to be 1,250,000—an average yearly increase of 70,000.

The study team found that the family car is a prized possession:

> The presence or absence of a car was a cardinal factor
> in our model [of the Hungarian family], not merely
> because the rate of car buying has accelerated but also
> because the car-owning consumer unit is expanding its
> scope so that its use of leisure, its travel and relaxation
> habits, are changing in both content and quality. As its
> experience widens, the family spends more time together
> and its experiences tend to become collective. All this,
> in our opinion, is leading to the development of closer
> family ties.

The proportion of families owning their houses or apartments is remarkably high, as the following breakdown shows:

Budapest*	32 percent
Towns	62.8 percent
Villages	91.5 percent

---

*Budapest is considered separately because it contains about one-fifth of the country's population, a proportion not approached elsewhere in Eastern Europe.

On 1 January 1974, some 70.8 percent of all households owned, or were engaged in purchasing, their own dwellings, and the average monthly installment payable on this account was 392 forint; average number of "years still to pay" was 13. In 1973, the average monthly rent was 192 forint and in the following year 205 forint. In light of income, however, housing takes a much smaller proportion of family expenditure than is the case in Western countries. The survey found that average monthly income per family was as follows:

Budapest	5,849 forint
Urban areas	4,802 forint
Rural areas	3,573 forint

It also showed that the average Hungarian family's attitudes are similar to those of its counterpart in the mass consumption societies of the West. The desire for home ownership, the importance attributed to the automobile, and the urge to purchase a multiplicity of labor-saving appliances are typical of industrially developed societies everywhere. Unfortunately the report on the survey is too generalized to enable one to discern the obviously important differences between higher- and lower-income families, but it throws considerable light on attitudes toward the control and planning of family spending in Hungary today.

It is doubtful whether the pattern of expenditure and the desire for consumer goods in the rest of Eastern Europe differ significantly from the Hungarian picture presented here. At the same time, however, it must be kept in mind that over the last 15 years Hungary was the only East European state in which the average annual growth rate for consumer goods production exceeded that of producer goods output. Also, as was noted in the case of Bulgaria, real personal income has grown faster than the availability of consumer goods. Despite the concern expressed by the leaders of Eastern Europe to increase the supply of consumer products, priority continues to be given to heavy industry and producer goods. Rising expectations will be difficult to satisfy under these conditions.

NOTES

1. Pravda (Moscow), 25 February 1976.
2. Ibid., 7 March 1976.
3. Rabotnichesko Delo (Sofia), 23 February 1976.
4. Rude Pravo (Prague) Special Supplement, 21 April 1976.
5. Neues Deutschland (East Berlin), 15 January 1976.
6. Karoly Nemeth, "Tasks of Economic Building," Tarsadalmi Szemle (Budapest), November 1975, and "Text of the Fifth Five-Year

Plan of the HPR, 1976-1980, Promulgated by Parliament on 18 December 1975," Nepszabadsag (Budapest), 21 December 1975, Supplement.

7. Piotr Jaroszewicz, report at the seventh Polish party congress on 9 December 1975 (Radio Warsaw domestic service, 9 December 1975).

8. Scinteia (Bucharest), 3 July 1976.

9. See R. N. (Bulgarian Unit), "CC Plenum Decisions on Standard of Living," Bulgarian Background Report/3, Radio Free Europe Research, 2 March 1973.

10. Rabotnichesko Delo, 12 February 1976.

11. On the difficulty of producing enough food items, see Ikonomichesko Zhivot, no. 4, 21 January 1976; and Bulgarian Situation Report/6, Radio Free Europe Research, 3 March 1976, Item 1.

12. The results of the study were published in Mrs. Istvan Hoffmann, "The Structure of Hungarian Household Management," Kozgazdasagi Szemle (Budapest) no. 4, 1976. The survey covered several thousand households and required some three years to complete.

CHAPTER

10

THE CURRENT CRISIS OF
THE CZECHOSLOVAK ECONOMY

Prokop Machan

During 1976, Czechoslovak leaders and the mass media showed increasing concern with the state of the country's economy. Not only was the anxiety economically well founded, but it had an important political dimension as well. Economic difficulties are politically dangerous to the present leadership of Gustav Husak, since his primary claim to acceptability is the ability to maintain a relatively high living standard. After taking over in 1969, the leadership correctly perceived the importance of improved wages and stable prices and concentrated on raising the standard of living as the best means of winning at least passive support for the party. The major targets of the plan that had set an improved standard of living as its main goal were reached. The subsidized prices of basic foodstuffs remained stable, although the supply of some was at times erratic. Supplies of consumer durables improved, but prices were rather high. The housing situation also improved; a record number of apartments were built, and though rents did increase somewhat, they remained low. There were, however, important flaws under the surface.

Widespread political apathy acted as a brake on labor productivity, which was further retarded by production inefficiencies and poor utilization of raw materials. During the 1971-75 plan period, these problems became increasingly apparent. They were mainly attributable to delays in putting new production facilities into operation, unplanned increases in capital investment costs, labor shortages, a steady

This chapter is a shortened and updated version of Prokop Machan, "Czechoslovakia's Economic Difficulties," RAD Background Report/228, Radio Free Europe Research, 5 November 1976.

increase of unsatisfied purchasing power, hidden price hikes, an
unsatisfactory supply structure, and a growing deficit in the foreign
trade balance. The situation deteriorated further in 1974 and 1975
as a consequence of world price increases for energy and raw materials, which, though after some delay, also ultimately affected Comecon
prices. Czechoslovakia's dependence upon imported raw materials
(especially from the Soviet Union) caused the terms of trade for
Czechoslovakia to deteriorate.

WARNING VOICES AND CRITICAL
ASSESSMENTS

In January 1975, the noted Czechoslovak economist Josef Goldmann[1] criticized certain phenomena in the economy and described
past "inertial trends" whose persistence involved serious risks for
the future, particularly in the sector of external economic relations.
He criticized delays in the introduction of new products and claimed
that their inadequate range and unsatisfactory composition had resulted
in a decrease in export effectiveness, and this was coupled with a
growing demand for imports of raw and semifinished materials.
Goldmann stated that the combined effect might be a chronically
unfavorable balance of payments, which could leave the economy
unstable and vulnerable, and even a relatively minor occurrence—
such as a bad harvest or the loss of a small trade outlet abroad—could
make it more difficult to import essential raw materials, food, and
machinery. The second bottleneck, according to Goldmann, was
manpower, and the replacement of old facilities posed additional
serious problems. He also noted that the fuel-energy balance might
become a barrier to further economic growth.

A year later Goldmann reiterated his warning, pointing out that
despite a considerable decline in the growth of the labor force, the
rate of increase in new production capacities remained approximately
the same. He cautioned against further increases in the rate of
investment in new facilities, predicting that such investments would
not only be wasteful but would also disrupt the stability of the economy
and hamper its development.[2] Other economists voiced similar concern.[3]

Although top party and state officials have criticized shortcomings
in the economy frequently in the past, their statements have begun to
be marked by increased frankness. The turning point seems to have
been the 15th CPCS congress in April 1976, when CPCS Secretary-
General Husak devoted a large part of his report to the economic
situation. He warned that extensive sources of economic growth,
such as labor reserves and the possibilities of added capital construc-

tion, were practically exhausted, and that the economy would have to rely increasingly on intensive growth factors—primarily higher labor productivity, better use of working hours, a higher shift coefficient, and improved labor morale.[4] CPCS Presidium member and federal Premier Lubomir Strougal, who delivered the economic report at the congress, also insisted that the economy must develop greater efficiency.[5]

A CPCS CC plenum in September 1976 revealed that the economic difficulties were increasing. The main agricultural crops had been adversely affected by the summer's drought, and in his report to the plenum Strougal linked the sorry state of the engineering industry to the poor harvest, warning that Czechoslovakia would have to spend "several thousand million crowns for agricultural imports, primarily from capitalist countries." He admitted indirectly that the engineering industry was not efficient or competitive enough to provide the necessary funds by increasing exports to the West.[6] In October 1976, Presidium member Antonin Kapek called the engineering industry the country's major source of foreign currency and a primary factor in safeguarding the standard of living. He deplored the fact that Czechoslovakia's share in worldwide trade in engineering products was declining, adding that this situation posed a danger to the future of the country. The causes are known, said Kapek: low engineering standards, low labor productivity, slow response to changing world market needs, and high production costs.[7]

The energy situation was also the subject of criticism. In September 1976, CPCS Presidium member and CC Secretary Josef Kempny spoke about the critical situation in regard to energy and power supplies, and criticized the fact that some plants had not been put into operation and others had fallen short of rated capacity.[8] The first restrictive measures for industrial as well as private users of electricity were introduced shortly afterward.[9]

These economic troubles could not fail to affect the standard of living, and the first signs of their impact began to appear. In October Strougal admitted that the demand for meat could not be met, that agricultural reserves would have to be mobilized in the coming months, and that the population would have to show understanding for temporary supply difficulties in some places. He attributed the shortage to the growing needs of the population, and added that to import meat in sufficient quantity to meet domestic demand would cost the state treasury more than 1 billion Koruna (Kcs).[10] Also in October the price of potatoes for winter storage was increased by 130 percent over the price that had been in effect for ten years, and to prevent hoarding no family was permitted to buy more than 50 kilograms per head for winter storage.[11] The price hike came into force less than two months after Husak's speech at the harvest festival in Nitra, in

which he announced that food prices would remain stable and said
there was no reason for "unnecessary panic over increased food
costs."[12]

FACTORS BEHIND HIGH PRODUCTION COSTS
AND LOW PRODUCTIVITY

One of the primary aims of Czechoslovak economic policy under
Husak was to reach a high degree of stability in growth rates. This
was achieved in a relatively short period of time, thanks to a relatively stable volume of capital investments.[13] At the same time,
however, in 1970 the rate of growth in nonlabor production inputs
began to exceed that of produced national income (output), as can be
seen from Table 10.1.

In 1968, 1969, 1974, and 1975, the GNP and national income
growth rates were higher than those of nonlabor production inputs,
but in the other years nonlabor input was higher than output, and
economic efficiency declined. The report on the development of the
economy in 1971-75[14] showed the same tendency (although the figures
differ slightly from those in Statisticka Rocenka CSSR 1975). It did,
however, explicitly state that "national income was produced with a
higher consumption of raw and other materials than had been assumed,"
and admitted that in the fifth five-year plan the growth rate of nonlabor inputs had exceeded that of the GNP and also that of produced
national income, and thus production costs were rising.

Another factor in the declining efficiency of the economy was
the slow increase in labor productivity during the 1971-75 plan period.

TABLE 10.1

Growth Rates of GNP, National Income, and
Nonlabor Production Inputs in CSSR, 1967-75
(in constant prices as of 1 January 1967; increase
in percent as compared with previous year)

National Accounts	1968	1969	1970	1971	1972	1973	1974	1975
GNP	6.6	5.4	7.7	5.8	6.3	5.5	5.4	5.7
National income	7.2	7.3	5.7	5.5	5.7	5.2	5.9	6.2
Nonlabor produc- tion inputs	6.2	4.1	9.1	6.0	6.7	5.7	5.1	5.3

Note: The figures for 1975 are preliminary.
Source: Statisticka Rocenka CSSR 1976, p. 157.

TABLE 10.2

Share of Labor Productivity in Production
Increase, 1971-75
(in percent)

Economic Sector	1971	1972	1973	1974	1975
Industry	94	91	88	88	88
Building construction	76	75	70	78	79

Sources: For industry, Statisticke Prehledy (Prague) no. 7,
July 1976; for building construction, Finance a Uver (Prague) no. 5,
May 1974 (1971-73) and Rude Pravo (Prague), 28 January 1975 and
27 January 1976.

According to the law on the plan,[15] increased labor productivity should
have been responsible for about 95 percent of the increase in national
income, but in fact it lagged behind the plan, as can be seen from
Table 10.2.

In view of the annual figures, it is surprising to find that labor
productivity was responsible for 93.3 percent of the increase in
national income, as was stated in the report on fulfillment of the
plan.[16] The report showed that labor productivity was responsible
for only 90 percent of the increase in industrial production, and for
only 78 percent of that in the building industry in the period between
1971 and 1975. The higher figure may be explained by higher productivity rates in other economic sectors, particularly that of agriculture.
The situation improved slightly in 1976, according to the report on
fulfillment of the state plan; the figures for industry and building construction were 90 and 85 percent, respectively.[17]

Another factor that added to the cost of production was ineffective
use of fixed capital assets, chiefly machinery and equipment. In
1971, the Federal Statistical Office carried out an investigation in a
large number of industrial enterprises and found that in 205,000
places of work machinery and equipment were not being used for
30 percent of the time in the main shift and 70 percent in other shifts.[18]
The nadir in this respect was reached in the engineering sector. With
this study used as a basis, it has been estimated that there were about
150,000 unmanned machines during the first shift in the processing
industry (excluding metallurgy and the chemical industry). Between
1960 and 1971, the utilization rate decreased considerably: In heavy
and general engineering, it fell from 60 and 54.9 percent, respectively,
to about 46.9 percent; in the consumer goods industry, the corres-

ponding figures were 58.9 and 50 percent, and in the food industry
54.2 and 51.9 percent. The actual number of hours during which
such equipment was in use was lower than in any other Comecon country.

The loss resulting from inadequate usage of capital goods is
enormous. According to Zdenek Karpisek, an official in the federal
ministry of Labor and Social Welfare, every percentage point decrease
in utilization means a drop of 1 percent in labor productivity and 1
percent in production, and over industry as a whole this represents
a loss of gross output amounting to 4 billion Kcs annually.[19] The
decrease in utilization of machinery and equipment is also an important factor in higher production costs.

Better utilization of capital investments is connected with the
shift coefficient. The shift rate is the average number of shifts worked,
and its coefficient—that is, the total number of workers in all shifts
divided by the number in the main shift—indicates the distribution of
manpower. Until 1962, the shift coefficient increased steadily,
reaching its maximum of 1.409 in that year, and of the total number
of working days 70.9 percent were worked in the main (first) shift.
The respective figures for the second and third shifts were 22 and
7.1 percent.[20] Since 1962, however, the shift coefficient has been
falling, and even the strenuous efforts of the authorities to reverse
the trend in the 1971-75 plan period were unsuccessful.

It has been admitted that one of the reasons for this unfavorable
development was lack of courage to discontinue technically obsolete
production programs, which would permit more efficient use of the
labor force in the second shifts in modern plants.[21] The labor shortage has made it increasingly difficult to man the second and third
shifts, and the degree to which the efforts of the authorities to stop
the decrease failed can be seen in Table 10.3.

The decreased utilization of machinery and equipment caused
by the decline in second- and third-shift work represents a considerable economic loss. It was admitted that a decrease of 0.05 points
in the shift coefficient would require additional investments in machine
assets amounting to 8 billion Kcs.[22]

The sociopolitical aspect of production—its organization and
management and the approach of workers to their tasks—plays an
important role in achieving production efficiency. The purges of
1969 and 1970 resulted in the dismissal of a good number of qualified
management cadres, and, in addition, many specialists left the
country. They were replaced in many cases by less experienced and
less well-qualified people. Labor morale is a major source of concern. Hardly a day passes without a mention in the press or on the
air of time lost through absenteeism, an indirect index of labor discipline. According to a spokesman for the Czech Ministry of Labor

TABLE 10.3

Shift Rate and Labor Distribution in
Industrial Enterprises

Shift Rate and Labor Distribution	1965	1970	1971	1972	1973	1974	1975
Shift coefficient	1.384	1.351	1.343	1.337	1.333	1.329	1.325
Percent of total number of working days:							
First shift	72.3	74.0	74.5	74.8	75.0	75.3	75.5
Second shift	21.1	19.9	19.5	19.4	19.2	18.9	18.7
Third shift	6.6	6.1	6.0	5.8	5.8	5.8	5.8

Sources: Statisticka Rocenka CSSR (Prague, 1973, 1975, and 1976).

and Social Welfare, roughly 100 million working hours are lost annually in the Czech Socialist Republic alone because people attend to their private affairs during working hours.[23]

The amount of absenteeism because of illness and accident, however, decreased during the 1971-75 plan compared to 1970, although the record in the first eight months of 1976 was less favorable.[24] A rather large percentage of this absenteeism can be put down to malingering. In 1975, more than 9,000 violations of sick-pay regulations were uncovered in the Central Bohemian region alone.[25] A check carried out one Friday between 11 A.M. and 12 noon revealed that out of a total of 1,190 persons leaving big cities for the weekend, 824 had left their places of work illicitly under various pretexts or were "sick."[26]

The authorities seem to have had little success in preventing such behavior. It has been repeatedly admitted that negative attitudes and even opposition to work have not been overcome, that there still exist those who are "irresponsible and lack discipline."[27]

DIFFICULTIES WITH INVESTMENT, MANPOWER, AND RAW MATERIALS

Despite its high degree of industrialization, Czechoslovakia spent huge sums on investments in the 1971-75 five-year period. According to the report on economic development in the fifth five-year plan,[28]

the total amounted to 606,200 million Kcs, of which 373,900 million
Kcs went on construction and 232,300 million on machinery and equipment. While this policy in itself is not unsound, the investment in
construction was of an extensive rather than an intensive character.
It was oriented mainly toward the construction of new production
facilities and the expansion of existing enterprises rather than modernization and rationalization. Moreover, the new or reconstructed
enterprises frequently did not correspond to the plan or meet world
standards, and as a result the process of substituting capital for labor
did not proceed rapidly enough.[29]

During the period 1971-75, another trend became visible in
Czechoslovak investment policy—an increase in the investment rate.
In 1970 and 1971, this amounted to 5.9 and 5.7 percent, respectively,
but it increased to 8.7 percent in 1972 and in the following two years
the figures were 9.2 and 9.3 percent. In 1975 the investment rate
slightly declined, to 8.3 percent[30]—still relatively high, given Goldmann's opinion that the volume of gross investments should rise by
approximately 5 percent annually.[31]

The problem of investments is the more delicate since, in the
five-year period 1971-75, new production facilities were put into
operation only with considerable delay and their costs exceeded the
planned estimates. Too many projects were under construction, and
the investment resources were too widely dispersed. Several important projects could not be finished, and it was necessary to continue
their construction to the sixth five-year plan. This was especially
true of the power industry, where, according to the plan, 3,700
megawatts (MW) of new generating capacities should have gone into
operation in the 1971-75 period. This target was not met: Newly
installed capacity amounted to 2,850 MW, and the actual utilized
capacity reached only 2,500 MW, owing to poor quality of fuel, low
operation levels, and so on.[32]

Shortcomings in investment in building facilities were a subject
of frequent criticism in Czechoslovak news media. Lack of efficiency
in investments was revealed by a check carried out in 1975 in 24
important construction projects. The rated output was not attained
by 22 of these projects, 21 did not reach various planned production
indexes, and in several cases the planned prime costs per production
unit were exceeded and the planned profit was not achieved.[33] The
excessive number of projects begun, the rise in construction expenditures, deviations from set production indexes, and other shortcomings
were criticized in a Radio Prague broadcast,[34] in which it was also
admitted that in 1975, there were important projects that failed to
go into operation.

Apparently, investment projects are not delayed primarily by a
lack of capital, although huge amounts are tied up owing to the length

of time it takes to complete their construction and the fact that too many are under construction at any one time. The weak spots are inadequate building capacities, a shortage of qualified workers, the general shortage of manpower, poor preproject preparation, and the failure of suppliers to deliver blueprints and specifications, raw materials, and machinery and other equipment on time.

Another major factor that limits economic development is the deceleration in the growth rate of the labor force. This point was made by, among others, Josef Goldmann,[35] who described it as a threat to future economic growth. Deputy Minister of Labor and Social Welfare Premysl Tomasek also said that the size of the labor force was one of the "limiting factors in the sixth five-year plan" and that by 1980 it was expected to increase by only 180,000 persons over the 1975 figure. The prospect for the seventh five-year plan (1981-85) was even less favorable; the expected increase will amount only to some 100,000. This represents a considerable drop from past figures. Some transfers from the agricultural sector can be expected, but the rate of shift is decelerating. In addition, larger numbers of workers are needed in the service and infrastructure sectors.[36]

Between 1971 and 1975, the practice of redistributing manpower among economic sectors continued. The share of the primary sector (agriculture and forestry) declined from 18 percent in 1970 to 15 percent in 1975, while that of the secondary (industry and construction) and tertiary (service) sectors increased—from 47 to 48 percent and from 35 to 37 percent, respectively.[37] Thus the ratio of workers in the production sphere continued to diminish, from 78.2 percent in 1970 to about 77.5 percent in 1975 (preliminary figures), and it can be expected that redistribution will continue at the same pace during the 1976-80 five-year plan and in the following years. The future increments to the labor force will be so small, however, that competition for workers between the production and nonproduction spheres is bound to arise. The redistribution of labor from agriculture to industry will be far less extensive than in the past, and already the labor situation has become so tight that prospective retirees are encouraged to continue working beyond retirement age.

Since 1948, the number of workers has risen at a much faster rate than the population. This was achieved by employing "free manpower," chiefly women who had previously remained at home. This source is now virtually exhausted, and the current extremely high employment rate among women may even decline slightly. Another important source of manpower was the population in the "postproductive age"—men over 60 and women over 55. This source seems also to have been largely exhausted, because between 1970 and 1975 their numbers declined from 625,000 to 607,000.[38] It is doubtful whether their number can be increased significantly by additional material incentives to continue or return to work, and since the number of young people attending institutes of higher education will have to rise in order to keep pace with scientific-technological progress, the shortage of manpower indeed seems to be a critical problem.

There are still "invisible" reserves of manpower in the economy, however. Although the CSSR's per capita industrial output equals that of the advanced industrial countries, its industry uses 20–25 percent more labor than they do. In addition, the slack in industrial working time runs as high as 25 percent.[39] Thus it will be necessary to exercise strict economy in the use of available manpower in the years ahead.[40]

Another problem is that the consumption of raw materials and energy in the creation of national income is much too high. To create the same value of gross national product, Czechoslovakia needs between 1.5 and 2 times as much energy and steel as the "capitalist" countries in Western Europe.[41] A comparison with neighboring socialist countries (the GDR, Poland, the USSR, and Hungary) is also unfavorable: In 1970, the CSSR had the highest rate of energy and steel consumption for the creation of the same unit of GNP. This is the result of the restructuring of the Czechoslovak economy in favor of heavy industry that has been going on since the early 1950s. Product designs requiring large quantities of raw materials also are a contributing factor. Between 1950 and 1970, the number of branches consuming large quantities of energy rose from 30.0 percent to 33.6 percent (but the figure has remained at roughly this level since).[42] Among the consequences is the fact that despite its long tradition in the automobile industry the CSSR imports a large number of cars from the USSR but exports to that country rolling mill equipment whose production requires large quantities of energy and raw materials.

The situation has become especially serious in the last two years. The Czechoslovak economy now depends to a great degree on raw material imports. There are domestic reserves of coal, lignite, uranium, and wood, but other materials such as high-grade fuels, iron ore, and nonferrous metals must be imported in ever growing quantities. As a result of world price increases and the consequent increase in Comecon prices, Czechoslovakia has to pay considerably more for its huge imports of Soviet raw materials. At the same time, the Soviets are no longer able or willing to meet in toto the CSSR's raw material requirements, and thus the latter must turn to nonsocialist markets, where raw materials are for the moment even more expensive. (And the Soviet Union's requirement that its Comecon partners prepay future deliveries of raw materials with investments in the development of resources in the USSR has not helped to ease the growing economic pressure on Czechoslovakia.)

Only negligible quantities of crude oil and natural gas are extracted domestically in the CSSR. The prime domestic sources of fuel and energy are coal and lignite. The "mixture" generally used to generate electricity consists of more than 20 percent hard coal, 70 percent brown coal and lignite, about 6.5 percent liquid hydrocarbons, and about 2 percent gaseous fuels. Although the amount of electricity generated has increased in the past few years, as noted earlier the size of the increase has been insufficient to meet domestic needs.[43]

THE FOREIGN TRADE PICTURE

Given its limited raw material base, high degree of industrialization, relatively narrow domestic market, and present production structure, the Czechoslovak economy is heavily dependent on foreign trade. It has been estimated that in the 1960s the share of imports represented about 13 percent of the national income, and that by 1970 this ratio had risen to about 16 percent.[44] Consequently, per capita exports were also relatively high. This dependence on foreign trade increased in the last five-year plan period, and with the advance of industrialization it will continue to rise. In fact, the vulnerability of the CSSR's economy to changing external conditions has increased substantially in the last few years.

The commodity structure shows that imports of fuels and raw and semiprocessed materials are of crucial importance. During the 1960s, their share of total Czechoslovak imports declined (from 53 percent in 1960 to 44.4 percent in 1969), but in the 1970s it began to rise, going from 43.1 percent in 1970 to about 46.7 percent in 1975.[45] In exports, the percentage share of this commodity group varied only slightly. In the 1950s and 1960s, Czechoslovakia was able to procure hard currency with which to pay for its imports of raw materials by increasing its exports of machinery and equipment, whose share of total exports rose from 45.1 percent in 1960 to 50.9 percent in 1969. In the 1970s, however, exports of machinery and equipment declined, falling to 46.6 percent in 1974, and there was only a slight increase in 1975, to 48 percent.[46] The decline in exports of machinery and equipment demonstrates the inability of this sector to adapt to changing conditions not only on world markets but also on Comecon markets.[47]

Similar difficulties with exports can also be seen in the industrial consumer goods sector. Their share of total exports changed almost not at all during the 1971–75 period; it was 18.0 percent in 1971 and 18.1 percent in 1975.[48] Imports of foodstuffs, including raw materials and semifinished products declined from 14.8 percent of total imports in 1970 to 9.4 percent in 1975, but the poor harvest in 1976 will tend to reverse this trend.

The 1971-75 period was marked by a steady worsening of the foreign trade balance. Since 1973, the trade surpluses registered in Group I commodities (machinery, equipment, tools) have not been sufficient to cover the deficits incurred by trade in commodities of Group II (fuels, raw and semiprocessed materials), and recently Czechoslovakia's foreign trade deficit has been increasing. Table 10.4 gives the picture.

Although the Czechoslovak authorities frequently point out the necessity to reduce the foreign trade deficit by increasing both production efficiency and exports, the tendency of imports to exceed exports seems to continue. In 1975, although exports grew faster than imports in trade with socialist countries, in relations with the "capitalist" states the volume of exports was lower and imports had increased.[49]

The deteriorating foreign trade balance affects the balance of payments and represents a potentially restrictive factor so far as the economy is concerned. Rising debt-servicing charges may lead to limiting imports of the raw materials needed by industry and other economic sectors and of machines and equipment designed to ensure higher productivity, improved efficiency of production, and higher competitiveness on foreign markets. In mid-1976, Prague did its first major borrowing from the West—a $60 million syndicated Euromarket loan,[50] and several months later a West German banking consortium arranged a $200 million credit for the Czechoslovak Foreign Trade Bank.[51] This will undoubtedly help the CSSR to meet its present difficulties, but it is hardly a substitute for long-term improvement.

It would be easy to blame external economic conditions for the CSSR's present economic troubles, to point to the growing competition it is facing on world markets or to the more difficult conditions under which its economy is operating. Changing external conditions obviously do affect the country's economy, but internal problems are at fault as well. The increase in the prices of raw materials on both world and Comecon markets have had a major impact. In 1973 and 1974, however, more than 74 percent of the increase in import prices could be covered by an increase in the prices of Czechoslovakia's exports. Other economies have also been affected by rising raw material costs.[52] Increased competition on world markets, however, necessitates higher standards of quality, better servicing, and prompt deliveries of spare parts. Not only are the CSSR's "capitalist" trade partners becoming more exigent in this respect, but so are its Comecon partners—particularly the Soviet Union. As long ago as 1972, Foreign Trade Minister Andrej Barcak was urging enterprise managers

TABLE 10.4

Czechoslovak Net Foreign Trade Balance,
1971-75
(in million Kcs)

Year	Total	Socialist Countries	Industrially Advanced Countries	Developing Countries
1971	+1,225	+1,039	-1,052	+1,238
1972	+1,676	+1,568	- 809	+ 917
1973	- 483	+ 568	-1,376	+ 325
1974	-2,761	- 799	-2,300	+ 338
1975	-4,065	-2,021	-3,244	+1,200

Source: Calculated on the basis of import and export figures
in Statisticka Rocenka CSSR 1976, p. 428.

to improve the quality of exported goods. He pointed out among other things that in the future Czechoslovakia would be able to export only products of top quality to the USSR.[53] It was easier to sell machines and equipment in the 1950s and 1960s, when demand seemed unlimited and most of the CSSR's Comecon partners were on a much lower level of industrialization. The situation in this respect has changed, however.

Domestic factors operating in the Czechoslovak economy and several built-in limitations are also responsible for the country's economic troubles. The Czechoslovak economy has developed in an extensive rather than in an intensive manner. Several "traditional" weak spots—for example, inefficient production, increased costs of capital investment, poor-quality products—have long hampered economic expansion, but their impact became more evident when changes in external conditions prompted foreign customers to be more stringent in their requirements. The inefficient production sketched earlier might be corrected by appropriate internal measures such as adequate economic stimuli and other steps designed to encourage greater cooperation from workers. But the limiting factors originating mainly in difficulties with modernization and rationalization of production capacities, in the shortage of manpower and lack of adequate supplies of raw materials, and in the worsening of Czechoslovakia's trade balance and terms of trade, especially in relations with "capitalist" countries, are even more serious barriers to future development. The CSSR needs top-standard equipment, which, in great measure, only "capitalist" countries are able to deliver, but it is increasingly difficult to buy such equipment in the West in view of the CSSR's increasing deterioration in trade relations with "capitalist" countries.

Thus the present situation is a vicious circle from which it is difficult to escape. Finding an adequate and rapid solution to all contemporary ills in the economic sector poses a serious challenge to Husak. If little improvement takes place, the standard of living— the one success of the leadership's normalization policy—is bound to suffer, and this will have both political and social repercussions. Unfortunately for the leaders and the Czechoslovak population, the room for economic maneuvering today is considerably smaller than it was in the big economic crisis of the early 1960s.

NOTES

1. Josef Goldmann, "The Czechoslovak Economy in the 1970s," Politicka Ekonomie (Prague), no. 1, January 1975. See Czechoslovak Situation Report/8, Radio Free Europe Research, 26 February 1975, Item 2; and Thomas E. Heneghan, "Czechoslovakia: The Economic Discussion Continues," RAD Background Report/51, Radio Free Europe Research, 19 March 1975, pp. 18-21.

2. Hospodarske Noviny (Prague), nos. 2, 3, and 4 (9, 16, and 23 January 1976), and Czechoslovak Economic Papers, no. 16 (Prague, 1976), pp. 7-18.

3. For example, Ruzena Vintrova in Politicka Ekonomie, no. 4, April 1976.

4. Rude Pravo (Prague), 13 April 1976. See Czechoslovak Situation Report/14, Radio Free Europe Research, 10 April 1976.

5. Rude Pravo, 14 April 1976. See Czechoslovak Situation Report/15, Radio Free Europe Research, 14 April 1976, Item 1.

6. Rude Pravo, 15 September 1976. See Czechoslovak Situation Report/38, Radio Free Europe Research, 22 September 1976, Item 1.

7. Rude Pravo, 5 October 1976.

8. Czechoslovak Television, 4 September 1976.

9. Vecerni Praha (Prague), 28 September 1976, and Radio Prague, 30 September 1976.

10. Czechoslovak Television, 6 October 1976; see also Czechoslovak Situation Report/41, Radio Free Europe Research, 14 September 1976, Item 2.

11. Rude Pravo, 12 October 1976.

12. Ibid., 30 August 1976.

13. Goldmann, op. cit.

14. Statisticke Prehledy (Prague), no. 7, July 1976, p. 193.

15. Collection of Laws, no. 101/1971.

16. Statisticke Prehledy, no. 7, July 1976.

17. Rude Pravo, 27 January 1977.

18. Planovane Hospodarstvi (Prague), no. 3, March 1973.

19. Ibid.

20. Statisticka Rocenka CSSR (Prague), 1966, p. 222.

21. Rude Pravo, 6 February 1975.

22. Planovane Hospodarstvi, no. 3, March 1973.

23. Czechoslovak Television and Radio Prague, 10 March 1975.

24. Zdravotnicke Noviny (Prague), no. 35, 26 August 1976, and Radio Prague, 10 October 1976.

25. Radio Prague, 12 July 1976.

26. Radio Hvezda, 24 June 1976.

27. Rude Pravo, 21 July 1976.

28. Statisticke Prehledy, no. 7, July 1976, p. 195.

29. See also Goldmann, op. cit.

30. Calculated on the basis of constant prices as of 1 January 1967 published in Statisticka Rocenka CSSR 1976, p. 194.

31. Czechoslovak Economic Papers, no. 16, 1976.

32. Svet Hospodarstvi (Prague), no. 33, 18 March 1976.

33. Radio Prague, 7 November 1975.

34. 18 July 1976.

35. In Goldmann, op. cit.

36. Czechoslovak Television, 7 March 1976.

37. For details see Planovane Hospodarstvi, no. 4, April 1976.

38. Statisticke Prehledy, no. 7, July 1976.

39. Planovane Hospodarstvi, no. 2, February 1975.

40. For details on the shortage of manpower, see Czechoslovak Situation Reports/14 and 22, Radio Free Europe Research, 10 April and 2 June 1976, Items 2 and 1, respectively.

41. Politicka Ekonomie, no. 4, April 1976. Planovane Hospodarstvi (no. 1, January 1975) admitted that in Western European "capitalist" countries energy consumption per unit of national income was only 52-75 percent of that needed by the Czechoslovak economy.

42. Planovane Hospodarstvi, no. 2, February 1976.

43. Revue Prumyslu, Obchodu, Hospodarstvi (Prague), no. 4, April 1976. For details on power problems see Czechoslovak Situation Report/34, Radio Free Europe Research, 25 August 1976, Item 1; on the regime's efforts to increase the output of coal see Czechoslovak Situation Report/40, Radio Free Europe Research, 6 October 1976, Item 1.

44. Oesterreichische Osthefte (Vienna), no. 2, 1975.

45. Statisticka Rocenka CSSR, 1973, p. 420, and Czechoslovak Foreign Trade (Prague), no. 3, March 1976.

46. Statisticka Rocenka CSSR, 1973 and 1976, pp. 419 and 440 respectively.

47. Goldmann, op. cit.

48. Czechoslovak Foreign Trade, no. 3, March 1976; for details on foreign trade commodity structure in 1971–75, see Czechoslovak Situation Report/23, Radio Free Europe Research, 9 June 1976, Item 1.

49. Radio Prague, 11 October 1976.

50. Journal of Commerce (New York), 18 March 1976.

51. According to a dpa dispatch dated 1 October 1976.

52. Revue Prumyslu, Obchodu, Hospodarstvi, no. 1, January 1976.

53. Nova Svoboda (Ostrava), 18 October 1972.

11

YUGOSLAV MEASURES TO COPE WITH THE WORLD RECESSION AND INTERNAL ECONOMIC DEVELOPMENT

Zdenko Antic

One can say without exaggeration that the outstanding feature of Yugoslavia's internal situation during the early 1970s was an increasing trend toward economic, social, and political instability. First, as a developing country changing rapidly from a rural-agricultural to an urban-industrial society, at the beginning of the decade, Yugoslavia had to cope with a huge exodus of labor from rural into urban areas. The situation was complicated by the fact that many of those who left the countryside were unable to find suitable employment in urban industry, and even less in the service sector or administration. Unemployment had already become a problem in the mid-1960s, when Yugoslavia decided to introduce measures designed to create a more profit-oriented economy and a more rapid entry into the world market. A number of enterprises and even entire branches of the economy released part of the so-called labor surplus in order to "rationalize" the labor force and achieve greater labor productivity, and, accordingly, during the decade from 1964 to 1974, the number of unemployed doubled to nearly 500,000 persons, or about 11 percent of the total labor force.[1] The number would certainly have been even higher had the authorities not permitted Yugoslav citizens to seek work outside the country, with the result that about 1 million became guest workers (Gastarbeiter) in West European countries.[2]

Economic development was also strongly affected by the rapid change in the socioeconomic system. The economic reform not only

This chapter is a revised and updated version of the following Radio Free Europe Research reports by Zdenko Antic: "Yugoslavia on the Way to Economic Recovery," RAD Background Report/229, 9 November 1976, and "Yugoslavia Confronted with Return of Gastarbeiter," RAD Background Report/89, 15 April 1976.

introduced completely new business and earning practices, which
took time to learn properly, but brought with it a number of problems,
all of which had been inherent in the old economic system. The
architects of the Yugoslav economic reform were well aware of the
need for it, and the resolution on socialist transformation in Yugoslavia adopted at the ninth LCY congress in March 1969 listed those
factors and instruments that would have to be changed.[3] It stressed
particularly the need to reform (1) the general investment fund or
the so-called state capital, which was the main channel through which
investments were financed; (2) the banking system, which involved
decentralizing the big Belgrade commercial banks; (3) the state-
controlled foreign currency system, which redirected the greatest
part of the foreign currency earned by enterprises; and (4) the manner
in which the federal budget was financed, by decreasing the direct
burden on the economy. Further development, "strengthening of
the material basis of the self-management system, limitation of
administrative interference," and development of the market instruments were also urged.[4]

It was no wonder, however, that the discussion over dismantling
the instruments of the old economic system and the forms and functioning of the new one rekindled old antagonisms and conflicts of
interest among Yugoslavia's nations, republics, and regions. It was
therefore no accident that the questions of "state capital," "Belgrade
banks," "foreign currency," and "financing underdeveloped regions"
were the very essence of the political confrontation between Zagreb
and Belgrade, Yugoslavia's two biggest financial centers; between
Croatia and Serbia, Yugoslavia's most influential republics; and between the developed north and the underdeveloped center and south.
At stake was the redistribution of the nation's wealth, and those who
were privileged under the old system (Belgrade and the underdeveloped
regions) obstinately defended their positions, while those who were
expecting to receive more urged immediate change. The national
sentiments that pervaded the country during 1970-71 were at first
mobilized in support of the republican leaderships, but they threatened
to become uncontrollable, and the political stalemate made any decision impossible.

Therefore, Tito's purges of the party and state leaderships of
Croatia in December 1971 and of Serbia in October 1972 were not
only directed against the rising nationalism of Yugoslavia's two
largest republics; they were also aimed at reshaping the national
leadership on the basis of a new consensus, in order to make it
capable of implementing the economic and social policies adopted at
the ninth party congress.

As the period of instability, at least in the political sphere, was
approaching its end, the famous letter to all LCY members issued in

October 1972 and signed by Tito and CC Executive Committee Secretary Stane Dolanc again drew attention to the urgent problems in the country's economy.[5] The letter called for transformation of the LCY into an organization of revolutionary action that would take the lead in the country's life and, at the same time, stressed "the need to reaffirm the principles underlying economic and social reform, market economy, and a system of deliberately planned direction of economic and social trends."

The accent the letter placed on the need to solve the outstanding economic problems was fully justified, since the situation of the economy as a whole was a gloomy one indeed. The letter did not mince words in listing the most urgent problems:

> In stabilizing the economy we are confronted with end-
> less obstacles. There is no sign of any change in the
> usual behavior [of enterprises]. Illiquidity still exerts
> pressure on the economy. The number of enterprises
> working at a loss is increasing. There are a lot of
> [not fully funded] investments. Sociopolitical communi-
> ties have not settled their obligations toward the economy,
> and the budgetary surplus was not returned. The solu-
> tion to our present difficulties is still seen to be increasing
> prices.

Given this unsatisfactory state of affairs, it was natural that the world economic crisis should have a deleterious effect on the situation in Yugoslavia. This negative influence began to be felt in 1974, and the year ended badly, particularly in regard to foreign trade, price stability, and the standard of living, while unemployment reached a new peak. Nevertheless, the economy as a whole continued to develop; the GNP rose, as anticipated, by 7 percent, and industrial productivity was 5 percent over the 1973 level.[6] The agricultural sector chalked up a record harvest, which had a beneficial effect on economic development. On the other hand, the trade deficit amounted to $3,735,000,000, and despite a high inflow of foreign currency attributable to invisible earnings, the 1974 balance-of-payments deficit was $1,310,000,000. By the end of the year the annual rate of inflation was 26 percent, and the number of unemployed neared the half-million mark.

These negative trends continued during 1975. The trade deficit amounted to $3,624,000,000,[7] but invisible earnings contributed largely to the reduction of Yugoslavia's adverse balance of payments, which fell from $1,310,000,000 in 1974 to $950 million—a real achievement in a year characterized by economic recession. Inflation reached a new peak in May, when the annual rate was about 30 percent, but, by the end of the year, it had dropped to about 17 percent. The number

of unemployed, however, continued to expand, and by the end of the
year was close to 600,000.[8]

Indicators published at the end of 1975 suggested one or two
positive developments, however, particularly in foreign trade and
in the drive against inflation. The world was on the way to economic
recovery, and this had a beneficial effect on Yugoslavia's domestic
development. Nevertheless, anticyclical measures introduced in
Yugoslavia during the 1974-75 period also brought about a change
for the better. A number of such measures were announced at the
10th party congress in May 1974, and a resolution on economic stabilization listed a series of specific goals that would have to be reached
if economic stabilization was to be achieved.[9] Although the resolution
stressed the need for more planning, particularly in the sphere of
investments, it also announced introduction of decentralizing measures
transferring a number of economic activities from the state to autonomous economic institutions. The resolution also called for more
effective penetration of the world market.

EMPLOYMENT POLICY AND THE PROBLEM
OF THE GASTARBEITER

A separate resolution adopted at the 10th congress outlined
measures to decrease the number of unemployed and the number of
citizens looking for work outside the country and to promote the
gradual return of those temporarily employed abroad. Thus employment and the absorption of returning Gastarbeiter from Western
Europe became priority number one in 1974-75.

During the 1960s, rising unemployment, an unwanted byproduct
of the profound economic reform measures passed, and the traditional
migration of labor from rural to urban areas were both effectively
offset by Yugoslavia's policy of permitting unlimited "export" of its
manpower. The number of unemployed during the late 1960s would
have been much higher had the authorities not agreed to permit the
"labor surplus" to seek employment in Western Europe. Initially,
this migration of labor was barely tolerated. Later, it was officially
organized and channeled through Yugoslav and Western labor offices.
Although in the beginning there were no precise statistical data available on the number of workers who had left the country to seek employment abroad, by the end of the 1960s it was estimated that about
150,000 workers were doing so annually.[10] The first official data
were provided by the census of 31 March 1971, which revealed that
at the beginning of that year there were 671,908 Yugoslavs temporarily employed in Western countries, but the number continued to grow,
reaching its peak of about 1 million by the end of 1973.[11] On the

basis of figures for the end of 1974, the largest number of Gastarbeiter were in West Germany (540,000) and Austria (170,000), which
together accounted for over two-thirds of the total. Large numbers
were also in France, Sweden, Switzerland, and other Common Market
countries.

This massive exodus of labor (equal to about 20 percent of those
employed at home) had many positive effects on the Yugoslav economy.
During the period of economic reform it helped absorb the growing
labor surplus. Those workers who later returned home used their
savings to build small family houses, introduced new farm machinery,
or expanded their own small workshops. In addition, from 1971 to
1975, Yugoslavs employed abroad sent home over $1 billion annually,
thus helping to reduce Yugoslavia's adverse balance of payments.[12]

The 1973-75 economic recession that affected the Western countries, however, reversed this positive trend. Most West European
countries prohibited the hiring of additional foreign labor; and with
the increased unemployment among the domestic labor supply, the
number of laid-off Gastarbeiter also increased. At the beginning of
1976, there were about 145,000 unemployed Gastarbeiter in the
Federal Republic of Germany. About 23,000 of them were Yugoslavs.[13]
A limit was put on the length of time unemployed Gastarbeiter might
remain in the Federal Republic as well as in other Western countries.
Following a six-month period of unemployment, their residence permits were usually revoked, forcing most of them to return home.
According to Western sources, by mid-1976 the European recession
had forced the return of about 200,000 workers,[14] and some Yugoslav
sources placed the number as high as 450,000,[15] at a time when
there were already about 500,000 unemployed in Yugoslavia.

The large number of unemployed (about 10 percent of the registered labor force) and the increasing number of returning Gastarbeiter
tended to create not only economic but also social and political uncertainty. There was widespread unemployment among young people
looking for their first jobs. Ways of meeting the problem were discussed at length in a resolution on economic development in 1975
adopted by the Federal Assembly in October 1974. This resolution
suggested a GNP growth rate of 7 percent over the preceding year
and increases of 8 and 3 percent, respectively, in industry and agriculture. This entailed a 3.5 percent increase in labor productivity
and a similar increase in the number of people employed. About
150,000 additional jobs would have to be created.[16]

Clearly aware at a fairly early stage of the potential dangers a
major recession posed to the country's economy, the Yugoslav leaders
pursued a two-pronged approach in an effort to blunt its impact. A
policy of expansive economic development was initiated at the outset
of the recession in Western Europe, supported primarily by a huge

increase in the quantity of money (about 22 percent per annum in the 1974-75 period), an increase in foreign loans, and greater outlays on investments (about a 50 percent average growth during the 1974-75 period); almost simultaneously, an effort was made to reorient Yugoslavia's economic relations, particularly in regard to business cooperation and construction, toward the markets of the East European and developing countries, in order to compensate for the stagnation on the West European markets.

The results would seem to indicate that measures initiated in 1974 were successful. A high rate of increase in employment was achieved (about 5 percent per year), and a good number of the returning Gastarbeiter as well as most of those looking for their first jobs (altogether about 250,000 annually) were employed. Indeed, from the beginning of 1974 to the middle of 1976, a total of 630,000 new jobs were created; with the return of about 350,000 Gastarbeiter, the net number of unemployed rose, however, by 200,000, from 400,000 to about 600,000—reaching some 10 percent of the labor force.[17] This program will probably continue to be successful provided the present expansive policy of maintaining a high growth rate in employment is not endangered by widespread domestic instability or an increase in discriminatory foreign economic measures, or by a jump in the number of returning Gastarbeiter above the 1974-75 level (about 100,000 per annum).

FOREIGN TRADE PROBLEMS

Foreign trade and economic relations with other countries in general also caused considerable trouble during the recession. Yugoslavia's broader entry into the world market, which followed the introduction of the economic reform in 1965, produced a continuing increase in its trade and economic cooperation with developed Western countries. The expansion of trade with Comecon, although desirable, was in the past hindered by a number of factors, the main obstacle to more rapid trade expansion with the Comecon countries being "differences between the Yugoslav self-managing socioeconomic system and the system of administrative socialism [prevailing in the Comecon countries] and the lack of an institutional framework that would ensure more dynamic development."[18]

On the other hand, trade with developed Western countries was in many respects important to Yugoslavia's overall economic development. Of primary significance was the fact that it provided access to modern technology, opened up the possibility of cooperation on third markets, and made it possible to acquire Western credits on very favorable terms. It was therefore natural that the share of these

TABLE 11.1

Regional Distribution of Yugoslavia's
Foreign Trade
(in percent)

Area	Exports				Imports			
	1973	1974	1975	1976 I-VI	1973	1974	1975	1976 I-VI
Developed Western countries	55.1	45.1	35.4	42.1	61.1	58.7	57.5	55.3
Comecon countries	32.3	38.6	46.8	43.3	24.4	22.7	24.2	29.1
Developing countries	12.6	16.3	17.8	14.6	14.4	18.6	18.3	15.6

Source: Ekonomska politika (Belgrade), 26 April and 28 June 1976.

countries in Yugoslavia's trade had always been large, particularly so far as imports were concerned. With the onset of the world-wide economic recession this situation changed, however. Table 11.1 gives a 3.5-year breakdown.

As can be seen, the economic recession in the West and the consequent relative reduction in trade with that area prompted Yugoslavia to intensify its trade exchanges with Eastern Europe and the developing countries, and the share of the developed Western countries dropped from 69 percent in 1971 to 53 percent in 1975.[19]

The gradual switch from industrialized Western to Eastern and developing countries did not solve the problem of Yugoslavia's growing deficit, however. As Table 11.2 indicates, reorienting Yugoslavia's trade did not meet problems caused by the economic recession, which resulted in a huge trade deficit.

In 1975, in an effort to curb the country's growing deficit, the federal government introduced a number of measures restricting imports of certain commodities. At the beginning of May, Yugoslav enterprises were obliged to deposit 30 percent of the value of the commodity they intended to import in advance at the National Bank. At the same time, the federal government placed a temporary limitation on imports of certain essential raw materials, semi-finished and finished products of the chemical industry, nonmetallic minerals, and products of the paper, building materials, and nonferrous metal industries.[20] The following month additional import restrictions were

TABLE 11.2

Yugoslavia's Trade Balance, 1972–75
(in millions of dollars)

Direction of Trade	1972	1973	1974	1975	1976 I-VII	1975 Index (1972 = 100)
Exports	2,236	2,853	3,753	4,072	2,700	183
Imports	3,226	4,511	7,488	7,696	3,819	240
Net balance	−990	−1,658	−3,735	−3,624	−1,119	−366

Source: Compiled from various issues of Indeks (Belgrade).

introduced, including certain types of food, consumer durables, and
agricultural machinery.[21] These decisions remained in force only
from 21 June to 31 December 1975.

In addition to limiting imports, the government also introduced
measures designed to encourage exports. Efforts were made to
broaden trade with traditional partners and to acquire new ones. To
this end, Premier Dzemal Bijedic visited Washington in March 1975,
and evidence points to the fact that his discussions were devoted primarily to bilateral economic relations. His visits to France, Belgium,
and Luxembourg and his session with representatives of the EEC in
Brussels in February 1976 had the same purpose. Concurrently, a
number of domestic measures were taken to ease the availability of
export credits,[22] and pressure was exerted on export organizations
to coordinate their representation on foreign markets.[23]

As a result, in 1975 export volume rose 7 percent over the 1974
figure, the expansion of imports was slowed down, marking about a
2 percent increase over the preceding year, and for the first time
in four years the foreign trade deficit dropped. The trend continued
during the first nine months of 1976: Exports increased by 22 percent
and imports were 8 percent lower than in the preceding year. The
trade deficit declined to about $1.2 billion, the chronic balance-of-
payments deficit was almost eliminated, and the foreign currency
reserves surpassed the old record of $1.7 billion.

It is of particular significance that these results have been
achieved mainly thanks to the expansion of trade with developed
Western countries. In the first eight months of 1976, such exports
increased 43 percent over the figure for the same period in 1975,
while imports were 20 percent lower.[24] The increase in trade with
the East European countries was 12 percent in both exports and imports; trade with the developing countries registered no significant
change.

In discussing this favorable change in foreign trade during the
first nine months of 1976, federal Minister of Foreign Trade Emil
Ludviger mentioned other contributing factors. In his opinion, the
new currency system, which obliged enterprises and export houses
to make extra efforts to earn foreign currency to pay for imports of
raw materials and new technology, was of great importance.[25] In
force since May 1973, it enabled an enterprise to retain from 20 to
50 percent of the foreign currency it earned, depending on the branch
of industry involved. Ludviger also mentioned the domestic stabilization policy and the revival of economic activity in Western Europe in
this connection.

THE STABILIZATION POLICY

The economic expansion introduced at the beginning of 1974 in
an effort to cope with the growing unemployment, made more critical
by the increasing number of returning Gastarbeiter, inevitably resulted
in price instability and inflation. For an underdeveloped country that
lacked adequate domestic financial resources and that continued to
refuse to accept fully the idea of external risk capital, there was
little choice left but to resort to inflationary financing.[26]

The steady rise in the prices of imported goods—particularly oil—
in 1974-75 resulted in a huge balance-of-payments deficit, which, as
a rule, was financed domestically through an expansive monetary
policy and externally through foreign loans, both of which tended to
increase the rate of inflation in Yugoslavia. By the end of 1973, the
annual rate was 20 percent, and in December 1974 it was 30 percent
over the preceding year's figure. A series of antiinflationary measures brought it down to 25 percent in May 1975, to 17 percent that
December, and to about 10 percent in June 1976.[27]

It is interesting that Yugoslavia managed to fight inflationary
trends without resorting to wage and price controls. The system of
prices introduced in 1965 remained in operation, and as the economic
reform progressed price controls were gradually removed, concurrently with the consolidation of the market. In fact, at the end of
1970 the prices of about two-thirds of Yugoslavia's products and
services were "freely" set. Producers' prices were liberalized for
57 percent of the industrial products, and in commerce the ratio was
76 percent of the turnover.[28] Direct administrative wage and price
control was imposed only on basic infrastructural products and services (electricity, steel, copper, cement, transport, and communication services) and some basic foods.

A deflationary monetary policy accompanied by temporary wage
and price controls was often resorted to by the government in the past.

It did so in 1972, freezing wages and prices for six months and calling
for greater discipline in regard to both. That year also saw the introduction of the Social Price Control Act, passed in May, which spelled
out the criteria on which prices would be set—through social compacts,
self-management agreements, and the price determination mechanism—
and stipulated which authorities would be responsible for direct price
control.[29] The basic aim of the act was to ensure associated labor
(economy) a dominant role in the formulation and implementation of
a price policy that would make it possible for market laws to influence
more comprehensively the flow of investments and at the same time
ensure implementation of the economic policy as determined by social
compacts. Thus the act not only gives organizations of associated
labor the right to determine independently the prices for their goods
and services, but also obliges them, by means of social compacts
and self-management agreements, to keep price relations in accord
with prescribed criteria and in conformity with the established development policy.

A similar policy was followed so far as wages were concerned.
They are no longer controlled directly, however; the 1975 Social
Contract obliged republics, provinces, and individual branches of
the economy to coordinate the system of personal income. This contract, which was agreed to by republics, provinces, branches of the
economy, and trade unions, provided for distribution of income on
the basis of results achieved—a stipulation of the utmost importance
for the Yugoslav economy, since it means that distribution is made
on the basis of decisions taken by the workers' assembly in each
enterprise.[30]

The beginning of 1976 was marked by an important new step in
Yugoslavia's antiinflationary policy, one that also represented a
further step in the reform of the economic system as a whole. Toward
the end of 1975, the Federal Assembly adopted two laws, which,
because of their far-reaching effect on the country's financial and
credit policies, had a decisive influence upon business practice.[31]
The Law on the Establishment and Determination of Incomes in Basic
Organizations of Associated Labor and the Law on Payments to Bene-
ficiaries of Social Property were in fact two faces of the same coin.
The aim of this new legislation was to ensure the proper functioning
of a new system of clearing accounts and settling commercial debts.
This system has made it possible to settle enterprise indebtedness
on a national scale and has introduced a range of commercial paper
as instruments of payment, and it should therefore help to reduce
enterprise expenditures, moderate and rationalize investments, and
stabilize incomes—all necessary preconditions for both fighting inflation and ensuring adequate liquidity. Despite growing pains and a
number of bankruptcies and forced mergers, the operation was an

essential step in the development of Yugoslavia's socialist market
economy and commercial relationships among enterprises.

Yugoslav commentators and economic experts maintain that the
legislative measures regulating the balancing of accounts and settling
of commercial debts are largely responsible for slowing down inflation
and for the favorable developments in foreign trade. The production
and trade enterprises have been forced to make more rational decisions about what to produce, how to buy, and how to distribute, and
they must adhere more strictly to market law.

In a speech to the 23d meeting of the LCY Presidium, Federal
Assembly President Kiro Gligorov, one of the country's leading
economic experts, described the new system as of the utmost importance because it obliges enterprises and the economy as a whole

> to distribute only earned income; the consequences of
> this new business practice are to be respected by every
> enterprise and should become the standard of behavior
> for all self-management units and factors. Moreover,
> our success in fighting inflation has tended to remove
> the basis for any criticism of our self-management
> system or the situation in our country.[32]

THE BALANCE SHEET

A balance sheet of Yugoslavia's economic development in the
years 1974-76, which saw economic recession in Western countries
and rapid changes in Yugoslavia's own economic system, brings two
main aspects into focus—one economic, the other political.

The economic recession in Western Europe began to affect the
Yugoslav economy at a moment of great political and social instability,
when a rapidly rising inflation rate and a dangerous increase in
domestic illiquidity, a huge trade deficit, and a rising number of
unemployed were placing an extra burden on an economy in the throes
of reform. The temptation to abandon the socialist market economy
system and return to a centrally planned and state-controlled socialist economic model must have been very great—especially since that
model had always been regarded by Yugoslavia's East European
neighbors as a panacea for all social and economic ills. But the
Yugoslav leaders resisted the temptation and adhered to their policy
of economic reform, developing and improving the instruments needed
by a socialist market economy. Their decision seems to have been
justified, since the latest results point to a recovery achieved with
the help of measures designed to strengthen commercial relations,
coupled with a limited degree of state intervention.

Politically speaking, Yugoslavia's self-management system and
socialist market economy were subjected to—and passed—a relatively
severe test. Despite negative domestic and foreign developments,
they proved their efficacy and usefulness, and this is what Gligorov
meant when he said the basis for criticism had been undermined.
An editorial in the LCY organ Komunist[33] was even more explicit.
In commenting on Yugoslavia's economic situation and the results
that have been achieved, the paper said:

> The value of the [Yugoslav] system and the strength of
> self-management socialism were manifested at the very
> moment when the country was being subjected to great
> external pressure. Thanks to self-management action
> on the part of all working people and the use of common
> social means of production, we have succeeded in re-
> buffing all external pressures and have developed new
> social and economic qualities.

The Yugoslavs, having had some success in stabilizing their
system of self-management socialism, were countering criticism
of their model with vigor and self-confidence. This was particularly
true in their polemics with Soviet and East European authors regarding the existence of various roads to socialism, a discussion that is
likely to reach new heights in the near future. On the other hand,
the success achieved last year does not mean that Yugoslavia is
about to solve all the problems inherent in its socioeconomic, self-
managing socialist market system. Still to be answered are such
questions as how to ensure further growth, eliminate unemployment
and the north-south development gap, and ensure modernization.
Even if the policies being followed are correct, a lot of energy and
skill, together with financial and technological aid and cooperation
from the economically developed countries, will still be needed.

NOTES

1. Statisticki godisnjak SFRJ 1975, and Indeks (Belgrade)
February 1975.
2. Ekonomska politika (Belgrade), 17 February 1975.
3. Deveti kongres SKJ (Ninth Congress of the LCY, Belgrade,
1969).
4. Ibid. A good analysis of the political and economic entangle-
ment in Yugoslavia was made by François Fejto in the June 1971 issue
of Le Monde Diplomatique (Paris); see also Zdenko Antic, "Economic
Aspects of the Yugoslav Crisis," Communist Area Analysis Research
Report No. 0999, Radio Free Europe Research, 6 May 1971.

5. Politika (Belgrade), 19 October 1972.
6. Ekonomska politika, 30 December 1974.
7. Indeks, February 1976.
8. Ibid.
9. Vjesnik (Zagreb), 31 May 1974.
10. Vjesnik u srijedu (Zagreb), 4 February 1970.
11. Ekonomska politika, 17 February 1975.
12. Statisticki godisnjak SFRJ 1975.
13. Vjesnik, 13 January 1976.
14. Journal of Commerce (New York), 13 May 1976.
15. Ekonomska politika, 17 May 1976.
16. Vecernje novosti (Belgrade), 18 October 1974.
17. Indeks, September 1976.
18. Delo (Ljubljana), 29 June 1974.
19. Ekonomska politika, 19 January and 26 April 1976.
20. Economic Review (Belgrade), no. 181, June 1975.
21. Politika, 21 June 1975.
22. Ibid., 28 March 1975.
23. Ibid., 24 May 1975.
24. Vjesnik u srijedu, 25 September 1976.
25. Ekonomska politika, 28 June 1976.
26. See Zdenko Antic, "Inflation and Stabilization Policy in Yugoslavia," Communist Area Analysis Research Report no. 2101, Radio Free Europe Research, 27 August 1974.
27. Indeks, September 1976.
28. Yugoslav Survey (Belgrade), August 1972.
29. Ibid., August 1975.
30. Politika, 19 March 1975.
31. Ibid., 25 December 1975.
32. Vjesnik, 7 October 1976.
33. 11 October 1976.

12

THE CONTINUING PROBLEMS
OF AGRICULTURE

Harry Trend
Rada Nikolaev
Roman Stefanowski
The Radio Free Europe
Research Staff

Prior to World War II Eastern Europe, excluding the Western
part of Czechoslovakia and what is now East Germany, was overwhelmingly agricultural. The greater part of its labor force was
engaged in agriculture, and conditions were far from idyllic—rural
overpopulation, primitive methods, and miserable standards of living
were prevalent. The communist governments that came to power
after 1945, however, were committed to rapid industrialization with
emphasis on heavy industry. In the economic policies that these
governments followed, agriculture was deliberately neglected and
the rural population was seen primarily as a labor pool from which
to supply the growing needs of industry. Collectivization, which
began in earnest after 1948, was aimed less at increasing efficiency
and output than at gaining political control of the rural population
and economic control of agricultural production, in order to supply
capital for industrial investment and food for the growing army of
urban workers. After the ruthless and disastrous policy followed in
the Stalinist era was abandoned, the situation generally improved,
though increases in agricultural output did not keep pace with export

---

This chapter is based on the following Radio Free Europe Re-
search Background Reports: Harry Trend, "Some Problems Affecting
Agriculture in Eastern Europe," RAD Background Report/211,
7 October 1976; R. N. (Bulgarian Unit), "Bulgaria's Agro-Industrial
Complexes After Seven Years," RAD Background Report/34, 14 Febru-
ary 1977; Roman Stefanowski, "Agricultural Perspectives," RAD
Background Report/19, 20 January 1976; and Radio Free Europe and
Radio Liberty Research Staffs, "Agricultural Cooperative Members'
Private Plots: A Statistical Summary," RAD Background Report/130,
4 June 1976.

requirements and domestic demands, owing to lower-than-necessary agricultural investments and the migration of farm workers to the industrial sector. In the 1960s investment in agriculture increased, however, and greater attention was paid to the sector, but investments remained below the required level, and incentives for those working in agriculture were generally inadequate to inspire greater productivity.

CURRENT PROBLEMS FACING EAST
EUROPEAN AGRICULTURE

An article in a Hungarian literary and political weekly[1] reviewed the agricultural situation with particular emphasis on Hungary, but what it had to say is applicable throughout Eastern Europe, where a "maturing" socialized agriculture is plagued by problems that threaten to inhibit any increase in production and efficiency.* During periods when the sector can be heard to sputter, increased attention is paid to tinkering with the engine: "crisis-problem planning" of this kind is frequently found in agriculture, as in other economic sectors. When, however, exogenous factors and improvements effected earlier combine to produce above-plan results, interest in improved performance seems to wane, and thus there is a cyclical shift from acute concern to benign neglect.

Among the obstacles to improved agricultural efficiency are the changes that have taken place in the behavioral patterns of the farm labor force. The material incentives used in the agricultural sector seem to be losing some of their effectiveness in influencing the attitudes and behavioral patterns of farm workers. There are several possible reasons for this. Farm workers in large agricultural enterprises have discovered that supplementary income can now be earned from nonagricultural pursuits more easily than in the past, and they are no longer exclusively dependent on farm work for their livelihood. At first glance, in fact, it appears that the success of the East European economies in providing improved incomes for farm workers and more opportunities to supplement these incomes from nonagricultural sources is one major reason for the decreasing effectiveness of the traditional incentives.

A second consideration is the willingness of the new generation of farm workers to swap income for leisure. Ironically, from the point of view of the party leaders, the drive to industrialize the farm

---

*Data and quotations cited hereafter in this section are from this article.

worker has brought with it a clock-punching approach to work and greater interest in a fixed workday and a five-day workweek. To deal with this situation, farm managers will have to rely on using larger numbers of workers coupled with a staggered workweek and on increased investments in machinery and equipment as means of bridging the work gap caused by what appears to have become a permanent modification in the work ethic under socialized conditions.

A third factor affecting work attitudes is the growing size of farms, which has fostered compartmentalization in large agricultural enterprises. The workers and managers of the crop-producing sector have become less interested in problems of animal husbandry, and vice versa. Hungarian figures for 1971-75 point up the problems here. In the production of slaughter pigs, where the plan was 117 percent fulfilled, the large farms fell short of target (87 percent) while the private plot farmers achieved 157 percent.

The author of the Elet es Irodalom article asks why the application of the industrialized production system has "such good results" in industry yet fails when it comes to farms. Technical equipment used on farms is necessarily less efficient productively, but one cannot ignore organizational and managerial factors. "Often enough the wrong persons in large agricultural enterprises make the crucial recommendations." Politically appointed officials outrank knowledgeable individuals actually engaged in agriculture, and this is but one of the obstacles to the application of technically beneficial knowledge.

Agriculture's inability to respond to changing market needs by rapidly modifying its production structure is also a problem. Changes in production structure should be relatively simpler than in industry. Nevertheless, there is a definite need to react more swiftly to changes in market demand, and during the next few years this will have to be done in a less favorable world market climate.

Specialization within the agricultural enterprises may result in improved production in one sector, but not necessarily in the operation as a whole. Faced with this situation, many East European planners are tempted to resort to an increased number of plan indexes covering detailed aspects of farm work, thereby reducing the range of alternatives available to managers and sacrificing flexibility at the operational level.

The relationship between the producers of agricultural commodities and commercial distributors also deserves examination. Market shortages, which frequently plague the East European consumer, can be as much the fault of the trade system as they are of the producers. "Supply difficulties are [originally] caused by the unreasonableness, greed, and inflexibility of the wholesale buyers." The middleman wants to appropriate too large a share of the takings.

Another problem is the acquisition and proper use of personnel by the large agricultural enterprises. In terms of number and quality, Hungary has a trained agricultural "intelligentsia" that is "the envy of most countries. Or would be if the effectiveness of its utilization were proportionate to the extent of its knowledge." There are, however, too few technicians, and the situation is especially critical in regard to irrigation; it resulted, for example, in the watering of only half the irrigable area during the late June 1976 drought. In Eastern Europe generally, there is a need for more and better technicians and for more efficient utilization of them. But the problem is still more extensive. The industrialization of these countries is rapidly reducing the rural work force.

Relatively poor harvests in some East European countries notwithstanding, for more than a decade the general trend has been one of steady improvement, and the growth rate achieved was noteworthy. In Hungary, for example, agricultural production increased at an average annual rate of 2.9 percent during the 1966-70 period and 3.4 percent between 1971 and 1975. A 3.2 to 3.4 percent average annual improvement is anticipated during the current (1976-80) plan period. With the possible exception of the Soviet Union, the East European countries can point to a similar order of improvement over the last dozen or so years, and much of this improvement is attributable to a policy shift that made it possible to funnel more resources into the agricultural sector rather than divert them from agriculture to the industrial sector.

As socialist agriculture "matures," it faces new obstacles to continued progress in agricultural production, which will make the task of matching past growth rates, which started from a much lower base, all the more difficult. Changing work attitudes, specialization-induced diversity of interests, restrictive organizational relationships, unresponsive management and the shackling effects of the economic control system, inadequate utilization of the agricultural intelligentsia, and a shortage of the middle-level technicians required by an "industrialized" agriculture—all these bar the way to continued improvement. A partial, patchwork technique of improvement—encouraged by the usual crisis approach to selected economic problems—is bound to hinder the successful implementation of solutions designed to deal with the problems that arise in a tightly organized and politically dominated agriculture such as that found in Eastern Europe.

Among the more significant and potentially far-reaching changes being introduced are those affecting the organization of agriculture. The institutional framework that surrounds agriculture is being modified in order to accommodate the specialization and integration programs of the countries concerned. The changes are related to the

degree of integration that obtains and range from simple forms such
as the development of private cooperation organizations or the establishment of loose interenterprise collaboration among socialized
economic units, up to the creation of agro-industrial complexes (AICs)
along horizontal organizational lines, or even vertical integration in
the form of industrial-agricultural complexes (IACs) or associations
between agriculture and interdependent industrial, commercial, and
service organizations. The type of institutional development taking
place in each country is tempered by the structure of its agriculture,
its technological level, the availability of investment resources, the
importance of the private sector, its determination to improve control,
the general institutional complex, and ideological and political considerations.

The two extremes in this process are undoubtedly Bulgaria and
Poland. The former has gone furthest in establishing a nationwide
system of AICs—the most extensive move toward specialization and
integration in Eastern Europe. Poland, on the other hand, has done
the least in this regard, and a very large proportion of Polish agriculture remains in private hands. The problems these two countries
face are thus a mocrocosm of the difficulties of all Eastern Europe.

THE BULGARIAN AGRO-INDUSTRIAL
COMPLEXES

In 1959, immediately after the collectivization of land in Bulgaria
had been completed, a drive to merge the cooperative farms into
larger units was carried out. The situation thus created lasted in
outline for a whole decade, until 1970. The establishment of AICs
took place only after the new organizational form had been tested on
an experimental basis. The first suggestion for their creation came
from party First Secretary Todor Zhivkov in July 1968, and the first
official recommendation to set up such "combines" in places "where
conditions allow it" was made later the same year at a CC plenum.[2]
Even before then, however, the first AIC in the country had been set
up in southeastern Bulgaria, and shortly thereafter two AICs were
established in the northwest area with an explicitly declared "experimental purpose." Toward the end of 1969 a few other, different types
of complex were replaced.[3]

In April 1970 the BCP CC held a special plenum on "concentration
and development of agriculture on an industrial basis." It recommended
the concept of AICs as "the most purposeful form of concentration of
agriculture" and laid down the character of these new management
units and the principles that should be observed when establishing
them. As a result of this recommendation, some 133 AICs were set

up by the end of 1970, varying in size between 10,000 and 40,000
hectares. Their average size was 24,290 hectares, and they employed
an average of 6,479 people.[4]

The plenum defined the priorities: Horizontal integration would
be furthered by joining several farms into one AIC—that is, essentially
territorial integration; vertical integration with industrial, procurement, and trade enterprises was to come "gradually" and would
initially operate through contracts before being formally introduced.
Certain prerequisites for vertical integration had yet to be created,
namely concentration and improvement of the territorial distribution
of food industry enterprises.

The plenum also laid down four principles to be observed in setting up AICs: (1) each farm had the right to decide whether or not to
join an AIC and to choose which neighboring AIC to join; (2) the composition, size, and productional composition of the AIC would be
worked out on scientific principles; (3) the independence (autonomy)
and original organizational forms of the cooperative and state farms
joining the AICs would be preserved; and (4) there would be territorial
unity.

Plainly, the second and fourth principles could not be applied if
the first was strictly observed.

From the beginning, it was explicitly stated that there would be
no obstacle to one AIC containing both cooperative and state farms,
and each farm had been promised that it would preserve its autonomy
and its own form of management within the AIC structure. Despite
political motivation to preserve the cooperative farms, the AICs in
fact speeded up their disappearance. Very soon the process of de-
priving both cooperative and state farms in the AICs of their autonomy
began. The reason for this move was the "scientifically well-founded
demand" for unified branch management: Within each AIC, a single
enterprise should be responsible for all cattle breeding, another for
all poultry breeding, and so on. In early 1971, the first five AICs
were reported to have introduced this system; by the end of 1975,
more than half the total number of AICs had abolished the autonomy
of their component farms, and during the 1976-80 period the branch
principle of management is to be generally introduced.[5]

Experimentation with More Advanced
Organizational Forms

This process was closely linked with an acceleration of vertical
integration, which had initially been treated as a remote goal, but,
as one of the AICs' main raisons d'être, was nonetheless being continually and strongly promoted both centrally and by local authorities.

As a means toward this end, early in 1973 a new type of complex was
created: Eight IACs were set up with sugar beet growing as their
main specialization, under the management of a new state economic
organization, the Bulgarian Sugar Industrial-Agricultural Association.
Seven of these IACs were attached to the country's seven sugar refineries and incorporated two or more of the existing AICs on adjacent
territory, or in some cases parts of them; the eighth, which special-
izes in seed production, is somewhat different.[6] The extremely large
average size of the AICs, about 24,000 hectares, was generally considered a problem that would be difficult to master, but it was greatly
exceeded by the IACs, which came to cover an average of about
47,000 hectares.[7] The sugar complexes have, thus far, remained
the only ones of their kind.

Another kind of experimental organizational form set up in March
1974 was a "scientific-productional complex" (SPC) for viticulture
and wine processing. It was based on parts of an AIC and sections
of a neighboring cooperative farm and a state farm, together with an
enterprise and its experimental and training element.[8] Two years
later, this pattern was followed with the establishment of two more
SPCs for viticulture and wine processing, one for maize growing,
and one for fruit and vegetable growing, and plans were revealed to
set up others for wheat and maize, soybeans, and barley, and for
attar-yielding roses, essential oil, and medicinal plants.[9]

The SPCs seem in structure and economic operation to be similar
to the sugar IACs. An important difference between them and the
IACs and AICs is that their territory is not on contiguous land but
includes areas that previously belonged to AICs in various parts of
the country. Thus, one of the basic principles governing the AICs
has been set aside in the SPCs, and the principle of territorial con-
tiguity and consolidation does not apply to them. There are also
indications that in certain respects their economic mechanism is
different, since the main element in them is a scientific institute
and the emphasis in their activities is placed on technology and its
links with production.

A completely different project from those just mentioned is the
AIC in Silistra, northeastern Bulgaria, which reflects not only territorial integration, and on a very large scale at that, but also vertical
integration. This AIC is probably the one best known abroad, and it
has aroused much interest in the West[10] because of its enormous
size and the efforts made and resources invested in an attempt to
make it a model of modern technology and efficient management.

The Silistra project was initiated by a governmental instruction
of 18 March 1974.[11] It provided for the merger of the six AICs that
had been set up in the district into one AIC and one IAC, the aim of
the operation being narrow specialization. The AIC was to specialize

in grain growing and livestock breeding and the IAC in fruit and vegetable growing. The autonomy of all farms on their territory was
abolished and the branch management system introduced.

Two years later, a step toward even greater integration was
taken by merging the IAC and the AIC into a single areawide AIC.[12]
In this way, for the first time almost the entire territory of an administrative district—which with its 170,000 hectares comes 15th among
the 28 Bulgarian districts in terms of arable land—has been given a
single organization to manage its agriculture. Before the merger,
the AIC was already a huge complex of 124,200 hectares.[13] Consequently, the Silistra AIC is now more than six times the size of an
average AIC.

The Functioning of the Agro-Industrial System

The vertical integration of agriculture and the food industry on
a nationwide scale was initiated at the end of 1968, when the Ministries
of Agriculture and the Food Industry were merged. There were
several things to be considered, however, in determining the structure of the national agro-industrial complex (NAIC); for instance,
which of the branches connected with servicing agriculture should be
included in it, and what form should its management structure take?

After much delay, the NAIC was formally set up in August 1976.[14]
The long list of units placed under its management—which is exercised
by the Ministry of Agriculture and the Food Industry—includes some
200 autonomous economic organizations and about 25 subdivisions
or "links" of lower status. The 200 include 13 state economic associations, most of them engaged in processing and marketing various
kinds of agricultural products, but some employed on servicing
agriculture—such as the associations for agrochemical servicing and
for the repair of agricultural machinery; there are five scientific
productional associations (for pig breeding, cattle and sheep breeding,
poultry breeding, veterinary medicine, and seeds and plants); four
SPCs (those mentioned above, which have not yet been set up; the
others are subdivisions of the corresponding state economic associations); the 144 AICs now in existence; and the agricultural departments
of each of the 28 district administrations. The subdivisions include
various scientific institutes, design organizations, and research
centers, as well as the advanced institutes and secondary and professional schools for agricultural education and the agricultural
newspapers and periodicals.

The NAIC is the largest economic management complex in Bulgaria. It is said to be producing at present 29 percent of the national
income, 27 percent of the gross national product, 32 percent of all

exports, and 45 percent of the goods for the home market.[15] Its huge
size inevitably arouses doubts about its capacity to operate efficiently,
but thus far there have been no indications of problems in this respect,
although de facto, if not formally, the NAIC has existed for several
years.

Indeed, the main problems existing at present are connected with
the structure of management of the individual AICs and with their
method of operation. Current regulations on the operations of the
AICs were issued in June 1972 and supplemented later the same year.[16]
These rules contain detailed provisions on planning, on procurement
prices and profitability, on the allocation of the AICs' income and
their funds, and so on. But they too were termed "temporary," and
there are indications that since then some changes have taken place.
The essence of the present system can be summarized as bringing
agriculture closer to industry in its system of management, method
of remunerating labor, and so on. The farmers have meanwhile
obtained (or are in the process of obtaining) the same rights to pensions, vacations, maternity leave, children's allowances, and so on,
as the workers in state enterprises. Many of the former characteristics of the cooperative farms have thus disappeared.

The very large size of the AICs permitted what is generally
described as industrialization, concentration, and specialization in
agriculture. It includes various measures to make better use of
mechanization, save labor, and achieve greater efficiency. For
example, soon after the first AICs were set up, boundaries separating
individual farms and fields sown with different crops were abolished
and enormous fields, described as "massives," sown with a single
crop were created. This trend toward enlargement has continued.
Increasing specialization, based on scientific analysis of natural
conditions in each area, is running parallel with this concentration.
The IACs specializing in sugar beet growing are a typical example
of this policy.

Large-scale concentration and specialization allow better and
more rational use to be made of modern machinery and equipment,
but demand increasing capital investments in the form of new equipment, construction of livestock-breeding farms, and so on. On the
whole, capital investments are still insufficient and do not match
the ambitious plans for the modernization of agriculture. According
to the statistics, the total volume of capital investments in Bulgaria
in 1974 had increased by 240 percent over 1960, but in agriculture
the corresponding increase was only 100 percent. In 1960, 27.9
percent of all capital investments went to agriculture, but in 1965
only 18.8 percent, in 1970 only 14.9 percent; after the introduction
of the AICs, however, there was some improvement and the figure
in 1974 was 16.3 percent.[17] Special efforts have been made to im-

prove the image of the "mechanizers"—that is, all those who work with machinery in agriculture—whom Zhivkov has described as "the central figures" in the sector. A decree on the subject was issued in 1976.[18] It also took up the question of expanding shift work in the fields, a practice that seems to have been applied with some success during the 1976 harvest season.

The industrialization of agriculture requires more machinery, more use of fertilizers and other chemicals, and expansion of the areas under irrigation. During the 1971-75 period, the number of tractors and combines available increased at a relatively high rate, but there was a decline in the use of fertilizers and almost a stand-still in the expansion of the irrigated areas. The plan for 1976-80 envisages a relatively modest increase in the tractor and combine fleet but sets ambitious targets for fertilizers and irrigation.[19]

Automated systems of management, based on computerization, are increasingly being used in the management of the huge AICs. Bulgarian propaganda takes great pride in this fact, but no information is available on how these systems work.

Results of the AICs

In an economic branch that depends so greatly on the weather and other imponderables, it is difficult to assess accurately the impact of organizational factors on results. It is clear that Bulgarian agriculture has made considerable strides in increasing overall pro- duction and average yields, but progress has been no more impressive during the early 1970s than it was in the late 1960s, so that it cannot be attributed to the AICs, or not to them alone. At the same time, however, it must be noted that the production results under the AICs were achieved in the face of a continuing decline in agricultural labor. Much of the success achieved has been due to improved technology and the help of technology, which have aided in reducing the influence of adverse weather conditions. The expansion of irrigation and the increased use of fertilizers and plant protection chemicals over the last 15 years can also be mentioned in this connection, and a very important role has been played by the introduction of new varieties of seeds. In animal breeding, too, efforts have been made to improve breeds by importing stock, but the results in this sector have been more modest, mainly owing to a continuing shortage of fodder.

Table 12.1 illustrates the progress made. These, however, are crops that have received a great deal of attention and for which 1976 figures have been released. To this privileged category should be added maize, which increased from an average of 1,782 kilograms per hectare in 1956-60 to 3,647 in 1966-70 and 3,833 in 1971-74, and

TABLE 12.1

Average Per-Hectare Yields, 1956-76
(in kilograms)

Commodity	1956-60	1966-70	1971-74	1976
Wheat	1,630	2,743	3,412	3,900
Barley	1,810	2,437	3,124	3,400
Sugar beets	20,504	32,052	31,918	32,500
Tomatoes	28,181	29,033	30,043	26,100
Grapes	4,044	5,476	5,420	6,000

Source: Statisticheski Godishnik, 1961, 1968, 1970, 1975; and Rabotnichesko Delo (Sofia), 3 February 1977.

an estimated yield of nearly 5,000 in 1976. The yields of many other crops, however, have hardly risen at all, and their total production has actually declined. This is particularly true of fruits like apples, pears, plums, and cherries (but not of apricots and peaches) as well as of some fodder and "technical" crops, melons, strawberries, and so on.

Total milk production in 1974 was about 60 percent more than in 1960, while egg production increased by about 44 percent in the period. Both increases took place at relatively stable annual rates.

Integration of agriculture with the food-processing industry might have been expected to yield more concrete results directly attributable to the creation of the AICs. By the end of 1976, it was reported that almost 25 percent of all AICs had their own canning factories for the processing of fruits and vegetables.[20] This does not seem to have increased the output of canned food significantly, however. According to the 1974 statistics, the production of canned vegetables in that year was 33 percent higher than in 1970, whereas that of canned fruit was at exactly the same level as four years earlier.[21] Possible increases in freezing and other processing methods, however, may reflect greater success, but no data are available.

The Bulgarian party and government are placing great hopes on the AICs and the NAIC, in spite of their lack of conspicuous success so far. But there is no reason to doubt that greater progress will soon result from the modernization on which the whole new system is based. Good central and local organization, efficient management, and strict discipline will of course be necessary and, last but not least, well-qualified managerial cadres and rank-and-file specialists will have to be found.

Bulgaria's embarkation on so impressive an experiment has given rise to speculation that the AIC system may have been inspired by Moscow (or Comecon) and that Bulgaria may have been selected as a proving ground for a scheme that, if successful, will be adopted by the other East European countries, although it is known that the Soviets have conducted experiments with similar forms of vertical integration in the Moldavian and other republics. In Eastern Europe generally, concern has been shown about increasing the efficiency and output of the agricultural sector, and there has been much interest in various organizational forms of specialization and integration. Bulgaria, nevertheless, is the only East European state to apply the system on a nationwide scale. Although there are differences among the agricultural organizations in each of the East European states, they have all closely followed developments in other countries; the Bulgarian approach is no doubt being watched carefully, and certain aspects of it have probably influenced developments in other Comecon states.

THE POLISH PERSPECTIVE

In contrast to Bulgaria, Poland has pursued an agricultural policy that balances the pragmatic with the political. Except during the period of collectivization in the early 1950s, agriculture has been permitted to retain its overwhelmingly private character within the socialist economy. Some collectivization was undertaken in the years 1949-55, but, after the crisis of 1956, agrarian policy-makers, under Wladyslaw Gomulka's leadership, adopted a new means of achieving it. They embarked on a program known as the "gradual socialization of agriculture"—that is, gradual reduction of private holdings and expansion of the collective and state farms coupled with a much higher rate of investment in the two forms of socialized unit.

Under Edward Gierek, the position of the private peasants has been enhanced by extending the state's social benefits to them, and productivity has improved. There has, however, been a concurrent drive toward further socialization of agriculture, and in contrast to the Gomulka era specific programs have been initiated to nudge the peasants toward selling their land to the state. Encouraged by the relative success of its program and by demographic trends that promised more of the same, the party incorporated its agricultural policy into the guidelines for its seventh congress;[22] at the congress itself (held in December 1975), specific goals in regard to the transfer of land from private to public hands were announced, and some of the means the party might use to achieve its ends—such as taking over poorly managed private farms—were hinted at.

Though forced collectivization appears to be out of the question, time is working in the state's favor. Voluntary land sales by peasants in recent years resulted in private ownership of agricultural land dropping to 74.9 percent of the total in 1974, while the land held by state farms increased to 16.2 percent and that held by collective farms went up to 1.4 percent.[23] By the end of 1976, private holdings were dropping rapidly toward a 70 percent level. At the same time, demographic trends and economic forces encouraged migration from the farm. Thirty years of industrialization created so many openings for peasants that between 1945 and 1975 over 5 million of them moved from the countryside to the cities.[24] This resulted in a lessening of the isolation of the villages and in the emergence of about 3 million peasant-workers—people who hold jobs in town while still clinging to their agricultural holdings, which are worked more and more on a spare-time basis with the help of wife and other family members, and in many cases only the wife.[25]

Despite their predominance in terms of area owned, the private peasants are greatly limited by the fact that private farming has been drawn into the orbit of socialist economic planning.[26] The dynamics and structure of agricultural production, investment, and income are determined by state-made plans. Though theoretically independent, the peasants are subject to the indirect effects of planning, since the state regulates the supply of means of production (credits and machinery), purchases much of the farm produce, influences levels of income (contracting prices, taxes, and subsidies), and controls the rate of technological innovation (better seed, advice, improvement of livestock, and obligatory purchase of fertilizers). The party places great emphasis on the socialization of agriculture, however, and the socialized sector—including both collective and state farms—attracts more attention, investment, and other resources and will continue to do so. In an effort to obtain better results, in terms of both production and return on investment, the industrialization of agriculture within the framework of the socialized sector's holdings will continue.

Owing to a number of factors, such as the aging of the peasantry as a result of the exodus of the youth to urban areas, the structure of the present rural population is quite different from that of the mid-1950s, when the state's collectivization drive was successfully turned back. Now older and with less of a vested interest in the continuation of private agriculture, the peasantry may offer less resistance to the state's policies in the future. (One should not, however, underestimate the resilience of the peasantry.) All things being equal, it is likely that in the foreseeable future the authorities will continue to preoccupy themselves with the problem of socialization, but only so long as it does not seriously hinder production. And it must be remembered that one factor limiting the rate of change is the availability of investment resources for agriculture.

The Private Sector

At the beginning of 1976, there were 3 million individual agricultural holdings in Poland on which 4,282,000 peasants were employed on a full-time basis, compared with 5,041,000 in 1950. At the end of 1974, the agricultural land in the private sector represented 74.9 percent of the total. Agricultural production thus comes largely from individual farms—in 1974, for instance, the private sector accounted for 81.7 percent of the crops and 81.8 percent of livestock.[27] Thus, despite any pending changes, this sector will have a decisive bearing on the level of Polish agricultural production for some time to come.

A two-pronged dilemma faces the authorities. On the one hand, the rural population demands a standard of living and conditions of work comparable to those of the industrial worker, and if these are not granted soon, the peasants will presumably protest by either leaving the countryside or reducing their efforts, which will result in a drop in production. On the other hand, improvements in this area inevitably strengthen the private sector, which, in turn, delays the socialization of agriculture, to which the party is committed. The authorities cannot afford any serious drop in production that would adversely affect market supply, and any gaps would have to be made good with imports, which would place an unacceptable additional burden on the economy.

It was in realization of all this that the sixth party congress resolved—and this was confirmed later at the 15th CC plenum[28]—that achievement of the basic aims of agriculture depends on the simultaneous realization of the following: an increase in agricultural production, creation of conditions for gradual socialist changes in the countryside, and gradual improvement in the quality of life in the countryside, so that it will eventually match that in urban areas. To achieve these goals, various economic instruments have been employed in the last few years, such as tax measures, easier credit, and upward revision of the procurement prices of some products.

The real and lasting chance to improve the peasants' living conditions (without having to juggle with the old trio of procurement prices, market prices, and subsidies), however, lies in a gradual decrease (about 4 percent per annum) in the labor force of the private sector,[29] which would mean a drop from the 28 persons per hectare employed in 1974 to 14 or 15 persons in 1990.

Solutions here hinge mainly on two related considerations—the rate of exodus from the countryside, and the willingness of the authori-

ties to counteract the consequences of the drift from the land by
changing their policies in regard to mechanization, land allocation,
and the availability of capital. There are indications, at least with
regard to ownership of tractors, that the policy vis-a-vis private
farmers is changing. In absolute terms, for instance, the number
of tractors on private farms almost tripled between 1970 and 1974
but in the latter year still represented only 42.3 percent of all tractors
in the country. (In 1970 only 24.3 percent were privately owned.)[30]

Another problem closely related to the question of creating a
viable agricultural economy is the size of farms. It is a curious
phenomenon that the peasant's traditional attachment to the land and
his passion to accumulate it seem to have waned somewhat, or even
to some extent been reversed. Between 1965 and 1976, the individual
sector transferred 1 million hectares of agricultural land to the state,
and it is significant that nearly a quarter of this transfer took place
in 1974. In the same period, 107,000 owners abandoned their farms;
67,000 opted for pensions, and of this number 24,000 did so in 1974.[31]
Forecasts for the future indicate more of the same.

Between 1950 and 1974, there was an overall drop of only 5 percent in the number of people employed in agriculture, but a decline
of about 750,000 (nearly 15 percent) took place in the private sector,
leaving 4,282,000 in 1974. The socialized sector more than doubled
its labor force during this time, reaching 916,000 in 1974.[32] Were
it not for the suspicion that it is often the wrong people, for the wrong
reasons, who are forced to abandon agriculture, one would have to
say that such movement is an essential factor in the transformation
of Poland from a country with a mixed economy to an industrial nation.
It is the structure and perhaps the uncontrolled fashion of the transformation that call for close examination.

Eugeniusz Kowalczyk of the Council of Ministers Planning Commission analyzed this trend on the basis of two projections.[33] First,
if the situation continues in much the same fashion as it has up to now,
he puts the exodus figure for the 1971-90 period at 1,306,000. His
second projection, based on the assumption that agriculture is going
to be radically transformed so far as both structure (socialization,
consolidation, industrialization) and cultivation methods (mechanization, chemicalization, intensification) are concerned, estimates an
exodus of 3,406,000. What is striking in both projections is that the
vast majority of these migrants would be in the productive age group,
while women predominate among those of retirement age who rejoin
their families in the cities.

Although the number of individuals engaged in private agriculture
continued to decline, the individual sector did not benefit from the
land left vacant by migration. In fact, specialists question whether
the individual farms will ever reach the projected average size of

12 hectares.[34] One reason for this is that over the last 30 years some 1.5 million hectares of agricultural land have been put to non-agricultural use.[35] Other factors inhibiting size were that the number of tractors available for the individual sector was proportionately much lower than for the socialist sector, and that spare parts and servicing for privately owned tractors were more difficult to obtain. As noted above, there has been some improvement in the availability of farm machinery since 1970, but the problem has certainly not been resolved.

Land available for private farming has also been limited by the fact that, despite continuing migration from the countryside, an over-whelming share of the land that becomes vacant is transferred to the State Land Fund. Although such land is theoretically available for individual agricultural use, in most cases it is given to private individuals only on a short-term tenancy basis, which appears to have negative effects on production in the long run. The State Land Fund clearly favors state and collective farms and agricultural circles over individuals in making permanent assignment of the land at its disposal.[36] It is unlikely that the situation will improve much, although it is expected that the fund will acquire an additional 2 million hectares over the next five years,[37] and the authorities have also pledged to return to agricultural utilization an additional 2 million hectares no longer required for industrial and other purposes.[38] The future of individual peasants who have a genuine wish to stay in agriculture depends on the state's decision on how to dispose of the land it has acquired.

One of the consequences of current policy toward private agriculture is the fact that about 32 percent of individual farm owners have a permanent secondary occupation outside agriculture. Estimates of the number thus employed vary depending on the source, but 3 million seems to be a reasonable figure.[39] The reasons for this phenomenon are many, but two seem to prevail. First, despite the improvements in the standard of living and other conditions in the countryside, the incomes of the peasants are still far below the national average; and second, both industry and urban services require cheap unskilled labor to do jobs that the qualified and comparatively more discriminating city dweller is no longer willing to do. In fact, the peasant-worker has become a kind of "Gastarbeiter of the great industrial and urban civilization."[40]

Ninety percent of all peasant-workers possess less than three hectares of land (the national average in the individual sector is 3.5 hectares per person working on the land),[41] and such a small unit cannot guarantee even a subsistence type of living. The combined income (from the smallholding and an outside job) of a peasant-worker, when counted on a per-capita family member basis, is almost equal to that of families owning bigger, self-sufficient farms.[42] This suggests that what prompts a peasant to take an outside job is the desire to earn a living wage.

There is no doubt that, given an opportunity to enlarge their holdings to an economic size, many peasant-workers would opt for full-time agricultural work, but even under the best of circumstances this can only be done if others leave agriculture. Predilection for the countryside apart, a peasant would probably tend to shy away from the sheer strain of commuting, hard city work, and then working his own land or plot on his return home. But there are also factors that discourage his abandoning agriculture completely. For instance, the difficulty of obtaining suitable accommodation in the city is enormous; the average waiting period for housing is four to five years if one hopes to buy, and eight to ten years for cooperative housing.[43] And, because of his unskilled status and slight possibility of improving his qualifications, the peasant-worker has little chance of obtaining allocated housing. In sum, if he had the opportunity to acquire more land he would probably remain in agriculture, but land is not likely to be made available.

Among the things that help to determine how long a peasant-worker can maintain his dual status are his efficiency and productivity, together with the condition of his land, property, stock, and farm buildings. That the state hopes to reduce the number of peasant-workers in the coming years was made quite clear by Agriculture Minister Kazimierz Barcikowski in his speech at the seventh congress, when he stated: "We are working on economic measures that will encourage reduction of peasant-worker holdings to the dimensions of building lots, or get rid of them entirely."[44] Provided the investment policy and industrial activity are maintained, the days of the peasant-worker are numbered.

The Collective Sector

There are 1,150 agricultural collective farms in Poland, with 51,000 members working 330,000 hectares of land. In 1975 alone, 120 new collectives were formed, adding almost 40,000 hectares to the collective sector, and in 1976 another 330 were formed.[45]

A policy of pumping additional resources into the system in order to make collective farms at least more productive, if not commercially viable, was introduced some time ago. In the years 1971-74, some 8 billion zloty were invested in the sector, compared with only 5 billion zloty in the whole of the previous five-year period. Fifty percent of the amount invested was in livestock and related expenditure, 28 percent went for machinery and equipment, 10 to 12 percent for members' housing, and the balance was used to increase fodder production in the collectives.46

Much is made of the alleged superiority of the collectives over the individual farms when it comes to productivity and efficiency, but in most cases the comparisons are not valid, since the accent in the collectives is on specialization and they are favored in investments. As a result, labor productivity is higher on collective farms. The importance the state places on the collective sector as the spearhead of the "gradual socialization of agriculture" may be gauged from the rate of increase in the collective members' income in the last five years, which far exceeded that in the industrial sector.* Despite vigorous efforts to make entry into the collectives more attractive, membership has grown very slowly in those places where no free land was given when collectivization started and where no incentives (such as tractors, credits, stock, and seeds) were provided later. In some voivodships (regional government units), not a single new collective was set up during 1975, and some of these have virtually no state farms (PGRs) either.

So far as the resources poured into the collective sector go, neither holdings nor returns on capital invested seem impressive. The collectives are promoted as a base for the future industrial integration of agriculture and as centers disseminating advice and encouraging cooperation with the individual sector—a kind of intermediary between the state and the peasant. Meanwhile, as they increase their stake, their impact on the countryside is bound also to increase, mainly owing to the consolidation of their position as monopoly suppliers of seeds and pedigree livestock.

In view of the present holdings, the prevailing trends, and the resources lavished on the PGRs, it seems very likely that these may play a bigger role in Polish agriculture in the future. This was confirmed by Premier Piotr Jaroszewicz's speech at the seventh party congress, in which he forecast that the state farm sector would improve its holdings by a further 10 percent, to reach 30 percent of all agricultural land by 1980.47

Undoubtedly, however, there is a distinct upswing in the number of private farmers who engage in some sort of cooperation. In 1975, the Ministry of Agriculture indicated that 32,000 teams of individual farmers had combined together for specific purposes, such as crop production, livestock breeding, general farming, or joint use of agricultural machinery.48 The latter purpose definitely predominates; two-thirds of all peasants join together in order to pool their machin-

---

*The average income doubled, to about 70,000 zloty per annum not counting emoluments in kind (<u>Glos Pracy</u>, 3 November, 1975.)

ery, and in any case a group finds it easier to obtain machinery than does an individual, since the state favors such groups. Because there were only 4,640 such teams in 1973, one may conclude that such "unions" reflect the members' own interests, and thus are likely to increase. Such cooperative groups are strongly supported by the authorities since, apart from enabling members to take advantage of technical advancement not available to individual peasants, they may well become a stepping stone to collectivization proper.

The agricultural circles, with a nominal membership of about 2.8 million, make up the last group in the collective sector.[49] Their original purpose was to provide services to the individual farmer, but instead they have been used to enforce conformity to state rules and regulations, since nonobservance would totally deprive the peasant of the circles' services. Agricultural circles also act as halfway houses. It is easier to transfer the patchwork pattern of peasants' land parcels into the cooperatives of the agricultural circles; they can be serviced more conveniently and in less time there than on a servicing collective or a state farm, and the time saved can be used for private needs. When a holding becomes geographically integrated, it may be transferred either to an existing socialized farm unit or to a new one set up for the purpose.

Whatever is decided, the extension of socialization will no doubt be circumscribed by industry's ability to generate sufficient investment capacity and production means; and the fact that any sudden policy changes are bound to create tensions that may affect the production of food must also be taken into account. Any dislocation would result in the necessity to increase the already very high imports, something the country can ill afford. Central authorities have assumed that socialization will initially adversely affect total output.

The current situation in Polish agriculture is marked by increased pressure to maintain and improve market supply. Rising purchasing power, the rural exodus, and disappointing harvests have accentuated the problem. The often pragmatic approach of the Gierek leadership has been accompanied by an unobtrusive but significant campaign to strengthen the party's influence. The socialization of agriculture is but the next step in the party's program of extending its influence in the Polish countryside. As things are, developments leading toward larger holdings and increased mechanization, carefully steered and controlled by the party, are working in its favor. Since the authorities cannot permit the private sector to lower the level of its production significantly, they do allocate to it the bare essentials—but they distinctly favor the collective and state farms. This grudging support given the private sector—that is, support conditionally determined rather than deliberately chosen—is the outcome of the party's belief that private agriculture has to be tolerated at this stage and supported within narrow bounds, but that the future points in the direction of further socialization.

PRIVATE PLOTS OF COOPERATIVE FARM
MEMBERS ELSEWHERE IN EASTERN EUROPE

Although Poland is the exception, with just over 70 percent of its agricultural land still privately owned and worked, private plots also play an important role in the remainder of Eastern Europe and the Soviet Union. In most cases they are associated with cooperative farms, since one of the concessions made to persuade peasants to join the cooperatives was the promise that they would be given such plots. In some countries, however, employees of state farms and other individuals are also given plots for personal use under specified conditions. These plots were originally provided in order to enable farm families to raise some of their own food. The demand for the kinds of agricultural produce raised on the plots, however, soon resulted in their becoming an important supplement to the domestic market. The statistical data on private plots given below deal only with those farmed by cooperative members, unless otherwise noted.

Table 12.2 shows the percentage of arable land given over to cooperative farmers' private plots in the various countries of Eastern Europe. The figure for Czechoslovakia (which is almost identical with that for the USSR) is only about a third of those for the other three countries, and in 1975 Otazky Miru a Socialismu[50] reported with evident satisfaction that 37 percent of the CSSR's cooperative farms no longer had any private plots.

In deciding how much land a collective farmer or his household may farm privately (see Table 12.3), the authorities usually adopt the principle that the scale should vary in inverse ratio to the productivity of the land and its suitability for the application of large-scale farming techniques.

While all the countries under review impose similar limits on the size of private plots, there are wide discrepancies in their attitudes to the number and type of livestock that may be bred on them. The Bulgarian government, for instance, abolished all restrictions of this kind in 1971, and this led to reports of workers, teachers, and other distinctly nonagricultural citizens leaving their posts to set up livestock farms on which they bred pigs by the hundred and poultry by the thousand.[51]

The restrictions imposed by the other countries are too heterogeneous to be presented in the form of a table. They are listed below.

Bulgaria: No restrictions since 1971.

Czechoslovakia: One cow; one to two pigs for fattening and slaughtering; goats, sheep, poultry, and bees in numbers defined by the collective farm statutes; the guiding principle is that such holdings must not be detrimental to collective farming in the area concerned.

Hungary: Limits are set separately by each cooperative farm's assembly and therefore vary widely from place to place; they are determined by the accommodation and fodder supply available rather than by doctrinal or national planning considerations.

Romania: Three cows; 15 sheep; unrestricted numbers of pigs and poultry.

Soviet Union: Kolkhoz households: One cow with calves up to one year of age; one calf up to two years; one sow with piglets of up to three months, or two hogs for fattening; up to ten sheep or goats; local limits on bees, poultry, and rabbits.

TABLE 12.2

Percent of Total Arable Land Covered by
Cooperative Farm Members' Private Plots

Country	Percentage	Date
Bulgaria	8.9[a]	End of 1973
Czechoslovakia	2.8	End of 1974
Hungary	8.9	End of 1973
Romania	8.1	Constant over last few years
Soviet Union	2.8[b]	1 November 1974

[a]Until the end of 1972, cooperative farmers' private plots in Bulgaria were statistically distinguished from other classes of private holdings (those farmed by artisans, industrial workers, and so on). For 1973, only one consolidated figure is available, and this has been split (for the purposes of the present survey) pro rata with the 1972 breakdown.

[b]This includes private plots farmed by nonagricultural workers.

Sources: Bulgaria: Statisticheski Godishnik (Sofia, 1973 and 1974); Czechoslovakia: Statisticka Rocenka CSSR (Prague, 1975); Hungary: Statisztikai Evkonyv (Budapest, 1974); Romania: Anuarul Statistic al RSR (Bucharest, 1970-74); Soviet Union: derived from Narodnoe Khozyaistvo SSSR v 1974 (Moscow, 1974), p. 337.

TABLE 12.3

Maximum Permitted Size of Collective
Farmers' Private Plots
(in hectares)

Country	Per Member	Per Household
Bulgaria	0.20–1.00[a]	–
Czechoslovakia	0.25–0.50[b]	0.50–1.00[b]
Hungary	0.60[c]	–
Romania	–	0.30
Soviet Union	–	0.20–0.50[d]

[a]The higher figure applies to mountainous regions, the lower to intensively cultivated ones; in grain-growing areas it is 0.50 ha. These maxima can be exceeded in certain circumstances—for example, 0.10 ha. of extra meadowland is permitted for each cow or buffalo bred on a private plot.

[b]The higher figure applies to mountainous regions only.

[c]Available only to a full member of a cooperative farm.

[d]Kolkhoz households are normally eligible for 0.50 ha., but on irrigated land the maximum is 0.25 ha. Households of workers and employees in sovkhozes and other state agricultural enterprises can farm a maximum of 0.30 ha.

Sources: Bulgaria: Model Statutes of Cooperative Farms, 1967; Czechoslovakia: Collective Farm Statutes and Czechoslovak Government Order no. 137, 4 December 1975; Hungary: Cooperative Farm Law, 1967; Romania: Cooperative Farm Statutes, 8 December 1965; Soviet Union: kolkhoz households—Selskaya Zhizn (Moscow), 30 November 1969; sovkhoz, etc., households—Ekonomika Selskogo Khozyaistva (Moscow), no. 2, 1965.

Table 12.4 shows the contribution to national outputs of selected products made by cooperative farmers' private plots in 1965, 1970, and 1974 (owing to the delay with which some countries publish their statistical annuals, at the time of writing, 1974 is the latest year for which figures are available for all countries covered by the table).

The authorities in Eastern Europe appear to be reluctant to release information on the total contribution made by the plots, though part of the reason may be the difficulty of collecting the information. In Hungary it is believed to be about a fifth of the country's total agricultural production value, and within this amount over a quarter of its animal-products output,[52] and Western estimates have put the proportion for the Soviet Union at 25 percent. "Official"—and relatively very low—figures are available in the case of Czechoslovakia, and it can be conjectured that they have been released precisely

TABLE 12.4

Percent Contribution of Cooperative Farmers'
Private Plots to Total Agricultural Output

Commodity and Year	Bulgaria	Czecho-slovakia	Hungary	Romania	Soviet Union[a]
Eggs					
1965	56		76	62	67
1970	50	See Note[b]	43	59	53
1974	49[c]		30	53	41
Milk					
1965	30		31	40	39
1970	23	See Note[b]	8	37	36
1974	22[c]		10	38	32
Meat					
1965	Un-		23[d]	43	40
1970	avail-	See Note[b]	12[d]	34	35
1974	able		15[d]	34	32
Potatoes					
1965	38		6	35	63
1970	41	See Note[b]	8	35	65
1974	47[c]		7	34	64
Vegetables					
1965	Un-		10	28	41
1970	avail-	See Note[b]	11	27	38
1974	able		13	27	33

[a]Includes kolkhoz private plots and livestock holdings and those of workers and employees in sovkhozes and other state agricultural enterprises and of nonfarm workers and employees.

[b]Figures for the categories in the table are not available from Czechoslovak sources, but Statisticka Rocenka CSSR (Prague, 1975) gives the following data, which although not comparable are of some interest in themselves:

	1972	1973	1974
Percentage share of private plots in total plant and animal production	9.0	8.8	6.6
Ownership of: Cows	7.3	6.6	5.8
Pigs	8.6	8.5	7.0
Poultry	18.5	17.2	16.4

[c]Figures for 1973.

[d]Beef, pork, poultry.

Sources: Bulgaria: Statisticheski Godishnik (Sofia, 1973 and 1975); Hungary: Mezogazdasagi Statisztikai Zsebkonyv (Budapest: 1966 and 1975); Romania: Anuarul Statistic al RSR (Bucharest, 1968 and 1975); Soviet Union: derived from Narodnoe Khozaistvo SSR v 1974 (Moscow, 1974), p. 315.

because they are so low and show the rapidity of the private sector shrinkage in recent years.

A juxtaposition of Tables 12.2 and 12.4 reveals an apparently enormous discrepancy between the small percentage of arable land allotted to the private plots and the high proportion of the national agricultural output for which they are responsible. In the Soviet Union, for example, the private farmers produce two-thirds of the country's potatoes and one-third of its eggs and milk on less than 2.8 percent of its arable land.

These figures should be read with caution, however. No doubt the "privateness" of the private plots and the knowledge that income is roughly proportional to effort play a considerable role in the private sector's success story, but the main reason for the discrepancy is that the private plots concentrate on high-value products that require relatively little hectarage. Products that are labor intensive are avoided by the socialist sector, and this contributes to the profitability of the private plots; for example, in 1973 the private plots provided 61 percent of Bulgaria's plums, but only 1.2 percent of its wheat.

NOTES

1. "Where Are the Fields?" Elet es Irodalom (Budapest), 10 July 1976. Data and quotations cited hereafter in this section are from this article.

2. Rabotnichesko Delo (Sofia), 25 July and 1 December 1968.

3. See R. N., "Organizational Experiments in Bulgarian Agriculture," Bulgarian Background Report/13 Radio Free Europe Research, 27 March 1969; and R. N., "Bulgarian Agriculture at the Turn of the Decade," Bulgarian Background Report/6, Radio Free Europe Research, 9 February 1970.

4. Rabotnichesko Delo, 30 April 1970. See R. N., "Central Committee Decision on Reorganization of Bulgarian Agriculture," Bulgarian Background Report/14, Radio Free Europe Research, 31 October 1969; Kooperativno Selo (Sofia) 7 January 1971; Statisticheski Godishnik (Sofia, 1973), p. 265.

5. Otechestven Front (Sofia), 23 January and 11 February 1971; Novo Vreme (Sofia), no. 2, 1976; Kooperativno Selo (Sofia), August 1975.

6. See Bulgarian Situation Reports/1, 4, and 6, Radio Free Europe Research, 4 and 25 January and 8 February 1973, Items 4, 2, and 3, respectively. For a review of the results of the activities of IACs in the fourth year of their existence, see Bulgarian Situation Report/28, Radio Free Europe Research, 4 November 1976, Item 1.

7. Kooperativno Selo, 30 October 1973.

8. Darzhaven Vestnik (Sofia), no. 25, 29 March 1974; see Bulgarian Situation Report/12 Radio Free Europe Research, 2 May 1974, Item 2.

9. Darzhaven Vestnik, no. 19, 5 March 1976; see Bulgarian Situation Report/2, Radio Free Europe Research, 21 January 1977, Item 1; and Rabotnichesko Delo, 12 June 1976.

10. Foreign Agriculture Magazine (Washington, D.C.), 9 February 1976; Financial Times (London), 2 March 1976; and others.

11. Darzhaven Vestnik, no. 28, April 1974; see Bulgarian Situation Report/16, Radio Free Europe Research, 6 June 1974, Item 1.

12. Darzhaven Vestnik, no. 14, 17 February 1976; see Bulgarian Situation Report/5, Radio Free Europe Research, 26 February 1976, Item 2.

13. Ikonomicheski Zhivot (Sofia), no. 23, 4 June 1975.

14. Decree no. 146 of 5 August 1976, published in Darzhaven Vestnik, nos. 75 and 76 of 21 and 24 September 1976; see Bulgarian Situation Report/26, Radio Free Europe Research. 30 September 1976, Item 1.

15. Rabotnichesko Delo, 23 September 1976, and Bulgarian Situation Report/26, Radio Free Europe Research, 30 September 1976, Item 1.

16. Rabotnichesko Delo, 27 June 1972, and Darzhaven Vestnik, no. 90, 17 November 1972; see R. N., "Decree on Economic Mechanism in Agriculture," Bulgarian Background Report/8, Radio Free Europe Research, 26 July 1972, and Bulgarian Situation Report/36, Radio Free Europe Research, 1 December 1972, Item 4.

17. Statisticheski Godishnik (Sofia, 1975), p. 105.

18. Darzhaven Vestnik, no. 39, 14 May 1976; see Bulgarian Situation Report/12 Radio Free Europe Research, 14 April 1976, Item 1.

19. For detailed figures, see R. N., "Bulgaria's Seventh Five-Year Plan," RAD Background Report/240, Radio Free Europe Research, 24 November 1976, p. 5.

20. BTA, 29 October 1976.

21. Statisticheski Godishnik (Sofia, 1975), p. 130.

22. See Nowe Drogi (Warsaw), September 1975.

23. Rocznik Statystyczny (Warsaw, 1975).

24. Argumenty (Warsaw) 20 July 1975.

25. Trybuna Ludu (Warsaw), 30 September 1974.

26. Mieczyslaw Mieszczandowski, "Indirect Planning in Polish Agriculture," a report delivered at the 11th Seminario Internationale Urbino organized by the Centro Studi e Ricerche su Problemi Economico-Sociali, Urbino, Italy, 3-5 July 1975.

27. Trybuna Ludu, 23 May 1975; Rocznik Statystyczny (Warsaw), 1975), pp. 243, 278, and 329.

28. See Polish Situation Report/34, Radio Free Europe Research, 25 October 1974, Item 1.

29. Zdzislaw Grochowski in Zycie Gospodarcze (Warsaw), 21 September 1975.

30. Rocznik Statystyczny, 1975.

31. These and the following data are taken from an article by Ryszard Manteuffel in Kultura (Warsaw), 26 October 1975.

32. Zycie Gospodarcze, 9 November 1975.

33. Ibid.

34. Kultura, 26 October 1975.

35. Radio Warsaw, 29 October and 24 November 1975.

36. See data on the State Land Fund's allocations of land in Rocznik Statystyczny, 1975.

37. Kultura, 30 November 1975.

38. Radio Warsaw, 4 January 1976.

39. Argumenty, 20 July 1975.

40. Ibid., 27 July 1975.

41. Ibid., 20 July 1975; Zycie Gospodarcze, 26 October 1975.

42. Wies Wspolczesna (Warsaw), October 1975.

43. Trybuna Ludu, 26 August 1975; Radio Warsaw, 24 September 1975.

44. Trybuna Ludu, 12 December 1975.

45. Radio Warsaw, 29 September 1975; Glos Pracy (Warsaw), 3 November 1975; Premier Jaroszewicz in talks with a Hungarian delegation, Radio Budapest, 31 January 1977.

46. Glos Pracy, 3 November 1975.

47. Radio Warsaw, 9 December 1975.

48. Ibid., 18 November 1975.

49. PAP in English, 3 November 1975.

50. (Moscow), no. 9, 1975.

51. For this and other examples of private enterprise in action, see Bulgarian Situation Report/32, Radio Free Europe Research, 21 November 1975, Item 2.

52. See Hungarian Unit/KK, "The Private Plots Today," RAD Background Report/156, Radio Free Europe Research, 11 November 1975.

IV

DOMESTIC POLITICAL AND SOCIAL DEVELOPMENTS

The variety of domestic political and social developments in
Eastern Europe is certainly greater than the space that can be devoted
to them in a volume of this nature. Therefore, rather than attempting to cover the entire domestic scene, which would mean giving
superficial treatment to all states in the area, we have chosen to deal
in somewhat greater depth with certain topics and countries that are
either of greater interest and significance or representative of the
entire region.

Chapter 13 considers the civil rights movement in Poland, East
Germany, and Czechoslovakia. The dissent movement in the Soviet
Union has a long history and has attracted a number of leading Soviet
intellectuals, but until 1976 it had only a limited impact on Eastern
Europe. In the middle of that year, however, it began to assume
greater importance. Civil rights became a central issue in Poland
after the June price protests and the formation of the Committee for
the Defense of the Workers. In the GDR, more than 100,000 persons
have reportedly applied for exit visas, citing the 1975 Helsinki agreement and the East German Constitution as the bases for their appeals.
The publication in early January 1977 of Charter 77 by a group whose
purpose is to monitor violations of internationally guaranteed rights
marked the beginning of a civil rights movement in Czechoslovakia.
These protests, all apparently inspired by the Helsinki conference
and the increasingly independent stance of the Eurocommunists,
caused considerable embarrassment to the East European governments, especially prior to the Belgrade review conference. The
authorities attempted to quiet the dissenting voices, but the civil
rights groups were determined to continue monitoring and publicizing
what they considered to be violations of the Helsinki Final Act.

One of the reasons for the emergence of a civil rights group in
Poland was the official reaction to the June 25 protests against price
increases. This reaction and its consequences can be considered
among the most important recent developments in Eastern Europe.
Chapter 14 examines the altered balance of forces that emerged after
the protests. The strikes, which were fairly widespread, forced the
government to retract its proposed price hikes and to leave the problem unresolved for an indefinite period. The leadership also promised
to promote party-people consultations on price policy, a move that
could mean fewer policy options for the party. These two concessions
were made against a background of growing pressure on the agricul-

tural sector, worker dissatisfaction, and increasing foreign financial burdens. If some of the existing trends in the economy and in party policy were to continue, the leadership might find itself pressed to offer concessions on certain policies or procedures in order to ensure implementation of others. These events have been watched carefully by leaders in other East European nations and the Soviet Union. It is too early to say what impact they have had or may have elsewhere, but their ripples will almost surely spread beyond the confines of the Polish People's Republic.

Chapter 15 is concerned with the range of issues facing the Czechoslovak regime. While some of these are unique to that country, others are of a more general nature and are to be found in other East European states as well. The starting point for this assessment is the 15th party congress, held in April 1976, at which Gustav Husak's position in the party was confirmed and continuation of the policies of the previous five years proclaimed. There was almost no mention—or sign—of the significant splits within the party, although this by no means signaled that they had disappeared. Rather, the congress avoided the problem, just as it left untouched such other troublesome questions as party-people relations, economic pressures, and the real nature of the "threat from the Right"—that is, the still influential individuals who were involved in and the ideas that prevailed during the 1968 Prague Spring. Among the most serious problems facing the CPCS are party and economic issues. The most probable course of development is economic stagnation without political change.

The final chapter (16) in this section is concerned with Romania's policy of ideological mobilization. Although Bucharest has pursued this issue with considerably more vigor than its neighbors, all countries of Eastern Europe have shown an interest in bolstering the ideological front since the campaign to hold the Conference on Security and Cooperation in Europe began to make headway in the early 1970s. A major factor behind the Romanian drive was the desire to use ideology to inspire greater economic effort and efficiency. Relieving the growing labor shortage, which is compounded by an increasing demand for workers with specialized technical knowledge, has been one of the main targets of the campaign. Concern with youth is another important element, as is the desire to bring the cultural elite under control. Members of the latter group have been instructed to produce socially useful works inspired by revolutionary zeal, and there is new stress on culture for the masses. Emphasis on patriotism and national history—albeit in socialist garb—is also being used to stimulate Romanians to sacrifice for their homeland. While Romania is perhaps an extreme example and has a number of unique features, what has happened there is in many regards similar to what has taken place elsewhere in Eastern Europe in the past few years.

13

CIVIL RIGHTS DISSENT
IN EASTERN EUROPE
Thomas E. Heneghan

In the three different countries in three different ways, civil rights dissent reached Eastern Europe in the second half of 1976 and early in 1977. About 300 Czechoslovaks—some prominent dissidents, but mainly unknown citizens—launched Charter 77, a group whose intention was to monitor Prague's compliance with Czechoslovak and international statutes on human rights. Polish intellectuals formed a Committee for the Defense of the Workers after the June 1976 price protests and, along with other intellectual groups and the Catholic Church, demanded a full inquiry into charges of police brutality against the striking workers. And, in the German Democratic Republic, more than 100,000 persons, citing the Helsinki Final Act and the United Nations Declaration of Human Rights, applied for visas to emigrate to the West. In all three countries, considerable numbers of citizens lost their fear of demanding the rights their governments guarantee them on paper. Supported by developments in regard to detente and in the communist movement, these dissidents began monitoring their countries' compliance with their own laws and publicizing the faults they found. Even in its initial stages, human rights dissent in Eastern Europe may present an even greater challenge to

This chapter is a shortened version of Thomas E. Heneghan, "Civil Rights Dissent Spreads in Eastern Europe," RAD Background Report/22, Radio Free Europe Research, 28 January 1977. It reflects the position at the end of January 1977, and although the situation will undoubtedly be altered by subsequent events, the chapter is included in order to indicate the scope and nature of dissent in Eastern Europe and the official reaction to it.

the communist authorities than the many individual letters of protest that appeared so regularly in the past.

These developments represent a significant change of focus for dissidence in Eastern Europe. Pre-Helsinki protests usually took the form of individual voices crying in the wilderness for ideals such as freedom and justice. But for all their power to embarrass their targets temporarily, these protests seemed not to present a serious challenge to the authorities. Post-Helsinki protests, however, have concentrated on documenting specific cases in which the human rights guaranteed in national constitutions and international agreements to which the country subscribes have been violated. Since it contains— at least on paper—a pan-European consensus on desirable goals in the field of human rights, the Helsinki agreement represented for the dissidents a standard against which their countries' humanitarian records could be judged. The West European countries will be doing this at the Helsinki follow-up conference in Belgrade in June 1977, and the East European dissidents seem to be acting with this in mind.

The dilemma for the East European governments is that they too must keep Belgrade in mind. The Warsaw Pact states have produced great quantities of material supporting the claim that they, and not the Western countries, have been the better disciples of the Helsinki message. But by providing documentation of alleged violations of the Helsinki agreement, the human rights groups in Eastern Europe challenge this official view in a way that supports Western criticism of communist compliance with the Final Act. They also confront their governments with a serious dilemma. If they try to break up the groups and imprison their members, the governments only under- score the dissidents' accusations that rights are being violated. But if they opt for restraint, the wave of protest could continue to roll on. The dissidents compound this dilemma by denying all political ambitions and concentrating solely on documenting alleged violations of human rights. This legalistic approach makes the more stereo- typed government accusations seem even more misplaced than usual. And, coming from within the country, it also deprives the govern- ments of the interference-in-domestic-affairs charge, their standard defense against criticism from abroad. Caught between the demands of international opinion and the need for domestic order, the govern- ments opted for harassment, house searches, and confiscations. This did not appreciably limit the demand for human rights, however.

CZECHOSLOVAKIA

Charter 77 was founded on 1 January 1977. The original signers, reported to number either 242 or 257,[1] were soon joined by others

whose names were not revealed because there was no guarantee they
would not be harassed for their action. Some of the signers are
prominent dissidents and figures from the reform movement; the bulk
of the group's support, however, comes from previously unknown
persons of various professions, including academics, scientists,
and some clerics. As the group stressed in its manifesto, "Charter
77 is a free, informal, and open association of people of various
convictions. . . . Charter 77 is not an organization, has no statutes,
no permanent agencies, and no formally organized members. . . .
[It] is not a basis for activity as a political opposition."[2] As Jiri
Hajek (who was Minister of Foreign Affairs during the Dubcek era)
explained, the manifesto is

> fully within the framework of our country's Constitution
> and laws. We want the application of these international
> agreements on civil and human rights—above all the
> accords signed at the Helsinki conference—which, once
> subscribed to by our representatives, became part of
> our legal system.[3]

The group based its monitoring activity on Law No. 120 of the
Czechoslovak Collection of Laws. Effective as of 23 March 1976,
this statute incorporates into Czechoslovak law the International
Covenant on Civil and Political Rights and the International Covenant
on Economic, Social, and Cultural Rights—two agreements drawn up
by the United Nations in the 1960s. Czechoslovakia signed these
covenants in 1968 and reconfirmed them at the Helsinki conference
in 1975. Taken together they express support for a wide spectrum
of human and civil rights, and Charter 77 carefully refers to both
covenant and article in its accusations of widespread official violation
of legally guaranteed rights. Among the rights violated, the manifesto lists freedom of expression, assembly, and religion; immunity
from slander and invasion of privacy; and freedom to receive and
impart information regardless of national borders, to travel freely,
and to strike. In cases where young persons are denied admission
to universities because of their views or those of their parents, the
right to education is also violated.

Official reaction to the group was swift and strong. Soon after
Charter 77's existence became known, six of its signers were detained
by the police for questioning. Although they were soon released, they
and other signers were routinely brought in for interrogation. Instead
of being questioned as suspects, however, they were asked to testify
as "witnesses," a formality that deprived them of the right to refuse
to testify, which they would have had if held in protective custody or
charged with a specific offense. In addition, a number of documents—

including sections of the Czechoslovak Collection of Laws concerning human rights—were confiscated during searches of the Charter 77 members. In a vehement editorial denouncing the Charter, Rude Pravo said on January 12 that it had been issued by "the discredited organizers of the 1968 counterrevolution on orders from anticommunist and Zionist headquarters." The "pamphlet," Rude Pravo continued, "is an antistate, antisocialist, antipopular and demagogical, libelous rag" based on "cosmopolitan postures."

As was to be expected, numerous protests against Prague's stand on Charter 77 came in from abroad. Criticism was expressed by the Italian, Spanish, French, Swedish, Danish, and Greek (Interior) Communist Parties. West European Socialist leaders lodged their parties' protests, and Socialist International President Willy Brandt did so in the name of that organization. Many West European and American intellectuals voiced their complaints, and the Austrian section of Amnesty International took up the case of the four Czechoslovaks charged with subversion (see below). Interestingly, a group of Hungarian intellectuals made the only East European contribution to the protests; over 30 signatories sent a letter to the Charter 77 group expressing solidarity with them. The Hungarians, in whose ranks not only "New Left" theorists in Budapest but many other cultural figures were to be found, made no comment about Hungarian conditions in their letter.[4]

Parallel to these denunciations was a mounting campaign against alleged West German and U.S. espionage activity against Czechoslovakia. In early January it became known that Josef Grohman, an important publishing official and chairman of the Czechoslovak Commission on Cooperation with UNESCO, was being tried on charges of spying for Western intelligence agencies. The Rude Pravo editorial of January 6 denouncing the alleged activities of Western intelligence agencies against Czechoslovakia also mentioned the cases of two West German citizens indicted for espionage, as well as a trial of four other persons accused of spying for West Germany. At the same time Czechoslovak Television began a four-part series on American intelligence activities. With so many espionage cases being revealed, some dissidents suspected they might soon be charged with the same crime. "They are apparently trying to implicate us in spy stories or something of that nature," Pavel Kohout told a French journalist. "It is absurd."[5]

Kohout's fears were confirmed on January 17, when Ceteka announced that four men—Vaclav Havel, Jiri Lederer, Ota Ornest, and Frantisek Pavlicek—had been arrested and charged with "serious criminal activities directed against the foundations of the republic." Apparently the four were to be charged under the first section of a special chapter of the Czechoslovak Penal Code that covers a wide range of crimes, from defamation of the republic to espionage and subversion. In the official announcement, they were accused of "having maintained contacts with foreign enemy forces and émigré circles for a long time and handing over to them materials damaging to the interests of Czechoslovakia."[6]

In making these arrests, Prague intended to show the other side of the double-edged sword known as Helsinki. On the one hand, detente and the Final Act have provided added support for East European dissidents. Their governments pledged to respect the human rights enumerated in the Helsinki document, and the distance between their words and their deeds has created a vacuum within which the dissidents feel they can act comparatively safely. But the Final Act also acted as a challenge to the governments of Eastern Europe, and exposed them to a more effective form of protest than they had known in the past. Prague evidently decided that it was this side of the Helsinki issue, and not the subtleties of East-West detente, that was more important for Czechoslovakia.

POLAND

The human rights discussion has had a longer and more complicated history in Poland. Unlike the Czechoslovak situation, Polish dissent involved a wide range of the population. By their protests against the June 1976 price increases, the workers demonstrated their discontent with economic shortages and their power to block unpopular measures to correct them. The Catholic Church resumed its protests against limitations on church construction, discrimination against believers, and bringing agriculture into the socialized sector, and expressed support for the imprisoned June strikers and their families. And the intellectuals, besides calling for a free press and trade union movement, formed a Committee for the Defense of the Workers and monitored official discrimination against and repression of the workers. The confluence of these three streams of protest represented a coalition of dissenting interests not seen in Poland since 1956.

The roots of this round of protest stretch back to December 1975. At that time constitutional amendments were formulated that were to codify the leading role of the Polish United Workers' Party PUWP, proclaim Poland's ties to the Soviet Union "unbreakable," and make a citizen's rights dependent upon the fulfillment of his duties toward the state. But even before Edward Gierek could give the amendments cautious support (in his address to the seventh party congress, which opened on 8 December 1975) 59 intellectuals had delivered their protests to the Sejm (the Polish Parliament). In the following weeks about 400 other citizens joined in the protest. Stefan Cardinal Wyszynski preached against the proposed amendments, seeing in them the basis for future legal discrimination against believers. When they were finally adopted in mid-February, the amendments had taken on a different form. The sections on the party and the Soviet Union had been watered down, and the connection between rights and duties replaced by an admonition to citizens to carry out their duties honestly.

The real impetus toward more active dissent came in June 1976. After workers' protests had forced the government to withdraw its dramatic price increase proposals, a group of 11 intellectuals called for an "authentic dialogue" between party and people and a "broadening of democratic liberties," including a free press and the right of free association.[7] After the first round of indictments was handed down against workers from Ursus and Radom in mid-July, historian Jacek Kuron appealed to PCI leader Enrico Berlinguer to intercede on behalf of the Polish workers. He also protested the extensive firings, "massive repression," and police brutality that followed the June protests. "Only a general amnesty for all participants in the June demonstrations can arrest the terror against the workers," the former student leader wrote. "It is only public opinion in the countries where it is truly independent that can take up the struggle for this amnesty."[8] In an unprecedented move, the PCI Central Committee immediately responded with a message to the PUWP pleading for "moderation and clemency."[9]

A decisive step came in mid-September, when 14 intellectuals formed the Committee for the Defense of the Workers.* The group stated that "repressive methods" against the strikers had been "coupled in most cases with infringement of the law by the authorities. The courts handed down verdicts without adequate evidence. The Labor Code was infringed. The authorities did not hesitate to use force to gain evidence." "The reprisals taken against the workers," the document continued, "violated human rights approved by international law and by laws that are binding on Poland. These are the right to work, the right to express opinions freely, and the right to take part in meetings and demonstrations." Because "society has no other defense against lawlessness except solidarity and mutual aid," the committee announced that it would provide financial, legal, and medical aid to imprisoned workers and their families. Furthermore, it would push for amnesty for all those arrested and reinstatement for workers fired from their jobs. "In every community, in every plant, people should be sought who have the courage to start collective forms of help."[10]

_____

*Subsequent additions have brought membership up to 23.

Committee activities concentrated on three areas. First, observers were sent to the trials of the strikers to document the prosecutor's charges, the defendants' testimonies, and the legality of the proceedings. These observers were sometimes roughed up outside the courthouses or pelted with eggs. The committee made public in numbered communiques the information it gathered at these trials, as well as any new information it received about the June protests and the official measures taken against the workers. According to the information provided in the first six of these communiques, by the end of January 1977 the committee had collected more than 2 million zloty to aid persecuted workers and their families. Over 400 workers were reported to have received aid from the committee. Of the aid money, more than 120,000 zloty were confiscated by police during searches of committee members' apartments.[11] In addition, the Polish Post Office was ordered to seize and turn over to public funds all money sent to the committee.[12]

The Catholic Church was also active in its defense of the workers. In the first weeks after the protests, Church leaders chose to exert their influence with the government privately. When the demands for amnesty were not heeded, however, the episcopate began publicizing its opposition to the government's policies. The communique on the episcopal conference of September 7 to 9 called for reinstatement of all workers fired for participation in the protest and compensation for their losses, and stated that those sentenced should be granted amnesty. Addressing themselves to the population, the bishops said that all citizens should strive to preserve the "internal peace and order required by the interests of the country." State authorities, however, they continued, should "fully respect civil rights and conduct a true dialogue with society."[13] When results were slow in coming, Cardinal Wyszynski began preaching sermons in favor of amnesty, saying that "it is painful when workers must struggle for their rights from a workers' government."[14] The episcopal call for amnesty was renewed on November 19, at which time the bishops also announced that "the Polish episcopate believes that giving aid to people and families deprived of work and means of livelihood is the duty of all people of good will and especially of a Christian community."

A demand for a full inquiry into cases of alleged police brutality became the central topic. In mid-November the committee submitted a motion to the Sejm requesting a full investigation; in a sermon on December 6 Cardinal Wyszynski accused the police of brutality and claimed to have a list of over 30 jailed Ursus workers of whom only 4 had not been beaten or sent through a police gantlet; 28 prominent professors appealed to the Sejm on December 21 for a parliamentary commission to study the issue ("only an objective and detailed investigation . . . by an authoritative body," they wrote, "followed by publication of its conclusions . . . will stop the rising tide of discontent"); and on January 3 the committee issued a statement charging that "terror and lawlessness" had reigned in Radom since June, and that the blame lay "not only with the local authorities but and above all with the Prosecutor-General's Office," which had been receiving complaints about beating and brutality from Radom workers since the beginning of September.

Reporting to a Sejm legal committee on January 5, Prosecutor-General Lucjan Czubinski gave a reply to these criticisms that was bound to provoke further protest. The charges of police brutality, he said, were "groundless," and the letters his office had been receiving were full of falsifications.[15] The next day 172 citizens, among them writers, professors, sociologists, engineers, and journalists, wrote to several Sejm deputies demanding a parliamentary commission "to investigate the abuse and tortures the whole country is talking about." In late January, 31 persons who had attended workers' trials complained in an open letter about police harassment, and 61 Catholic priests "in their own names and in the names of their parishioners" demanded that police activities be investigated.[16]

The authorities first said they would use "intellectual means" to combat the civil rights efforts of the committee, but as noted above several committee members attending trials of workers were roughly handled, and almost all were brought in for interrogation at least once; some were questioned several times. Besides committee funds, house searches and confiscations netted several documents and 11 typewriters. Other attacks have run a gamut of accusation. Zycie Warszawy, for example, charged that committee member Jerzy Andrzejewski and his colleagues represented "a terrible chaos and mixture of ideas." Among them, the paper claimed, "you can find everything: Utopia and Trotsky, Social Democratic odds and ends, bits of [Soviet Russia's] New Economic Policy, and the latest anticommunist ammunition, a slice of Zionism, and a bite of Christian Democracy."[17]

It is highly unlikely that these accusations were intended as the basis for Czechoslovak-style political trials. Warsaw has always shied away from such extreme measures, and, when one considers the leadership's shaky position, it would certainly have been inadvisable to start turning to them. In mid-January officials began fining committee members for participating in "illegal collection of money"—that is, fund-raising for the committee. According to Polish law, the group should have applied for authorization to collect funds, a step it did not take. Committee members called before "people's courts" to answer these charges did not appear, but were fined 5,000 zloty in absentia.[18]

The government, of course, considered the committee and its activities illegal, but apparently felt that it would have more to lose than to gain if it pressed serious charges against committee members.

THE GERMAN DEMOCRATIC REPUBLIC

In the GDR dissidence seemed to have both a smaller and a larger base than it did in Poland and Czechoslovakia. On the one hand, the number of active dissidents was small (one of the most prominent, balladeer Wolf Biermann, was expatriated while on a concert tour of West Germany in November 1976, and another, Professor Robert Havemann, was put under house arrest after the Biermann incident and thereafter subjected to harassment). On the other hand, by the end of 1976 more than 100,000 GDR citizens had reportedly applied for visas to emigrate to the West since the Helsinki summit in mid-1975. Citing the Final Act and the United Nations Declaration of Human Rights as the basis for their appeals, these citizens, although unorganized, had in effect given the East German government a mass vote of no confidence. The authorities tried various methods to keep citizens from exercising their legal right to apply for exit visas, but the pressure for permission to emigrate continued.

The crackdown on unruly intellectuals began in November. During his first concert tour in West Germany in 11 years, Biermann, a critical but committed Communist, was stripped of his East German citizenship and forbidden to return to East Berlin. In retrospect, the decision to issue Biermann a passport seems to have been made with expatriation in mind. The 40-year-old singer, prohibited from giving public performances in the GDR since 1965, is one of the country's most persistent critics, and his songs and poetry denouncing the party bureaucracy and supporting "communism with a human face" are popular on both sides of the Wall. His rather radical communist beliefs may not have made him acceptable to all East German youth or intellectuals, but his popularity was apparently wide enough to worry the orthodox leadership of the Socialist Unity Party (SED). And, as a talented singer and perhaps the East German dissident best known in the West, Biermann was able to attract international publicity out of proportion to the strength of dissent in the GDR.

It was Biermann's expatriation, rather than Biermann himself, that rallied East German intellectuals to protest. In late November 1976, a dozen intellectuals petitioned the SED leadership to "rethink the measures taken." Their letter, the first known protest of its kind in East German history, was signed by a number of the GDR's most prominent writers.[19] Others soon joined the group, and the number of signers rose to about 100. In a separate statement, Professor Robert Havemann, a friend of Biermann and perhaps the only other well-known dissident in East Berlin, protested against the singer's expatriation and repeated his oft-stated demands for amnesty for political prisoners, a free press and free trade unions, and a socialist opposition party. Soon afterward, Havemann was placed under house arrest and his telephone service was cut off.

The official reaction against the other Biermann supporters was also harsh. About 50 persons were reported to have been arrested for signing a petition protesting the expatriation, and six prominent writers were expelled from the Writers' Union.20 As the protests increased, the party organ Neues Deutschland published several pages of statements by prominent cultural personalities supporting the government. This campaign was abruptly stopped, however, when it became clear that the ambiguity of many of the comments suggested even further discontent among GDR intellectuals.

Why, after 11 years of ignoring him, did East Berlin decide to expatriate Biermann? Why did it risk such an unpopular step? Although it must have expected criticism, the party leadership certainly did not anticipate such strong protests, especially from within East Germany itself. But it seems that the party leaders felt that Biermann would have to be removed if other problems in the society—the rising number of emigration applications, the growing uneasiness in the Protestant Church—were to be countered. Ironically, Biermann has consistently argued against Abhauen ("taking off," that is, emigrating to the West), but a growing number of East Germans have ignored this part of his message and applied to leave their country.

Far more widespread, but also more unorganized, was the wave of exit visa applications. Most people applying for permission to emigrate brought with them a copy of the Helsinki Final Act or quoted the United Nations Declaration of Human Rights. Some took the novel approach of applying for discharge from East German citizenship, a procedure provided for in the country's Constitution; of the 79 signers of the "Petition for the Full Attainment of Human Rights," at least seven were jailed for trying this method. As noted above, over 100,000 East Germans are reported to have applied for exit visas since the Helsinki summit, and about 10,000 have been permitted to leave each year.21

Only about half the recent emigrants went to join relatives in the West; the rest simply wanted to leave the GDR and were willing to put up with the discrimination and harassment that accompany applications for visas. Late in 1976, in an attempt to limit the wave of applications, the SED announced that only real cases of family reunification would be considered. Then, in January 1977, East German guards appeared in front of the West German Permanent Mission in

East Berlin to prevent "unauthorized" East German citizens from
seeking advice on emigration. Under the terms of the 1974 agreement under which they were established, GDR officials claimed, the
permanent missions in East Berlin and Bonn were not authorized to
advise the citizens of the other country; the West German mission's
activities therefore represented direct interference in the affairs of
the GDR.[22] The guards were removed after strong Western protests,
and the citizens began returning for advice regarding emigration.

   This growing restlessness was paralleled in other sectors of
society. The East German Protestant Church, long a rather compliant
organization, began to express mild criticism of the government
shortly before the Ninth SED Congress in May 1976. Church-state
tension increased in August when Pastor Oskar Bruesewitz immolated
himself in protest against what he called official repression of youth
and discrimination against Christians. In its response the Church
stated that it did not agree with Pastor Bruesewitz's "desperate act"
but admitted that it illustrated the "deep cleft" that had developed
between episcopate and congregation. At a synod in late September
the Church reiterated its demands for a "discussion on principles"
with the East Berlin authorities. Also in September, a Protestant
church in Prenzlau acted as host for Wolf Biermann's first concert
in the GDR since 1965. Biermann followed the performance with
some unexpectedly positive remarks about the Church. There was,
he said, a "Red Church" developing that "emphasizes the communist
dimensions of the Gospels and thus criticizes [the East German]
situation from a Christian-communist standpoint and takes a position
that is really progressive and constructive."[23] In response, the
progovernment Catholic magazine Standpunkt claimed that churches
in the GDR, under the influence of West Germany and psychological
warfare, were trying to shake one of the foundations of Church-state
relations—that is, "all-round loyalty to the GDR and its policies."[24]

   Economic considerations provided another source of tension.
The rise in Comecon prices for raw materials and East Berlin's
growing debts in the West, which amounted to about $4 billion[25] by
the fall of 1976, began to strain the GDR's economy. The long drought
in the summer of 1976 left the country's harvest 10 percent smaller
than the year before. Instead of a planned growth of 5.3 percent in
national income, the figure for 1976 was only 3.7 percent[26]—a fact
that undoubtedly had an adverse effect on the standard of living. The
personnel changes in October, in which Prime Minister Horst Sindermann was replaced by veteran politician Willi Stoph, were presumably
necessitated by Sindermann's unsatisfactory handling of the growing
economic problems. In addition, while an experimental new wage
system introduced in about 100 large industrial plants reportedly
raised the basic wage of the workers, it did so in such a way that
taxes took out even more than the new increases provided.[27]

The question of "all-round loyalty" strikes at the heart of East Berlin's problems. The GDR has had some difficulty developing specifically <u>East</u> German loyalties among its citizens. West Germany is far too visible for the East German authorities to prevent "German-German" comparisons. Greater numbers of West Germans have traveled in the GDR in recent years as a result of Bonn's <u>Ostpolitik</u>, creating even better opportunities for East Germans to maintain contact with relatives and friends in the West. West German radio and television broadcasts can be received in most of East Germany, and since late 1974 West German radio and television reporters have been working in East Berlin and providing East Germans with an alternative look at daily events in their own country. Many East Germans who dislike their government are strongly tempted simply to move next door. International agreements such as the Helsinki Final Act and the International Covenant on Civil and Political Rights—both documents signed by the GDR—guarantee them the right to do so, and now that the GDR, after years of isolation, has been accepted into the international community as an independent nation, many of its citizens have apparently concluded that it should honor the international agreements it has signed. The resulting grass-roots movement toward emigration is probably the most widespread and specifically Helsinki-oriented demand that has appeared in Eastern Europe, and the SED cannot disregard it.

FOREIGN AND DOMESTIC INFLUENCES

Probably the prime catalyst for the growth of human rights protests in Eastern Europe was the Helsinki Conference's Final Act. Vague and inadequate though its provisions may be, its Declaration on Principles Guiding Relations between Participating States (in Basket One) and the provisions for "cooperation in humanitarian and other fields" (Basket Three) provided the first internationally recognized standard by which progress in East-West detente could be measured. Of course, most of the principles contained in the Final Act are also part of the Constitutions of East European countries, as are those in the Charter of the United Nations and the Universal Declaration of Human Rights, to which all East European states subscribe. The human rights activists, one could say, did not have to wait until Helsinki. But it was probably the fact that the Final Act concentrated solely on European, not universal, issues that made it a more suitable vehicle for protests. Perhaps most important of all was the prospect of the follow-up summit in Belgrade in June 1977. Because of the infrequency and importance of such follow-up meetings, charges that the Final Act had been violated would arouse more inter-

est than, for example, protests lost in the daily operations of committees at the United Nations.

Another contributing factor was the rise of Eurocommunism.
This outlook, represented most strongly by the Italian, Spanish,
and French communist parties, emphasizes respect for human rights
and the independence of each national party. The differences between
the loyalist and autonomous parties became dramatically clear at the
conference of European communist and workers' parties in East
Berlin in June 1976. While the East European and some Western
parties defended the Soviet model of communism, PCI leader Enrico
Berlinguer underlined the autonomy of each party and argued for a
"secular, nonideological" state, political plurality, trade union
autonomy, and the freedoms of religion and of expression.[28] Santiago
Carrillo, leader of the outlawed Spanish CP, said, "We are beginning
to lose the characteristics of a Church." As for "fundamental freedoms," Carrillo declared that "those of us who suffered under Franco's
dictatorship for 40 years have learned the value of these freedoms,
which deserve to be defended with the utmost vigor."[29] As the official daily of the host party, Neues Deutschland was obliged to publish
these speeches in full, and this, Wolf Biermann later reported, led
to "passionate discussions of the speeches of Comrades Berlinguer,
Carrillo, and Marchais" among young people.[30]

Another factor promoting Eurocommunism in Eastern Europe
is the solidarity of its leaders with the dissidents. The Eurocommunists have long been critical of the Soviet invasion of Czechoslovakia
and in recent years steadily increased their denunciations of repression in Eastern Europe. The PCF was instrumental in securing the
release of Soviet dissident Leonid Plyushch, and the PCI responded
immediately to Jacek Kuron's appeal for investigation on the party
level on behalf of the striking workers on trial. These moves made
the Eurocommunists not only ideological brothers but significant
political allies of the dissidents in their struggles with their own
governments. The fact that influential communist parties in the West
aid dissenters in the East makes it extremely difficult for Moscow
to attack this "fraternal assistance" without endangering the unity
of the communist movement.

For all the common influences, though, there seemed to be no
coordination between the protests in the different countries. The
main influences—Helsinki and Eurocommunism—were present in each
protest wave, the others in varying degrees depending on the country.
But there are significant national factors that make each protest movement different. With the restlessness of the workers and the power
of the Church behind them, the Polish human rights activists were
able to act far more openly and boldly than, for example, the Charter
77 members in Czechoslovakia, where dissent in any form besides

apathy has little root among the people. The division of the German nation spawned a post-Helsinki emigration trend almost unique to the GDR.

In the long run, two other problems will face the East European governments. The first is a strengthening of the disappointment with detente that has developed in the West. The Helsinki agreement has come under heavy fire from conservative circles in several Western countries. If the Helsinki-based demands of the current protest wave are rejected by the local governments, there could be pressure for Western countries to give some sort of suitable response to indicate their disapproval. Judging from editorials in the East European press, the communist leaders already see an anti-detente trend in the West; they would presumably expect increased tension if detente turned sour.

The second problem concerns the unity of the communist movement itself. The Eurocommunist parties have regularly criticized official measures against dissent in Eastern Europe. As the anti-dissident campaign grows in that area, however, the West will call not only for Eurocommunist criticism of specific issues, but for a rigorous Eurocommunist analysis of the whole system—that is, a formal break with the loyalist parties and a full-scale critical review of their system. The Italian communist press, for example, has observed that "there are many who urge the West's Marxists—and Communists in particular—to face up to a closely reasoned confrontation with the reality of the socialist countries."[31] One writer recently suggested that the "instruments of the most radical criticism of capitalism" that the Marxists possess "should be applied to the very countries that have begun the construction of 'real socialism.'"[32] If these pressures pushing the Eurocommunists toward a real critique of the Soviet model are successful, the heresies that would result could lead to open dispute and possibly schism. Thus, two Soviet policy priorities—detente and the unity of the communist movement—have been endangered by the protests cropping up in Moscow's backyard.

NOTES

1. Most reports cited the figure 242 (see The Times [London], 12 January 1977), but the Frankfurter Allgemeine Zeitung (7 January 1977) stated that the document contained 257 signatures.
2. See The Times, 7 January 1977.
3. Stampa Sera (Turin), 10 January 1977.
4. Reuter, 21 January 1977
5. See Le Monde (Paris), 12 January 1977.

6. International Herald-Tribune (Paris), 18 January 1977.

7. Agence France-Presse (AFP), 29 June 1976.

8. For the text of Kuron's letter, see Agencia Nationale Stampa Associata (ANSA), 19 July 1976.

9. United Press International (UPI), 20 July 1976.

10. For text, see ibid., 28 September 1976.

11. Neue Zuercher Zeitung, 4 January 1977; Die Zeit, 7 January 1977; and UPI, 5 January 1977.

12. Le Monde, 18 January 1977.

13. UPI, 10 September 1976.

14. Frankfurter Allgemeine Zeitung, 28 September 1976. Soon afterward, seven Ursus workers were set free.

15. Trybuna Ludu (Warsaw), 6 January 1977.

16. UPI, 29 January 1977.

17. Polska Agencja Prasowa (PAP), 8 January 1977.

18. Le Monde, 18 January 1977, and Reuter, 22 January 1977.

19. Deutsche Presse-Agentur (dpa), 18 November 1976.

20. Frankfurter Rundschau, 21 December 1976.

21. By comparison, the (pre-detente) figure for 1970 was 500. For more on the exit visa problem, see Deutsches Allgemeines Sonntagsblatt (Hamburg), 21 November 1976.

22. Frankfurter Allgemeine Zeitung, 13 January 1977.

23. Der Spiegel (Hamburg), 20 September 1976.

24. AFP, 24 November 1976.

25. Reuter, 12 November 1976.

26. Sueddeutsche Zeitung (Munich), 24 January 1977.

27. Die Zeit (Hamburg), 31 December 1976.

28. Allgemeiner Deutscher Nachrichtendienst (ADN), 30 June 1976.

29. Radio Independent Spain, 30 June 1976.

30. Der Spiegel, 20 September 1976.

31. Rinascita (Rome), 14 January 1977.

32. l'Unità (Milan), 29 December 1976.

14

THE POLISH PRICE
INCREASE PROTESTS
Thomas E. Heneghan

The 25 June 1976 price protests are gone but not forgotten in Poland. The worker unrest, directed against the dramatic price increases proposed in the Sejm on June 24, caused more problems than the price hikes were meant to solve. After revoking the proposals, the government was in the unenviable position of having the same problems waiting to be solved and decreased authority with which to do so. In addition, the government's retreat carried political implications as well, since concessions to one social group could bring demands from another. Warsaw's immediate reaction was to hold support rallies around the country and promise to consult more with the people before any increases were reproposed. In the weeks that followed, the leadership was at pains to keep all the factors involvod in this issue in some sort of acceptable balance.

An examination of these factors reveals how complex was the issue that faced the Polish leadership. The first problem appeared in connection with the June 25 events themselves. Just what did happen? Were the proposed price increases necessary? Did the leadership think they would be accepted without difficulty? The aftermath of the protests also led to important questions. Why did the government decide to try certain strikers, and why were the sentences so severe? Would the intellectuals' protests, as well as those of the Italian CP, have any effect on further court proceedings? Looking to the longer term, what effects would this whole episode have on leadership in Poland? Not all these questions can be answered now

---

This chapter is a shortened and updated version of Thomas E. Heneghan, "The Summer Storm in Poland," RAD Background Report/176, Radio Free Europe Research, 16 August 1976.

with certainty. But the events of June 25 can be seen with a somewhat more critical eye and, perhaps, with a bit more understanding.

THE EVENTS

Perhaps the best way to start is to review the events surrounding
the price-increase issue. Basic food prices, frozen since 1966, had
become a sensitive political issue for Gierek by the mid-1970s. Unwilling to strain the post-December (1970) social contract, the party
leadership continued to subsidize basic food commodities despite
bad harvests, a worsening international financial standing, and the
growing buying power of the population. The housewives' protest
against food shortages in early 1975 was a warning the leadership
accepted seriously. That December, at the seventh party congress,
Gierek announced that basic food prices would be increased after
consultations with the workers. Although occasional reports claimed
that surveys[1] or meetings[2] had taken place, there was little indication
of wide consultation before Premier Piotr Jaroszewicz presented
the government's price proposals to the Sejm on June 24. The motion,
which was immediately accepted, provided for dramatic increases
in the prices of many products—for example, a 69 percent average
increase for meat, and 40 percent for grain. The package, which
was to go into effect on June 28, also foresaw immediate increases
in wages, allowances, and pensions to offset the price rises.

Twenty-four hours later, Jaroszewicz was forced to announce
the withdrawal of the price proposals. In the interim, workers in
several factories around the country expressed their disapproval in
meetings, through strikes, and in some instances by destruction
and vandalism. Workers at the Ursus Tractor Factory outside Warsaw ripped up railroad tracks and held up traffic on the main rail
line to the west. In Radom, strikers' protests were accompanied by
vandalism and looting, and the local party headquarters was set on
fire. In announcing the withdrawal of the planned increases that
evening, Jaroszewicz argued that some sort of price rise remained
necessary. It would come, however, only after further consultation
with the workers, a process that would require several months to
complete. Although official reaction to the disturbances began with
criticism of "rowdies and unsocial elements," it soon turned to the
issue of consultation and concentrated on this question and on the
inevitability of price increases. In rallies around the country, support was expressed for the leadership's policies and its practice of
consulting with the workers.

Gierek, who had stayed on the sidelines on June 24, made his
first statement on July 2, at a rally in Katowice. The speech was

rather conciliatory in tone, with appeals to Polish patriotism and economic rationality and special emphasis on party-people consultations. In a speech on July 5 Jaroszewicz said that prices for meat, sugar, fish, and poultry would not be raised as high as planned, but that those of other products, such as bread and baked goods—which were not supposed to rise—would be increased by a small amount. The government would include these suggestions in a draft law it would present for discussion in Sejm committees. Another round of consultations with the workers would take place before the government presented its final draft bill to the Sejm for approval. It was in these speeches that the leadership outlined the offensive it planned to take on the price issue.

In mid-July Jaroszewicz gave further details of the government's price plans. Reporting to the Politburo "in agreement with the announcement of 25 June 1976,"[3] the premier announced that the government had decided to raise only the prices for meat, meat products, and poultry, and only by 35 percent. When these increases would take effect was not stated. All other increases, the premier continued, would be delayed until 1977, and then introduced in steps. In a related development, the Council of Ministers announced that agricultural procurement prices and the cost of "agricultural means of production" would rise immediately. These increases are identical to those introduced in the controversial price-increase package. By authorizing these increases without retail price hikes, the government subjected itself to further economic burdens in the form of higher subsidies for food products, but the need for added investment in agriculture was evidently great enough to warrant this expensive step.

WERE PRICE INCREASES NECESSARY?

If nothing else, the cost of the food subsidies alone justified some sort of price increase. The most interesting revelation in the preprotest articles was that the state had paid out more than 100 billion zloty for food subsidies in 1975. Only 22 billion zloty were spent on subsidies in 1970, and yearly increases have oscillated between 20 and 40 percent since then. Owing to the increase in the price of slaughter livestock in 1975, one paper went on to explain,[4] the state would probably spend only about 37 billion zloty on subsidies in 1976. Nevertheless they represent a burden, since they "limit the economic resources for stepping up agricultural output and . . . unreasonably boost demand for food products, making them 'competitive' in relation to other goods and services and seriously hindering increases in consumption and real incomes."

The consumption structure problem, another factor making price increases advisable, was a direct result of the freeze on basic food products. Since Gierek came to power, average wages have risen 40 percent while basic foodstuffs have remained at their pre-December 1970 levels. Meat and meat products seemed to be favorite purchases for Polish consumers, especially since prices were relatively low and became even lower—comparatively speaking—with each wage increase. This put special pressure on this sector of the food market, and this pressure led to recurring shortages of meat in the cities.

Polish agricultural authorities have had to spend more foreign currency in order to increase domestic production. Because of the poor harvests in 1974 and 1975, Warsaw has been forced to buy grain abroad to feed its animal population, whose meat is one of the country's successful export items. The Soviet Union, normally a supplier of grain to Eastern Europe, also had poor harvests, and therefore failed to fulfill its contractual obligations to Warsaw. As a result, Poland bought about 2 million tons of grain from the United States in 1975 before sales were stopped.[5] In November of that year Poland signed a five-year agreement with the United States that provided for Polish purchases of 2 million to 2.5 million tons of grain annually. It should be noted that, in all, Poland imported 4.4 million tons of grain in 1975, most of which came from the West and 70 percent of which was used as fodder.[6] Imports represented 24.3 percent of that year's grain supply. Jaroszewicz underlined the importance of such imports in his speech before the Sejm in March, when he said that "the rapid increase in the rate of meat production in the last five years was mainly attributable to higher grain and fodder imports."

Viewed against Poland's trade difficulties, such dependence on imported goods presents considerable problems. It is not only grain but also technology and credits that Poland needs from the West. The turn toward the West for trade and credits characteristic of the Gierek economic outlook reached a point in late 1974–early 1975 when trade was almost equally divided between East and West. Although this acted as an important catalyst for Poland's domestic development, it also put Warsaw deeply in debt to the West and tilted the country's balance of trade to its own disadvantage. Its overall debts in the West were estimated at $6.0 billion to $6.5 billion in the summer of 1976, and Western bankers calculated the total trade deficit with the West at $2.5 billion in 1975, a sizable jump over the estimated $1.8-billion deficit in 1974.[7]

The oil-price problem created difficulties for Poland as well. With the price of Soviet oil rising by 131 percent in 1975 and then pegged to a sliding price mechanism that follows adjusted world prices, the cost of Polish imports of Soviet oil will rise in the present five-year period. The original Polish-Soviet contracts for 1976–80

oil deliveries, which provided for about 50 percent of Poland's oil
needs by 1980 (as opposed to 85 percent in 1975)[8] at first seemed
to indicate that Warsaw would have to make major purchases of oil
in the West to take up the slack. A subsequently announced plan to
cut Poland's refineries expansion program and give added emphasis
to coal will help reduce the bill for oil imports. But since Poland
will be paying roughly twice as much for relatively less Soviet oil,
there will still be a need for substantial imports from the West.
And, since the Soviet oil must be paid for under bilateral-bicommodity
arrangements (or, for above-quota sales, in hard currency or export-
able goods), the rising Comecon prices will also have the effect of
drawing Poland back toward closer trade relations with the other
Comecon countries. This could hinder the export offensive in the
West, which the planners had foreseen as the method by which the
debts of the import boom would be repaid.

Since the prices of imported oil and grain are forces outside
Poland's control and the export offensive intended to repay Western
debts has been delayed, Warsaw has turned to agriculture as the
sector in which a solution could most probably be found. The emphasis is on agricultural self-sufficiency, but this is a goal the leadership admits is a rather difficult one to reach. The delayed price
increases were supposed to help foot the bill for the increase in agricultural procurement prices, which planners felt was necessary to
encourage higher production. The fact that procurement prices were
raised later, without a parallel rise in retail prices, stands as further
proof of the need to give the peasants added incentives. Interestingly,
procurement prices for cattle increased during the previous five-year
period by 250 percent, and for pigs the figure was 230 percent, while
procurement prices for grains rose only by 21.2 percent.[9] Since
grain used for fodder is such an important element in meat production,
one wonders why meat production was emphasized while grain production was not.

Another area in need of investment is agricultural mechanization.
The need to expand it was never put as clearly as in Trybuna Ludu[10]
after the withdrawal of the June 24 price proposals. Only about 40
percent of all farms are fully mechanized, the paper said, and this
means that Polish agriculture is about ten years behind developments
in Romania and Bulgaria, 15 years behind Czechoslovakia and the
GDR, and up to 20 years behind such Western states as France and
Italy. At present, the socialized sector of agriculture is heavily
favored in the distribution of agricultural machinery. Of 3 million
private farms, 250,000 are fully mechanized, 500,000 have adequate
facilities, and the rest either depend on equipment-sharing arrangements in the local agricultural circle or use horses and human labor.

A third means by which the party hopes to boost agricultural production is socialization of agriculture. Almost 80 percent of all agricultural land is in the hands of private peasants, and the average plot is about five hectares in area. Since private farming is such a sensitive political issue in Poland, official policy since Gierek came to power has been to foster the "socialist transformation of agriculture" by offering pensions to older farmers who sell their land to the state. Approximately one-third of Poland's private farmers are close to retirement, and many of them have no one to whom they can transfer the land, since modernization has drawn many youths from the country into the cities. Demographic trends indicate that this method of transforming private farming into socialist agriculture could make significant changes in the Polish countryside in the coming decades.

Interestingly, the socialization program has political boundaries on both sides. On the one hand, the Polish bishops have spoken up against the program, and it seems that the episcopate has become an unofficial spokesman for the unorganized (but mostly church-going) peasantry. On the other hand, CPSU party leader Leonid Brezhnev made Moscow's views on Polish agriculture clear at the PUWP's Seventh Congress in December 1975, when he said that one of the tasks facing the Polish party was "the continuation until final victory of socialist relations in town and country." Wedged in between these pressures are the country's economic difficulties. It seems that Gierek is trying to promote the socialization of agriculture as much as possible, but his ability to push the program on to further stages depends on the state of agricultural production and the political mood of the population at the time.

WEAK LINKS IN THE CHAIN OF COMMUNICATION

Press commentaries after the June 25 protests consistently argued that the people understood the need for price increases. Peaceful and constructive consultations on the price proposals had been taking place on that day, the media contended, but handfuls of individuals disturbed the proceedings in several places. In fact, the economic necessity of the price increases does seem clear enough. But if the leadership had so many understandable reasons for wanting to raise prices, why did it withhold most of them and attempt to introduce the increases in a single swoop?

It is improbable that the government was unaware of the implications of the price increases. Although he originally let the Gomulka price increases stand, Gierek realized—after about two months of

unrest—that the Polish workers were opposed to them and he finally
rescinded them. Since then, price increases have been so sensitive
a topic that they have rarely been discussed publicly. Every year
wages have been allowed to rise while prices have remained stable,
and Gierek kept promising an improvement in the standard of living.
That he felt the 1970 increases—which averaged only 17 percent—were
necessary and still did nothing about new price hikes until 1976
indicates how cautious he has been in this regard. For all his caution,
however, he knew that increases would have to be introduced. The
only question was how this should be done, and it was probably here
that serious mistakes were made.

One of the official explanations for the workers' rejection of the
price proposals was that there was not enough prior consultation
between party and people. This line of argument was taken up indirectly by Gierek, who had the idea of consultations and said that
the next round of price increases would be preceded by wider discussion than—it was implied—was previously the case. The crucial
variable here is the meaning of the word "consultation." Gierek had
promised at the party congress in December 1975 that prices would
only be raised after the party had consulted with the people. It seems,
however, that while the party took steps to test the waters of public
opinion, it did not actually consult with the people. In an interview
with the West German weekly Stern, [11] Deputy Premier Mieczyslaw
Jagielski said that the price increase problem "was discussed and a
public opinion poll was conducted, but on a limited basis." Thus,
when Premier Jaroszewicz spoke on June 24 of "a lively discussion
and national debate," he presumably was referring to the discussions
within the party hierarchy, the polls mentioned above, and the press
campaign shortly before the price increases were proposed.

A poll was presumably taken of the party organizations in the
voivodships and in the large industrial enterprises, and it may be
that the reports from this level were more positive than the situation
actually warranted. This is perhaps understandable, since local
party organizations might be inclined to paint a rosier picture of
conditions in their areas than actually existed. Caught between the
economic and the political considerations of the increase, the party
leadership might have seen Gierek's popularity, the successful trip
to West Germany, and the favorable reports from the party organizations as a sufficient buffer against the discontent the economically
necessary steps would arouse.

The possibility of communication difficulties at the local level
was discussed in an interesting Zycie Partii article, [12] which questioned whether the accepted practice of filling managerial posts with
party officials was perhaps not the best solution to the problem of
ensuring party influence within the government and the economy.

One significant problem seems to be posed when a party post has been taken over by a leading manager. Although the party official may be interested in his party duties, the tendency to emphasize the managerial and economic aspects of a decision is strong. Furthermore, since local party officials—for example in the Office Committees—often hold both party offices and high managerial posts, "it is difficult to expect that during a basic party organization meeting criticism will be directed against a director who is presiding over the meeting in his capacity of Office Committee secretary." In addition, the territorial administration reform of 1975 and numerous events since then have left local party officials with "not always enough time to think about how to raise the efficiency of party operations in the voivodship offices or on other administrative levels."

The territorial administration reform evidently caused problems at the parish level as well. According to the article, the inexperience of the parish office staffs led to "a great deal of controversy," and

> a certain amount of time will have to pass before the parish office staffs finally achieve the necessary level of experience in administrative affairs. On the other hand, one is often confronted with the opinion, current in the parish offices, that the voivodship office and the people working for it treat the parish officials with indifference, disregard their opinions, go so far as to curb their authority, and so on.

Trybuna Ludu took up the observations made in Zycie Partii. In its August 3 edition, the party daily carried an article about the Ursus plant that contained excerpts from the plant committee's report on the events and aftermath of the June 25 protests.* After detailing the extent of losses attributable to the protests, the report said:

> The seventh congress resolution stated that there would be adjustments in the prices of goods. We take the view that each action of this kind must be shored up by the necessary economic analyses, which should be presented to the people and must be preceded by preparatory political work carried out by extensive political-economic aktifs.

---

*The report "did not conceal the fact that out of 14,000 Ursus workers, only 1,200 loyalists stayed behind to man the foundries and other essential facilities."[13]

It must be clearly stated that the sociopolitical and economic aktifs of the Ursus plant were not prepared for
such contingencies. It is absolutely necessary to create
a system of liaison between the administrative and
sociopolitical leadership and all the plant workers.

The picture these two articles paint clashes only apparently with
Gierek's reputed connection with the workers. The enthusiasm of
the Katowice rally, at which Gierek spoke one week after the protests,
attests to the more than formal support he enjoys among them. But
while the connection between the party leader and the grass roots
may be good, apparently the intervening levels—in the plant and between administrative bureaucracies—may not be as efficient and
communicative as they should be. If contacts between the party aktifs
and the workers were as faulty as the Trybuna Ludu article portrays
those in Ursus, then a considerable amount of the reporting "from
the base" may have been inexact. Zycie Partii implies that some
of the problems at the local level are the result of the 1975 reforms.
It may be that the elimination of the districts—the administrative layer
between the parishes and the voivodships—inhibited the efficiency of
reporting from the base. Thus a situation may have developed in
which the party leadership was misled by the inadequate reporting of
its own local organizations.
An immeasurable but real possibility is that Warsaw may have
been under pressure from abroad to raise its prices. Such pressure
could have come from both East and West. Seen through Comecon
eyes, the Polish economy cannot be considered totally in order, with
about 80 percent of the country's agriculture in private hands, trade
roughly balanced between East and West, indebtedness still on the
rise, and prices uneconomically low. Soviet party leader Leonid
Brezhnev presumably gave the official Comecon opinion on Polish
agriculture at the PUWP's congress in December 1975 when he cited
as one of Poland's main tasks "continuing until final victory to set
up socialist relations in town and country." Since Comecon—and
especially Soviet—indebtedness is also climbing, no pot could call
any kettle black; caution is presumably the work throughout Comecon.
But if debts from trade and credits continue to rise, then presumably
other factors, such as domestic prices, must be called on to take up
the slack in the state treasury. From the Comecon side, it could be
argued that Warsaw must bring its domestic prices more into line
with those prevailing in the other East European countries. Coordination of prices is one of the goals set out in the Comecon Comprehensive Program, and the question has become even more topical since
the 1975 changes in Comecon raw material prices. Equally, Poland's

extensive trade dealings with the West may have exerted pressure
on the domestic price situation.* Western observers have been
speculating about Poland's credit ceiling, and the difficulties the
Poles had in tying up all the credit lines they hoped to receive during
Gierek's visit to Bonn may have represented a watershed beyond
which credits would become increasingly difficult to arrange. This
sort of pressure could also have moved Warsaw to opt for an economically more rational system of basic food prices.

In retrospect, the urgency of the economic arguments, bolstered
by the reports that increases would be accepted by the people, was
probably the deciding factor in the government's decision to announce
the fateful price proposals. From an economist's point of view, the
price package presented an opportunity to raise prices, increase
agricultural procurement rates, shunt demand away from the scarcer
items, introduce flexible pricing practices, and maintain the average
standard of living, all at the same time. The neatness of it all was
probably very attractive to the economists and managers, and the
political leaders, apparently hoping to get the long-delayed price
increases taken care of in one swoop, finally agreed with the economists' suggestions. As is now evident, this was a grave miscalculation of the people's mood, and the leadership will now probably delay
all the longer before trying to solve the price problem again.

THE TRIALS AND THE PROTESTS

After the rallies in support of the government passed, the trials
of workers who participated in the strikes began. In the Radom case,
six men were sentenced to prison terms of four to ten years for
"taking a particularly active part on last June 25 in street riots,
attacks on militia officials, and plundering public property."[15] The
seven men tried for the Ursus disturbances received sentences ranging
from three to five years for destroying railroad tracks, derailing a
locomotive, and threatening its engineer.[16] The court's severity in
the Radom cases was expected, since official statements had attempted
to portray the active dissenters there as "antisocial elements" and
"hooligans." But it was assumed that the Ursus workers would not
receive such harsh sentences. In handing down his opinion, the judge
in the Ursus trial reportedly told the court that the sentences would
have been more severe had the workers not had such good records.[17]

---

*There were no known cases of direct pressure from Western
creditors before the price proposals were made on June 24. Soon
afterward, however, Reuter reported that Western bankers were
reviewing their rates for credit to Poland.[14]

In subsequent statements, Jaroszewicz continued to insist on harsh treatment of criminal elements. Late in July the premier said that the party would continue its attempts to win over those persons who did not understand the government's policy. But the leadership would have to take appropriate measures against "all destructive elements that do not shy away from a conflict with the law." Action would also have to be taken, the premier continued, against "careless people who take under their protective wings persons who do not deserve to belong to the work forces of our leading enterprises."18

The "careless people" Jaroszewicz referred to were presumably the Polish intellectuals who had protested against the government's handling of the workers. The first open letter, written shortly after the strikes, called for an "authentic dialogue" between party and people and "a broadening of democratic liberties" within society. "The events of the last few days," the letter stated, "indicated that under the present system of rule the only way in which the real views of the citizens emerge is in dangerous outbursts of social dissatis- faction. This kind of system cannot be continued without risking incalculable catastrophe."

"The trade unions did not truly represent the workers during the latest events, thus proving that they are fictitious," it continued. To remedy the situation, nationwide discussions must be more authen- tic, and a "broadening of democratic liberties," including a free press and the right of free association, must be allowed.19

In mid-July, after the sentences in the Radom and Ursus trials were announced, dissident historian Jacek Kuron appealed to Italian communist leader Enrico Berlinguer to support the workers who had been tried for their participation in the protests.20 In his letter Kuron described the events of June 24–25 and stated that "workers reacted spontaneously with an almost general stoppage of work. In various localities there were street demonstrations." He continued:

> In the cities and in the countryside massive repression
> has begun against the participants in the demonstrations
> and the strikers. . . . Thousands of workers were fired,
> there were numerous arrests in Radom and Ursus, and
> those who leave the police offices show evidence of physi-
> cal maltreatment, very serious in some cases.

Blame for the damage done during the protests did not lie with the demonstrators, Kuron argued. Rather, he said, it should be placed on a system that did not allow the workers any means of expressing their opinions. To hold "the participants in the workers' demonstrations morally and legally responsible" for damage that was actually caused by the system, he continued, "has nothing to do with

legality. . . . Crimes must be punished, but it is inadmissible to
punish demonstrators who resist the police when the authors of the
bloody massacre of workers on the Baltic Coast have escaped all
punishment." Kuron seemed particularly concerned about what would
happen at the local level. "We have no possibility of controlling the
conduct of legal proceedings [at this level]," he complained. Therefore, "only a general amnesty for all participants in the June demonstrations can arrest the terror against the workers. It is only public
opinion in the countries where it is truly independent that can take
up the struggle for this amnesty."

The PCI responded promptly to this appeal. In a message to
the PUWP, its secretariat expressed concern about the trials and
expressed the "hope that measures tending to show moderation and
also clemency may be adopted and publicized." The Italian Communists reiterated their belief that "it must be possible in the socialist
countries to resolve social contrasts and even conflicts without serious disturbances through a continuous search for active collaboration
by the workers." In a report criticizing government spokesman
Janiurek's press conference statements for "not coming to grips with
the political problems" raised by the PCI's message, the PCI daily
l'Unità21 wrote that the Italian party's secretariat had "assumed the
role of spokesman for the concern evoked by the sentences and increased by the restrictions placed on news coverage."

Dissident intellectuals changed tactics in late September with
the creation of the Committee for the Defense of the Workers. The
14 founding members declared in their first statement that the workers who protested on June 25 had been subjected to "repressive
measures and physical terror." The police handled them brutally,
they were forced to confess to acts of violence, and courts passed
verdicts without sufficient evidence. The authorities, the statement
continued, "infringed human rights approved by international law and
laws binding in Poland—i.e., the right to work, the right to freely
express opinions, and the right to participate in meetings and demonstrations." Since the fired workers could no longer expect help from
the state, the communique announced, the committee had been formed
to provide them and their families with financial, legal, and medical
aid. It also intended to pressure the government to grant amnesty
to those workers jailed after the protests and reinstate those who
had been fired. To back up its work, the committee began collecting
money within Poland and abroad, sending observers to workers' trials,
and reporting on these trials as well as on the events of June 25 in
carefully documented subsequent communiques.22

These developments posed special problems for the leadership.
Protests from the workers appeared only when economic issues were
at stake, and the leadership could expect them to fade when economic

concessions were granted. Church opposition is an important factor
in People's Poland, and Warsaw is often careful not to antagonize
the bishops needlessly, since they can cause problems for the government. But the Church is also wary of appearing to be in total opposition to the government, lest its opposition to certain policies in the
long run do harm to the economy or the standard of living the Poles
enjoy. This is part of the Church's role as a "loyal opposition."
But intellectual protest, usually the most ineffective of the three,
can present radical critiques of Polish society and offer alternative
plans for development. All shades of political opinion are represented
in the protests; many of the committee members, for example, were
leftist critics who did not want to get rid of the system as much as to
reform it according to their own designs. These critics can attract
the interest of certain Western groups such as the Eurocommunists,
whose criticism of Polish policies is more damaging to Warsaw than,
say, Vatican complaints about the small number of permits issued
for the construction of new churches. With these intellectuals firmly
established in the troika of protest against party policies, the stakes
for the PUWP have gone beyond economic policy to issues such as
the unity of the communist movement.

THE IMPLICATIONS

Longer-range domestic considerations also figured in the leadership's actions. The price protests gave concrete expression to a
process visible since early 1975—that is, the deterioration of the
economic base of the post-December social contract and the resultant
rise of various political tensions. The central legitimizing element of
of the Gierek team was its dedication to economic expansion and
material improvement. Gierek came to power at a time when detente
and East-West trade were on the upswing, and his economic and
diplomatic skills enabled him to use these trends to improve Poland's
standard of living and expand its relations with other countries. The
effects of international inflation and recession, as well as Poland's
debts and poor harvests, began to slow the boom, however, and this
caused political tension. In the coming years, this change will probably force Gierek to draw in his horns on several issues. Unpopular
measures—such as price increases—will have to be pushed through,
and policies formerly considered too controversial—such as the
socialization of agriculture—will probably receive greater emphasis.
The focus of Polish domestic politics is shifting from economic to
political issues, and Gierek will have to become more of a mediator
between interest groups than he has been in the past. This form of
"consensus socialism" could prove very difficult for the PUWP, and

the consultation method now being promoted by the party may not
cover all the bases in the emerging political constellation.

This fluidity in Polish politics is probably the most important
result of the price protests. Whereas the Gierek leadership at one
time could almost disregard all social groups but the workers, the
price issue and the earlier constitutional issue have proven that every
group has definite interests that will have to be satisfied in some way.
And since Warsaw has only limited resources at its disposal, the
satisfaction of one group's demands can mean postponement of another
group's satisfaction.

The danger this presents for the party leadership is that the need
for minimum consensus among the various social groups might lead
to a greater role for consultation. Shortly after the protests, party-
people consultations were being held up as the central means of
political decision-making in Poland and the constitutionally guaranteed
right of all citizens. If held within the limits the party seems to have
put around them, such consultations could help to keep the leadership
closer to the pulse of public opinion and also offer the workers a means
of peacefully expressing their opinions. Indeed, if managed properly,
a certain degree of consultation could help the party in formulating
and presenting its decisions, and this could even become a means of
legitimizing the party's leading role comparable—although not equal—
to the economic means used in the first phase of the Gierek era. Of
course, the inherent problem in all this is that the leading role of
the party, which party-people consultations should legitimize, could
become diluted by workers taking the "principle of consultations" too
literally. The uncertainty involved in the consultation option will
presumably move the leadership to use this new tool only when necessary, and neglect it whenever possible.

The coming years will probably present fewer opportunities to
neglect it, however. The need to introduce food price increases is
the most obvious example of problems whose solution the consultation
procedure should help to bring about, but there are several other
problems that will have to be acted upon in the years ahead. For
example, Gierek has spoken about a "flexible price policy" for some
time, and it would seem logical to introduce such a price mechanism
before another backlog, with the obvious political complications,
develops. But will the workers accept this innovation, or will they
insist on the rather ideal situation of frozen prices and rising wages?
Owing to bad harvests and the cancellation of Soviet grain deliveries,
Polish agriculture has come under growing pressure.

Warsaw sees the quickest and most effective solution of agriculture's present problems in accelerated socialization of private
agriculture—a program that has moved from the voluntary stage
of its initial years to the point where the inefficient private farmers

might be required to sell their land to the state. At some point in this program, the Church may feel compelled to draw a line beyond which it will no longer accept without opposition the socialization of agriculture and the transformation of traditional rural life in Poland. The Church may expand criticism of the educational system as the 1973 reforms come into effect in the majority of schools. The episcopate has already made several announcements criticizing the limitations these reforms have imposed on religious instruction and the changes evident in the way the nation's history and literature are presented to the students.[23] And, with the founding of the Committee for the Defense of the Workers and the continuing criticism from the PCI, Polish intellectuals will probably continue to express their disapproval and demands more frequently and forcefully. All these problems could cause situations in which the leadership might have to increase rather than decrease the role consultations play in decision making. Although Gierek, of all the East European leaders, may be the one most able to cope with such a situation, it could still present serious problems for the party and its position in society.

The specific conditions of the Polish situation probably explain why the June events did not have much direct effect on Warsaw's neighbors. In fact, Hungary introduced measures to deal with problems similar to those in Poland, and the transition was noticeably smoother. On July 1, while the Polish events were still fresh in people's minds, the Hungarians went ahead with the scheduled 30 percent increase in meat prices. Budapest even introduced wage and pension supplements to offset the higher prices. But the Polish and Hungarian situations differed in two essential points. First, the domestic situation in Hungary was not as strained as that in Poland. Secondly, the style in which the Hungarian increases were introduced also contributed to the smooth transition. General price increases were announced last November, and a program of gradual price changes was introduced. Budapest's well-publicized method of raising prices stands in strong contrast to Warsaw's proposals for dramatic and immediate increases. As for other neighbors, Czechoslovakia, in which there was also a certain tension between party and people, reacted to the Polish events with reassuring statements about the stability of Czechoslovak prices, while the GDR seemed to show no direct reaction. The internal situation in the latter country—both economically and politically—was less tense than in Poland, and thus the need to take noticeable compensatory measures was small.

In relations with the Soviet Union, signals moving from Moscow to Warsaw will probably be more important than vice-versa. The price protests were certainly watched with great interest in the Kremlin, and the Soviet Union, with its recent bad harvests and meatless Thursdays, also faced serious agricultural problems. But,

again, internal conditions are not comparable, and the same complications need not be expected in the Soviet Union. More important
were the Kremlin's statements of support for the Gierek leadership.
This support was underlined in early November when the Polish party
leader visited the Soviet Union with a delegation representing not only
the PUWP but also the United Peasant and Democratic Parties. During
this visit, Soviet party leader Leonid Brezhnev reiterated his support
for Gierek, to which the Polish leader responded with frequent praise
of the Soviet Union and of Polish-Soviet relations. On the economic
side, the Soviet Union promised to deliver about 1 million tons of
grain and to increase its deliveries of consumer goods. The visit
was important for Gierek for both the economic and the political
support it gave him. What it left unclear was what political price,
if any, the Polish leader might have to pay for this support.

If the June events do have an effect on the other East European
countries, it will be mainly a long-term one. Just as the protests
marked the end of the expansionist phase of the Gierek era, so they
may come to mark a similar shift in the rest of Eastern Europe as
well. The problems of rising oil prices and growing debts with the
West affect all Comecon states. It is difficult to predict whether
the still hypothetical "consensus socialism," of which vague outlines
have appeared in Poland, will really take root in that country, and
even more difficult to state with certainty whether it might then spill
over into the neighboring states. But if Gierek chooses to continue
down this path and succeeds in overcoming the problems on the horizon, some elements of his policy—or a combination of the Gierek-
Kadar approach to increasing prices—may appeal to the East European
leaders. On the other hand, Eastern Europe may not follow this path
at all. But the changes to be expected if it does would be great, and
this eventuality is surely on the minds of Poland's neighbors as they
read the news from Warsaw.

NOTES

1. Newsweek (New York), 26 January 1976.
2. Frankfurter Allgemeine Zeitung, 24 June 1976.
3. Polska Agencja Prasowa (PAP), 13 July 1976.
4. Trybuna Ludu (Warsaw), 23 June 1976.
5. See Polish Situation Report/30, Radio Free Europe Research,
26 September 1975, Item 2. Purchases were deferred because Washington felt that Poland was also buying for the Soviet Union, which
had been barred from making any further purchases in July in order
to avoid a repetition of the 1972 "wheat deal."
6. Trybuna Ludu, 9 April 1976.

7. See the International Herald-Tribune (Paris), 2 July 1976.
By the end of the year, these estimates had risen to $8 billion to
$10 billion.

8. See PAP, 28 February 1975, and the Journal of Commerce
(New York), 14 October 1975.

9. PAP, 14 July 1976.

10. 6 July 1976.

11. (Hamburg), 15 July 1976.

12. (Warsaw), April 1976.

13. Reuter, 10 August 1976.

14. See the International Herald-Tribune, 2 July 1976.

15. PAP, 19 July 1976.

16. Agence France-Presse (AFP), 20 July 1976.

17. Reuter, 20 July 1976.

18. Deutsche Presse Agentur (dpa), 25 July 1976.

19. See AFP and United Press International (UPI), 29 June 1976.

20. All quotations are taken from the Italian text transmitted by
Agencia Nationale Stampa Associata (ANSA), 19 July 1976.

21. (Milan), 30 July 1976.

22. For more information on the committee, see Chapter 13.

23. Radio Vatican, 3 August 1976, and Washington Post, 9 July
1976.

15

CZECHOSLOVAKIA AFTER
.THE 15TH PARTY CONGRESS
Thomas E. Heneghan

"As you see," said Gustav Husak, announcing his reelection to
the 15th party congress, "there were no surprises. You do not change
horses in midstream." And indeed the Communist Party of Czechoslovakia (CPCS) did not change horses at its congress in April 1976.
Except for retiring Ludvik Svoboda, the entire Presidium was reelected and Husak was retained as its head. Touches of Husak's
policies were also evident at the congress, such as a partial amnesty
for purged party members. There was ample praise for him from
the foreign delegates, and the tone of most speeches was compatible
with his policies. In short, the congress reconfirmed Husak's position
and the continuance of the present policies in Prague.

Although hidden behind the facade of unity, there was a second
horse also trying to lead the party across the stream. The hard-line
faction* within the party was quiet at the congress, and two of Husak's

---

*Characterizing politicians and their policies is often difficult,
and the factions of the normalization period are no exception here.
For clarity's sake, "hard-line" will be used in this chapter to describe
the orthodox policies most commonly associated with Vasil Bilak,
while "conservative" will be used for Husak's position. The party
leader is often referred to as "moderate," which, simply in relation
to the hard-liners, can be said to be true. But a truly moderate
position in Eastern Europe would presumably be more like that of

---

This chapter is a shortened and updated version of Thomas E.
Heneghan, "Czechoslovakia After the 15th Party Congress," RAD Background Report/165, Radio Free Europe Research, 27 July 1976.

main opponents, Vasil Bilak and Alois Indra, did not even address the gathering. This detail could be taken as a plus for Husak, who thus dominated the congress stage. But could it not also be taken as a sign of his weakness, because he could not let the two men speak for fear of the divisive orthodoxy they might air in their addresses? It is probably indicative of the present constellation of power in Prague that either of these possibilities could be true.

This analysis attempts to examine the postcongress balance of forces in Prague. As the first section will show, the split within the party stands at the center of the problems facing the country now and in the future. This split fostered instability within the leadership and prevented decisive action being taken to deal with the challenges the economic and social situations present. Such central instability makes prediction impossible and speculation a tenuous enterprise. But it is a subject worth consideration because of the problems waiting in the future. (Because it is dealt with in detail in Chapter 10, the Czechoslovak economy will not be extensively analyzed in this chapter.)

THE PARTY

If prestige and protocol equaled influence, Gustav Husak would be in clear control of the CPCS today. During 1975 and 1976, he chalked up a series of impressive coups that should have enhanced his status as leader and strengthened his hand within the party. To a minimal extent they did so, but, despite the new titles and the repeated statements of Soviet support, the party leader was still unable to extend his power and influence beyond the formal boundaries of party leadership. He is opposed by a strong hard-line faction within the leadership, and is confronted with a party base that, if not actively hard line, is certainly not actively pro-Husak. The problem is further compounded by hard-line predominance within the party apparat and in important areas of party policy. These positions are not strong enough to serve as a springboard for a hard-line takeover of the party. But they do provide their patrons with sufficient influence to launch repeated attacks on policy initiatives by the conservatives, and have more than once allowed them to squeeze significant policy concessions from the leader they cannot oust.

Janos Kadar in Hungary, or Husak's own policies as he presented them during the Prague Spring. Since a later section will argue that Husak has not been able to achieve a Kadarite balance between party and people, it would be somewhat misleading to continue calling his policies moderate.

It is necessary to ask whence these two competing factions in the party leadership derive the power and authority to wage these battles against each other. In each case Soviet support plays an important role, but there are also significant domestic factors that add to each faction's base.

Numerous visits and words of praise in recent years have underlined time and again that Leonid Brezhnev considers Husak the most capable and dependable politician within the leadership of the CPCS. But his initial years as party leader were plagued by lack of a clear and decisive imprimatur from the Kremlin. Other factions within the Soviet leadership seemed to favor the hard-line group, an ambivalence that gave the orthodox elements in the CPCS added leverage in the early 1970s. By 1973, however, a number of developments—the political trials, the eclipse of some hard-line supporters in Moscow, and Brezhnev's growing power—had shifted Moscow's backing more decisively toward the conservative group. Since that time Husak has often been upgraded on the scale of Soviet praise and backing; his position, as far as the Soviets are concerned, is now fairly well secured.

Two arguments initially spoke in Husak's favor. First, in the months after the August 1968 invasion, he showed a talent for outmaneuvering the reformers—as can be seen in his campaign against Josef Smrkovsky—without falling in with the hard-liners. This bridge-building function was certainly necessary in the transition from reformist to orthodox leadership, and here Husak showed himself well qualified. Secondly, since all the popular and experienced politicians to the liberal side of his then moderate stand were disqualified for the leadership, Husak had little competition as the "lesser evil." Many of the orthodox politicians were either discredited by their ties to Novotny or simply unpopular because of their policies. This put Husak, himself only moderately popular, in an advantageous position.

Although this power base was limited at the beginning, the passage of time saw it grow. The most plausible reason for Husak's increasing influence was the fact that his policies worked. Despite the problems posed by unruly dissidents and apathetic workers, the normalization course brought order back into Prague's political life, satisfied consumer demands, and kept the country out of international headlines. By 1973, Western dignitaries had again begun visiting Prague, and little fuss was made about Czechoslovakia at the Conference on Security and Cooperation in Europe. Some of the more prominent reformist writers even went through the obligatory self-criticism and reappeared in print.

One area where Husak seems to have been less successful is in building a base within the party. Here the hard-line faction seems to have either made or retained a core of power that gives it the influence it needs in Prague. At the top, of course, this faction is represented by such politicians as Vasil Bilak, responsible for ideology and foreign affairs, and Antonin Kapek, the Prague municipal party leader. But this power seems to extend further down through the party ranks. After the exchange of party cards in 1970, CPCS membership dropped by 28 percent, and one can safely assume that this 28 percent represented the progressive element in the party. The remaining 72 percent of the prepurge party presumably falls into a smaller group that supports party policy actively, and a larger one that hopes a minimum of political activity will ensure a maximum of private privilege. One may also assume that the members who joined the party since 1971—in 1976 they accounted for 24.1 percent of total membership[1]—are not reformist. They are probably younger-generation careerists going along with the current party line.

Another imprecise reading can be made by tracing possible lines of influence within the party organization. This activity again must remain to a great extent speculative, since the bureaucratic nature of the Soviet-type party and information systems leaves little opening on the lower levels for affinity or disagreement to become apparent. In the regional party organizations, hard-line connections can be inferred from the backgrounds of several of the 12 regional first secretaries. All four Czechs brought in to replace reformers in 1969 had previously been connected with the hard-line Czech Party Bureau. Two of the three Slovak regional party secretaries were also replaced that year, so that half the regional party secretaries were changed in the 1969 purges. A fifth politician connected with the bureau became a regional party secretary in 1971. It may be that this level and still lower ones in the party ranks represent the sphere in which the most prominent hard-liners in Prague find additional support for their cause.

In view of the backing the hard-liners enjoy within the party, it is difficult to see how Husak will be able to overcome the split within the leadership and proceed to carry out policies clearly of his own making. The seven years of his tenure have produced a pattern of initiative and counter-initiative from both sides, with the struggles centering around ideological and power-politics issues. This split within the leadership could present greater problems in the future if the structure supporting the upper reaches of the party hierarchy becomes less stable. The plans for dealing with just such an eventuality are antithetic and contradictory, and there seems to have been little effort—especially on the part of the hard-liners—to make provision for a possible shift at the base.

FOREIGN POLICY

Within the framework of Czechoslovak diplomacy, two main currents can be seen. The first is that of detente between states. Although domestic differences kept Prague from joining the general upswing of East-West relations in the early 1970s, recent diplomatic initiatives have been making up for any lost time. Relations with other European states have intensified rapidly, and the frequency of visits between Czechoslovak and West European statesmen—at home and abroad—is rightly seen by the leadership as a sign of its slow return to diplomatic respectability. On the other hand, Prague has become for many an uncomfortable partner in ideological relations. During the preparatory meetings for the June 1976 conference of European communist parties, Czechoslovak representative Vasil Bilak often led the loyalist parties in their debates with the more independent parties, such as those of Italy, Yugoslavia, and France. Relations with the first two deteriorated markedly in early 1976. Although these ideological differences between Prague and its foreign counterparts cannot negate the progress made on the state-to-state level, they act as a recurring reminder of the nature of normalized Czechoslovakia and encumber relations with Western countries ready to forget the past.

The cornerstone of Prague's diplomacy is, of course, its relationship with the Soviet Union. The 15th CPCS Congress was the latest in a series of opportunities the Soviet Union has taken to exhibit its support for Husak. Politburo member and CC Secretary Andrei Kirilenko, who represented CPSU leader Leonid Brezhnev at the congress, announced that the party, under the leadership of Gustav Husak, had successfully consolidated Czechoslovak society and strengthened its leading role. Another demonstration of Soviet support came in November 1975, when Husak led a high-level delegation on an official visit to the Soviet capital. In an advance article about the visit, Pravda[2] wrote that the "crisis" into which "revisionist forces hostile to the people" had brought the CSSR in 1968 had been overcome and that the "leading role of the working class" had been restored, and a few days later,[3] the Soviet paper stated that Czechoslovakia's recent successes were "unbreakably linked with Gustav Husak's name."

These displays of Soviet support have emphasized two important trends. The first is the growing identification of Gustav Husak with the successes of normalization. This is an understandable development, since the party leader has been generally successful in bringing the country back into the orthodox line the 1968 invasion was meant to protect. The hard-liners have by no means lost their influence, but the real threat to Husak's power that they seemed to present in the early years of normalization seems to have waned. The second element evident in this praise is the presentation of Czechoslovakia as a model friend and ally, which, after a period of confusion, regained its self-confidence and sense of direction. Prague is now able to return to full diplomatic activity, the commentaries seem to be saying, and it should now be treated as an equal partner in all European endeavors.

Adapting to detente with Western Europe was not easy for Prague.* One problem was that many Western statesmen were unwilling to accept the Husak leadership. The invasion, the fall of Dubcek, and the purges that followed were strongly criticized in the West, and the representatives of the new order in Czechoslovakia were avoided in diplomatic circles. Paralleling the West's lack of interest in relations with Prague came domestic hard-line resistance to contacts with that area. The Prague Spring's lively contact with Western ideas presented a threat to the orthodox faction of the CPCS, and its members therefore sought to minimize such contacts once they had returned to positions of power and influence within the party. The development of East-West detente made this isolation seem more and more irrational, however, and Western countries began to seek better relations with the CSSR. In April 1973, British opposition leader Harold Wilson visited Prague and said it was time for the Western countries to "turn their backs on 1968." At roughly the same time, there was movement by Washington to improve relations. After the first session of the European security conference took place in Helsinki that July, U.S. Secretary of State William Rogers traveled to Prague to sign a consular agreement before returning to the United States.

Detente had its greatest effect on Prague's relations with its neighbors to the west and south. In 1973, after two years of bilateral discussions, Bonn and Prague finally reached a settlement that removed the last obstacle to the establishment of relations represented by the infamous Munich Agreement of 1938. Although Prague had wanted the agreement to be totally nullified, the two sides compromised on a statement that the 1938 document was no longer valid. The tension of the negotiations hung over the visit paid by West German Chancellor Willy Brandt in December 1973 to establish diplomatic relations, and developments thereafter were undramatic.[4] Diplomatic relations were resumed with Vienna in 1974. The question of compensation for former Austrian property in Czechoslovakia had hindered this step for 20 years, but each side finally made concessions to the other's position. Foreign Minister Bohuslav Chnoupek traveled to

---

*Relations with the Warsaw Pact countries will not be discussed here because they are generally devoid of any serious problems.

Vienna in December 1974 to raise ties from the legation to embassy level. When Austrian Chancellor Bruno Kreisky visited Czechoslovakia in February 1976, he expressed his pleasure that the atmosphere between the two neighbors was "clear at last."[5]

Especially among the West European states, however, the stigma of invasion and normalization endures. This is in fact somewhat ironic, because Prague's isolationism in the early 1970s almost succeeded in making the Prague Spring a nontopic in international relations. But as Czechoslovak diplomacy becomes more active in the West, the memory of 1968 revives. Many commentators throughout Western Europe have sharply criticized Czechoslovakia when delegations have paid official visits. The Times of London called a Czechoslovak parliamentary delegation visiting the British capital "not our favorite guests" and said that "no Czechoslovak member of parliament should expect to be received with respect when there are so many people in prison in his country for their political beliefs, and when so many people are excluded from useful work or persecuted in various ways."[6] Commentaries from other countries were similar.[7] Of course, newspaper commentaries are synonymous with neither public nor official opinion, and states often go about their business as if editorials did not exist. But they do represent a certain circle of opinion in any country, and this is often an influential one.

Prague's ideological orthodoxy also irritates some other communist parties. At the preparatory meetings for the East Berlin communist conference, the Czechoslovaks frequently called for a "militant document" to be signed at it, "militancy" presumably consisting of the presence of an attack on China and strong support for proletarian internationalism. In its attacks on the more autonomous forms of communism, Prague has refrained from naming particular parties. But the objects of its criticism are fairly recognizable. Vasil Bilak has warned communist parties against making alliances with "views that are at variance with communist ideology. Even if these alliances seem beneficial in the short run, their long-term effect can only be harmful for the party." At the party congress, Antonin Kapek warned that "the struggle to gain a socialist perspective cannot be waged only under a national flag; it must always be the red flag." In addition, the Czechoslovak press often prints articles defending positions that are only slight reformulations of the Brezhnev Doctrine. A typical example is a Nova Mysl[8] article entitled "International Legal Relations Among Socialist Countries," in which the author argued that a new system of socialist international law is evolving whose core is the socialist principle of state sovereignty. This includes recognition not only of a country's independence but also of its duty to protect "socialist achievements" at home and abroad. In response to Prague's orthodoxy, the Yugoslav, Italian, and French CPs have been increasingly critical of Czechoslovakia. The LCY concentrates on the ideological position taken by the CPCS, especially its support of the Brezhnev Doctrine, while the Italian and French parties reiterate their criticism of the 1968 invasion and the ensuing normalization and publicly support the reformers now serving jail sentences or being subjected to job discrimination.

Relations with the Vatican are equally strained because of Czechoslovakia's orthodox policies. In a speech to the College of Cardinals last December, Pope Paul named Czechoslovakia as the first of the areas "where certain badly disturbed relations have long been awaiting [a solution]."[9] Archbishop Casaroli visited Czechoslovakia early in 1975, but the results of his visit were meager and relations have worsened since then. A meeting in Rome in December 1975 was equally unproductive. In 1976 a very active atheistic campaign got under way in Slovakia, where the Catholic Church has its strongest following. The clergy are subject to bureaucratic chicanery, seminarians are encouraged to give up their religious studies, and pressure is exerted on parents who send their children to religious instruction classes. Considering the size of the target, the campaign often seems to be shooting at flies with cannon. But religion is another area in which orthodox objections will not be stilled until no trace of the "deviation" remains. The party may succeed in lowering the number of church-going Czechoslovaks, but one must ask whether here, as well as with the dissidents, the vigor of the attacks merely serves to strengthen the true believers.

POLITICAL AND CULTURAL DISSIDENCE

Before Charter 77 rose above the horizon, dissent was a low-magnitude star in the Czechoslovak skies.[10] The dissidents' voices could be heard more clearly in 1975 and 1976 than at any time since Husak's rise to power, but they remained so isolated that they could be treated as a political football to be lobbed back and forth between the conservative and hard-line factions. A protest letter would give the hard-liners an opportunity to beat the orthodox drum; the self-criticism of an erstwhile reformer would be used to justify the conservatives' policy of distinguishing between those who were capable of being saved and the incorrigibles.

In postcongress Czechoslovakia, isolation was (as it has largely remained) the dissidents' main problem. Cut off from any real exercise of power, the reformists have little opportunity to deal with the fundamental issues facing the Czechoslovak state. This isolation is probably also the reason for the relative lack of concrete proposals for gradual change of the present situation. Seen as a whole,

Czechoslovak dissidence is predominantly of a cultural and moral
nature: Playwright Vaclav Havel said that normalization had created
a moral crisis more dangerous than any in Czechoslovakia's recent
history. "The much-advertised normalization is phony," he concluded,
"the crisis is real."11

Husak's approach toward the reformers seems to reflect a realization of this isolation. After the reformers were removed from
their positions of influence, it seemed that the conservative approach
evolved into a search for maximum cooperation and minimum confrontation. Alexander Dubcek's case can be used as an example to
illustrate this outlook. The hard-liners, however, seem to feel that
their isolation is either nonexistent or irrelevant. Dissidents' letters
are often used as a pretext to initiate an orthodox campaign, and it
seems that the chain of protests in 1975, which began with the publication of Josef Smrkovsky's "memoirs" in February and continued
through the summer, moved the hard-liners to consider seriously
the possibility of political trials. It is surprising that they should
even have contemplated another round of these, which would certainly
have aroused strong protest in the West and impeded Prague's otherwise successful normalization of relations with its neighbors in Western Europe. But, having lost their control over the party in the
reform period, the hard-liners were wary of any development—at
home or abroad—that might have challenged them again. This "any-
trickle-could-become-a-flood" approach left no room for reconciliation or any other movement but a retrograde one.

The policy resulting from these two stands has been an unstable
mixture. On the whole, a slight predominance of the conservative
outlook has been visible. Except in 1972, when Husak was forced to
consent to them to secure his own position, there have been no political
trials. Below this level there have been house searches, interroga-
tions, and confiscations of manuscripts, but the symbolic ultimate
goal of the hard-liners, the show trial, has been avoided. In the
cultural sphere, the "differentiation" policy has had certain successes;
the writers Bohumil Hrabal and Jiri Sotola have reappeared, as has
Oscar-winning film director Jiri Menzel. But no wide-scale reconciliation has taken place, and it is difficult to see one coming. The
cultural field seems fated to continue under the star of total politiciza-
tion, of interest to the factions in Prague only insofar as it serves
them in party in-fighting.

PERSPECTIVES FOR THE FUTURE

Do the trends and policies outlined in the previous sections
indicate future patterns of development? Is there a possibility of

liberalization? Will hard-line influence grow? Or will the stagnation that observers say cannot last forever continue for some years to come?

The majority of Prague's policies are dependent on trends within the party, and here the pattern of decision-making and implementation is erratic. Since neither faction is supreme within the party, much time and effort are invested in power politics in which neither side can win decisively. As long as this essential instability continues, it is almost impossible to foresee which direction policy will take.

Despite these reservations, however, there are four basic patterns that must be considered as future possibilities for Czechoslovakia. The country could muddle through a continuing state of "normalization," or it could begin a slow stagnation and decline. Both these possibilities emphasize economics and the domestic political stalemate. The second set of options considers the outlook for change within the party, either independently—a sort of Kadarization—or as a result of pressure from outside. Each pattern has a chance of being followed but none has the level of probability needed for it to be called the future.

One possibility that must be considered is that things might not change very much at all. The party has been stalemated ever since Husak came to power, and there seems to be little leeway for real policy initiatives by either side. If Husak were in complete control of the party, he would probably tend toward a less orthodox position than the hard-liners. But the power of the hard-line faction, especially in the party apparat, is great; if the hard-liners in its leadership were not able to stop movement toward liberalization, then their colleagues lower down in the party ranks would presumably be able to do so. This split between the party leader and the party could have even further consequences. If Husak were to begin an energetic campaign to implement the conservative line, he could jeopardize his own shaky position at the top of the divided CPCS. The threat of thwarted intentions could expand to the threat of a thwarted incumbency.

The second major split—that between party and people—would have an equally constraining effect on Husak. If any liberalization were to take place, the demand for an investigation of the normalization period would presumably arise. Here, Husak would find himself ironically in the company of the people who put him into prison in the 1950s; too involved in an unpleasant period in the country's history, he could not allow any inquiry that would expose his own hand in it. Of course, this applies even more to the hard-liners, a fact that only strengthens the coalition opposing any opening toward the people. This inner party opposition to change gained strong roots during the normalization purges. With the expulsion of almost 500,000 reform-

minded party members, the basis within the party that would have
supported evolutionary change was shut out. This means that Husak
not only has no more liberal group within the party to which he could
turn if he wanted, but also that he has created a large number of
former party members who could now be expected to oppose present
policy.

In a situation where little change can be expected from the party,
it is the economy that often provides the impetus for new policies.
That was how the reform movement of the 1960s got its start. Faced
with the specter of almost negative growth in the 1961–65 plan, then
party leader Antonin Novotny agreed in 1963 to a thorough study of the
economy and management. The study group, led by economist Ota
Sik, suggested the reforms and adjustments that led to the liberalization of 1968. These conditions are obviously not present today. The
economy, although not dynamic, has not done badly since Husak's
coming to power. Growth has been steady and the standard of living
is high. The two main causes of the slump of the early 1960s—
insufficient investment and lack of adaptation to changing export
markets—do not present an imminent threat to the economy. There
are, however, some disturbing trends. Productivity is still relatively
low, and modernization of the industrial base is progressing too
slowly. Rising oil prices and falling manpower reserves are beginning to gnaw at the base of the country's industry and will probably
sharpen the edges of the existing difficulties and strain the social
contract that now exists between party and people. But, if these
strains do not break that contract, or if the economy can absorb the
pressure, then there is a chance that the leadership could muddle
through the coming years without having to make any substantial
changes.

The second possibility works with the same assumptions as the
first but sees them more negatively. Party policy may continue its
present course, or it may even take a further turn toward orthodoxy.
The evolution of this sector is basically irrelevant. But the second
option sees a trend toward economic deterioration. Here the negative
trends in the economy gain predominance, and the party is unable to
deal with the pressures this development creates.

Oil and manpower play the main roles in this option. Prices for
Soviet oil will rise throughout the 1976–80 period, and the growing
deficit Prague now has with the Soviet Union could continue to mount.
The energy imports from the Soviet Union will put indirect pressure
on Prague's hard-currency reservoir by demanding more Czechoslovak
exports in order to meet the energy bill. Given the decline in hard-
currency income, Prague will be hard put to it to continue importing
consumer capital goods from the West. The economy will also be
faced with a dramatic fall in the number of young people entering the

job market. If, as official estimates predict, labor's growth rate in the coming years will be only about 15 percent of its 1950-70 level, then the inefficiencies of the present system will become even more visible. Thirdly, the falling rate of production efficiency would seriously affect Prague's foreign trade. If Prague finds it increasingly difficult to modernize its industrial base via imports of Western technology, it will not be able to keep its production up to the standards needed for exports to the West. Thus, at a time when rising raw material prices make it imperative for Prague to export more, it could find that it has less to offer than importers want to buy.

The danger in this scenario is not the economic deterioration itself but rather the party's inability to cope with it. If the present constellation within the party remains, there will be little leeway for real change. Developments in socialist economics in the 1960s offer several alternatives to stagnation. Two models—the Czechoslovak and the Hungarian—offered some sort of decentralization and marketization, while the third—the GDR example—aimed at progress through technocratization. Having had its experiences with decentralization, the party would presumably hesitate before giving this idea another chance. The East German model might also be rejected since under it the economy would be "largely exempt from subordination to ideologists and party apparatchiks and would be turned over to technical and economic experts who pursue purely pragmatic, rather than ideological, aims."[12] It seems that the party might opt for recentralization rather than any of these alternatives.

This chain of events, if it occurred, could produce a high level of instability. It is probably only under these circumstances that the possibility of strong public protest would be considered. The population has traded liberalism for materialism, and most probably the loss of the material benefits of normalization would make the political aspects of it unacceptable. While this is the logical conclusion of the hypothetical development just portrayed, a few realities of Czechoslovak history must also be considered. It is possible that the economic situation could become dramatically worse without arousing strong popular protest. The Czechoslovak people have endured several defeats and periods of hardship without staging protests of the Hungarian and Polish variety. It is difficult to argue that they will necessarily start now.

The Kadar example is sometimes held up as a possible path for Gustav Husak to follow. Coming to power under far more divisive circumstances than Husak, Janos Kadar managed to bring Hungary back to orthodoxy and then venture out on his own series of reforms. In the process, Kadar evolved from a discredited "puppet" to an accepted leader. Could Husak forge a reconciliation between people and party in Czechoslovakia as Kadar did in Hungary?

The different circumstances in which he must work make it unlikely that he could repeat Kadar's performance. Perhaps the most decisive of the different circumstances is the difference in the Kremlin. Kadar came to power during the Khrushchev era. The new Soviet leader, anxious to secure his position and also ensure a more viable relationship with Eastern Europe, introduced de-Stalinization in 1956 and pushed for its implementation for several years thereafter. Within this framework innovation and diversity were fostered, and thus Kadar was able, after the initial consolidation period, to advance toward reconciliation with full support of the Kremlin. The Brezhnev era has been different. The new leadership responded to the threat of revisionism in Czechoslovakia with the invasion and continued to consolidate its leadership within Eastern Europe from then on. The experimentation and diversity of the Khrushchev era were replaced by caution and increased emphasis on ideological orthodoxy. The coming of detente also played a role. Although they considered detente with the West desirable, the Soviet leaders felt it should be accompanied by increased vigilance at home against the "harmful influences" that increased contacts with the West would bring. Since Eastern Europe was a more closed system in the late 1950s, the specter of growing Western influence was not one of the major problems facing Kadar when he began his reforms.

The structure of Kadar's party also provided him with a greater basis for change. The Hungarian Communist Party disintegrated in 1956, and a rump party known as the Hungarian Socialist Workers' Party was formed. Kadar, who enjoyed immediate Soviet support, was able to purge it of the Stalinist elements that still remained and initiate a course of reform. In the Czechoslovak case, however, the reformers were expelled from the CPCS; this action went so far that almost the whole faction standing to the more liberal side of Husak was removed from the party. When the purge period finally ended, Husak found himself not at the head of a unified party, but rather off to one side of a divided one. Since strong Soviet support was withheld until 1973, he was forced to straddle both factions in order to keep his position of leadership. A progressive faction, to which Husak could ally his followers in an effort at liberalization, no longer exists within the party. The partial amnesty for members struck off party lists in 1970 could be the first step toward rebuilding this progressive faction within the CPCS, but the possibility of such a faction's growing without hard-line resistance is dim.

The possibility of external pressure for change in Prague provides the base for the fourth alternative. Considering the difficulties of an independent evolution within the CPCS, this alternative seems to offer the most promise for change. But where will the pressures come from? How will they develop? And what would be the result?

The most obvious and most effective source of outside pressure on Prague is Moscow. The Soviet leaders have proved, time and again, that they are capable of creating conditions that have a crucial meaning for East European policy-makers. Both the de-Stalinization of the 1950s and the reideologization of the 1970s were the result of Soviet policy decisions. It is perhaps natural, then, that several of the most prominent reform politicians look to the Soviet Union for change. The most detailed proposals made by a reformer to the Kremlin came from Josef Smrkovsky, who reportedly had several contacts with Soviet officials before his death in 1974. In a letter to Brezhnev in July 1973,[13] he characterized the invasion as the "last gasp of the cold war." The international situation had changed since then, he said; the invasion was supported by "persons who are no longer in decisive positions in public life."* The initial steps of normalization were probably unavoidable, he admitted, but they have now become a system that is stifling the growth of real socialist democracy. Smrkovsky argued that it was time to extend the party's base from a position of power to a relationship of trust between party and people. "Decisive steps must be taken in the Czechoslovak question and the initiative must come from the Soviet side. In my opinion, this would be the easiest, if not the only, way." Such an initiative would be appreciated by the Czechoslovak people, Smrkovsky wrote, and he would do all within his power to start the necessary negotiations.

Rather than emphasize the achievements of the Husak years, as Smrkovsky did, Alexander Dubcek accused the present leadership of factional activity and stated that it was corrupt and based on a "system of personal power." "The present party line," he wrote, "has been 'successful' in the sense that social values have been successfully destroyed, but none of the conflicts which led to the crisis in the party and society in the 1960s [that is, before 1968] have been resolved." The former leader reiterated his loyalty to the Soviet Union and seemed interested in finding an explanation for the "misunderstandings" that led to the Soviet invasion in 1968. Moscow's actions were excused because its information was wrong. Interestingly, although the former leader strongly criticized the present regime, he made no mention of other reformers who were oppressed—some much more than he—by the present leadership. Dubcek did not echo Smrkovsky's explicit offer to help find a solution to the present dilemma, but his interest is evident.[14]

At one time the Soviet Union seemed interested in using its influence for change. This phase reached its high point in 1973, after

---

*The context implies that Wladyslaw Gomulka and Walter Ulbricht are meant here.

the 1972 trials had brought Czechoslovakia to its most hard-line
positions of the normalization period. Soviet support for Husak was
not so unequivocal as it is today, and there were reportedly several
contacts with Josef Smrkovsky concerning possible liberalization
moves.[15] European detente was still a widely accepted concept
then, and Moscow was about to see the realization of one of its long-
term diplomatic goals, the European security conference. If the
time were ever ripe for the West to influence Eastern Europe, it was
then. And yet little changed in Czechoslovakia. The atmosphere
calmed somewhat, and Husak was finally given clear Soviet support.
But nothing really changed. Communist participation in governments
in Italy and France would present a different type of influence, a more
persuasive model for democratic change, since a communist party
would be a main actor in the process. But the international atmosphere seems less favorable now than in 1973-75, and Prague's
polemics against the Western CPs seem to be a type of preventive
medicine. In the end, it will probably be to Moscow that Prague will
have to look for impetus toward significant change.

If there is any guess to be made about the coming years in Prague,
it is that the muddling will probably persist. Dissidents have consistently argued that the present situation cannot continue, but it is
an undeniable fact that it has lasted for seven years, and no real
change is now in sight. Husak has survived the stormy period of
normalization, the euphoric period of detente, and two party congresses without losing his position; in fact, by attaining the presidency,
he has strengthened his standing, if only minimally. If there is to
be any significant change, it will probably be the result of external
pressure.

Here there are several unknowns that could be important for
Czechoslovakia's future. For example, what will happen after Leonid
Brezhnev leaves the Kremlin scene? Could the departure of his team
mean a loss of support for Husak and a strengthening of the hard-line
faction? Similarly, how will the post-Tito era in Yugoslavia affect
Eastern Europe? If Yugoslavia should become a center of conflict,
would the Soviet reaction be to increase cohesion within Eastern
Europe? Will unifying trends increase if the present Western disappointment with detente grows stronger? And what if some sort of
popular turmoil or a new stage in party-people consultations should
develop in neighboring Poland? Would a consolidation similar to the
one after 1968 be introduced?

Thus, behind the outward stability of the Husak leadership, an
inherent insecurity prevails. That the post-Dubcek leadership has
been unable to sink deep roots is probably the price the party has
paid for normalization. The situation in 1976 was the result of the
invasion and the purges, two factors that have split the party and

alienated the people. It is hard to see how the party can evolve by itself into an accepted ruling power, and it is even more difficult to see international factors fostering such a change. What they will probably foster is further economic difficulty and a sharpening of the present problems. Whether they will produce the surprises absent from the congress is a question whose answer is unknown.

NOTES

1. Rude Pravo (Prague), 21 April 1976

2. (Moscow), 22 November 1975.

3. 25 November 1975.

4. For more on Czechoslovak-West German relations, see Robert W. Dean, "Bonn-Prague Relations: The Politics of Reconciliation," World Today (London), April 1973.

5. Radio Prague, 17 February 1976.

6. 22 November 1974.

7. See, for example, Le Monde (Paris), 13-14 November 1975, and Vrij Nederland (Amsterdam), 22 November 1975.

8. (Prague), February 1976.

9. Frankfurter Allgemeine Zeitung, 26 February 1976.

10. This section deals with the dissident scene before Charter 77 appeared. For more information on this issue, see Chapter 13, "Civil Rights Dissent in Eastern Europe."

11. For the text of this letter to Husak, see Encounter (London), September 1975.

12. Radoslav Selucky, Economic Reforms in Eastern Europe (New York: Praeger Publishers, 1972), p. 51.

13. Reprinted in Frankfurter Rundschau, 21 June 1975.

14. See his letter to the Federal Assembly, published in The Observer (London), 13 April 1975.

15. Der Spiegel (Hamburg), 9 December 1974.

16

**IDEOLOGICAL
MOBILIZATION
IN ROMANIA**
Robert R. King

In Eastern Europe the last few years have witnessed an increase in ideological activity and growing criticism of ideological relaxation, both within the individual communist parties and in society as a whole. In large part, this ideological campaign is related to, and in fact a counterpart of, the successful campaign to hold the Conference on Security and Cooperation in Europe, the final session of which was held in Helsinki in the summer of 1975. The emphasis on ideological orthodoxy is primarily directed against the "harmful" impact of "bourgeois-capitalist-imperialist" ideological influences. Although there has been some effort to combat Western ideologies beyond the border of Eastern Europe, the primary concern is with shoring up the home front. The Helsinki Final Act's provisions on the exchange of information, ideas, and people among all countries of Europe are thought to pose a particular threat to the communist parties, although the Warsaw Pact states can hardly be said to have been conscientious about fulfilling their Basket Three commitments under the accord. The statement that there can be "no ideological coexistence" has frequently been made.[1]

Although the Romanians have been out of step with their Warsaw Pact allies on a number of issues related to European security and to East-West relations in general, they have for the most part been in agreement on ideological issues. They have shown a certain selectivity in regard to attending or not attending various conferences involving the members of the Warsaw Pact, but generally speaking

---

This chapter is a shortened version of Robert R. King, "Ideological Mobilization in Romania," RAD Background Report/40, Radio Free Europe Research, 21 February 1977.

they have participated in conferences involving ideological issues and been more willing to forgo attendance at gatherings dealing with other topics.[2]

The Romanians have not only been willing to cooperate with their East European neighbors on ideological problems, but have also given higher priority and greater emphasis to ideology than have the other European communist states. The year 1976 in particular was marked by a flurry of ideological activity in Romania unmatched elsewhere. In early June, for instance, a Congress on Political Education and Socialist Culture was held in Bucharest. This was a massive event organized by the Front of Socialist Unity and involving almost 6,500 participants, including members of the RCP Central Committee, the State Council, and other government agencies, representatives of mass organizations, and activists from the spheres of propaganda, education, and culture; over 300 of them spoke during the plenary sessions and in the special sections into which the congress was divided. The year-long build-up for the congress was likewise massive—meetings of local party organizations, trade unions, nationality councils, youth organizations, and the Front of Socialist Unity were held throughout the country, and in the final month before the congress, conferences of all county party organizations and the municipality of Bucharest took place. The congress was followed in September by the publication of an "Action Program for Implementing the Decisions of the 11th Party Congress and of the Congress on Political, Cultural, and Educational Work." The Action Program— a summary of which occupied several pages in the party daily—was submitted for discussion to party organizations and to the public. At a two-day Central Committee plenum in early November, it was discussed and approved. Between June and November, specialists in various areas related to ideology had held meetings to consider their role in implementing the campaign and to receive encouragement and inspiration from the party leadership. In July, in order to emphasize further the concern with ideology, RCP Secretary-General Nicolae Ceausescu was appointed to head the CC Ideological Commission, and personnel changes involving various cultural, propaganda, and ideological organizations were made at the November CC plenum.[3]

The pace of ideological activity in Romania was particularly hectic in 1976, but this was not the first time such an extensive campaign had taken place. Five years earlier, a similar program had been initiated with the publication of Ceausescu's 17-point program calling for intensification and strengthening of ideological, cultural, and educational activity along Marxist lines. In many respects the 1976 campaign is an outgrowth and continuation of the earlier one and represents a new impulse to follow up on programs and concerns originally put forth in 1971.

Although the general post-Helsinki concern with the effects of Western influence upon East European society is obviously an important consideration behind Romania's ideological drive, there are others unique to Romania.

THE ECONOMICS OF IDEOLOGY

One key motivating factor behind the campaign is the expectation that renewed emphasis on ideology will yield concrete results in terms of economic efficiency and output. Although there is considerable evidence that ideological mobilization yields limited economic results, it is quite apparent that Ceausescu thinks otherwise. Although higher personal incomes, coupled with greater availability of consumer goods, are generally recognized as being more effective in stimulating output and efficiency, Ceausescu's rapid industrialization program calls for devoting only minimal resources to such material incentives. Thus ideological stimulation provides one of the few alternatives that holds some hope of inspiring achievement of economic goals.

It is probably no coincidence that major ideological efforts were made in 1971 and 1976, each the first year of a five-year plan period. Having set ambitious economic targets, the party undoubtedly felt that a massive effort was required to induce the population to reach them. Ceausescu explained this in his speech at the June 1976 cultural congress:

> Socialism and communism are built with the people
> and for the people. . . . This is why our party centers
> on shaping the new man . . . to arm the builders of
> socialism with the most advanced achievements of
> human genius [modern science and technology] and
> with knowledge of the objective laws of social develop-
> ment [i.e. Marxism-Leninism]. Only if they know
> these laws and universally valid truths, will the work-
> ing people be able to act consciously to transform
> nature and society.[4]

In a speech to social science and political education cadres, he was equally explicit. After stating that economic efficiency, labor productivity, and product quality were matters deserving "great attention," he continued, "It is obvious that political and ideological activity must attach primary importance to these basic and essential problems for our country's development in the next stage."[5]

The approach of the party in utilizing ideology and education for the benefit of the economy has been twofold. First, the work ethic must be firmly established. This involves eradicating negative attitudes toward work—laziness, avoidance of manual labor, procrastination, poor-quality workmanship, slovenliness, bureaucracy, and so on. Party officials have been directed to take measures against such things, and the mass media publish stories about success in dealing with the problem.6 All this has been balanced with efforts to promote a "positive" approach to work. To quote Ceausescu again, work "must therefore be viewed as a necessity, as an honorable duty for each citizen; at the same time it must be seen as the chief means of asserting the human personality and the creative capability of each citizen."7 Coupled with this effort to upgrade the status of labor is a new stress on the principle that "each man receives a share from society that is in keeping with his concrete contribution to society's progress."8

A second element that has been emphasized is the importance of establishing closer links between education and research and production—that is, education must be geared to satisfying the labor and technological requirements of the economy. This has been a recurring theme in Romania for some years, but in the context of the recent ideological, cultural, and educational campaign, it has received additional emphasis. Past efforts in this direction have obviously not achieved the desired result, and the new scheme of restructuring party education and the new focus on general education represent attempts to come to grips with the problem. The Action Program called for the introduction of practical activities, starting at the preschool level. The "technical" activities of children in grades 5 through 8 will be geared to the requirements of the areas in which their schools are located; in vocational schools 80 percent of course time is to consist of activities in production; and students in the last two years of the ten-year compulsory educational program will be required to participate in "compact and continuous two- to four-month periods of activity in production in order to ensure that students have reached the skilled-worker level by the time they graduate." In addition to his scientific and cultural training, every student will be taught a trade.9

Linking education to production is not only a task for the state educational system; it will also be a matter for the party to deal with. The new three-year program of evening courses in party education set up under central direction focuses clearly on economic tasks. The three basic areas to be covered in the party education program are "basic problems of party-state activity," which Ceausescu explained means "production relations, production forces, and related

problems pertaining to party-state structure"; "scientific socialism
and Romania's socioeconomic development"; and "questions of dialectical and historical materialism and the role of science and technology in the country's socioeconomic progress."[10]

The first major problem with which the RCP is attempting to
deal in its educational and ideological program is the growing demand
for skilled labor. A rapidly developing economy requires a constantly
increasing number of skilled workers. The party's emphasis on the
work ethic and its glorification of labor are intended to encourage
more individuals to participate in the economy, and the educational
system is charged with providing them with the required skills. The
concern with raising labor productivity, also a key aspect of the
ideological-educational programs, is prompted by the need to reduce
the demand for manpower by increasing the efficiency of those currently employed and of new entrants into the labor market.

An indication of the need for new labor is given by the estimates
for 1977. Government figures indicate that some 426,000 new workers
will be required, of whom 315,000 should be skilled workers, 38,900
technicians and foremen with mid-level specialized training, and
30,600 highly trained specialists.[11] This heavy demand is one of
the major factors behind the ideological-educational programs
recently introduced. Although nonmaterial incentives and ideological
mobilization are techniques to be used in this campaign, measures
to increase the labor force have included the adoption of laws intended
to limit voluntary labor migration, assignment of jobs to the unemployed and graduating students, and imposing on all citizens the
obligation of working from the age of 16 until retirement.[12] Reports
in Romanian media[13] indicate that the laws are being enforced by
the police.

The training and retraining of the labor force have also received
considerable attention from economic specialists.[14] Thus the
ideological-educational program's emphasis on such training is an
integral part of over-all economic policy. As Ceausescu said:

> Our society's progress and the carrying out of the program
> to forge a multilaterally developed socialist society are
> conditioned by personnel, by people! Man is the main
> force in all that we forge; consequently we must first con-
> cern ourselves with training him, with creating the person-
> nel for all fields of activity.[15]

The second problem related to the economic implications of the
ideological program is also a complicated one. Since party activists
are required to take the lead in industrialization, they need two
basic qualities—a strong political commitment to the party, its leaders,

and its policies, and the technological expertise to deal with the growing complexities of a modernizing economy. This red-versus-expert
question has faced most communist parties, and it is hardly new even
in Romania. At the beginning of the 1971 ideological campaign,
Ceausescu tipped the balance in favor of the committed party member
over the technocrat, although he insisted that both political commitment and technical competence were necessary.16 That this view
has not changed is apparent from recent observations by the party
leader: "It should be clear to everyone that specialists must have a
thorough political and ideological background," and in a speech to
county party leaders Ceausescu said that while both "professional
and political" qualifications of party and state cadres must be raised,
"increasing their awareness and their political and ideological level"
should be given higher priority.17

Ceausescu's speeches and the party documents call for a combination of technical competence and revolutionary élan. In a speech at
the Stefan Gheorghiu Party Academy, the Romanian leader said that
henceforth party activists will be required to increase their knowledge
of the economy by actively participating in the organization and actual
practice of management while they are still students at the party
academy. At the same time, it is hoped that narrowing the gap between manual and intellectual labor will result in greater social
homogenization and the molding of the new man, "armed with the
most advanced achievements of modern science and technology and
a keen socialist awareness." But the task of molding this new man
is far from completed, despite the fact that it is considered "the
party's most significant and most noble goal, to which greater efforts
than previously must be devoted."18

For both the present and the foreseeable future, the conflict
between political and technical competence is likely to remain unresolved, however. Merely raising the level of the technological training of party cadres and stepping up the ideological indoctrination of
specialists is not the answer. The root of the difference lies in
approach. The party man gives priority to carrying out party policy,
whereas the expert tends to resolve problems on the basis of his
technical knowledge. Theoretically it would be possible to narrow
the gap between the two approaches, but this would be difficult to
achieve in view of the fundamental differences in outlook.

THE QUESTION OF YOUTH

Economics was undoubtedly a major reason for the ideological
mobilization, but a second important factor was concern about the
younger generation. This was a major one, heard especially often

in 1971, but frequently since that time as well. During the initial stages, in July 1971, Ceausescu was sharply critical of the educational system and the youth organizations, and his censure was followed by criticism and self-criticism on the part of those responsible for the country's youth.[19] This concern was reiterated during the upsurge of ideological activity in 1976, but with somewhat less stridence. In his speech to the cultural congress in June, Ceausescu included the Ministry of Education and Instruction and the youth organizations among those suffering from organizational shortcomings, and at the same time he noted deficiencies in ideological work with youth.[20]

Both before and after the cultural congress, the youth organizations were among those that met to discuss implementation of the party's ideological tasks. In preparation for the congress the Union of Communist Youth (UCY) arranged meetings on all organizational levels. Following the RCP CC's approval of the ideological Action Program in November 1976, the UCY and the students' organization met again to adopt a program for fulfilling their responsibilities in regard to the political-ideological education of youth.[21]

The motivation behind the concern to involve youth in the ideological mobilization is complex. In the first place, young people represent the key to the future, and their political socialization is essential if party authority in Romania is to remain firmly established. The ideological indoctrination of youth is a primary concern of communist regimes everywhere. The persistence of a "bourgeois mentality" and the appearance of "capitalist ideological influences" (which have been intensified by contact with Western tourists and the infiltration of Western styles of dress, music, behavior, and so on) are no doubt important factors behind regime concern.

A second aspect is related to the desire to increase the participation of youth in the work force and to upgrade the skills and interest of young workers in order to increase labor productivity. Among the topics raised during the youth organization meetings prior to the cultural congress was the fact that some young people adopt a "parasitic" way of life and refuse to work, while others fail to observe labor discipline or do not fulfill established norms. The importance of youth to the economy and the demand that they take on special tasks in building the new Romania have been constant themes in the propaganda that has accompanied the renewed emphasis on ideology.[22]

The concern to involve young people more actively in productive labor is not conditioned solely by the need for additional workers in the economy, however, although this is an important element. Those whose energies are not expended on socially useful work are much more subject to undesirable influences and have time to develop and cultivate "decadent Western tastes," and thus work is a "positive" aspect of their political socialization.

At the same time, the ideological measures set forth in the Action Program called for increased attention to political education; youngsters will begin such study earlier in their school programs and greater attention will be devoted to it; social science teachers will be better trained; institutes will be made to keep their knowledge up to date; and new and better teaching materials will be prepared. Youth organizations will devote considerably more attention to the political education of their members, as will the Ministry of Education and Instruction. Thus, emphasis on productive labor and political education are visualized as two sides of the same coin so far as the indoctrination of youth is concerned.

THE CULTURAL ELITE AND CULTURE
FOR THE MASSES

Another important group involved in the ideological campaign is the cultural elite—writers, musicians, artists, and so on. The party's primary concerns here are to win their support for its policies and to utilize their talents in the mobilization of the masses. Traditionally, however, such intellectuals are not known for their wholehearted and uncritical support, and the RCP has had problems with them in the past.

In late 1968, there were signs that the party leadership was anxious to bring the cultural elite—and the writers in particular—under firmer control. This became much more evident with the launching of the ideological campaign of 1971, and has continued to be the principal aspect of the party's cultural policy since that time. In part it reflects a fear that intellectuals who get out of hand can pose a serious problem, and it is no coincidence that the party began trying to curb cultural liberalization not long after the Czechoslovak events of 1968, in which the Czech intellectual community played a major role. On the other hand, there has also been a strong desire to harness the cultural elite to the massive campaign to create the new socialist man and to build the new socialist Romania.

The call for politically committed creative works was heard frequently in the past, but it has been made with increasing insistence since the 1971 campaign, and with the rash of ideological activities in 1976, it has been voiced still more urgently. In essence, it is primarily a demand that art contribute to the party's goal of mobilizing the masses. This Ceausescu made clear in his speech to the cultural congress: "The working people need a truly revolutionary art . . . that is permeated by a strong mobilizing attitude and militates fervently for the improvement of society and of man." The artist must, therefore, take a revolutionary position—one that "presupposes a deliberate orientation of his work toward making an active contribution to bringing about a renovating and progressive change in society and in man."[23]

To ensure the impact of a committed creative elite upon the masses, the 1976 ideological campaign stressed two elements. First, inspiration must be drawn from the masses. "The working people want to recognize their own moral image in artistic and literary creations. . . . Those who think this means that these wonderful creators of material and cultural values—the working people—cannot provide the most important source of inspiration are completely wrong."[24] The Action Program approved by the Central Committee directed all unions and associations of creative workers "to promote art and literature inspired by the people's socialist ideals, by their heroic lives and work," in order to "make a greater contribution to shaping the consciousness of the new man." The Writers' Union, in particular, was directed to take steps "to intensify contacts and ties between writers and working people." Perhaps the reductio ad absurdum was the decision to assign all graduates of music, drama, and other artistic institutes to "socially useful work related to their training," in order to ensure their awareness of "real life" and "prevent early professionalism, which can sterilize their talents."[25]

Another means of harnessing the creative elite to the party's mobilization campaign and at the same time strengthening the party's hand is having them participate in amateur cultural groups. One of the new aspects in the recent ideological campaign is the emphasis on mass and nonprofessional cultural activities. "We must," Ceausescu declared, "give greater impetus to the creative spirit of the masses." Shaping the "new man" cannot be accomplished only by activists in the cultural area or by intellectuals, "no matter how ingenious or talented they may be." What is required is "the creation of a broad popular movement in the spheres of education and culture." This requires members of the creative elite and their party-led unions "to establish close links with the mass artistic movement, to participate in organizing and carrying out amateur group activity in enterprises and institutions, in towns and communes."[26] Directives to this end were contained in the Action Program.

Thus, creative works—literature, drama, music, art, and so on—are not valued for the mirror they hold up to life; they are useful only to the extent that they help to inspire and mobilize the masses to achieve the party's goals. Like history, culture and art must serve utilitarian ends.

Perhaps the best illustration of the mass concept in ideology and culture is the national festival "Hymn to Romania" that was presaged in Ceausescu's address to the cultural congress and announced in the Action Program. The festival began in October 1976, and will reach its climax in June 1977, in connection with the celebration of the centennial of Romanian independence. The various cultural activities inspired by the festival took place on judet (country), interjudet, and republic-wide levels.[27] In the future, such festivals are to be held every second year, and beginning in 1978 there will be sports contests as well as cultural and scientific activities.

The response of the Romanian cultural elite to the program can hardly be described as enthusiastic, although no one has been outspokenly critical—no doubt largely because the party controls the cultural press, thus restricting the potential forum for dissent. Some mild and implicit criticisms have been published, however,[28] and few if any artistic works that both possess aesthetic merit and give evidence of revolutionary commitment have appeared. In fact, there have been clear signs that the new directives on cultural policy, particularly with regard to popular music and the theater, have resulted in a decline in interest on the part of audiences.[29]

PATRIOTIC EDUCATION AND NATIONAL HISTORY

Another theme that appears prominently in all the ideological, cultural, and educational speeches and documents of 1976 is the emphasis on Romanian history. This, however, is hardly a new element. The RCP Program[30] adopted at the 11th party congress in November 1974 stressed these elements, and after the congress greater emphasis was laid on national history, in addition to party history, in party education. The concern with patriotism and history can be traced still further back, however—to the mid-1960s, when Romania's adoption of a more autonomous course in its foreign policy was accompanied by greater emphasis on nationalism, in which history played an important part.

The recent ideological campaign, however, seems to put greater stress on the teaching of history as contributing to "positive" national awareness and patriotism. The resolution adopted at the cultural congress in June 1976[31] stated that "the education of all working people regardless of nationality, and primarily of youth, in the spirit of love for country and of revolutionary and socialist patriotism" must be a matter of "central concern." History was described as a "powerful element in patriotic education and advanced thinking":

> By cultivating gratitude to and appreciation of our forefathers—who defended our people's national existence at the cost of great sacrifice and raised the banner of the struggle for freedom and independence and national and social justice—education must instill in the people's

minds a feeling of responsibility for our forefathers'
inheritance and a determination to continue to carry the
beacon of progress and civilization in Romania under
new historical conditions.

At the same time, however, it was made clear that the study of
history "must always be guided by the dialectical materialist concept
of Marxism-Leninism." What this means in practice is well illustrated
by the way Romanian historians have recently interpreted various
episodes of their national past. Regardless of the historical details,
medieval and Renaissance Romanian princes are interpreted in
Ceausescu-ian terms. Furthermore, historical events and person-
ages held up as models for emulation are artificially shown to be
similar to contemporary Romanian phenomena.[32] Thus, the study
and teaching of history are not undertaken in order to understand the
lessons of the past but to use past events to illustrate those things
the party considers important in the present. Another example of
this is the coupling of two anniversaries in 1977—the centennial of
Romanian national independence (a real national holiday) and the 70th
anniversary of an important peasant uprising (the kind of commemora-
tion communist historiography has traditionally emphasized as an
example of the class struggle).
    At the same time, however, the party is turning the Marxist-
Leninist interpretation of history to its own ends. Ceausescu made
this clear in his speech to the cultural congress[33] when he observed
that "serious mistakes were made in interpreting our country's
history, the formation of the Romanian people and language, and of
the nation itself." The reason he gave for these distortions of the
nation's past was that "for a considerable time . . . foreign [that is,
Soviet] systems and methods were copied mechanically." In general,
his criticisms of the evils of Stalinist education and historiography
were brief and nonspecific, but the point was made that Romanians
would interpret their own past. While an ideologically conditioned
view of history will undoubtedly be propagated, it will be determined
by the needs of the Romanian Communists, not those of the Soviet
Union.
    Using the Romanian national past can no doubt be an effective
tool in the political socialization of the Romanian people, but there
are potential problems with the national minorities, who constitute
some 10 to 12 percent of the country's population. Ceausescu's
ideological addresses and the party's ideological documents have
always included frequent and favorable references to the "coinhabiting nationalities." Emphasis was also placed on the beneficial mutual
influence and harmonious relationship between "the indigenous population and the peoples who passed our way or who settled side by side

with the Romanians." Despite favorable references to the minorities
and pledges to perpetuate their national rights, however, Ceausescu
has made at least two comments that may have raised eyebrows.
Once he stated that migration of "certain Asiatic peoples [Hungarians?
Slavs?] to Europe . . . greatly hampered social progress in this
area," and on another occasion he observed that the coinhabiting
nationalities "did not bring with them a higher civilization" but found
in Romania an advanced one that "constituted a primary factor in
their development."[34] Such sentiments, though coupled with other
positive statements, plus the emphasis on Romanian history, are no
doubt seen by the minorities as an effort to erode their separate identi-
ties. This feeling may well be reinforced by the Action Program's
directive: "More attention will have to be paid to having children of
the coinhabiting nationalities master both the Romanian language and
their mother tongue, to educating them in a spirit of fraternity and
unity, of love for the common fatherland—Socialist Romania."[35]

Concern has been focused, however, on ensuring that patriotic
education is a "positive" phenomenon. Ceausescu has said more than
once that the aim is to inculcate revolutionary, socialist patriotism,
which is quite different from bourgeois nationalism. It means "consistently militating against national discrimination, against chauvinism,
against racist concepts. . . . Under no circumstances can patriotism
be described as narrow nationalism; it cannot be opposed to solidarity
and friendship among peoples."[36]

The didactic use of history and the emphasis on patriotic education, like the remainder of the ideological campaign, are designed to
serve the party's ends. Once again the key seems to be the concern
with implementing party directives, particularly regarding the economy. Ceausescu has made no secret of the ultimate goal: "Being a
patriot, loving one's fatherland, means doing everything possible to
increase the national wealth and socialist property, sparing no effort
in carrying out the communist party's policy, which is fully in keeping
with the vital interests of the entire nation."[37] In other words,
patriotism is something that leads people to sacrifice for the good
of the nation; since it motivates the population to carry out party
policy, it is to be encouraged. This was put even more clearly by
the Romanian party leader in response to a West German journalist's
question about the contemporary importance of cultivating historical
traditions. Ceausescu maintained that it is

> an important factor in the creative and active stimulation
> of the work of building a better and more equitable
> world. . . . The study of history is closely connected
> with the development of the forces of production, with
> the struggle of peoples for national and social libera-
> tion, with their efforts to achieve progress.[38]

Among other benefits accruing to the party from its interest in inculcating patriotism and its respect for national traditions are increased support and credibility. By linking itself to the national tradition, the RCP seeks to gain legitimacy in the popular mind and strengthen its base of support among the population. By publishing authentic historical documents and paying great attention to national celebrations, it acquires a degree of credibility as a defender of the national interests.

IMPLICATIONS OF THE IDEOLOGICAL MOBILIZATION

The scope of the latest ideological mobilization is broader than in any other East European country. Its aims also go beyond the defensive concern to isolate the East European societies from the infection of Western bourgeois ideological influences, which are ever more present as a consequence of expanded East-West intercourse. Romania's concern with the political socialization of youth and bringing the cultural elite under firmer party guidance is shared with the remainder of Eastern Europe, but its insistence on ideological mobilization in order to achieve economic goals certainly goes beyond what is taking place elsewhere in the European communist states.

In this respect the Romanian campaign suggests Satlinist approaches of the early 1950s, its focus on economic development and industrialization being perhaps the most striking parallel. At the same time, there are important distinctions. Earlier the focus was upon quantity—greater investment in machinery and producers' goods, higher output, more rapid development. While there is still an echo of these quantitative indicators, the economic progress achieved during three decades of communist modernization and the growing sophistication of the economic system have reduced the impact extensive inputs can have and increased the need to pay more attention to intensive economic development. Greater labor productivity, more efficient use of raw materials, higher standards of production quality are the current requirements of the Romanian economy, and to meet these demands, the mobilization campaign has stressed such aspects as specialized education, efficiency, and the use of modern science and technology. It has become increasingly apparent, on the basis of official exhortations and figures, that greater qualitative improvement must be achieved in order to reach the goals that have been set. Nevertheless, it is primarily through ideological appeals rather than material incentives that these goals are to be achieved.

How successful the campaign will be remains to be seen. In the West, and even in other East European states, material incentives have had a more powerful effect in inspiring qualitative improvements. Even in Romania, among workers with an awareness of the role of ideological incentives, material remuneration seems to be a more important factor.* The vast effort being made by the Romanian regime to further its industrialization, reflected in the high growth rate and investment allocations, will no doubt have some impact regardless of what is done in terms of improving economic efficiency. But greater economic efficiency and higher product quality are essential if the goals the party has set are to be achieved.

In addition to the stress on quality input and output, the current ideological mobilization differs from those of earlier periods in its stress on patriotism and Romanian nationalism. The instrumental use of Romanian nationalism by the party serves a number of purposes. It is a means of inspiring greater efforts to fulfill the party's goals; of bridging the gap between party and population by identifying the former with the national traditions of the latter; of legitimizing the party's goal of industrialization by linking it to the nation; and of establishing the RCP's uniqueness in international communism. At the same time, the party's ideological purity could be threatened by this emphasis on the national past. In fact, one can question whether this is even Marxism-Leninism. The best way to deal with the matter, of course, is to emphasize the new socialist character of the Romanian nation, thus using selectively those aspects of the national past that suit the current ideology, and reinterpreting that past in such a way as to satisfy the needs of ideology. It remains to be seen, however, how successful this approach will be in linking the party and its leader with Romanian nationalism in the popular mind and in preserving ideological purity in the face of the potentially eroding effects of nationalism.

Perhaps more than anything else, the campaign shows the pragmatism of the party. Ideology is not pursued for its own sake, but because it is useful, because it is successful—or at least holds out some hope of success—in achieving party goals. Thus nationalism and patriotism are linked with the drive to create the new socialist man not because they are consistent with the orthodox Marxist-Leninist view, but because they exert a powerful influence on the

---

*A study of agricultural workers who were aware of the role of nonmaterial incentives in the economy indicated that they were far more concerned about the material incentives they received. The authors of the report blamed this upon the unsatisfactory level of their socialist awareness.[39]

masses. In the long run, it may be pragmatism rather than patriotism that undermines ideology in Romania.

NOTES

1. On this topic, see Charles Andras, "European Cooperation and Ideological Conflict," in Robert R. King and Robert W. Dean, East European Perspectives on European Security and Cooperation (New York: Praeger Publishers, 1974), pp. 17–49.
2. See Romanian Situation Report/37, Radio Free Europe Research, 22 October 1976, Item 6.
3. These developments are discussed in the following Radio Free Europe Research papers: Anneli Maier, "Final Preparations for the Congress on Political Education and Culture," RAD Background Report/123, 31 May 1976; Anneli Maier, "The Romanian Congress on Political Education and Socialist Culture," RAD Background Report/155, 7 July 1976; Romanian Unit, "Ceausescu's Ideological Role Is Strengthened," RAD Background Report/167, 29 July 1976; Anneli Maier, "Action Program for Ideological, Political, and Cultural Educational Work," RAD Background Report/208, 5 October 1976; and Romanian Situation Report/39, 5 November 1976, Item 1.
4. Scinteia (Bucharest), 3 June 1976.
5. Ibid., 8 October 1976.
6. See, for example, Ion Iliescu, "Aspects of the Development of Socialist Awareness and the Promotion of Principles of Communist Ethics," Era Socialista (Bucharest), no. 17, September 1976.
7. Scinteia, 3 June 1976.
8. "Resolution of the Congress on Political Education and Socialist Culture," Scinteia, 9 June 1976.
9. Summary of the Action Program, Scinteia, 19 September 1976; see also Ceausescu's speech to the conference of social science and political education cadres, Scinteia, 6 October 1976.
10. A description of the party education program is to be found in the Action Program, and Ceausescu's amplification in his speech to social science and political education cadres.
11. Agerpres, 11 January 1977.
12. The texts were published in Buletinul Oficial (Bucharest) I: 98, 11 November 1976. The laws are analyzed in Romanian Situation Report/40, Radio Free Europe Research, 15 November 1976, Item 1.
13. For example, Radio Bucharest, 10 February 1977.
14. See, for example, Ana Dragan, "Strategies for the Training and Utilization of Labor Resources," Revista Economica (Bucharest), no. 4, 30 January 1976; and Ioan Totu, "Party Policy on Education

and Occupational Training of the Labor Force," Revista Economica, no. 7, 20 February 1976.

15. Quoted by Dragan, op. cit.

16. Scinteia, 13 July 1971.

17. Ibid., 15 May and 8 October 1976.

18. Ibid., 2 October 1976.

19. See Romanian Situation Report/27, Radio Free Europe Research, 20 July 1971, Item 1.

20. Scinteia, 3 June 1976.

21. Scinteia Tineretului (Bucharest), 14 December 1976; Romanian Situation Reports/13 and 2, Radio Free Europe Research, 14 April 1976 and 20 January 1977, Items 6 and 2, respectively.

22. See, for example, Revista Economica, no. 15, 16 April 1976, pp. 3-5; the RCP Political Executive Committee approved proposals of the UCY to involve young people in the building of a section of the Danube-Black Sea Canal, construction of which is to be initiated during the 1976-80 plan period (Radio Bucharest, 29 September 1976; see also Romanian Situation Report/34, Radio Free Europe Research, 1 October 1976, Item 2).

23. Scinteia, 3 June 1976.

24. Ibid.

25. Ibid., 19 September 1976.

26. Ibid., 3 June 1976.

27. See Romanian Situation Report/5, Radio Free Europe Research, 10 February 1977, Item 1.

28. See Romanian Situation Reports/26, 1, and 3, Radio Free Europe Research, 5 August 1976 and 12 and 28 January 1977, Items 4, 2, and 1 respectively.

29. See Anneli Maier, "'Revolutionary' Music and 'Revolutionary' Morals," RAD Background Report/188, Radio Free Europe Research, 30 August 1976; and Romanian Situation Reports/33 and 37, Radio Free Europe Research, 23 September and 22 October 1976, Items 8 and 1, respectively.

30. Programul Partidului Comunist Roman de faurire a Societatii Socialiste multilateral dezvoltate si inaintare a Romaniei spre comunism (Program of the Romanian Communist Party for Constructing a Multilaterally Developed Socialist Society and Romania's Progress Toward Communism) (Bucharest: Editura Politica, 1974).

31. Scinteia, 9 June 1976.

32. In this regard, see the following papers by George Cioranescu: "Michael the Brave—Evaluations and Revaluations of the Walachian Prince," RAD Background Report/191, Radio Free Europe Research, 1 September 1976; "The Political Significance of the Thracians," RAD Background Report/218, Radio Free Europe Research, 22 October 1976; and "Vlad the Impaler—Current Parallels with a Medieval

Romanian Prince," RAD Background Report/23, <u>Radio Free Europe Research</u>, 31 January 1977.

    33. <u>Scinteia</u>, 3 June 1976.

    34. Ibid., 3 June and 8 October 1976.

    35. Ibid., 19 September 1976.

    36. Ibid., 3 June 1976.

    37. Ibid.

    38. <u>Frankfurter Rundschau</u>, 27 July 1976.

    39. See <u>Revista Economica</u>, no. 7, 20 February 1976, and Romanian Situation Report/7, <u>Radio Free Europe Research</u>, 3 March 1976, Item 4.

The relationship between Church organizations in Eastern Europe and the communist regimes is a complicated and interesting aspect of the domestic political scene. The two, of course, have quite different views of the nature of the world. At the same time, the Churches are among the few "precommunist" institutions that have managed to retain a degree of independence from the party. Church-regime relations vary considerably from country to country, depending on the religious affiliation of the population, their religious history, the course of communism, and the attitude of a given party. On the whole, the Roman Catholic Church has fared better than Protestant or Orthodox denominations so far as the retention of institutional autonomy is concerned, thanks in large part to the international nature of Roman Catholic organization.

The two chapters that compose this section deal with the relations between the Catholic Church and the governments in Poland and Hungary. In these two countries, somewhat different approaches have been adopted by both Church hierarchy and government bureaucracy in regard to the problem of coexistence. In Poland, the Church is a formidable force beyond direct party control. Its strength comes from the fact that the population is overwhelmingly Catholic. Also, Polish nationalism is closely identified with the Church, and there is a sizable conservative religious peasantry. In the early days of communist rule, the state provoked major confrontations by attacking the Church head on. After Gierek came to power in 1970, however, the party chose to foster a long-term transformation of Polish society with the double goal of promoting socioeconomic modernization and undermining the traditional strength of the Church. The episcopate's response has been to play the role of loyal opposition—loyal to programs to improve the material side of life in Poland, but opposed to the increasing emphasis on Marxism-Leninism in society. Chapter 17 outlines the religious implications of the party's program for the socialization of Polish life and the Church's response to it.

The course of Church-state relations in Hungary has been somewhat different. There the Roman Catholic population forms only about 60 percent of the total, and various Protestant groups are also influential. The Church was never as closely linked with Hungarian nationalism as was the case in Poland. The Church-state reconciliation in Hungary described in Chapter 18 required that two major steps be taken. First the Church had to admit the existence of the communist regime and accept the fact that the government had the power to impose limitations on its activity, and the government had to recognize the right of the Church to exist and function; second, the Primate of Hungary, Cardinal Mindszenty, who had become a symbol of irreconcilable differences, had in some way to be taken out of the picture. The state refused to acknowledge him as head of the Roman Catholic Church in Hungary but the Vatican continued to regard him as occupying that position. With the negotiation of a partial agreement between the regime and the Vatican in 1964 and the death of Mindszenty in 1975, these two obstacles were removed, and the two sides were able to effect a degree of reconciliation. The Hungarian regime's policy of seeking support from all segments of society in developing the country—reflected in party leader Janos Kadar's statement that "those who are not against us are with us"—is manifestly different from that of the Polish party so far as the Church is concerned.

17

THE LOYAL OPPOSITION: PARTY PROGRAMS AND CHURCH RESPONSE IN POLAND
Thomas E. Heneghan

Edward Gierek has occasionally claimed that no Church-state tension exists in Poland. In a speech to workers in Mielec in September 1976, for instance, he declared: "There is no conflict between Church and state in Poland. There are great opportunities for fruitful cooperation between Church and state in implementing important national goals." He himself had "always been in favor of such cooperation," he said, and added that this was "not only my own personal conviction; it is also the standpoint of the Politburo of the Central Committee of our party and the viewpoint of the supreme authorities of the state."[1] The Church, of course, sees the situation differently. A communique issued by the episcopate in late November 1976, apparently in answer to Gierek's comments in Mielec, contained a litany of Church complaints about the government's "secret conspiracy against God." The indictment covered the spectrum of Church-state difficulties, ranging from job discrimination against believers and hindrances to new church construction to an increase in atheistic propaganda and what the episcopate saw as the use of immorality in the official information media to break down society's moral fiber.

Relations between the Catholic episcopate and the communist government are—almost by definition—predestined to be tense, and this they have been during the 31-year existence of People's Poland. What emphasized these tensions in recent years was Gierek's policy of socializing Polish society. Since 1974 the party leader has been stressing programs and measures designed to foster a transforma-

This chapter is an abridged version of Thomas E. Heneghan, "The Loyal Opposition: Party Programs and Church Response in Poland," RAD Background Report/45, Radio Free Europe Research, 28 February 1977.

tion of Polish society and a strengthening of the leading role of the party. One of the main obstacles to perpetuating this role was the strong influence of the Church, but although some attacks were made on it, the main thrust of the drive was to undermine its influence through a broad program of long-term social transformation rather than through direct attacks and challenges. This approach on the part of the regime has both dominated party policy toward the Church and determined the character of the Church's response to it.

THE SOCIALIZATION OF POLISH SOCIETY

To understand the leadership's drive to socialize Polish society, one must realize the influence the Catholic Church has within it. The Church in Poland is historically so intertwined with the fate of the Polish nation itself that the two sometimes seem to be natural complements of each other. During the years when the Polish state did not exist (1795-1918), the Church was essentially the only institution that represented Poland in the German, Russian, and Austrian areas of occupation. It also pitted the faith of the Poles against the beliefs of their two traditional enemies—Germany (Protestantism), and Russia (Orthodoxy).

These experiences fused the Church and the Polish nation in a way unknown in the rest of Eastern Europe. In the first years after World War II, the communist authorities tried to eradicate its influence in Polish society through direct repression, but this ended in 1956, when Wladyslaw Gomulka came to power and made major concessions to the episcopate. When Edward Gierek took over from Gomulka in 1970, he also found it expedient to make initial concessions to the Church. The bothersome inventories pastors had to keep for government inspection were abolished, as was the turnover tax on transactions involving Church property. But while Gierek acceded to some of the Church's demands, he began to develop means of undermining its influence without directly confronting the institution itself. Specific programs such as socialization of agriculture and an overhaul of the educational system were launched to bring both of these sectors into closer harmony with the rest of Poland's socialist system, and a few years later an ideological offensive was begun. None of these programs seemed aimed directly at the Church, but each would obviously serve, among other things, to undermine its influence within society while expanding the role of the state.

AGRICULTURE

Socialization of agriculture might seem an unlikely way of challenging Catholic influence, but its long-term effects could bear significantly on the Church's future. When Gierek came to power, 84 percent of Poland's farmland was in private hands, and thus somewhat removed from the socialized economy. As a step toward remedying this situation, the new party leader offered pensions to those private farmers who, on retirement, would sell their land to the state instead of passing it on to younger heirs. Since nearly half those who work in Polish agriculture are over 50 and about 500,000 farms no longer have heirs to inherit them,[2] the outlook for the success of such a program was promising. By December 1975, at the seventh party congress, Gierek could announce that private farm ownership had dropped to 80 percent, and by 1980, he said, this figure should fall to 70 percent. Along with this increased emphasis on socialization of agriculture, special measures were introduced to draw private peasants into closer contact with the socialized sector. Because of Poland's agricultural difficulties, however, the leadership was forced to give production precedence over ideological goals, but it retained its interest in expanding state influence in this by no means socialist area of Polish society, and socialization will undoubtedly be accelerated when the food supply becomes more dependable.

The episcopate did not overlook the effect the socialization of agriculture would have on village life. The Church's strongest support comes from the rural areas, where the traditional piety of Polish Catholics and the customs of the village intertwine. In introducing economic modernization to the villages and drawing the private peasants closer to the socialized economy, the government began to gnaw at the pillars of traditional life in the country. And the introduction of pensions for private peasants probably helped to accelerate another type of erosion in the villages—the migration of rural youth to the cities. The bishops recognized the problems the socialization program could present for the Church, and in April 1976 they appealed to the authorities to stem the "unhealthy and disastrous mass migration of rural youth into the cities" and called for an increase in material supplies.[3] The government tried to expand supplies to the peasants, and even went so far as to offer pensions to those who farm efficiently but do not sell their land to the state—a step that should help improve the situation in agriculture. But the state authorities took these measures in order to increase agricultural productivity, not to benefit the Church, and the bishops cannot expect future agricultural policy to continue to be one of compromise.

The Church also sees its influence weakened among the young people who migrate to the cities. Urbanization has had secularizing influences in other countries, and this has certainly been the case in Poland as well. The authorities compound this problem for the Church by issuing far fewer building permits for new churches than the episcopate feels it needs.[4] They do occasionally issue permits, as a concession to Church demands, but general practice is to withhold them. The episcopate has put the building permits issue among its central demands in talks with the government but has made little headway.

EDUCATION REFORM

School reform is also a facet of Gierek's modernization program that could lessen the Church's influence in society. While it was almost unanimously agreed that the old system needed an overhaul, different views existed as to what form the reform should take. The government chose to transform the existing eight-year basic schools into ten-year general-education schools. In the rural areas, according to this plan, many of the small village schools would be closed and their pupils transferred to comprehensive community schools in the larger villages. What was unacceptable to the Church was the fact that the afternoon classes introduced with the reform would prevent children from attending religious instruction, since classes could hardly find time for religious instruction back in their home villages. The bishops opposed the education reform when it was announced and their opposition delayed its implementation, but it was slowly put into practice and reached about half the parish (gmina) schools by the beginning of 1977. Full implementation is scheduled for the autumn of 1978.[5]

IDEOLOGY

The move toward educational reform was accompanied by a reemphasizing of ideological education for the young. Increased stress was put on ideology, and according to Church reports, children at summer camps were prevented from attending religious services and believing students were harassed and threatened by the officials.[6] This amounted to a program of "imposed atheism" for the young, according to Cardinal Wyszynski, and gave rise to a general "mistrust of the authorities."[7] The Church leadership was also very worried about the manner in which Polish history and culture were presented in the schools. In the bishops' view, the new Polish literature and history courses played down the cultural values of the nation in favor of ideological tenets, a development they saw as a threat to the survival of Polish culture.

The ideological drive in the schools was part of a general ideological offensive that became evident in 1974. After three years of relatively pragmatic rule, the Gierek team began to place increasing stress on ideological issues. It was about this time that the Warsaw Pact countries' view of detente as peaceful coexistence accompanied by a sharpening ideological struggle began to be propagated, and the international connection certainly fostered this drive in Warsaw. But the increased emphasis on ideology also fitted into Gierek's program for the socialization of Polish society, and a renewed rhetorical offensive against the Church was launched. In a speech in March 1974, Politburo member Jan Szydlak lashed out at the "reactionary wing of the episcopate," saying that

> the main organized antisocialist power in this country, a veritable center uniting all the antistate currents while at the same time representing their last hope, is the reactionary wing of the episcopate, which derives its support from the institutional structure of the Roman Catholic Church. The latter is the only center of rightist social forces that has at its disposal a coherent philosophical outlook, a strong organizational base, and numerous cadres. . . . Its political strategy is aimed, above all, at exploiting our difficulties and failures.[8]

THE LAY CATHOLIC ORGANIZATIONS

A special chapter in the party's socialization program had to do with official policy toward the various lay Catholic organizations that represented some form of nonsocialist public opinion in the country. These organizations cannot be called representative of the average Polish Catholic; they are groups of Catholic intellectuals and politicians who exhibit varying degrees of agreement with the episcopate and presumably less with the traditionally pious Polish peasantry. They had always been able to publicize their views through the Znak circle of Catholic Sejm deputies, in the discussion forums of the Clubs of the Catholic Intelligentsia, or in the columns of publications such as Tygodnik Powszechny, Znak, and Wiez, but the government undertook to split the lay movement by isolating the more critical Catholic centers from their own organizational basis. Thanks to its control over such technicalities as election lists and company licenses, the state was able to make significant progress toward endangering the lay organizations' foundations and undermining their long-term influence within Polish society.

The complicated network of lay Catholic organizations had its roots in the events of 1956. In October of that year, Catholic laymen founded the All-Polish Club of Progressive Catholic Intelligentsia

(OKPIK). This loose organization encompassed Catholics of all outlooks except those of the discredited progovernment Pax movement. By March 1957, when it held its first national congress, OKPIK had 14 chapters around the country. The group dropped the adjective "progressive" at the congress, came under increasing government pressure in the months following, and was finally disbanded on government order late in the year. In its stead, five autonomous clubs, known as the Clubs of Catholic Intelligentsia (KIKs), were established in Warsaw, Cracow, Wroclaw, Poznan, and Torun; a coordination center was set up in Warsaw to facilitate communication between the clubs, and the Libella cosmetics and chemicals firm was created to support them. Through their control of Libella stock, the KIKs were able to finance their own operations and, later, the publication of the monthly Wiez.

DIFFERENT CURRENTS

Two centers of opinion developed within the lay movement. The first, in Cracow, was centered around the weekly Tygodnik Powszechny and the monthly magazine Znak. This group was close to the episcopate, and generally accepted the traditional Church approach in theological questions. The Cracow group was also the base for the Znak parliamentary circle, led by Cracow University law professor Stanislaw Stomma. Znak, which had also emerged from the events of 1956, was the only independent parliamentary club in the Sejm, and its members often added dissenting voices to the debates. A younger group with a closer attachment to aggiornamento, or renewal, was formed in Warsaw and found expression in Wiez (founded in 1958) and in the Center for Social Studies and Documentation (ODiSS) established in 1968. Roughly speaking, the Cracow group placed more emphasis on Catholic contributions to Polish cultural life, whereas the Warsaw laymen were more concerned with modern Catholic input into political life. ODiSS, which launched a bimonthly publication, Chrzescijanin w Swiecie, in 1970, had as its special goals documenting the postconciliar dialogue between the Church and the world, especially in the socialist countries, and promoting study and research in this area. Originally, ODiSS controlled three shares of Libella stock and KIK the remaining ten.

A certain rivalry existed between the more liberal Wiez group and the more traditionalist Znak leaders, but there were no essential policy differences. Where significant fissures appeared in the lay movement was between the Znak-Wiez-KIK people and ODiSS. In 1970 Janusz Zablocki, the director of ODiSS, resigned as chairman of the Libella audit council, and the shares were divided so that the

KIKs retained seven and <u>Wiez</u> and ODiSS received three each. Zablocki
was known to wish to form a lay Catholic movement midway between
the traditionalist Znak and the progovernment Pax organization—
"a model of collaboration" between Catholics and Communists.[9]

THE CONSTITUTIONAL ISSUE

The 1976 debate over proposed constitutional amendments defined
the contours of the debate between the lay movements. The Stomma-
led traditional Znak group opposed the amendments on philosophical
grounds, arguing that the changes would make ideological commitment
the duty of all citizens. They wanted all Znak members to sign a
statement supporting the episcopate's criticism of the amendments,
but three members, all belonging to the ODiSS group, refused. When
the amendments came before the Sejm, Stomma was the only deputy
to abstain from voting; Konstanty Lubienski, another Znak deputy,
delivered a mildly critical speech but led the rest of the group in
supporting the changes. Stomma's name failed to appear on the list
of candidates for the March elections, and all the Znak seats in the
new Sejm went to the Lubienski-Zablocki group. In a letter to
Zablocki, three Znak representatives—Stomma, Tadeusz Mazowiecki
(editor-in-chief of <u>Wiez</u>), and Jerzy Turowicz (editor-in-chief of
<u>Tygodnik Powszechny</u>)—argued that the "new Znak" deputies had been
"neither elected nor accepted" by the majority of KIK groups. They
therefore could not be considered the real continuation of the Znak
circle and should stop using the group's name.[10] The Warsaw KIK
confirmed the split between the "new" and the "old" Znak groups at
its annual meeting on March 28, and after what appears to have been
a controversial meeting the club elected a new board of officers.
No ODiSS personalities were returned to it, and the <u>Wiez</u> group
remained prominent.[11]

MOVES AGAINST THE KIKs

The countermeasures against the KIKs began in June 1976 with
the closing of the Coordination Center in Warsaw. The Poznan KIK,
whose chairman was one of the new Znak members, began gravitating
toward the ODiSS approach during the constitutional amendment debate,
and this became more apparent after the closing of the center. In
July Ryszard Bender, who was connected with ODiSS, was allowed
to open a KIK chapter in Lublin, something the original KIKs were
never permitted to do. In the following months some Znak publicists
were refused permission to travel to the West, while others connected

with ODiSS were issued exit visas. One of these, according to the West German Catholic weekly <u>Rheinischer Merkur</u>,[12] told West German Catholics that Libella funds were being used to support the Committee for the Defense of the Workers.

The decisive move against the KIK began in December, when the authorities informed its leadership that it would no longer be permitted to use Libella funds to finance its activities.[13] The decision was sealed with the publication of a government decree dated 21 January 1977, which transferred all Libella shares to the Polish Club of Catholic Intelligentsia (PKIK), a more progovernment splinter group said to be led by "new" Znak parliamentary leader Lubienski. This move cut off the KIKs' means of support and thus struck at the root of the groups' independent existence. <u>Wiez</u> was also affected, and it appears that the journal will now be controlled by ODiSS, a development similar to what happened to <u>Tygodnik Powszechny</u> (which was taken over by the Pax group from 1953 to 1956). Indeed, the funds switch and the reorganization of the Znak parliamentary group constitute the toughest measures taken by the authorities against laymen's organizations since the early 1950s.

One cannot say that the KIKs' alleged financial support of the Committee for the Defense of the Workers was the motivating force behind Warsaw's strong move against the laymen's organizations. If it were the only reason, then why were some active committee members allowed to continue publishing their weekly newspaper columns or appearing on Warsaw stages? Like other programs in Gierek's socialization drive, the measures against the KIKs and the Znak parliamentary circle seem to be part of a wider attempt to strengthen the leading role of the party in the remaining nonsocialist areas of Polish society. By transforming the Znak circle and undermining the work of the KIKs, the authorities apparently hoped to weaken the "only center of rightist social forces" referred to by Szydlak in 1974. Unwilling to risk a frontal confrontation with the Church, they chose to attack some of its "numerous cadres." This was a more direct move than programs such as the socialization of agriculture and could be taken as indicating the government's future policy vis-a-vis the Church.

THE CHURCH AS LOYAL OPPOSITION

The Church's role in Polish politics became increasingly evident as Gierek's socialization policies unfolded. Politically speaking, the Church is concerned to defend its present position and expand its influence within society. In concrete terms, this means that the episcopate must act to counter or alleviate the effects of certain

government policies and press for such practical concessions as
permission to construct more new churches, greater access to the
public communication media, and more—or at least not less—
opportunity to provide religious instruction for children. This
combination of interests makes the Church, in effect, a sort of political opposition. For both political and doctrinal reasons, however,
the episcopate wants to avoid giving the impression that it is a political force agitating against the government. The Church leaders,
knowing there is a time to keep silence and a time to speak, use
their influence in a highly political way, often pressing for changes
when no real Church-state tensions are evident and refraining from
comment when the strains in society are greatest. As a result, it
can represent both a challenge to and support for government policy,
depending on how it assesses the stability of a given political constellation. In certain especially tense situations such as the initial post-
protest period in the summer of 1976, Gierek has even depended on
the episcopate's sense of responsibility to help calm the political
waters.

If the Church does represent an opposition, however, it would
have to be called a loyal one. Not loyal to the PUWP, but loyal to
what it sees as the interests of the Polish nation as a whole. The
Church sees itself as the protector of the country's national interests,
the defender of the faith and of the nation. This dual self-image has
led the episcopate to agree with the government when the overriding
interests of the Polish nation are concerned; for example, it always
supported Warsaw's claim to the former German territories. The
bishops also recognize the necessity of finding a modus vivendi with
the neighboring superpower to the east, the Soviet Union. But when
the boundaries of strategic necessity are overstepped, or Warsaw
seems, for example, to come too close to Soviet ideology or practices,
then the agreement between Church and state ends.

THE CONSTITUTION AND ZNAK

The period of unrest in Poland that began with the constitutional
issue in December 1975 illustrated the subtle interplay between
Church and state very clearly. In an open letter to the Sejm, 59
intellectuals took a stand against proposed constitutional amendments,
which were to institutionalize the leading role of the party, define
Polish-Soviet ties as "unbreakable," and make a citizen's rights
dependent on fulfillment of his duties toward the state. While this
and other letters exerted pressure on the government publicly, the
episcopate made two private requests for an explanation of the proposed changes and submitted suggestions to a parliamentary commis-

sion on the Constitution. By the time Cardinal Wyszynski spoke out against the amendments in a sermon on 11 January 1976, the 59 original protesters had been joined by 12 legal experts and 300 intellectuals and students. As the issue developed, the Church made more and more public statements criticizing the amendments, contending that they represented long-term dangers for believers and bound the Polish state too closely to the Soviet Union. When the amendments were finally accepted by the Sejm, the three controversial passages had been watered down and the Church, by its protests and with the help of the Znak parliamentary group, was credited with playing an important role in gaining the final concessions. 14

AFTER THE JUNE EVENTS

The events of 25 June 1976 changed the complexion of Church-state relations. The government, surprised by the strikes and protests against the announced price increases, was forced to make a quick and embarrassing retreat. The workers—and soon afterward the intellectuals—angered by the government's secretive approach to price increases and its brutal repression of those who protested, were restless. The gulf between rulers and ruled became very apparent, and the leadership was visibly insecure. Such an explosive situation could result in further unrest, which would be harmful to Poland's interests as a whole. Recognizing this situation, the Church initially refrained from issuing public demands for a party-people dialogue, as some intellectuals did immediately after the protests, or for amnesty for jailed workers, as others did later. Privately, however, the hierarchy protested against the government's policy and criticized the mid-July sentencing of strikers. Because of the sensitive nature of the question, the Church did not admit that it had done this until mid-August, and only late in that month did Cardinal Wyszynski make a public appeal for leniency toward the protesters. 15

The communique on a bishops' conference that took place from September 7 to 9 deftly illustrated the Church's two-pronged approach to the price protest question. The bishops called upon the people to be "ready to make sacrifices for the common good." "Solid work is a moral obligation and the ability to make sacrifices a Christian virtue," the communique continued. "It is only by common effort that we can overcome the difficulties the country is facing." To the government, the bishops issued the following appeal:

> The plenary conference of the episcopate asks the state
> authorities to cease the oppression of workers who took
> part in the antigovernment protests. Workers who partici-

pated in the protests should have their rights and their
social and professional positions restored. They should
receive compensation for their losses. Those sentenced
should be amnestied.

The evenhandedness of this communique indicated the episcopate's
desire to calm the domestic situation and help both party and people
to find a way of resolving the nation's difficulties. Almost all national
newspapers published the first part of the bishops' appeal—something
almost unknown in People's Poland. But the call for amnesty was
left out of the media reports, and this selectivity presumably served
to heighten rather than lessen the tensions the party leader had denied.
By late September, Cardinal Wyszynski had begun contradicting the
party leader's words in his sermons, demanding amnesty in the
sharpest terms to date. "It is painful," he declared, "when workers
must struggle for their rights from a workers' government." Soon
afterward, seven Ursus workers were released from prison.[16]

CHURCH AND COMMITTEE

It was also in September that 14 Polish intellectuals founded the
Committee for the Defense of the Workers. The committee, they
said in their initial communique, was designed to provide financial,
legal, and medical aid to jailed workers and their families. The
communique demanded complete amnesty for those in jail and reinstatement of those fired after the June events and called upon the
citizenry to support them by making financial contributions and providing information about the June events until the committee's goals
were met. Interestingly, the communique clearly supported the
September 9 demands of the episcopate; while not declaring wholehearted support for the Church, some former radical student leaders
among the human rights activists praised the Church's commitment
to the cause of civil and human rights in Poland.[17]
Although there is no evidence that there was any planned coordination between the Church and the committee, their actions seemed to
complement each other. During October, the committee issued several
communiques documenting what it said were the facts of the June
events and of the trials that followed. The communiques concentrated
on cases where workers' rights were disregarded and brutal methods
used to repress the protests. On November 16, the committee handed
in a motion to the Sejm recommending an official inquiry into the
charges of brutality. Three days later, the episcopate, complaining
that its earlier appeals for amnesty had gone largely unheeded, announced that "giving aid to people and families deprived of their work

and means of livelihood is the duty of all people of good will and especially of a Christian community."[18] Collections for the fired workers and their families were to be taken up in the areas where the workers in question lived, so as to avoid the impression of a nationwide Church campaign in defiance of the authorities. But this formality could not disguise the fact that the bishops had decided to support the committee's tactics.

Just as Church-state relations were not characterized by total disagreement, Church-committee relations were not models of unanimity. The two groups shared a concern for the jailed workers and the general question of liberties in Poland. But essential differences existed. Most of the committee members were left-wing intellectuals, and several were Marxists or former party members. Their opinions and personal programs were far more overtly political than the programs of the Church. For the intellectuals, tacit Church support of their efforts for human rights is crucial, because without it they would represent too small a group to effectively pressure Warsaw into making policy concessions. The Church, however, is careful to keep a certain distance from the intellectuals, not only for reasons of opinion but also to avoid giving the impression that the bishops were engaging in overtly political activity. This subtle interplay between Church and committee became evident in the weeks before Christmas 1976. On November 28, an episocpal letter stating that "one is constantly aware of a secret conspiracy against God" listed Church complaints against government policy. On December 6 Cardinal Wyszynski added his voice to those demanding an inquiry into charges of police brutality against the strikers. The inquiry demand drew wider and wider support in December and January, but the Church leadership refrained from further pronouncements on the issue. There seems no doubt that the episcopate shared the committee's opinion about the brutality charges. But, in conjunction with its image as protector of both faith and people, it was wary of becoming too closely identified with groups it felt did not have the same relationship to the people, no matter how sympathetic some of their views might be.

By pursuing what one might call a "responsible" or "apolitical" line, the Church has sometimes become an indispensable factor in carrying out Gierek's policies. But the episcopate has also shown that it expects concessions in return for its responsible stance, and that it can switch to the offensive, as it did in November 1976, if it feels its demands are not being heeded. The question arises whether Gierek's socialization programs will begin to catch up on the shaky balance that has evolved. If the transformation of Polish society proceeds to the increasing disadvantage of the Church, the "responsible" posture of the episcopate may seem less and less productive.

The bishops might someday conclude that they were receiving far less in terms of accession to their demands for religious freedom than the government was in response to its appeal for national unity. When and if this point should come, the episcopate might have to reconsider its modus operandi on the Polish political scene. There is no alternative in sight, but neither is there any indication of immediate need to find one.

CONSIDERATIONS FOR THE FUTURE

For the near future, the Church's position in Poland seems strong. Church attendance remains high, and there are apparently more than enough vocations to fill the ranks of the clergy. At 75, Cardinal Wyszynski seems to be in good health and to have every intention of working vigorously for several years to come. The entire clergy seems to stand more or less behind his approach to the state. There presumably are differences of opinion on many practical questions, but the clergy does not seem to be significantly divided from the episcopate on the major issues.

Despite this positive picture, however, the Church must remain true to the Vatican practice of thinking in centuries, and this is where problems begin to emerge. Although the Church in Poland has been slow to react to them, changes are taking place in the society in which it operates, and this is bound someday to have an effect on the Church's influence. The party realizes the effects social changes could have and seems convinced that, if properly fostered, these changes will undermine the Church's influence and allow that of the party to expand. An analogous development, albeit without the key factor of a "leading party," has taken place throughout Western Europe. Poland is presumably already being affected by this trend, and the party's policies are designed to accelerate the development.

The more Polish society is changed by urbanization, education, and economic development, the more important the character of Polish Catholicism will become. Since the Communists came to power, the two organizations—Church and state—have become stuck in opposite roles. Roughly speaking, the Church has become the defender of society's traditional values while the party has arrogated to itself the concepts of progress and modernization. The influence of the Catholic Church has been based on its rapport with a large section of Polish society that either hopes to preserve traditional values or rejects the values and modernization offered by the party. By retaining its traditionalist approach, the Church has so far been able to maintain this rapport. But there may come a time when the conservatism that has helped it maintain its position within society for so long falls out of step with ever increasing numbers of the population. The need for aggiornamento will then have caught up with the Church. Even the experiences of such traditionally Catholic countries as Ireland and Italy have shown that the sea change necessary at that point can corrode the unity and influence of the Church.

If the episcopate approaches the problem flexibly, the change need not be too disruptive. But a major problem looms ahead for even the most talented clergymen. Any real aggiornamento within the Church will require widespread communication between the bishops and the believers. The episcopate will have to redefine its policies in such a way that they find the support of both the traditionalist base of Church members and the urbanized workers and educated class to whom both party influence and the forces of modernization have greater access. In Poland, the Church's opportunities to spread its views and foster Catholic thinking have been limited by government measures against Catholic publishing and religious education. As has become evident in recent years, party policy is to restrict these opportunities even more. If present trends continue, the Church may find its communication with the people shrinking while its need to communicate with them grows.

It is unclear how long it will be before pressure to change begins to mount, and it is impossible to predict how great an effect the changes will have on the Church in Poland. Through its role as the loyal opposition, the Church will probably be able to stave off some of the more controversial measures for some time to come. But the role of loyal opposition might decrease in effectiveness as the socialization of the country proceeds. It has become clear that party policy aims at a long-term isolation of the Church, and the episcopate will need a long-term plan of action if it is to retain its present influence. Neither side seems to know when the present social trends will begin significantly to affect the Church, and presumably neither side knows how the other will react when these changes begin to be felt. Both party and episcopate seem to recognize that they will come, however, and the next few years may be dominated by a Church-state struggle between accelerating and delaying the inevitable.

NOTES

1. Trybuna Ludu (Warsaw), 6 September 1976.
2. Radio Warsaw, 2 April 1975, and Polska Agencja Prasowa (PAP), 12 August 1975.
3. Reuter, 30 April 1976.
4. See Renate Marsch, "Bleibende Staerke trotz Kommunismus," Herder Korrespondenz (Freiburg/Br.), January 1977.

5. For more on the school reform, see Ewa Celt, "Poland Reforms Its School System," Polish Background Report/19, <u>Radio Free Europe Research</u>, 13 November 1973.

6. <u>La Croix</u> (Paris), 27 July 1976, and Reuter, 28 November 1976.

7. <u>The Guardian</u> (London), 27 August 1976.

8. <u>Nowe Drogi</u> (Warsaw), May 1974.

9. Reuter, 21 December 1973.

10. <u>Informations Catholiques Internationales</u> (Paris), 15 April 1976.

11. <u>Tygodnik Powszechny</u> (Cracow), 16 May 1976.

12. (Koeln), 6 January 1977.

13. dpa, 15 December 1976.

14. See, for example, the New York <u>Times</u>, 19 March 1976.

15. <u>The Guardian</u>, 27 August 1976.

16. <u>Frankfurter Allgemeine Zeitung</u>, 28 September 1976.

17. See Jacek Kuron in <u>Le Monde</u> (Paris), 29 January 1977, Karol Modzelewski in <u>Politique hebdo</u> (Paris), 6-12 December 1976, and Adam Michnik in <u>La Repubblica</u> (Rome), 16 November 1976.

18. United Press International (UPI), 20 November 1976.

CHAPTER

18

THE PATH OF CHURCH-STATE
RECONCILIATION IN HUNGARY

Charles E. Kovats

On 12 February 1976, Radio Bucharest and Radio Vatican reported the appointment of Laszlo Lekai as Archbishop of Esztergom. This decision was in some regards the most significant in the protracted course of reconciliation between the Roman Catholic Church and the communist government of Hungary. That an improvement has gradually been worked out is attributable in part to the recognition by Church officials that pastoral work requires a certain accommodation with the existing Hungarian regime, however much the Church and its teachings may be in conflict with that regime. But it is also partly owing to recognition by the party and government of the tenacity and reality of Roman Catholic institutions and the strength of popular religious convictions despite communist antipathy to religion in any form. Although the party has not by any means abjured its ultimate goal of eliminating all trace of religion, it nevertheless has had to reconcile ideological activities designed to achieve this end with the political desire for some kind of modus vivendi with the Roman Catholic Church, at least in the current phase of socialist construction in Hungary.*

---

*Some 65 percent of Hungarians are Roman Catholic; 21 percent are Protestant (primarily Calvinist, with some Lutherans), and about 1 percent are Jewish. A factor that further bolsters the Catholic Church is the strength of its ties with the Vatican and with Catholics

---

This chapter is a revised and updated version of Hungarian Unit/ KK, "Laszlo Lekai Named Archbishop of Esztergom," RAD Background Report/47, Radio Free Europe Research, 19 February 1976.

The communist seizure of power and the upheaval represented
by the revolution of 1956 left particularly difficult problems to be
resolved. During the later 1940s, as the communist regime was
consolidating its hold, a number of measures were taken against the
Church in order to weaken it as a center of power competing with the
communist party. These measures were similar to those taken elsewhere in Eastern Europe against religious institutions—Church schools
were nationalized (in 1945 some 60 percent of all schools in Hungary
were Roman Catholic); Church property was seized; monastic institutions were prohibited or their activities were severely restricted;
traditional sources of Church income were eliminated; many seminaries and other institutions for the training of the clergy were closed,
and the number of novices permitted to enter those that were allowed
to remain in operation was strictly limited; and clergy and officials
who resisted these measures were imprisoned. The Church was
further troubled by regime sponsorship of the so-called peace priests,
who for various personal and political reasons were willing to cooperate with the government and opposed the actions of the Vatican and
the Church hierarchy. Conflict arose between Church and government
over the latter's refusing to recognize Church officials whom the
Vatican continued to recognize as incumbents.

Among the most serious points of conflict between the Catholic
Church and the Hungarian state was the question of Jozsef Cardinal
Mindszenty, who had been appointed Archbishop of Esztergom and
Primate of Hungary in October 1945. In February 1949, he had been
tried on dubious charges of conspiracy against the state, high treason,
and illegal dealings in foreign currency, and sentenced to life imprisonment. The government refused thereafter to acknowledge his
religious office, but the Vatican continued to recognize him as primate,
although he remained incarcerated. He was released from prison
during the course of the 1956 revolution, but when the Soviet Army
arrived to quell the uprising he sought refuge in the U.S. legation in
Budapest, where he remained a virtual prisoner for many years.
He continued to be a very visible symbol of the difficulties in Church-
state relations, but as time went on he became an obstacle to their
improvement.

Two major steps prepared the way for the appointment of Lekai:
first, the 1964 partial agreement between the Vatican and the Hungarian government; and second, resolution of the Mindszenty problem—
a highly complicated issue which was really only settled with the
cardinal's death in 1975.

----

outside Hungary; the Protestants have far fewer significant ties with
groups outside the country.

THE PARTIAL AGREEMENT OF
SEPTEMBER 1964

The September 1964 agreement was a partial one because of the host of questions that had accumulated between the Hungarian government and the Church; agreement could be reached on only a few.[1] These included the following: a degree of normalization in the top hierarchy of the Church; the taking of an oath of allegiance to the state by all priests; new statutes for the Papal Hungarian Institute in Rome, which was removed from the control of émigré priests and put under the supervision of the Bench of Bishops in Hungary, and hence became subject to the influence of the government. The limited scope of the agreement is evident, though it was the upshot of difficult negotiations and hard bargaining that had dragged on since the spring of 1963. With the completion of the document, both sides expressed the hope that "other problems may also be solved in the future through further talks." Jozsef Prantner, then president of the Hungarian State Office for Church Affairs, attributed the partial agreement to a more "realistic" appreciation by the Holy See of the progress achieved by the Hungarian People's Republic and the enhanced reputation of the socialist countries.

After the conclusion of the agreement, there was a gradual improvement in relations between the Hungarian government and the Church, and a new era was ushered in. This did not mean, however, that hostility ceased or that the Church was permitted to pursue its pastoral tasks unhindered. Until September 1964, the government and the Holy See had pretended to ignore each other. The Vatican took decisions regarding the Church in Hungary—for example, by making ecclesiastical appointments (of apostolic administrators and bishops), which were valid de jure but could not be implemented in practice because they were made without previous consultation with the Hungarian government; the latter regarded such measures as inadmissible interference by a "foreign power" in Hungary's domestic affairs. Conversely, the "accord" concluded under duress between the Church and the government in August 1950[2] was regarded as valid by the Hungarian state but considered null and void by the Holy See. The Church had to develop "peaceful coexistence" with the Hungarian government, which became possible only after the Holy See and the government decided to recognize each other in some way. This was the breakthrough that underlay the partial agreement of September 1964. Thereafter it became a strictly-adhered-to practice to refrain from unilateral action and to resolve all pending problems by mutual agreement.

Among the positive results of the partial agreement were the renovation of the upper levels of the Church hierarchy through the appointment of new bishops and other officials; the lifting of government restrictions on travel to Rome by various ecclesiastical officials and the granting of permission for a number of priests to study abroad in Rome and elsewhere; and an increase in state subsidies for the Church, although they remained at a level that was far from adequate. Certain problems, however, persisted. One such issue was religious instruction for Catholic children, a sensitive area since the party was actively propagating its atheistic ideology among the young. Another problem was the dwindling number of young people entering the ranks of the clergy. The government continued to utilize various means at its disposal to discourage them from entering seminaries, and the rigors of religious life are such that only the most dedicated would wish to enter it.[3]

THE QUESTION OF CARDINAL MINDSZENTY

One important problem the partial agreement did not resolve was the status of Cardinal Mindszenty and the position of Primate of Hungary. Although as a consequence of the agreement an apostolic administrator for the Archdiocese of Esztergom was appointed by the Holy See with the approval of the Hungarian government, Mindszenty continued to be recognized by the Vatican as archbishop and primate, although the government refused to acknowledge him as such.

The first step in resolving this impasse was an agreement between the Vatican and the Hungarian government in September 1971 under which the cardinal left Hungary for Rome, where he was received by Pope Paul VI. Thereafter he took up residence in a monastery in Vienna. The Radio Budapest[4] announcement of his departure noted that he had "left Hungarian territory forever." Although the Vatican reports did not mention that his departure from the country was permanent, there is no reason to doubt that this was part of the agreement.

It is clear why the Holy See omitted any reference to the move being irreversible. A statement[5] issued with the announcement of Midszenty's departure from Hungary emphasized that the cardinal "retains the titles, conferred upon him on 2 October 1945, of Archbishop of Esztergom and Primate of Hungary." In other words, despite its tacit acceptance of the fact that his departure from Hungary was final, the Vatican refused to countenance any change in Mindszenty's status. He remained the de jure head of both the Estergom archbishopric and the Catholic Church in Hungary.

In the eyes of the Hungarian government, however, he had lost both positions when his sentence of life imprisonment was handed down on 8 February 1949.[6]

Although Mindszenty's departure from Hungary went far toward improving the government's relations with the Church, the Vatican's continued recognition of him as archbishop and primate was a constant source of irritation. This was no doubt heightened by the cardinal's frequent trips in the West, during which he was enthusiastically greeted by large crowds, and by his criticism of the Hungarian regime in his sermons. The government became increasingly insistent that canon law be invoked to remove him from his positions before further progress in relations with the Church could take place, and ultimately made his removal a conditio sine qua non for "normalization" of the Church's hierarchy.

This step was finally taken by the Vatican in February 1974, when the Holy See declared the see of Esztergom vacant, thus removing Mindszenty as archbishop and primate de jure as well as de facto.[7] Regime news media stressed the fact that the changes in the Church leadership were made by the Vatican with government approval and announced at the same time that they had been possible only because Pope Paul VI had declared the see of Esztergom "vacant."[8] State Secretary Imre Miklos wrote an article[9] in which he said that the appointments made after Mindszenty's dismissal had clearly proved that even "complicated questions can be resolved" and pledged that the party and government would continue to pursue a "principled policy" that would make it possible to settle further issues through negotiation.

The Vatican issued two documents on the subject. The first specified that

> in consideration of the pastoral problems of the archdiocese of Esztergom and after having had an ample exchange of correspondence with Jozsef Cardinal Mindszenty, archbishop of the metropolitan see, the Holy Father has decided to declare the above-mentioned archdiocese vacant and to appoint as its apostolic administrator . . . Titular Bishop Laszlo Lekai, hitherto apostolic administrator of the vacant see of Veszprem.

The second document was the text of a letter addressed by Pope Paul to Cardinal Mindszenty on 30 January 1974. Both documents stated that the archbishopric of Esztergom had been declared vacant in consideration of pastoral problems.

There was "an ample exchange of correspondence" with the cardinal and a "prolonged study of the circumstances," indicating that the Holy See made vigorous efforts to persuade Mindszenty to retire voluntarily but without success. Mindszenty, in fact, issued a statement explaining why he could not abdicate and stating that the decision to remove him was taken "by the Holy See alone." The Vatican responded to the cardinal's statement by reiterating that

Pope Paul's decision to dismiss him had been taken only in the interest of the diocese—that is, in order to promote the spiritual well-being of both priests and faithful in Hungary. The measure was intended to satisfy "the primary requirement of every Church community—that it be able to enjoy the guidance and active, encouraging, fortifying presence of a shepherd of its own in a normal regime of canonical administration."[10]

Despite the Vatican's removal of Mindszenty, no successor was designated. Declaring the see of Esztergom vacant was a condition imposed by the government if Church affairs in Hungary were to be regularized, but the Holy See was understandably reluctant to appoint a replacement while Mindszenty was still alive, though there was no legal obstacle to its doing so. The Hungarian government, on the other hand, seemed anxious to have an archbishop appointed, as a token of further normalization. The death of Cardinal Mindszenty in May 1975 opened the way for this to be done.

LEKAI NAMED ARCHBISHOP OF ESZTERGOM

Some nine months later, Laszlo Lekai, who since February 1974 had been apostolic administrator of the diocese of Esztergom, was appointed its archbishop by the Holy See with the approval of the Hungarian government. Traditionally and under the terms of the Church's statutes, the archbishop is Primate of Hungary and president of the Bench of Bishops. Also in keeping with tradition, Lekai was named a cardinal in April 1976, at the next consistory following his appointment.[11]

The agreement was preceded by an unusual number of consultations. In July 1975 Archbishop Poggi went to Budapest; in November Pope Paul received Prime Minister Gyorgy Lazar in a private audience (he was the first Hungarian head of government to pay a visit to the Holy See since World War II), and the development of relations ranked high on the agenda of their talks;[12] a few weeks later, Imre Miklos, head of the Hungarian Office for Religious Affairs, led a delegation to the Vatican for two days of secret talks with Archbishop Agostino Casaroli, the Vatican's "foreign minister"; and Archbishop Poggi again visited Hungary in January 1976, spending five days in Budapest during which he had talks with Archbishop Jozsef Ijjas of Kalocsa, president of the Hungarian Bench of Bishops, and was received by Miklos, with whom he discussed "questions of interest to both sides."[13] In all probability, these talks tied up the last "loose ends" and paved the way for Lekai's appointment.

It might be asked why so many consultations were needed in order to reach agreement on a single appointment. It is probable, however, that other topics also came up for discussion. It is also possible that the Hungarian government would have preferred someone else to be appointed—Jozsef Cserhati, for example, who was bishop of Pecs and secretary of the Bench of Bishops and on very good terms with the government (he also seemed to enjoy the confidence of the Holy See). It is probable, however, that while the Vatican obviously had to choose someone who was persona grata to the Hungarian government, it preferred someone who was less publicly so. Another point in Lekai's favor may have been the fact that he had been in charge of the archdiocese since February 1974. In any case, a number of men senior to him who had been residential archbishops or bishops for a number of years were bypassed. Lekai himself was virtually unknown abroad until February 1972, when he was raised from the rank of parish priest in the diocese of Veszprem and appointed titular bishop and apostolic administrator of the see.

Lekai's elevation to the rank of archbishop went a long way toward normalizing the situation of the upper-level hierarchy of the Catholic Church in Hungary. Previous steps in this direction had been taken in January 1975,[14] when new appointments brought the number of residential archbishops to two (out of a possible three) and of residential bishops to seven (out of a possible eight). Nine titular bishops were then in office, five of whom were attached to the various Church provinces as auxiliary bishops to ease the burden on their residential superiors. One might say that if the number of bishops is a yardstick of "normalization" of relations between the Holy See and a socialist government, Hungary ranks second only to Poland in this respect.

Lekai was explicit about his plans and policies in a statement made when he took his oath of allegiance to the Hungarian Constitution and afterward in a lengthy interview with the Hungarian news agency.[15] He expressed his "profound gratitude" to the pope for having appointed him to the see of Esztergom and added his "grateful thanks" to the Presidential Council for having given prior consent to the appointment. The outstanding feature of his nomination, he said, lay in the fact that through it the full hierarchy of the Catholic Church in Hungary had been restored in accordance with ancient tradition. He pledged that he and his fellow bishops would do their best to confirm Hungary's Catholics in their faith and cooperate conscientiously in the "peaceful and blessed" building of "our Hungarian fatherland."

His interview was marked by an awareness of the present limitations on the Church in Hungary. "The realities of the situation are that in our present socialist society believers and nonbelievers must live together," and although their Weltanschauungen are opposed to each other, they can provide an impetus for joint effort. Catholics, said Lekai, respect the views of others, but expect similar consideration from them—especially when it is found that "starting from our religious <u>Weltanschauung</u> we too can cherish aspirations similar to those of a developed socialist society." While it is accepted that fundamental differences of outlook cannot be a matter of compromise, this should not lead to rigidity or the marking of time. "The sincere road of dialogue," Lekai said, "will bring us together in the interest of our country."

The new primate expressed his satisfaction that religious freedom is ensured by the Hungarian state. While there are still some unsolved problems, he said, there is hope that they can be settled gradually and in a quiet atmosphere, on the basis of the mutual understanding and cooperation that characterize the present relations between Church and state. In this context, he referred particularly to the teaching of the catechism introduced in January 1975. He admitted that the existing settlement does not resolve all difficulties or preclude the misunderstandings that can arise in everyday life, and said that Church and state must therefore continue their efforts to remove the difficulties gradually and work out satisfactory practical solutions.*

During the interview, Lekai was questioned about the repeated appeals made by the party and government to all citizens to cooperate in "building a new Hungary." He answered that such appeals always kindled keen interest among the leaders of the Church and the masses of the faithful—even outside Hungary. In this connection, he quoted from the circular letter issued by the Bench of Bishops on the eve of the 30th anniversary of the "liberation of our native land,"[18] which stated that the Church, together with the people, had found a new place in socialist society and, again together with the people, "shared in full a community of concern for the future." Then he went on to say:

> I can hardly praise highly enough the realistic policies
> and efforts of the Holy See. The grinding pressure of

------

*Agreement on the teaching of the catechism in church buildings was negotiated between the government and the Bench of Bishops in the fall of 1974.[16] The practice is hedged about with restrictions—both the number of catechumens and the frequency of instruction are limited—and the agreement has therefore evoked strong criticism from both clergy and laity. It has not replaced the teaching of the catechism in the general schools and Gymnasiums.[17] These classes are still formally maintained even though the teaching of the catechism has virtually ceased. It is interesting that Lekai's flexible but nonetheless firm reference to the unsatisfactory solution reached in this matter was included in the summary of his interview published in <u>Nepszabadsag</u>.

earlier times has been lifted, and the souls of the bishops and the faithful have received a sense of reassurance and calm thanks to which we can now serve both our faith and our country in a harmonious way.

THE CHURCH AND THE POLICY OF ALLIANCE

The appointment of Lekai can in many respects be considered the high point to date in the reconciliation between the Catholic Church and the communist regime in Hungary. At the same time, however, significant differences persist. Although the appointing of fully empowered residential archbishops and bishops has for the most part been completed, the members of the hierarchy are generally advanced in age (at the time of Lekai's appointment, the average was nearly 63), and thus the question of new appointments is one that will continue to require attention. Much more is at stake, however. If the Church is to prosper, it will have to be given greater latitude to provide religious instruction, publish Church views, work among youth, and train new members of the clergy. The Church has shown its willingness to make the best of a bad situation, but there can be no question that the conditions under which it must operate are less than optimal, although the improvement in relations with the state has been accompanied by the creation of better circumstances for the Church.

For the Hungarian regime, improving its relations with the Church has involved certain concessions, primarily in the ideological and propaganda fields. The party has been anxious to enlist nonparty members, and especially religious believers, in the promotion of Hungary's social and economic development—a program known as the "policy of alliance," in referring to which First Secretary Janos Kadar inverted a phrase from the New Testament: "Those who are not against us are with us." CC Secretary Imre Gyori explained that building a "developed socialist society" cannot be left to Communists alone; it requires the cooperation of the overwhelming majority of the Hungarian population, party members and nonmembers, believers and nonbelievers.[19]

The regime takes pride in the fact that since 1945 relations with believers and their Churches have never been "as well ordered and tranquil as they are at present [1976]," and reference is frequently made to further agreement with the Roman Catholic Church on the settlement of "still pending" questions. Jeno Farago, one of Nepszabadsag's senior commentators on domestic political and ideological affairs, attached to this optimistic assessment of the current situation some comments that shed an interesting light on the everyday problems that arise in regard to cooperation between party and state and the ordinary Church member.[20] He said there are still people on both sides whose approach to cooperation is erroneous; some party members fail to discern that the "main line of division" runs between the supporters and the opponents of socialism, not between atheists and believers. He also said that "one still encounters people who want to take administrative measures against the influence of the Churches' representatives" instead of relying on ideological and educational work, which, he conceded, "is much more difficult but at the same time much more to the point."

The "other side," however, is not without its "misunderstandings." Farago criticized those who regard the settlement of relations between state and Church as a sort of armistice and hold that it is wrong to disturb the improved relations that have been achieved by continuing to propagate scientific socialism. This, he said, is a mistaken view of the situation. The party can never abandon its ideological struggle to attract newcomers to its cause. Some people complain about the ideological and educational influence exerted by the state, which they regard as inconsistent with Church-state rapprochement, but tolerate the Church's "methods of exerting influence, which are not only out of keeping with such agreements but directly contrary to them." He added that he wished the improved atmosphere now obtaining at the top also existed lower down.

As Deputy Prime Minister Gyorgy Aczel noted, "there are differences of views between . . . the Churches and the state, and it is natural that all problems cannot be solved satisfactorily. But patience on both sides helps us to bridge the gaps that exist."[21]

NOTES

1. See RE/Hungarian Unit, "The Hungarian-Varican Accord," Hungarian Background Report, Radio Free Europe Research, 18 September 1964.

2. Kis Ujsag (Budapest), 1 September 1950.

3. On the consequences of the 1964 agreement, see KK/Hungarian Unit, "The Partial Agreement Between Budapest and the Holy See: Ten Years Later," Hungarian Background Report/11, Radio Free Europe Research, 10 October 1974.

4. 28 September 1971.

5. L'Osservatore Romano (Vatican City), 28 September 1971.

6. See Szabad Nep (Budapest), 4 and 9 February 1949.

7. Radio Budapest, 5 February 1974.

8. See, for example, Magyar Nemzet (Budapest), 6 February 1974.

9. Nepszabadsag (Budapest), 3 March 1974.

10. See Hungarian Unit/KK, "Cardinal Mindszenty Removed as Primate of Hungary," Hungarian Background Report/3, Radio Free Europe Research, 13 February 1974.

11. Nepszabadsag, 28 April 1976; Uj Ember (Budapest), 2 May 1976; see also Hungarian Situation Report/15, Radio Free Europe Research, 5 May 1976, Item 2.

12. Katolikus Szo (Budapest), 23 November 1975.

13. Nepszabadsag, 21 January 1976.

14. Ibid., 11 January 1975.

15. The statement was broadcast over Homeland Radio, 13 February 1976; his interview was published in Nepszabadsag, 15 February 1976.

16. See the Bench of Bishops' circular letter issued in December 1974 and published in Uj Ember, 12 January 1975.

17. See the statement by Archbishop Ijjas in Magyar Hirlap (Budapest), 22 December 1974.

18. Katolikus Szo, 30 March 1975.

19. Nepszabadasag, 20 August 1976.

20. Ibid., 18 August 1976. See Hungarian Situation Report/31, Radio Free Europe Research, 1 September 1976, Item 1.

21. Vilagossag (Budapest), October 1976; excerpts translated in "The Socialist State and the Churches in Hungary," RAD Background Report/256, Radio Free Europe Research, 14 December 1976.

SELECTED DEMOGRAPHIC
DATA ON EASTERN EUROPE
Compiled by
William F. Robinson

TABLE A.1

Area

Country	Sq. Km.	Sq. Miles
Bulgaria	110,912	43,325
CSSR	127,877	49,952
GDR	108,178	42,257
Hungary	93,030	36,340
Poland	312,677	122,139
Romania	237,500	92,773
Yugoslavia	255,804	99,923
Total	1,245,978	486,709

Note: Unless otherwise noted, the Appendix tables have been compiled using data from the sources listed in the Bibliography at the end of the Appendix.

This appendix appeared in the Radio Free Europe Research series as "Selected Demographic and Economic Data on Eastern Europe," RAD Background Report/90, 30 April 1977.

TABLE A.2

Population
(in thousands)

Country	1960	1965	1970	1975
Bulgaria	7,906	8,231	8,515	8,730
CSSR	13,698	14,194	14,366	14,856
GDR	17,188	17,040	17,068	16,820
Hungary	10,006	10,166	10,354	10,572
Poland	29,795	31,551	32,658	34,180
Romania	18,495	19,083	20,361	21,353
Yugoslavia	18,402	19,434	20,371	21,352
Total	115,490	119,699	123,693	127,863

Note: All figures as of December 31 except those for Yugoslavia, which are as of July 1.

TABLE A.3

Population Density, 1975

Country	Persons per Sq. Km.	Persons per Sq. Mile
Bulgaria	78.7	201.5
CSSR	116.2	297.2
GDR	155.5	398.1
Hungary	113.6	290.9
Poland	109.3	279.8
Romania	89.9	230.1
Yugoslavia	83.5	213.7
Eastern Europe	102.6	262.7

Note: All figures as of December 31 except those for Yugoslavia, which are as of July 1.

TABLE A.4

Population Increases, 1966–75
(net increase per 1,000 population)

Year	Bulgaria	CSSR	GDR	Hungary	Poland	Romania	Yugoslavia
1966	6.6	5.6	2.5	3.6	9.4	6.1	12.3
1967	6.0	5.0	1.5	3.9	8.5	18.1	10.8
1968	8.3	4.2	0.2	3.9	8.6	17.1	10.4
1969	7.5	4.3	-0.3	3.6	8.2	13.2	9.6
1970	7.2	4.3	-0.2	3.1	8.5	11.6	8.9
1971	6.2	5.0	±0	2.6	8.5	10.0	9.6
1972	5.5	6.2	-2.0	3.3	9.4	9.6	9.1
1973	6.7	7.3	-3.0	3.2	9.6	8.4	9.5
1974	7.4	8.1	-3.0	5.8	10.2	11.2	9.7
1975	6.3	8.0	-3.5	6.0	10.2	10.4	–

Note: All figures based on average annual population except those for Romania and Yugoslavia, which are as of July 1.

TABLE A.5

Refined Fertility Rates, 1966–75

Year	Bulgaria	CSSR	GDR	Hungary	Poland	Romania	Yugoslavia
1966	–	65.6	80.5	54.5	68.0	55.7	79.2
1967	–	62.2	76.0	57.7	65.0	105.5	75.2
1968	–	60.3	73.5	58.7	64.0	102.9	72.0
1969	64.3	61.9	71.1	58.1	63.0	89.6	70.5
1970	62.8	63.5	70.1	56.6	64.0	81.2	66.4
1971	61.3	65.8	69.0	55.9	65.0	75.3	68.5
1972	59.6	69.4	58.6	56.9	66.0	72.7	68.7
1973	63.4	75.8	52.4	58.2	68.0	70.4	67.9
1974	68.0	80.5	51.9	69.6	69.0	79.3	68.1
1975	–	79.8	–	73.0	71.0	77.5	–

Note: Births per 1,000 females aged 15–49, based on end-of-year population figures except in the case of the GDR, where age bracket is 15–45 and population figures are as of January 1.

315

TABLE A.6

Urban/Rural Breakdown of Population
in Percent
(at end of year)

Country	1960	1965	1970	1975
	u : r	u : r	u : r	u : r
Bulgaria	38:62	47:53	53:47	58:42[a]
CSSR	57:43	61:39	62:38	66:34
GDR	72:28	73:27	74:26	75:25
Hungary	42:58	45:55	47:53	50:50
Poland	48:52	50:50	52:48	56:44
Romania	32:68	38:62	41:59	44:56
Yugoslavia	50:50[b]	—	62:38[c]	—

[a] 2 December 1975.
[b] 1961.
[c] 1971.

TABLE A.7

Suicides, 1966–75

(per 100,000 inhabitants, based on end-of-year population)

Year	Bulgaria	CSSR	GDR[a]	Hungary	Poland[b]	Romania	Yugoslavia
1966	9.9	23.0		29.6	9.9		12.3
1967	10.3	23.9		31.3	10.2	U	12.8
1968	9.8	24.5	29.5	33.7	10.5	N	13.2
1969	11.3	23.2	28.7	33.1	11.2	K	13.9
1970	11.9	25.3	30.5	34.9	11.3	N	13.5
1971	12.3	24.2		36.1	11.7	O	13.8
1972	11.4	24.6		36.9	12.0	W	13.7
1973	11.5	22.4		36.9	11.7	N	13.1
1974	12.6	22.9[c]		40.7	–		13.1
1975	–	22.0[c]		38.4	–		–

[a]Wolf Oschlies, "Selbstmorde in der DDR und in Osteuropa" (Suicide in the GDR and Eastern Europe), Deutschland Archiv, no. 1, 1976, p. 39.

[b]The Polish suicide rates cited here are lower than those appearing in Table XI of William F. Robinson, comp., "Selected Demographic Data on Eastern Europe," RAD Background Report/225, Radio Free Europe Research, 3 November 1976, p. 9. The higher figures reflect attempted suicides, both successful and un-successful, registered with the domestic police authorities. Owing to an oversight, this was not explained in the earlier publication. The lower figures in the table above reflect only deaths by suicide.

[c]Demografie, no. 2, April–June 1976, p. 171 (preliminary).

TABLE A.8

Induced Abortions per 1,000 Women in 15–49 Age Group

Country	1960	1965	1966	1967	1968	1969	1970	1971	1972	1973	1974	1975
Bulgaria	—	49.7	—	—	—	58.3	64.5	69.5	70.1	62.4	65.9	—
CSSR	27.7	23.7	26.3	27.5	27.9	28.3	27.6	27.0	25.2	22.4	23.1	—
GDR[a]	—	—	—	—	—	—	—	—	33.6	31.7	27.6	24.4
Hungary	65.1	71.6	73.0	72.1	75.9	78.7	71.7	69.9	66.6	63.3	38.1[b]	36.1
Poland	—	—	28.6	28.0	25.7	25.0	25.1	23.5	23.2	23.6	24.0	—
Romania						UNKNOWN						
Yugoslavia[c]	24.8[d]	—	—	53.7	—	—	—	—	—	—	—	—

[a] Based on absolute figures given by Radio DDR, 9 March 1977.
[b] Sudden drop is a result of new legal restrictions.
[c] Wolf Oschlies, Jugendprobleme in Jugoslawien (Cologne: Bundesinstitut für Ostwissenschaftliche und Internationale Studien, December 1976), p. 13.
[d] 1959.

318

TABLE A.9

Religious Denominations as Percent of Population

Denomination	Bulgaria[a]	CSSR	GDR[b]	Hungary	Poland[c]	Romania	Yugoslavia
Roman Catholic		60	7.6	65	88	5	31.8
Orthodox	57	1		0.4		66	41.4
Protestant[d]		8	49.8	21		1.7	2.2
Muslim	11						12.3
Greek Catholic						7	
Jewish	<0.08	0.1	0.005	0.8	0.03	0.4	<0.03
Unitarian		1					

Note: These are current estimates based on past data, fragmentary evidence from recent years, and the judgment of RFE analysts.

aProtestant, Jewish, and Catholic believers in Bulgaria probably constitute no more than 2 percent of the population combined.

bEvangelische Pressedienst—Landesdienst Berlin, 25 January 1974, 15 March 1977; Begegnung, no. 2, 1974.

cMinority denominations, including Polish Autocephalic Orthodox Church (457,000 members), equal no more than 2 percent of the population.

dPrimarily Lutheran and Calvinist, although Baptists equal 0.7 percent of the population in Romania.

319

TABLE A.10

Ethnic Composition of Population
(in percent)

Ethnic Group	Bulgaria[a]	CSSR[b]	GDR[c]	Hungary[d]	Poland[e]	Romania[f]	Yugoslavia[g]
Albanian							6.4
Byelorussian					0.5		
Bulgarian	88.2					0.1	0.3
Czech		65.0					0.1
German		0.6	c.99	2.3	h	2.0	0.1
Hungarian		4.0		94.2		8.5	2.3
Polish		0.5			c.98		
Romanian				0.4		87.7	0.3
Slovak		29.2		1.3			0.4
Sorbs and Wends			0.2-0.4				
South Slavs:	0.1			1.3			86.7
Of whom:							
Serbs							(39.7)
Croats							(22.1)
Slovenes							(8.2)
Macedonians	(0.1)[i]						(5.8)
Other							(10.9)
Turks	9.1					0.1	0.6
Ukrainians		0.4			0.5	0.3	0.1
Other	2.6	0.3	0.6-0.8	0.5	0.2	1.3	2.7

[a]Census of 1 December 1965.
[b]Census of 1 December 1970.
[c]Estimated for 1975.
[d]Census of 1 January 1970.
[e]Estimated for 1969.
[f]Census of 15 March 1966.
[g]Census of 31 March 1971.

[h]The Polish source for data on ethnic minorities in Poland did not mention any ethnic Germans since all were supposed to have been expelled from Polish territory after 1945 and any who remained claimed Polish nationality. On the basis of agreements between the governments of Poland and the Federal Republic of Germany in the 1970s, however, a large number of Polish citizens of ethnic German origin sought permission to emigrate to West Germany. The FRG Red Cross reported in mid-1975 that some 284,000 Germans living in Poland—or 0.8 percent of the population—had applied to emigrate (Frankfurter Allgemeine Zeitung, 1 July 1975), and hence the number of ethnic Germans in Poland undoubtedly exceeds this figure.

[i]The Bulgarian and Yugoslav governments have made quite different claims about the number of Macedonians living in Bulgaria. The 1956 Bulgarian census reported 187,789 (or 2.5 percent of the population), but the 1965 census reported only 8,750 (0.1 percent). During the interval between the two censuses, the Bulgarians changed their views regarding the existence of a Macedonian nationality. Until 1956, they acknowledged its existence, but thereafter they maintained that Macedonians were Bulgarians, not a separate nationality. The 1965 census figures reflected this decision. The Yugoslavs, on the other hand, have vigorously maintained the separate identity of the Macedonians and criticized Bulgaria for failing to grant them minority rights (see, for example, Nova Makedonija, 6 February 1967).

Sources: Bulgaria, Rezultati ot prebroiavane na naselenieto na 1.XII.1965 g. (Sofia, 1967); CSSR, Predbezne Vysledky: Scitani, lidu, domu a bytu k 1. prosinci 1970 v CSSR (Prague, 1971); GDR, Gesamtdeutsches Institut, Bonn; Hungary, Kritika, June 1975; Poland, Argumenty, 14 September 1969; Romania, Recensamintul populatiei si locuintelor din 15 martie 1966 (Bucharest, 1966); Yugoslavia, Popis stanovnistva i stanova 1971 (Belgrade, 1974).

TABLE A.11

Social Structure

(classes and strata as percent of working population)

Category	Bulgaria[a]	CSSR[b]	GDR[c]	Hungary[d]	Poland[e]	Romania[f]	Yugoslavia[g]
Blue-collar workers[h]	43.7	62.7	56.0	58.0	41.5	45.5	34.5
White-collar workers[i]	16.2	28.0	34.0	24.0	22.9	13.5	16.4
Cooperative peasantry	38.7	8.3	7.3	14.6	—	34.1	2.9
Private peasantry	0.5	0.8	0.1	1.7	32.9	5.0	41.5
Other private	0.9	0.2	2.6	1.7	—	1.9	4.7

[a]December 1965.
[b]December 1975.
[c]30 September 1975.
[d]January 1975.
[e]December 1970.
[f]1972: based on average annual number of active earners.
[g]April 1971.
[h]Includes state farm workers and cooperative artisans.
[i]Includes intelligentsia and government bureaucracy.

Special sources: Demografie (Czechoslovakia), no. 2, 1976, p. 177; Alexander Matejko, Social Change and Stratification in Eastern Europe (New York: Praeger Publishers, 1974), p. 6 (for Poland); Era Socialista (Romania), no. 4, February 1975, p. 18.

TABLE A.12

Contribution to National Income by
Economic Sector
(in percent)

	Bulgaria				CSSR			
	1960	1965	1970	1975	1960	1965	1970	1975
Industry	45.6	45.0	49.1	51.0	63.4	66.4	62.1	64.4
Construction	7.1	7.3	8.7	8.8	10.7	9.3	11.3	12.1
Agriculture	32.2	33.4	22.6	22.0	14.7	12.0	10.1	8.3
Transport/ Communications	4.2	4.5	6.9	8.2	3.0	2.4	3.8	2.2
Trade	8.7	7.7	9.9	7.8	7.0	8.5	11.3	11.9
Other	2.2	2.1	2.8	2.2	1.2	1.4	1.4	1.1

	GDR				Hungary			
Industry	56.4	59.2	60.7	62.2	36.6	42.1	43.2	47.0
Construction	7.0	7.4	8.2	8.0	11.6	10.7	12.1	12.9
Agriculture	16.4	13.8	11.6	10.0	30.8	24.2	17.7	16.3
Transport/ Communications	5.5	5.4	5.2	4.9	5.6	6.0	6.5	6.1
Trade	13.0	12.5	12.6	13.3	14.1	13.7	15.0	15.0
Other	1.6	1.7	1.6	1.6	1.3	3.3	5.5	2.7

	Poland				Romania			
Industry	39.5	45.0	49.8	52.1	42.1	48.6	58.6	57.1
Construction	10.5	10.2	11.4	13.3	8.9	8.4	11.1	8.4
Agriculture	30.3	23.2	17.5	12.6	34.9	28.3	19.1	16.6
Transport/ Communications	5.9	6.3	6.5	7.4	5.2	5.7	5.8	5.6
Trade	12.4	11.5	11.8	12.6	6.2	7.5	3.5	10.6
Other	1.4	3.8	3.0	2.0	2.7	1.5	1.9	1.7

	Yugoslavia			
Industry	45.6	50.3	35.3	35.0
Construction	4.5	6.8	9.7	10.8
Agriculture	28.1	19.3	21.7	17.9
Transport/ Communications	6.4	6.2	6.7	7.3
Trade	10.0	12.1	20.5	23.1
Other	5.4	5.2	5.2	6.1

Distribution of Investment Funds by
Economic Sector
(in percent)

Sector	Bulgaria				CSSR			
	1960	1965	1970	1975	1960	1965	1970	1975
Industry	34.2	44.8	45.2	39.9	40.1	42.8	38.0	36.1
Construction	1.6	2.7	2.9	4.1	3.3	2.9	3.7	4.2
Agriculture[a]	29.7	19.7	15.7	14.8	16.9	14.0	10.7	12.3
Transport/								
Communications	5.8	6.7	8.7	13.4	9.4	11.3	12.4	13.6
Trade	2.2	3.1	3.5	3.1	3.1	3.9	5.1	4.7
Communal[b]	26.4	23.0	23.8	24.7	27.0	25.1	30.1	28.9
	GDR				Hungary			
Industry	49.7	55.1	52.1	50.5	40	42	36	35
Construction	2.6	2.0	3.2	3.1	3	2	3	2
Agriculture[a]	12.0	13.5	13.3	12.7	21	17	23	19
Transport/								
Communications	10.7	9.5	8.8	10.8	12	15	13	15
Trade	3.0	4.4	4.8	4.0	3	3	4	5
Communal[b]	22.0	15.5	17.8	18.9	21	21	21	24
	Poland				Romania			
Industry	37.6	39.8	39.0	45.2	42.8	48.9	47.5	49.3
Construction	2.7	3.3	3.9	5.5	1.9	3.9	4.5	5.3
Agriculture[a]	12.6	16.4	16.3	13.5	19.6	16.9	16.4	13.5
Transport/								
Communications	9.6	10.5	12.0	11.8	8.0	9.4	10.6	10.7
Trade	3.0	3.1	2.5	2.3	2.7	2.6	3.5	3.5
Communal[b]	34.5	26.9	26.3	21.7	25.0	18.3	17.5	17.7
	Yugoslavia							
Industry	35.4	36.4	31.8	44.8				
Construction	2.3	1.6	2.2	4.2				
Agriculture[a]	13.4	9.4	7.6	7.8				
Transport/								
Communications	17.6	11.6	12.1	14.9				
Trade	5.2	5.2	13.2	7.2				
Communal[b]	26.2	35.8	33.1	21.0				

[a]Includes fishing, forestry, and water conservation.

[b]Includes housing (usually over 50 percent of the total sum for communal investment), education, health and welfare, government, public utilities, culture, insurance, police and fire protection, etc. In the case of Yugoslavia it also includes 1.4 (1960), 1 (1965), 1.3 (1970), and 1.5 (1975) percentage points for investment in artisanry.

TABLE A.14

Labor Force by Economic Sector
(in percent)

Sector*	Bulgaria				CSSR			
	1960	1965	1970	1975	1960	1965	1970	1975
Industry	22.4	27.0	30.7	33.3	37.3	38.3	38.0	38.5
Construction	4.7	6.3	8.1	8.2	8.3	8.0	8.5	9.2
Agriculture	55.5	45.3	35.7	28.1	25.9	21.1	18.3	15.2
Transport/								
Communications	4.1	5.1	6.0	6.4	6.0	6.6	6.8	6.5
Trade	4.0	5.2	6.1	7.8	7.9	8.4	9.1	10.3
Nonproductive	9.2	10.8	13.1	15.7	14.2	17.3	18.9	19.8

	GDR				Hungary			
Industry	42.1	42.6	42.6	42.4	28.5	33.9	36.0	35.5
Construction	6.2	6.0	7.0	7.1	5.5	6.4	7.2	8.4
Agriculture	17.2	15.2	13.0	11.4	38.9	29.7	26.4	22.7
Transport/								
Communications	7.1	7.3	7.4	7.5	6.2	6.9	7.2	7.7
Trade	11.6	11.4	10.8	10.5	6.6	7.3	8.0	9.0
Nonproductive	15.3	17.1	18.8	20.6	14.3	15.8	15.2	16.7

	Poland				Romania			
Industry	25.4	28.4	30.2	30.7	15.1	19.2	23.0	30.6
Construction	6.8	7.0	7.4	9.0	4.9	6.3	7.8	8.1
Agriculture	44.2	39.4	34.7	30.6	65.6	56.7	49.3	38.1
Transport/								
Communications	5.3	5.8	6.1	6.3	3.1	4.1	4.8	5.6
Trade	6.0	6.1	6.5	7.5	3.4	4.0	4.3	5.5
Nonproductive	10.2	11.2	12.8	13.5	7.6	9.2	10.2	11.4

	Yugoslavia			
	1961	1965	1971	1975
Industry	17.5	–	22.0	25.9
Construction	4.6	–	4.5	4.8
Agriculture	59.2	–	47.3	40.5
Transport/				
Communications	3.2	–	3.4	3.6
Trade	3.9	–	6.0	7.0
Nonproductive	7.4	–	9.5	10.7
Working abroad	?	–	7.2	7.8

Note: Based on the average annual labor force except for Yugoslavia, which is based on the labor force as of September 30. Excludes those working abroad except for Yugoslavia.

*Columns do not necessarily add up to 100 percent owing to omission of miscellaneous productive branches that do not readily fall into the major sectors listed.

TABLE A.15

Arable Land per Capita

Country	1960		1965		1970		1975	
	Hectares	Acres	Hectares	Acres	Hectares	Acres	Hectares	Acres
Bulgaria	0.62	1.49	0.59	1.42	0.56	1.35	0.55	1.33
CSSR	0.37	0.89	0.36	0.87	0.35	0.84	0.33	0.80
GDR	0.28	0.67	0.28	0.67	0.27	0.65	0.28	0.67
Hungary	0.53	1.28	0.50	1.20	0.49	1.18	0.47	1.13
Poland	0.54	1.30	0.48	1.16	0.46	1.11	0.43	1.04
Romania	0.53	1.28	0.52	1.25	0.48	1.16	0.46	1.11
Yugoslavia	0.55	1.33	0.52	1.25	0.50	1.20	0.47	1.13

TABLE A.16

Output of Selected Agricultural Products

Country	WHEAT (thousand metric tons)				(per capita, in kg.)			
	1960	1965	1970	1975	1960	1965	1970	1975
Bulgaria	2,379	2,921	3,032	2,771	301	355	356	317
CSSR	1,503	1,992	3,174	4,202	110	140	221	282
GDR	1,456	1,802	2,132	2,736	85	106	125	163
Hungary	1,767	2,343	2,718	4,007	177	231	263	381
Poland	2,303	3,422	4,608	5,207	78	109	142	153
Romania	3,450	5,940	3,360	4,840	187	311	165	227
Yugo-slavia	3,460	3,570	3,730	4,404	187	183	186	206

	MAIZE							
Bulgaria	1,505	1,238	2,375	2,822	190	150	279	323
CSSR	572	393	513	843	42	28	36	57
GDR	4.6	—	14.5	1.8	0.3	—	0.9	0.1
Hungary	3,504	3,564	4,013	7,172	352	351	388	682
Poland	47	15	12	79	1.6	0.5	0.4	2.3
Romania	5,531	5,877	6,536	9,241	301	309	323	435
Yugo-slavia	6,160	5,920	6,933	9,389	334	303	340	439

	OTHER GRAINS[a]							
Bulgaria[b]	975	1,141	1,430	2,199	123	139	168	252
CSSR	3,660	2,851	3,510	4,235	267	201	244	285
GDR[c]	4,918	4,929	4,310	6,173	286	289	253	367
Hungary[b]	1,588	1,384	809	1,009	159	136	78	95
Poland	11,962	12,298	10,791	12,828	401	390	330	375
Romania[b]	849	776	735	1,100	46	41	36	52
Yugo-slavia	962	1,445	932	1,203	52	74	46	56

	POTATOES							
Bulgaria	478	285	374	318	60	35	44	40
CSSR	5,093	3,678	4,793	3,565	372	259	334	240
GDR	14,821	12,857	13,054	7,673	862	754	765	456
Hungary	2,656	1,485	1,430	1,630	267	146	138	155
Poland	37,855	43,263	50,301	46,429	1,281	1,374	1,547	1,365
Romania	3,009	2,195	2,064	2,716	164	115	102	128
Yugo-slavia	3,270	2,380	2,964	2,394	178	122	146	112

Country	SUGAR BEETS (thousand metric tons)				(per capita, in kg.)			
	1960	1965	1970	1975	1960	1965	1970	1975
Bulgaria	1,650	1,392	1,714	1,758	209	169	201	201
CSSR	8,368	5,662	6,644	7,735	611	399	463	521
GDR	6,837	5,804	6,135	6,414	398	341	359	381
Hungary	3,370	3,452	2,174	4,089	338	340	210	389
Poland	10,262	12,314	12,742	15,707	347	391	392	462
Romania	3,127	3,013	2,921	4,905	170	158	144	231
Yugo-slavia	2,290	2,620	2,948	4,213	124	134	145	197
MILK[d]								
Bulgaria	1,115	1,388	1,632	1,803	142	169	192	207
CSSR	4,093	4,188	4,978	5,562	300	296	347	376
GDR[e]	5,780	6,282	6,763	7,417	335	369	396	440
Hungary	1,652	1,573	1,726	1,835	166	155	167	174
Poland	12,658	13,475	14,988	16,395	426	428	461	482
Romania	3,343	3,353	3,912	4,581	182	176	193	216
Yugo-slavia[e]	2,283	2,303	2,567	3,588	124	119	126	168
MEAT[f]								
Bulgaria	148	207	271	400	19	25	32	46
CSSR	472	590	712	974	34	42	50	66
GDR	684	859	1,052	1,435	40	50	62	85
Hungary	234	315	401	678	23	31	39	64
Poland	1,004	1,248	1,376	2,328	34	40	42	68
Romania	313	358	471	778	16	19	23	36
Yugo-slavia	629	686	820	1,031	34	35	40	48

[a]Unless otherwise indicated, includes barley, oats, and rye only.
[b]Also includes rice.
[c]Also includes miscellaneous grains.
[d]Includes milk from cows, buffaloes, goats, sheep, camels, and mares, as well as the milk fed to young animals. Does not include milk sucked by young animals.
[e]Cows' milk only.
[f]As produced at slaughterhouses. Refers to the freshly killed weight of disemboweled carcass cattle without fat, blood, hide, head, legs, and entrails. Includes (besides cattle) pigs, sheep, goats, horses, domestic poultry, game fowl, rabbits, and other animals.

TABLE A.17

Output of Artificial Fertilizer[a]
(in thousand metric tons of active substance)

Country	1960	1965	1970	1975
Bulgaria	125	340	434	626
CSSR	287	483	709	1,039
GDR	2,166	2,507	3,244	3,985
Hungary	102	265	518	629
Poland	477[b]	738	1,629	2,581
Romania	71	293	895	1,729
Yugoslavia	219	346	671	764

[a]Includes nitrogen fertilizer (N_2), phosphate fertilizer (P_2O_5), and potassium fertilizer (K_2O).
[b]Includes bone meal used as fertilizer.

TABLE A.18

Comsumption of Artificial Fertilizer[a]
(in kg. of active substance per hectare of arable land)[b]

Country	1960	1965	1970	1975
Bulgaria	33.8	79.1	160.7	126.2
CSSR[c,d]	91.4	166.3	242.1	268.1
GDR[c]	197.4	262.7	319.4	227.7
Hungary	29.5	62.5	147.9	240.5
Poland[c]	49.0	83.1	168.0	229.3
Romania	8.1	25.4	56.5	86.5
Yugoslavia	27.9	54.8	78.7	87.4

[a]Includes same type of fertilizer as Table A.17.
[b]Includes orchards and vineyards.
[c]Data pertain to "fertilizer years"–generally beginning July 1.
[d]Includes phosphate rock.

Extraction of Selected Natural Resources

Country	Metal Content (percent)	IRON ORE (thousand metric tons)			
		1960	1965	1970	1975
Bulgaria	38–50	415	1,804	2,409	2,337
CSSR	34	3,120	2,446	1,606	1,773
GDR	25–30	1,642	1,630	422	59
Hungary	24–28	516	762	629	642
Poland	30	2,182	2,862	2,554	1,254
Romania	32–40	1,460	2,479	3,206	3,065
Yugoslavia	40	2,200	2,504	3,694	5,239
BAUXITE					
Hungary		1,190	1,477	2,022	2,889
Romania		88	12	250	350
Yugoslavia		1,025	1,574	2,098	2,306
MANGANESE ORE					
Bulgaria	27	25	42	33	35
CSSR	<30	154	80	86	Ex-hausted
Hungary	26	123	213	169	131
Romania	30	175	126	102	140
Yugoslavia	35	13	8	15	17
COPPER ORE[a]					
Bulgaria		30.1	49.1	82.0	?
CSSR		?	452.0[b]	663.0	669.0
Yugoslavia		2,228	6,003	9,420	14,576
LUMBER (thousand cubic meters)					
Bulgaria		3,858	4,343	3,950	2,188[c]
CSSR		3,971	3,624	3,638	4,257
GDR		2,826	1,749	1,819	2,007
Hungary		1,568	1,993	2,495	3,136
Poland		6,272	6,451	6,818	8,012
Romania		3,928	5,004	5,305	4,660
Yugoslavia		8,997	11,955	11,557	12,495

[a]Hungary also produces copper ore, but no data are available.
[b]1966.
[c]1974.

TABLE A.20

Production of Selected Basic Industrial Goods

Country	CRUDE STEEL (thousand metric tons)			
	1960	1965	1970	1975
Bulgaria	253	588	1,800	2,265
CSSR	6,768	8,599	11,480	14,323
GDR	3,750	4,313	5,053	6,472
Hungary	1,887	2,520	3,108	3,671
Poland	6,681	9,088	11,795	15,004
Romania	1,806	3,426	6,517	9,549
Yugoslavia	1,440	1,770	2,228	2,916

	REFINED COPPER (thousand metric tons)			
Bulgaria	14.0	23.9	38.3	50.0
CSSR	10.0	11.9	16.7	22.8
GDR	40.0	40.0	40.0	50.0
Hungary	8.2	12.0	12.0	10.0
Poland	21.7	37.4	72.2	248.6
Romania	7.0	15.0	25.0	38.0
Yugoslavia	35.1	56.4	89.3	137.9

	PRIMARY ALUMINUM (thousand metric tons)			
CSSR	20	26	31	50
GDR	35	45	56	60
Hungary	50	58	66	70
Poland	26	47	99	102
Romania[a]	—	9	107	204
Yugoslavia	25	39	48	168

	SMELTER PRODUCTION OF LEAD[b] (thousand metric tons)			
Bulgaria	40.4	93.4	98.6	110.0
CSSR	12.0	15.3	17.6	18.5
Poland[c]	39.7	41.4	54.5	76.2
Romania[c]	12.0	15.0	40.0	45.0
Yugoslavia	89.1	101.6	97.4	126.1

Country	REFINED ZINC[d] (thousand metric tons)			
	1960	1965	1970	1975
Bulgaria	16.9	65.8	76.1	86.0
GDR	4.0	14.0	15.0	15.0
Poland	176.0	190.4	209.0	240.0
Romania	16.0	25.0	40.0	55.0
Yugoslavia	35.9	46.1	65.0	97.9

CEMENT (thousand metric tons)				
Bulgaria	1,586	2,681	3,668	4,358
CSSR	5,051	5,713	7,402	9,305
GDR	5,032	6,087	7,984	10,653
Hungary	1,571	2,383	2,771	3,759
Poland	6,599	9,573	12,180	18,544
Romania	3,054	5,406	8,127	11,520
Yugoslavia	2,398	3,120	4,398	7,066

PLASTIC MATERIALS[e] (thousand metric tons)				
Bulgaria	7.3	33.2	89.2	156.0
CSSR	64.0	126.0	245.0	428.0
GDR	115.0	219.0	370.0	605.0
Hungary	9.9	27.2	55.9	123.0
Poland	40.1	91.1	224.0	433.0
Romania	12.4	75.5	206.0	347.0
Yugoslavia	15.0	57.0	97.0	160.0

SULFURIC ACID[f] (thousand metric tons)				
Bulgaria	123	318	502	854
CSSR	553	933	1,110	1,245
GDR	730	985	1,099	1,002
Hungary[g]	178	393	484	650
Poland	685	1,062	1,901	3,410
Romania	226	541	994	1,448
Yugoslavia	130	435	747	936

(continued)

Country	TRACTORS[h] (units)			
	1960	1965	1970	1975
Bulgaria	–	2,800	3,493	5,112
CSSR	32,492	30,534	18,480	29,585
GDR	4,440	2,474	6,298	4,076
Hungary	2,649	2,961	1,930	551
Poland	8,673	21,622	40,998	57,553
Romania	17,102	15,836	29,287	50,003
Yugoslavia	7,309	7,430	12,047	33,207

	GRAIN COMBINES[i] (units)			
GDR	1,972	1,585	900	1,500[j]
Hungary	2,266	–	–	–
Poland	564	1,781	2,155	3,591
Romania	5,500	2,012	1,179	5,659

[a]Includes aluminum alloys.

[b]Lead produced from domestic and imported ores and concentrates, excluding scrap (secondary) metals.

[c]Probably including some secondary metal.

[d]Electrolytic and distilled (including redistilled) zinc produced from domestic and imported ores, scrap and other secondary material.

[e]Not including polymers used for the production of fibers and elastic, nor the actual goods made from plastic.

[f]Pure (monohydrate) sulfuric acid (100% H_2SO_4).

[g]Including oleum.

[h]Wheeled and caterpillar tractors of all types.

[i]Self-propelled and tractor-drawn. Includes only those combines with all necessary accoutrements.

[j]1974.

Production and Consumption of Primary Energy
(in million metric tons of coal equivalents)

Country	1960	1965	1970	1975
Bulgaria				
Production	7.7	9.6	10.0	8.8
Consumption	9.5	17.0	24.8	34.8
Deficit/Surplus	−1.8	−7.4	−14.8	−26.0
CSSR				
Production	49.8	61.8	66.0	65.8
Consumption	54.4	69.6	82.9	95.4
Deficit/Surplus	−4.6	−7.8	−16.9	−29.6
GDR				
Production	73.6	81.4	85.2	89.6
Consumption	84.0	96.4	107.6	122.7
Deficit/Surplus	−10.4	−15.0	−22.4	−33.1
Hungary				
Production	14.7	18.7	20.1	19.7
Consumption	18.6	24.7	30.1	36.2
Deficit/Surplus	−3.9	−6.0	−10.0	−16.5
Poland				
Production	93.4	110.9	136.9	165.9
Consumption	85.1	96.9	122.9	149.2
Deficit/Surplus	+8.3	+14.0	+14.0	+16.7
Romania				
Production	34.5	47.0	62.5	77.6
Consumption	25.7	39.8	60.6	83.2
Deficit/Surplus	+8.8	+7.2	+1.9	−5.6
Yugoslavia				
Production	15.5	21.2	24.0	29.4
Consumption	15.8	23.1	29.3	41.6
Deficit/Surplus	−0.3	−1.9	−5.3	−12.2

Note: Taken from and based on Tables 78 and 79 in Central
Intelligence Agency, Research Aid: Handbook of Economic Statistics
1976 (Washington, D.C., CIA). Data include coal, crude oil, natural
gas, and hydroelectric and nuclear electric power expressed in terms
of coal equivalents (calorific value of 7,000 kilocalories per kilo-
gram) and exclude such minor fuels as peat, shale, and firewood.

TABLE A.22

Production and Consumption of Coal
(net output in thousand metric tons)

Country	1960	1965	1970	1975
Bulgaria				
Produced				
hard coal[a]	571	553	397	307[b]
soft coal[a]	15,416	24,489	28,854	23,998[b]
Imported				
from USSR	—	2,154	2,149	2,462[b]
from elsewhere	—	100	—	—
Exported	—	—	—	—
Consumption				
(and reserve)	15,987	27,296	31,400	26,767[b]
CSSR				
Produced				
hard coal[a]	26,400	27,755	28,195	28,119
soft coal[a]	57,888	72,329	81,298	86,272
Imported				
from USSR	1,028	2,902	2,688	2,818
from elsewhere	3,306	2,318	2,920	2,888
Exported	3,638	3,563	4,220	5,349
Consumption				
(and reserve)	84,984	101,741	110,881	114,748
GDR				
Produced				
hard coal[a]	2,721	2,212	1,049	539
soft coal[a]	225,465	250,839	261,482	246,706
Imported				
from USSR	5,060	5,833	3,471	4,411
from elsewhere	3,075	3,631	4,721	2,029
Exported	—	—	—	—
Consumption				
(and reserve)	236,321	262,515	270,723	253,685
Hungary				
Produced				
hard coal[a]	2,847	4,362	4,151	3,021
soft coal[a]	23,676	27,075	23,679	21,867
Imported				
from USSR	266	1,000	386	—
from elsewhere	1,592	2,240	2,046	1,992
Exported	63	79	91	96
Consumption				
(and reserve)	28,318	34,598	30,171	26,784

Country	1960	1965	1970	1975
Poland				
Produced				
hard coal[a]	104,438	118,831	140,101	171,625
soft coal[a]	9,327	22,626	32,766	39,865
Imported				
from USSR	459	909	802	813
from elsewhere	317	301	293	283
Exported	22,952	26,244	32,788	41,921
Consumption				
(and reserve)	91,589	116,423	141,174	170,665
Romania				
Produced				
hard coal[a]	3,405	4,658	6,402	7,320
soft coal[a]	3,363	5,633	14,129	19,771
Imported				
from USSR	—	—	—	—
from elsewhere	416	706	728	2,419
Exported	—	—	—	—
Consumption				
(and reserve)	7,184	10,997	21,259	29,510
Yugoslavia				
Produced				
hard coal[a]	1,280	1,170	640	600
soft coal[a]	21,430	28,790	27,780	34,940
Imported				
from USSR	801	1,055	1,115	1,444
from elsewhere	424	1,130	706	865
Exported	—	—	—	—
Consumption				
(and reserve)	23,935	32,145	30,241	37,849

Note: Net output refers to coal delivered to the consumer, plus that utilized by mining enterprises for their own productive technical, economic, and human needs.

[a]Hard coal includes anthracite and bituminous, soft coal includes brown coal and lignite.

[b]1974.

TABLE A.23

Production and Consumption of Crude Oil
(in thousand metric tons)

	1960	1965	1970	1975
Bulgaria				
Produced	200	229	334	144*
Imported				
from USSR	—	2,154	4,759	9,009*
from elsewhere	12	46	937	1,620*
Exported	—	—	—	—
Consumption				
(and reserve)	212	2,429	6,030	10,773*
CSSR				
Produced	137	192	203	142
Imported				
from USSR	2,253	5,960	9,402	15,503
from elsewhere	4	136	396	336
Exported	—	—	—	—
Consumption				
(and reserve)	2,394	6,288	10,001	15,981
GDR				
Produced	200	229	334	144
Imported				
from USSR	1,811	4,908	9,233	15,097
from elsewhere	130	224	1,101	1,900
Exported	—	—	—	—
Consumption				
(and reserve)	2,141	5,361	10,668	17,141
Hungary				
Produced	1,217	1,803	1,937	2,006
Imported				
from USSR	1,401	2,087	3,951	6,500
from elsewhere	55	164	398	1,931
Exported	—	—	—	—
Consumption				
(and reserve)	2,673	4,054	6,286	10,437

Country	1960	1965	1970	1975
Poland				
Produced	194	339	424	553
Imported				
from USSR	714	3,216	7,011	10,882
from elsewhere	–	–	–	2,424
Exported	–	–	–	–
Consumption				
(and reserve)	908	3,555	7,435	13,859
Romania				
Produced	11,500	12,571	13,377	14,590
Imported				
from USSR	–	–	–	–
from elsewhere			2,291	5,085
Exported	–	–	–	843
Consumption				
(and reserve)	11,500	12,571	15,668	18,832
Yugoslavia				
Produced	944	2,063	2,854	3,692
Imported				
from USSR	252	528	1,476	1,801
from elsewhere	182	578	2,990	6,595
Exported	–	–	–	–
Consumption				
(and reserve)	1,378	3,169	7,320	12,088

*1974.

TABLE A.24

Production and Consumption of Natural Gas
(in million cubic meters)

Country	1960	1965	1970	1975
Bulgaria				
Produced	—	73	473.5	179.6[a]
Imported				
from USSR	—	—	—	1.0[a]
from elsewhere	—	—	—	—
Consumption				
(and reserve)	—	73	473.5	180.6[b]
CSSR				
Produced	1,443	965	1,204	800
Imported				
from USSR	} 4	7	1,334	3,790
from elsewhere		—	23	31
Exported	9	14	86	?
Consumption				
(and reserve)	1,438	958	2,475	4,621[b]
GDR				
Produced	negl.	130	1,230	8,000
Imported				
from USSR	—	—	—	3,302
from elsewhere	—	—	—	—
Exported	—	—	—	—
Consumption				
(and reserve)	negl.	130	1,230	11,302
Hungary				
Produced	342	1,108	3,469	5,182
Imported				
from USSR	—	—	—	600
from elsewhere	186	186	200	206
Exported	—	—	—	—
Consumption				
(and reserve)	528	1,294	3,669	5,988

Country	1960	1965	1970	1975
Poland[c]				
Produced	541	1,312	4,975	5,776
Imported				
from USSR	241	379	1,002	2,510
from elsewhere	—	—	—	—
Exported	—	—	—	—
Consumption				
(and reserve)	782	1,691	5,977	8,286
Romania				
Produced	10,330	17,450	25,030	31,200
Imported				
from USSR	—	—	—	—
from elsewhere	—	—	—	—
Exported	204	200	200	194
Consumption				
(and reserve)	10,126	17,250	24,830	31,006
Yugoslavia				
Produced	52	333	977	1,554
Imported				
from USSR	—	—	—	—
from elsewhere	—	—	—	—
Exported	—	—	—	—
Consumption				
(and reserve)	52	333	977	1,554

Note: Data include gas from natural gas wells and petroleum fields only. Figures refer to gross production less losses and waste.
[a]1974.
[b]Gross consumption and reserve (that is, without exports).
[c]Production from gas fields only.

Production and Consumption of Electric Power
(in million kilowatt-hours)

Country	1960	1965	1970	1975
Bulgaria				
Produced	4,657	10,244	19,513	22,806[b]
Imported	28	37	101	4,074[b]
Exported	?	?	?	?
Consumption (and reserve)[a]	4,685	10,281	19,614	26,880[b]
CSSR				
Produced	24,460	34,190	45,163	59,277
Imported	187	1,427	3,905	4,852
Exported	450	665	509	640
Consumption (and reserve)	24,197	34,952	48,559	63,489
GDR				
Produced	40,305	53,611	67,650	84,505
Imported	103	490	1,230	1,380
Exported	481	430	830	697
Consumption (and reserve)	39,927	53,671	68,050	85,188
Hungary				
Produced	7,617	11,177	14,542	20,457
Imported	?	?	4,058	5,802
Exported	?	?	663	1,678
Consumption (and reserve)	?	?	17,937	24,581
Poland				
Produced	29,307	43,801	64,532	96,862
Imported	659	937	1,560	2,411
Exported	357	1,391	1,505	2,924
Consumption (and reserve)	29,609	43,347	64,587	96,349
Romania				
Produced	7,650	17,215	35,088	53,721
Imported	?	?	?	?
Exported	28	577	2,334	2,918
Consumption (and reserve)	?	?	?	?
Yugoslavia				
Produced	8,928	15,523	26,023	40,040
Imported	—	—	negl.	?
Exported	—	—	—	?
Consumption (and reserve)	8,928	15,523	26,023	?

Note: Gross production at electric power stations of all types and by generators at all locations. Both production and consumption include transmission line losses and power station use.

[a]Gross consumption (that is, before export).

[b]1974.

Foreign Trade by Political Region
(in percent)

Country	1960	1965	1970	1975
Bulgaria				
USSR	53.1	51.1	53.0	46.9[b]
Comecon (w/o USSR)[a]	27.4	21.9	21.4	23.3[b]
Other communist states	3.4	3.8	3.4	2.7[b]
Industrially developed states	13.2	19.1	16.6	17.4[b]
Developing countries	2.9	4.1	5.6	9.7[b]
CSSR				
USSR	34.4	36.9	32.5	32.5
Comecon (w/o USSR)[a]	29.4	31.2	31.8	33.5
Other communist states	8.0	5.2	5.8	4.6
Industrially developed states	17.8	17.9	22.4	22.3
Developing countries	10.4	8.8	7.6	7.0
GDR				
USSR	42.8	42.8	39.1	35.7
Comecon (w/o USSR)[a]	24.8	26.7	28.2	30.6
Other communist states	7.0	4.4	4.2	3.5
Industrially developed states	21.1	21.7	24.4	25.9
Developing countries	4.3	4.5	4.0	4.4
Hungary				
USSR	29.5	35.6	33.6	36.8
Comecon (w/o USSR)[a]	32.8	35.4	28.6	28.4
Other communist states	8.5	3.7	4.1	3.7
Industrially developed states	20.7	21.5	24.5	23.2
Developing countries	8.5	3.9	9.2	8.0
Poland				
USSR	30.3	33.1	36.5	28.1
Comecon (w/o USSR)[a]	27.0	27.6	26.8	21.6
Other communist states	5.8	4.0	2.9	2.5
Industrially developed states	29.1	26.6	27.1	41.3
Developing countries	7.1	8.7	6.7	6.5
Romania				
USSR	40.1	38.8	27.0	18.6
Comecon (w/o USSR)[a]	26.5	21.5	21.9	19.4
Other communist states	6.4	4.6	7.0	6.8
Industrially developed states	21.6	27.6	34.8	37.3
Developing countries	5.4	7.5	9.3	17.9
Yugoslavia				
USSR	7.9	12.5	9.6	15.4
Comecon (w/o USSR)[a]	20.7	22.3	16.9	16.0
Other communist states	0.1	0.5	0.5	1.2
Industrially developed states	58.0	51.4	62.0	52.5
Developing countries	13.3	13.3	11.0	14.9

[a]Including Cuba after 1972. Prior to this time Cuba was included in the group "Other communist states."

[b]1974.

TABLE A.27

Export and Import Structure
(in percent)

Group A: Machinery and equipment, including means of transport and transport equipment, electronic equipment, buildings, laboratories, medical instruments, bearings, abrasives, tractors, and agricultural machinery.

Group B: Fuels, mineral raw materials, ferrous and nonferrous metals, including electric power, oil products, clay, ores, concentrates, semifinished products, and precious metals.

Group C: Nonmineral raw materials, products made by processing such materials, foodstuffs, and raw materials for the production of foodstuffs, including wood, paper, cellulose, raw materials for textiles, pelts and furs (but not final products), leather, seeds, fats, animal and vegetable oils, tobacco, livestock and livestock products, sugar, fruit, vegetable and grain crops, etc.

Group D: Industrial consumer goods, including clothing, hats, footwear, dishes, furniture, perfume, cosmetics, vitamins, medicaments, fabrics, consumer durables, and the "necessities and luxuries" of everyday life.

Group E: Chemical products, fertilizer, rubber, and construction materials, including paint, explosives, standard houses, photographic materials, isotopes, resins, and plant protection agents.

Group	Exports				Imports			
	1960	1965	1970	1975	1960	1965	1970	1975
Bulgaria								
A	12.9	24.8	29.0	40.7	43.9	43.7	40.6	41.4
B	9.2	7.6	8.1	7.8	24.3	26.7	29.1	33.5
C	56.4	49.9	43.4	33.8	16.7	17.3	15.9	12.7
D	17.9	13.6	14.7	10.3	7.6	5.1	5.7	5.1
E	3.6	4.1	4.8	7.4	7.5	7.2	8.7	7.3

Group	Exports				Imports			
	1960	1965	1970	1975	1960	1965	1970	1975
CSSR								
A	45.7	49.1	50.4	48.0	21.7	30.0	33.4	36.1
B	19.1	19.7	18.6	19.3	27.9	27.4	23.5	27.8
C	10.4	9.1	7.3	7.2	37.1	28.4	24.1	17.4
D	20.4	16.6	16.6	18.2	3.4	5.3	8.5	7.7
E	4.4	5.5	7.1	7.3	9.9	8.9	10.5	11.0
GDR								
A	49.0	49.8	51.7	50.7	12.7	18.0	34.2	30.6
B	15.7	12.9	10.1	12.1	38.5	39.1	27.6	30.5
C	5.9	6.0	7.4	9.1	39.2	33.1	28.1	22.6
D	15.1	19.1	20.2	15.6	5.3	4.0	4.5	5.8
E	14.3	12.2	10.6	12.5	4.3	5.8	5.6	10.5
Hungary								
A	38.6	33.2	32.6	36.9	28.5	28.8	30.9	32.2
B	12.8	14.1	14.4	11.9	27.7	27.9	23.6	27.3
C	27.4	26.9	26.7	25.2	29.2	27.8	24.4	19.0
D	17.8	21.3	21.3	20.5	5.1	5.3	7.7	7.1
E	3.4	4.5	5.0	5.5	9.5	10.2	13.4	14.4
Poland								
A	28.3	34.8	38.5	39.0	27.1	32.9	36.2	37.4
B	34.0	24.7	23.9	29.1	25.3	24.7	26.6	30.0
C	23.0	22.6	15.9	10.5	33.9	27.4	21.4	17.7
D	10.1	12.4	16.1	14.7	5.5	6.8	6.4	5.3
E	4.6	5.5	5.6	6.7	8.2	8.2	9.4	9.6
Romania								
A	16.7	18.8	22.8	25.3	33.6	39.9	40.3	34.7
B	36.9	25.1	22.7	22.3	34.3	31.4	30.4	38.3
C	35.9	35.3	26.8	22.6	18.4	14.3	15.6	15.6
D	5.8	11.0	18.1	16.1	5.2	6.7	5.5	3.8
E	4.7	9.8	9.6	13.7	8.5	7.7	8.2	7.6
Yugoslavia								
A								
B				COMPARABLE DATA				
C								
D				NOT AVAILABLE				
E								

TABLE A.28

Foreign Trade Per Capita
(in U.S. dollars)*

Country	1960	1965	1970	1975
Bulgaria	152.1	285.5	450.4	1,143.2
CSSR	273.3	377.6	521.8	1,173.0
GDR	256.0	345.0	552.0	1,271.0
Hungary	185.7	299.0	467.2	1,254.2
Poland	95.5	145.0	220.0	670.6
Romania	74.2	114.5	188.2	502.8
Yugoslavia	72.0	118.0	223.0	551.0

*Converted from the national currency at the official exchange rate.

TABLE A.29

Bilateral Aid Commitments to
Developing Countries
(in millions of U.S. dollars)[a]

Country	Annual Average 1966–70	Annual Average 1971–75	1971	1972	1973	1974	1975[b]
Bulgaria	40	52	55	40	43	117	7
CSSR	114	126	14	100	303	108	104
GDR	100	51	25	23	–	46	162
Hungary	47	98	42	45	148	110	142
Poland	28	109	65	100	247	107	27
Romania	40	350	141	385	36	752	438

[a]Converted from the national currency at the official exchange rate.

[b]Preliminary.

Source: UN Department of Economic and Social Affairs, World Economic Survey (New York, 1976), p. 178.

TABLE A.30

Percent of National Income Used for Science,
Research, and Development

Country	1960	1965	1970	1975
Bulgaria	?	?	1.5[a]	2.0[a]
CSSR	?	?	3.7	3.7
GDR	Unknown			
Hungary	1.5	2.3	2.8	3.5
Poland[b]	0.2	0.2	0.2	0.3
Romania[c]	1.2	0.4	0.6	0.7
Yugoslavia	0.2	1.4	1.0	1.5

[a]Estimate.
[b]Percentage of state budget expenditures for science.
[c]Percentage of state budget expenditures for science and scientific services.

TABLE A.31

Tourism to and from West

(in thousands)

Country	1960	1965	1970	1971	1972	1973	1974	1975
FROM THE WEST								
Bulgaria	c. 26	133	364	366	356	344	369	?
CSSR	?	618	731	792	895	833	891	905
GDR	?	?	119	114	130	150	180	173
Hungary	72	430	735	875	988	1,103	1,180	1,166
Poland	44	95	279	313	375	582	672	767
Romania	?	200	?	513	606	573	620	?
Yugoslavia	838	2,658	4,255	4,802	4,665	5,495	4,715	5,129
TO THE WEST								
Bulgaria	9.4	27	45	53	64	86	99	?
CSSR	?	169	212	197	204	256	317	294
GDR	?	?	Several hundred per year, maximum					
Hungary	35	165	184	216	250	234	263	252
Poland	51	81	114	157	209	259	280	316
Romania				Unknown				
Yugoslavia				Unknown				

Note: Excludes transit travelers, and in the case of the GDR also excludes inner–Berlin tourist traffic.

346

APPENDIX BIBLIOGRAPHY

Unless otherwise noted, all data given in this appendix have been taken from the statistical sources given below.

General

Sovet Ekonomicheskoi Vzaimopomoshchi, Statisticheskii Ezhegodnik Stran-Chlenov SEV (Statistical Yearbook of the COMECON Member-States). Moscow: Statistika Publishing House, 1974-1976.

UN Department of Economic and Social Affairs, Statistical Office. Demographic Yearbook. New York, 1974.

Central Intelligence Agency. Research Aid: Handbook of Economic Statistics. Washington, D.C., 1976.

Bulgaria

Narodna Republika Bulgaria Ministerstvo na Informatsiata i Suobscheniata. Statisticheski Spravochnik (Statistical Manual). Sofia, 1975.

Narodna Republika Bulgaria Ministerstvo na Informatsiata i Suobscheniata. Statisticheski Godishnik (Statistical Yearbook). Sofia, 1959, 1965-1975.

People's Republic of Bulgaria, National Information Office. Statistical Yearbook: Statisticheskii Ezhegodnik. Sofia, 1969, 1971.

The Bulgarian census of 1956 is partially reproduced in the 1959 Statistical Yearbook (Bulgarian-language).

Czechoslovakia

Federalni Statisticky Urad, Cesky Statisticky Urad, Slovensky Statisticky Urad. Statisticka rocenka Ceskoslovenske Socialisticke Republiky (Statistical Yearbook of the Czechoslovak Socialist Republic). Prague, 1965-76.

GDR

Staatlichen Zentralverwaltung fuer Statistik. Statistisches Jahrbuch (Statistical Yearbook). East Berlin, 1966, 1971, 1973, 1974, 1976.

Materials from the Gesamtdeutsches Institut, Bundesanstalt fuer Gesamtdeutsche Aufgaben, Bonn, West Germany.

Hungary

Hungarian Central Statistical Office. Statistical Yearbook: Statisticheskii Ezhegodnik 1974. Budapest, 1976.

Magyar Kozponti Statisztikai Hivatal. Magyar statisztikai zsebkonyv (Hungarian Statistical Pocketbook). Budapest, 1975, 1976.

Magyar Kozponti Statisztikai Hivatal. Statisztikai evkonyv (Statistical Yearbook). Budapest, 1965-1976.

Poland

Central Statistical Office of the Polish People's Republic. Concise Statistical Yearbook of Poland. Warsaw, 1975.

Rocznik statystyczny (Statistical Yearbook). Warsaw, 1965-76.

Glowny Urzad Statystyczny Polskiej Republiki Ludowej. Maly rocznik statystyczny (Concise Statistical Yearbook). Warsaw, 1974, 1975.

Romania

Romania. Directia Centrale de Statistica. Anuarul Statistic al Republicii Socialiste Romania (Statistical Yearbook of the Socialist Republic of Romania). Bucharest, 1965-76.

Romania. Directia Centrale de Statistica. Recensamintul populatiei si locuintelor din Martie 1966 (Census of the Population and Households of March 1966). Bucharest, 1969.

Yugoslavia

Statisticki Godisnjak Jugoslavije (Yugoslav Statistical Yearbook). Belgrade, 1965-76.

ROBERT R. KING is Assistant Director, Research and Analysis Department, Radio Free Europe, Munich, Federal Republic of Germany. His previously published works include East European Perspectives on European Security and Cooperation (coedited with Robert W. Dean), Minorities Under Communism, and Yugoslav Communism and the Macedonian Question. Dr. King holds a Ph.D. from the Fletcher School of Law and Diplomacy.

JAMES F. BROWN is Assistant Director of Radio Free Europe for Policy and Research, and is stationed in Munich, Federal Republic of Germany. His publications include Relations Between the Soviet Union and Its Eastern European Allies, Bulgaria Under Communist Rule, and The New Eastern Europe. Mr. Brown studied at the University of Manchester, England, where he earned his BA and MA degrees.

*THE INTERNATIONAL POLITICS OF EASTERN
EUROPE
                        edited by Charles Gati

*POLITICAL DEVELOPMENT IN EASTERN EUROPE
                        edited by Jan F. Triska and
                        Paul M. Cocks

THE SOCIAL STRUCTURE OF EASTERN EUROPE:
Transition and Process in Czechoslovakia, Hungary,
Poland, Romania, and Yugoslavia
                        edited by Bernard L. Faber

CURRENT RESEARCH IN COMPARATIVE COM-
MUNISM: An Analysis and Bibliographic Guide
to the Soviet System
                        Lawrence L. Whetten

PERIODICALS ON THE SOCIALIST COUNTRIES
AND ON MARXISM: A New Annotated Index of
English-Language Publications
                        Harry G. Shaffer

GROWTH AND REFORMS IN CENTRALLY PLANNED
ECONOMIES: The Lessons of the Bulgarian Experience
                        George R. Feiwel

*Also available in paperback as a PSS Student Edition